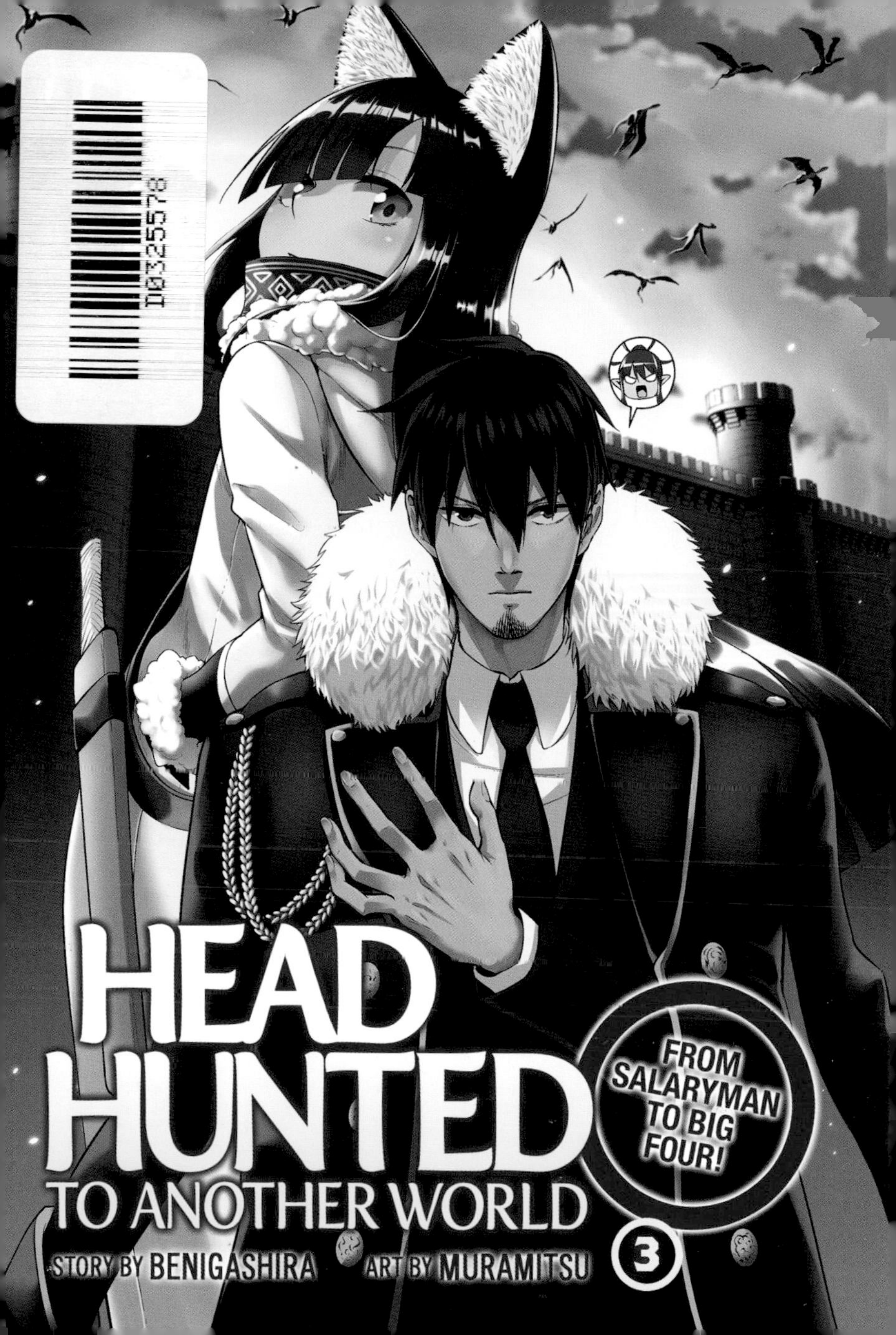

HEAD HUNTED TO ANOTHER WORLD

FROM SALARYMAN TO BIG FOUR!

3

STORY BY BENIGASHIRA ART BY MURAMITSU

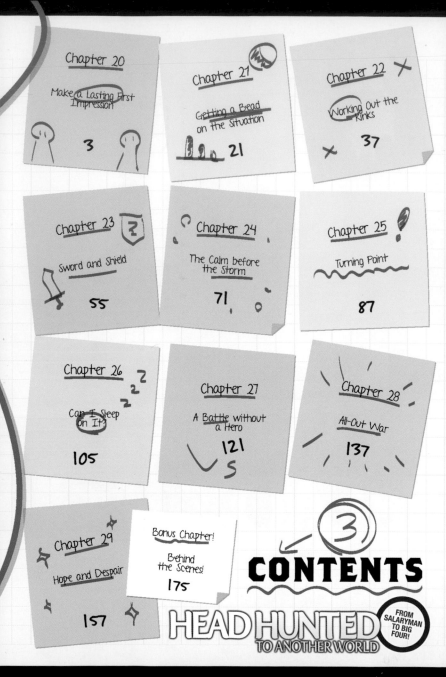

CONTENTS

3

HEAD HUNTED TO ANOTHER WORLD

FROM SALARYMAN TO BIG FOUR!

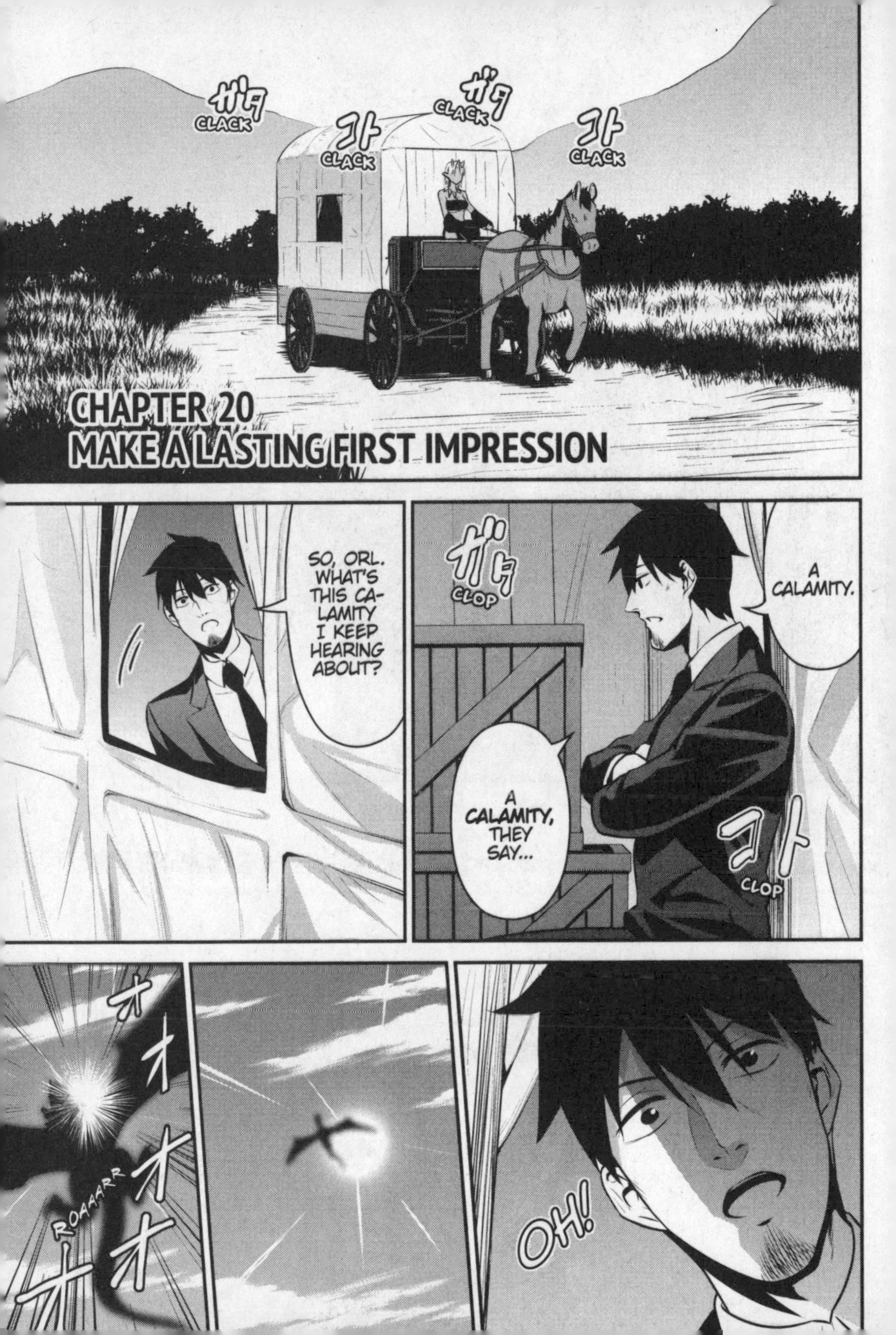
コト
CLACK
ガタ
CLACK
コト
CLACK
ガタ
CLACK
CHAPTER 20
MAKE A LASTING FIRST IMPRESSION
A CALAMITY.
ガタ
CLOP
A CALAMITY, THEY SAY...
コト
CLOP
SO, ORL. WHAT'S THIS CA-LAMITY I KEEP HEARING ABOUT?
OH!
オオオオ
ROAAARR

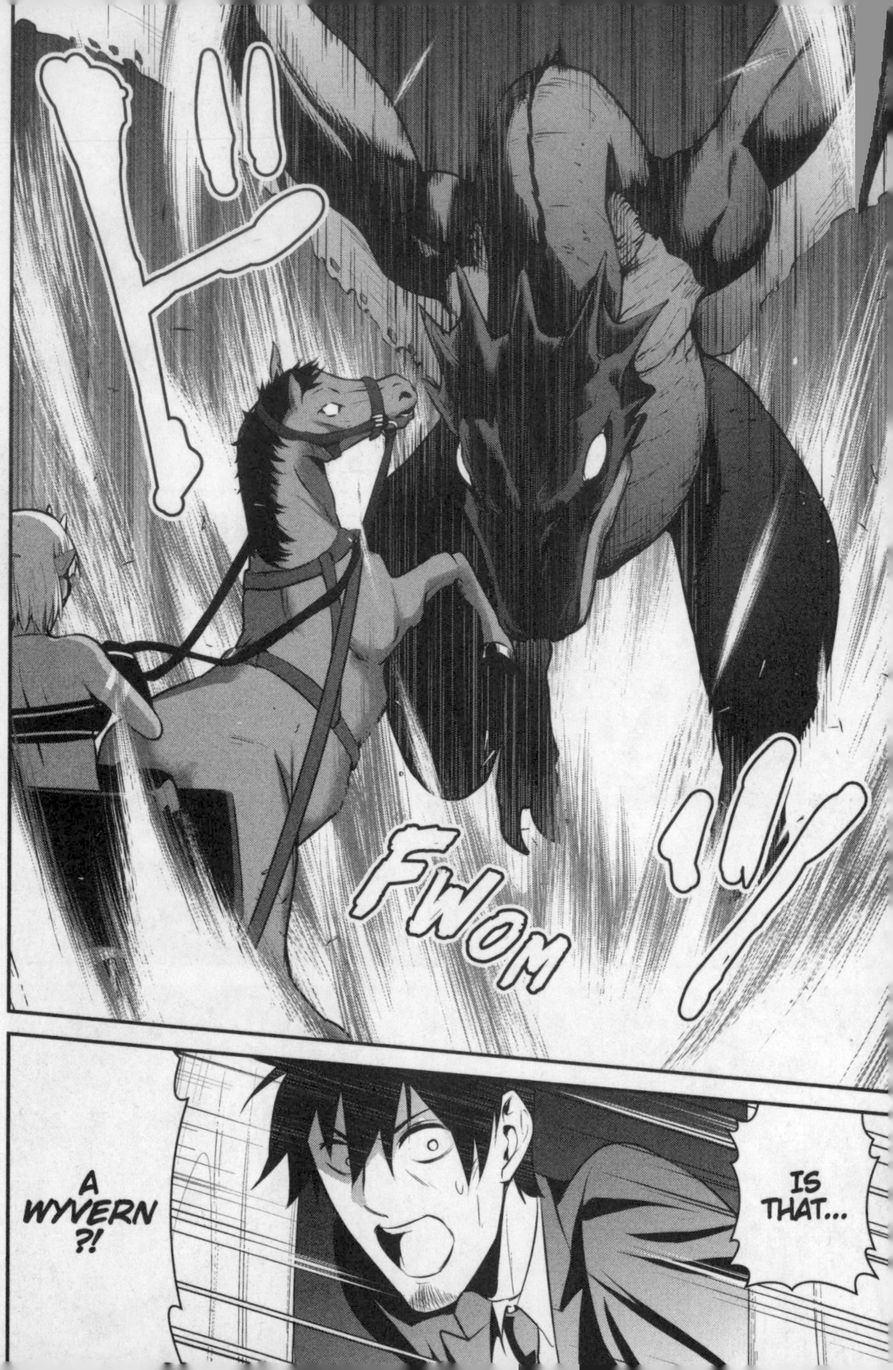
FWOM
IS THAT...
A WYVERN ?!

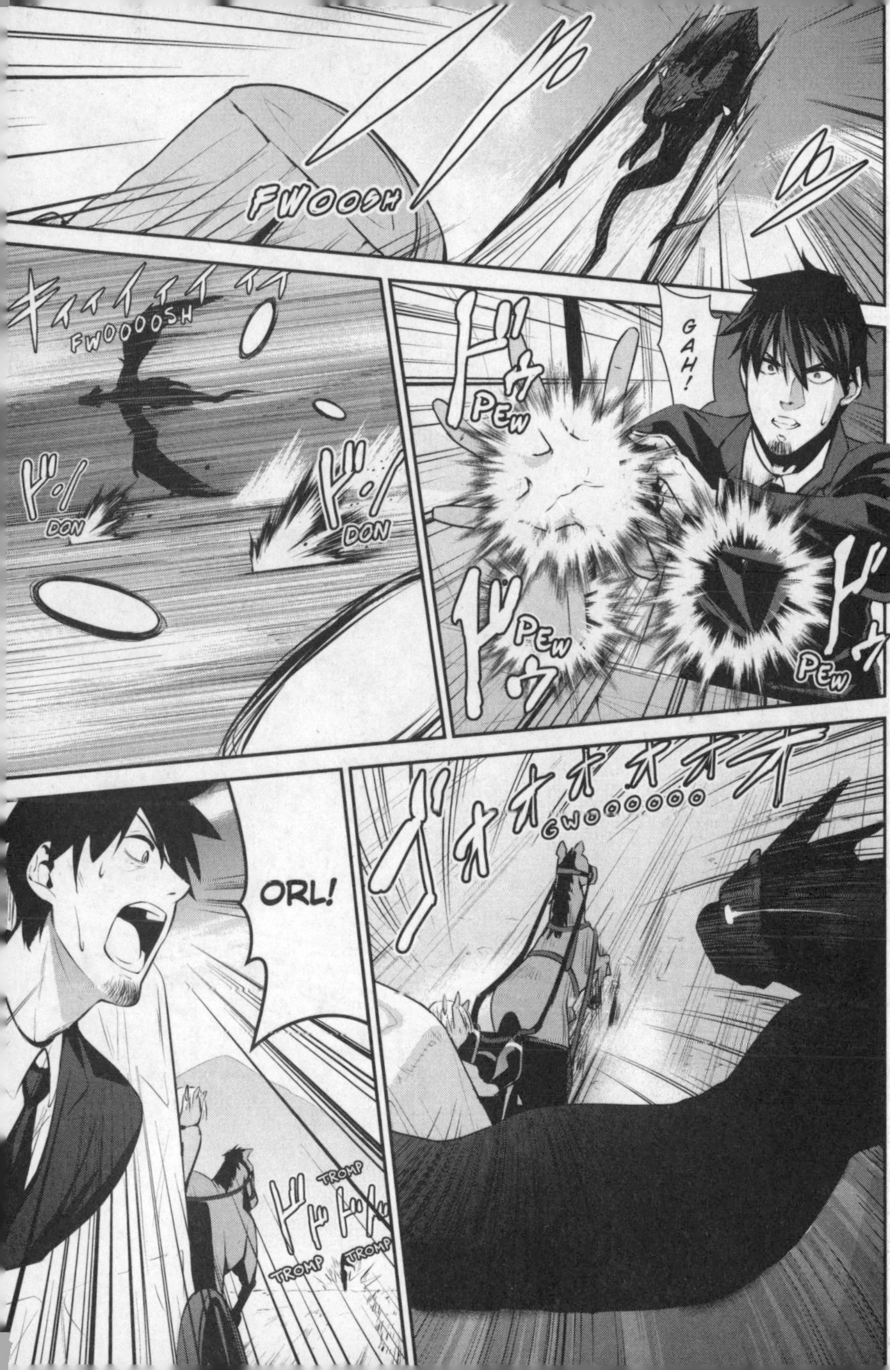
FWOOSH
GAH!
PEW
PEW
PEW
FWOOOOSH
DON
DON
GWOOOOOOO
ORL!
TROMP
TROMP
TROMP

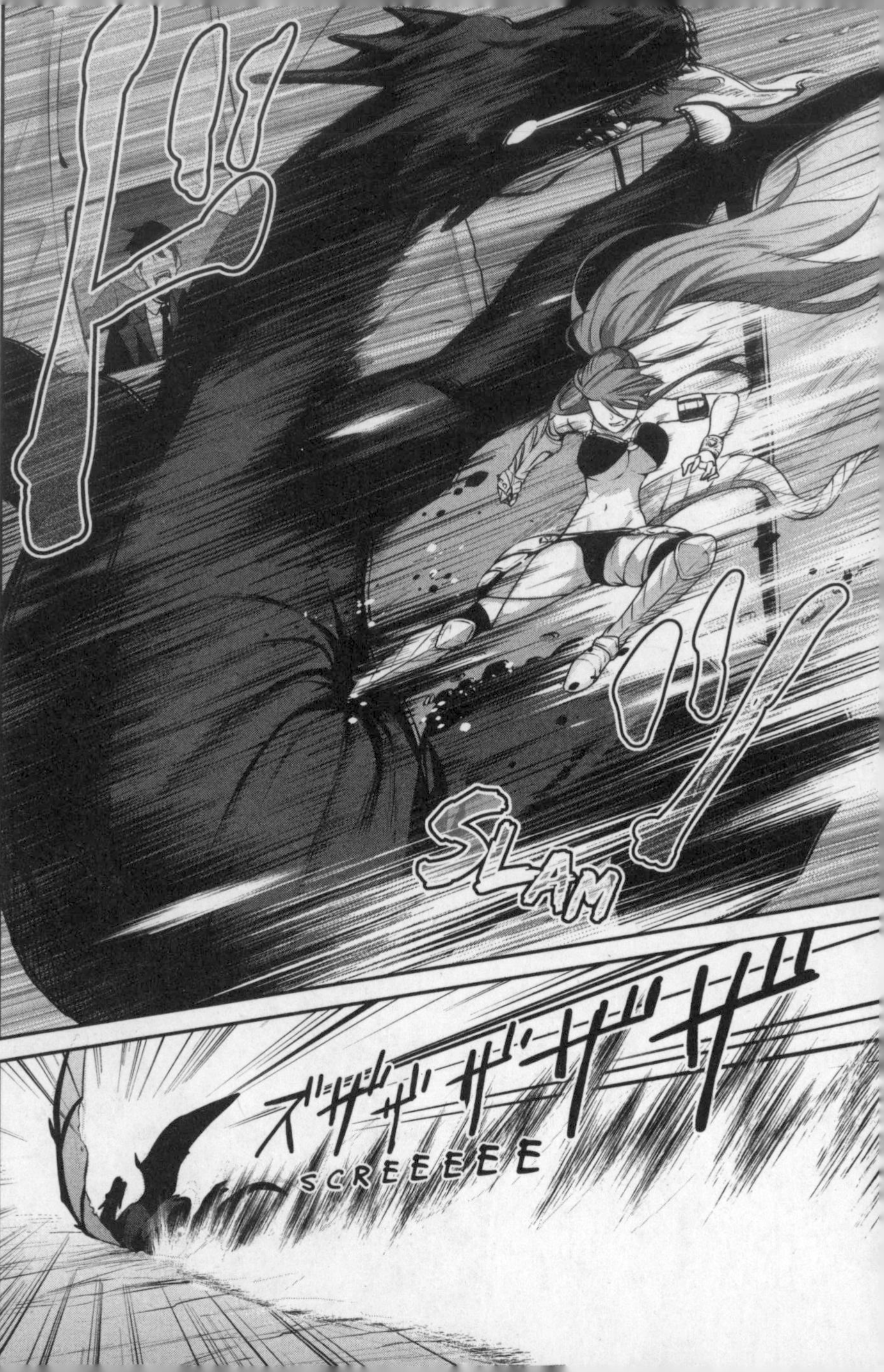
SLAM
SCREEEEEE

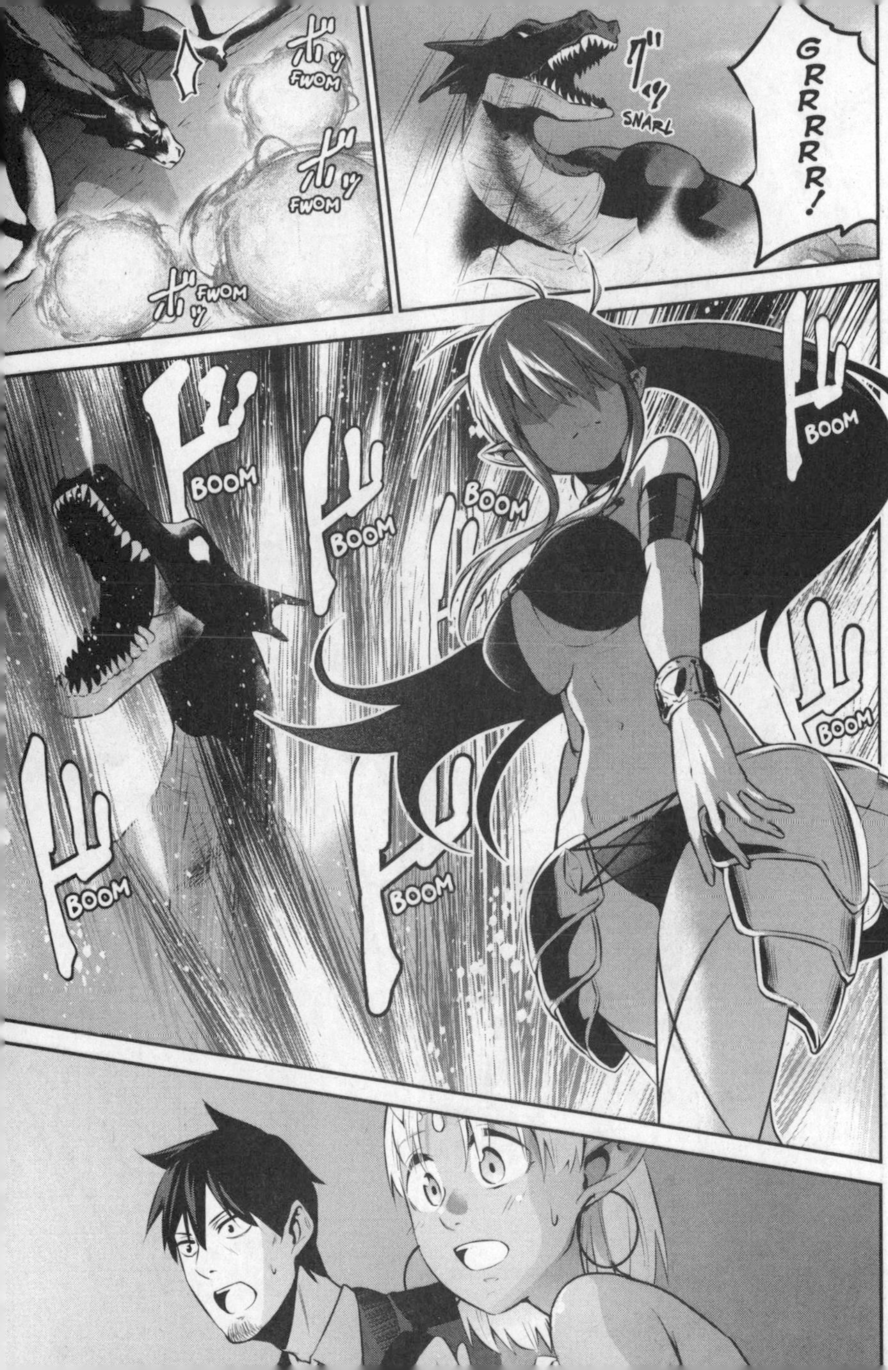
GRRRRR!
SNARL
FWOM
FWOM
FWOM
BOOM
BOOM
BOOM
BOOM
BOOM
BOOM
BOOM

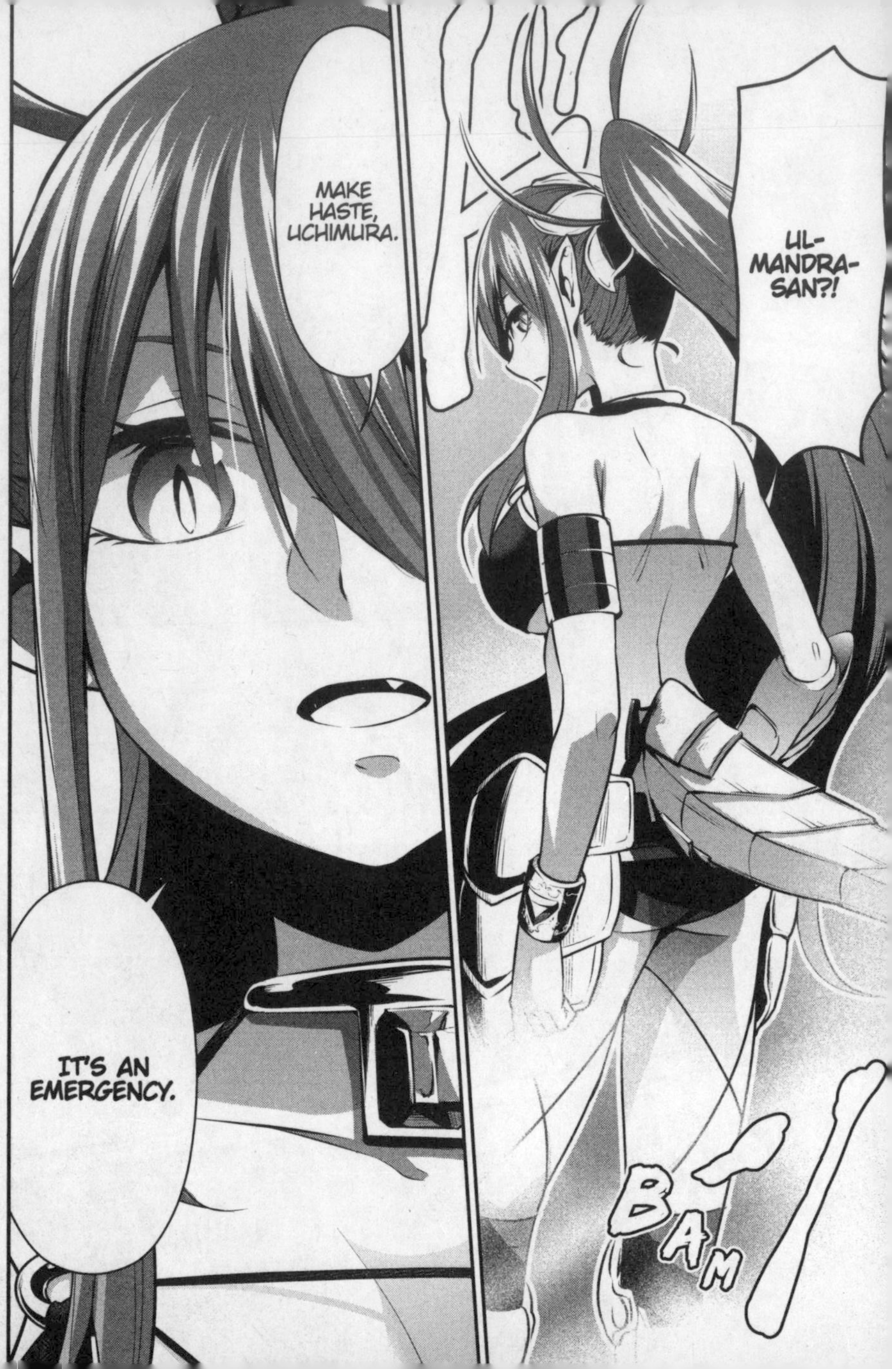
UL-MANDRA-SAN?!
BAM
MAKE HASTE, UCHIMURA.
IT'S AN EMERGENCY.

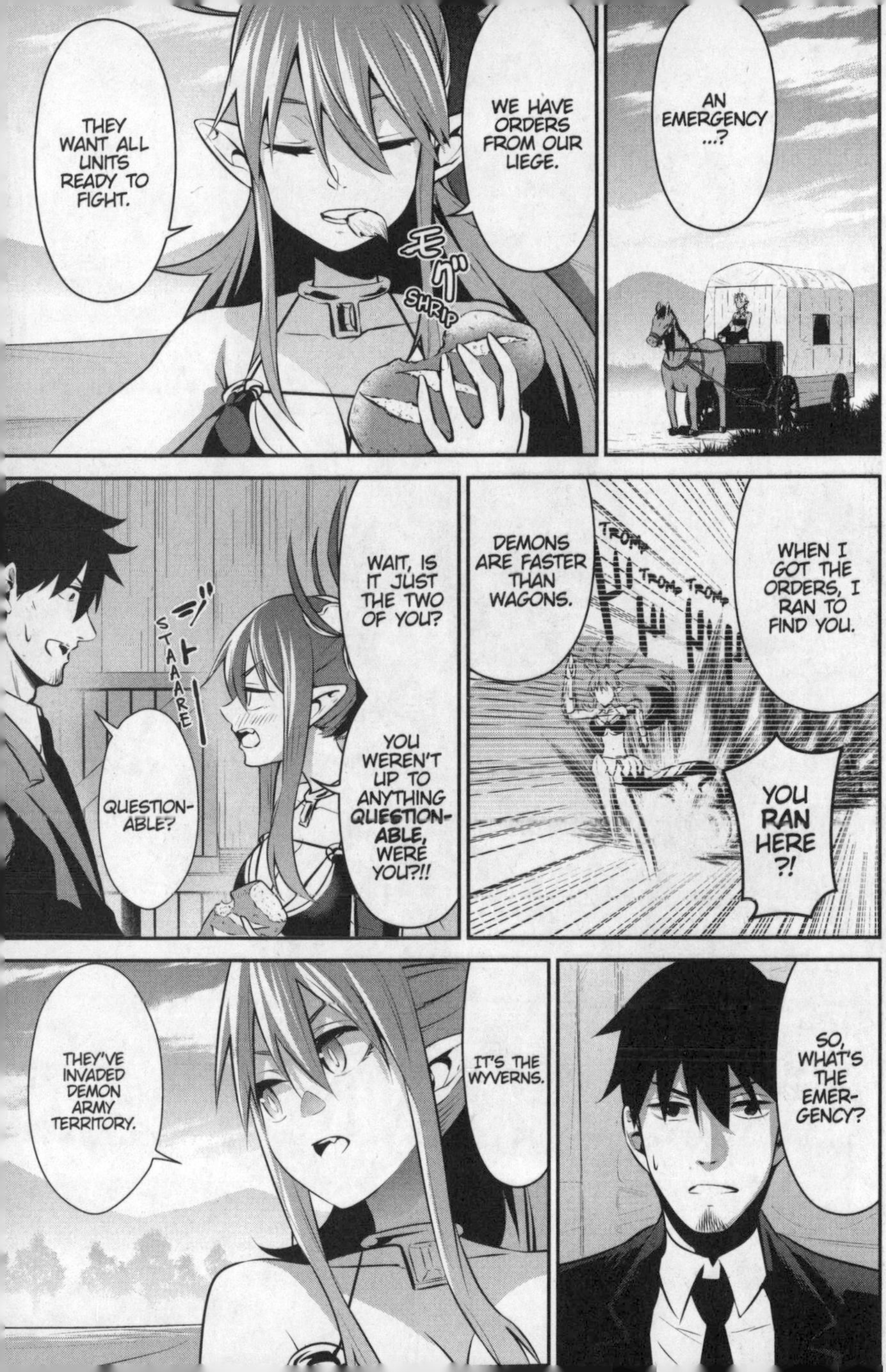
AN EMERGENCY ...?
WE HAVE ORDERS FROM OUR LIEGE.
THEY WANT ALL UNITS READY TO FIGHT.
モグ
SHRIP
WHEN I GOT THE ORDERS, I RAN TO FIND YOU.
YOU RAN HERE?!
DEMONS ARE FASTER THAN WAGONS.
TROMP TROMP TROMP
WAIT, IS IT JUST THE TWO OF YOU?
YOU WEREN'T UP TO ANYTHING QUESTIONABLE, WERE YOU?!!
STAAARE
QUESTIONABLE?
SO, WHAT'S THE EMERGENCY?
IT'S THE WYVERNS.
THEY'VE INVADED DEMON ARMY TERRITORY.

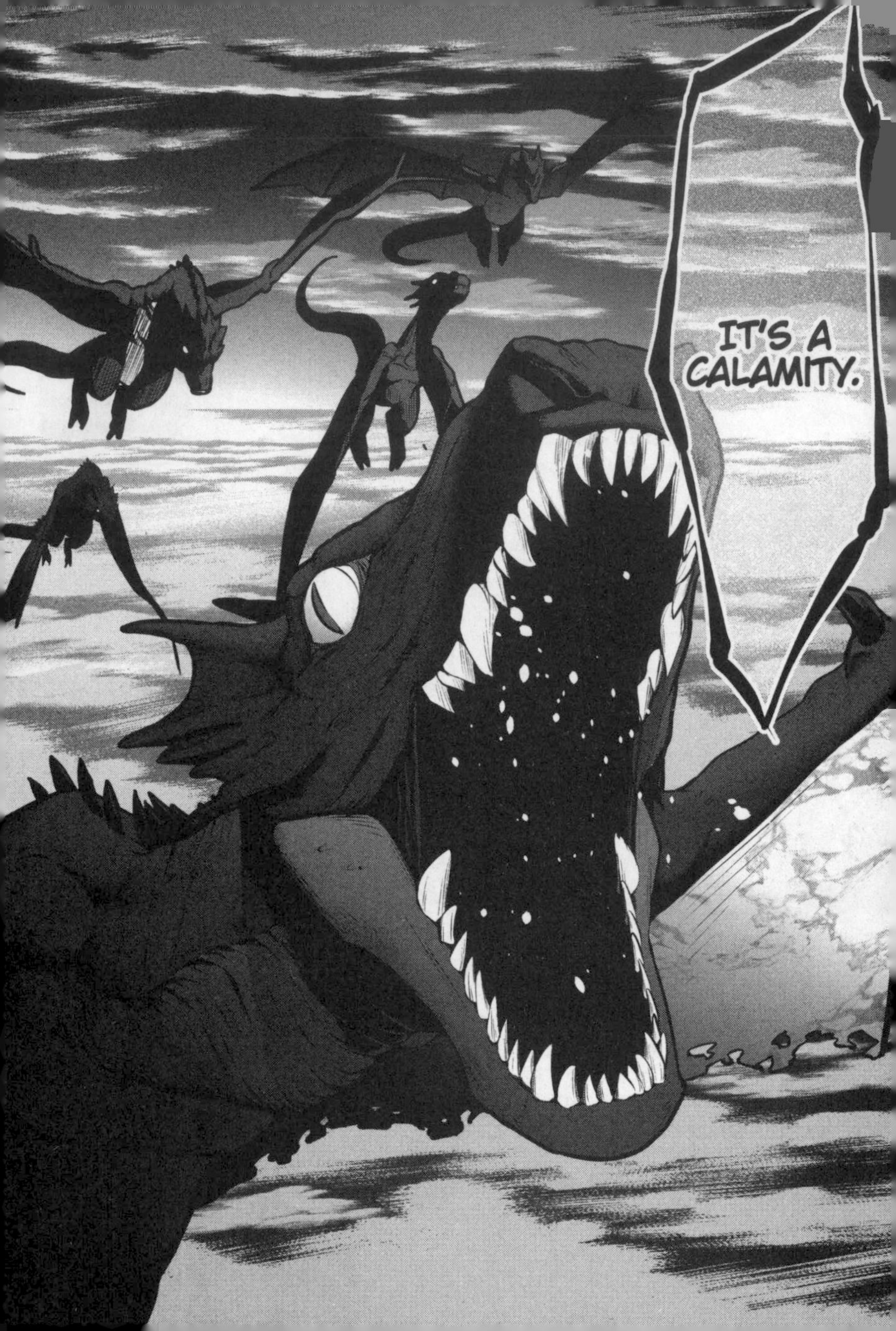
IT'S A CALAMITY.

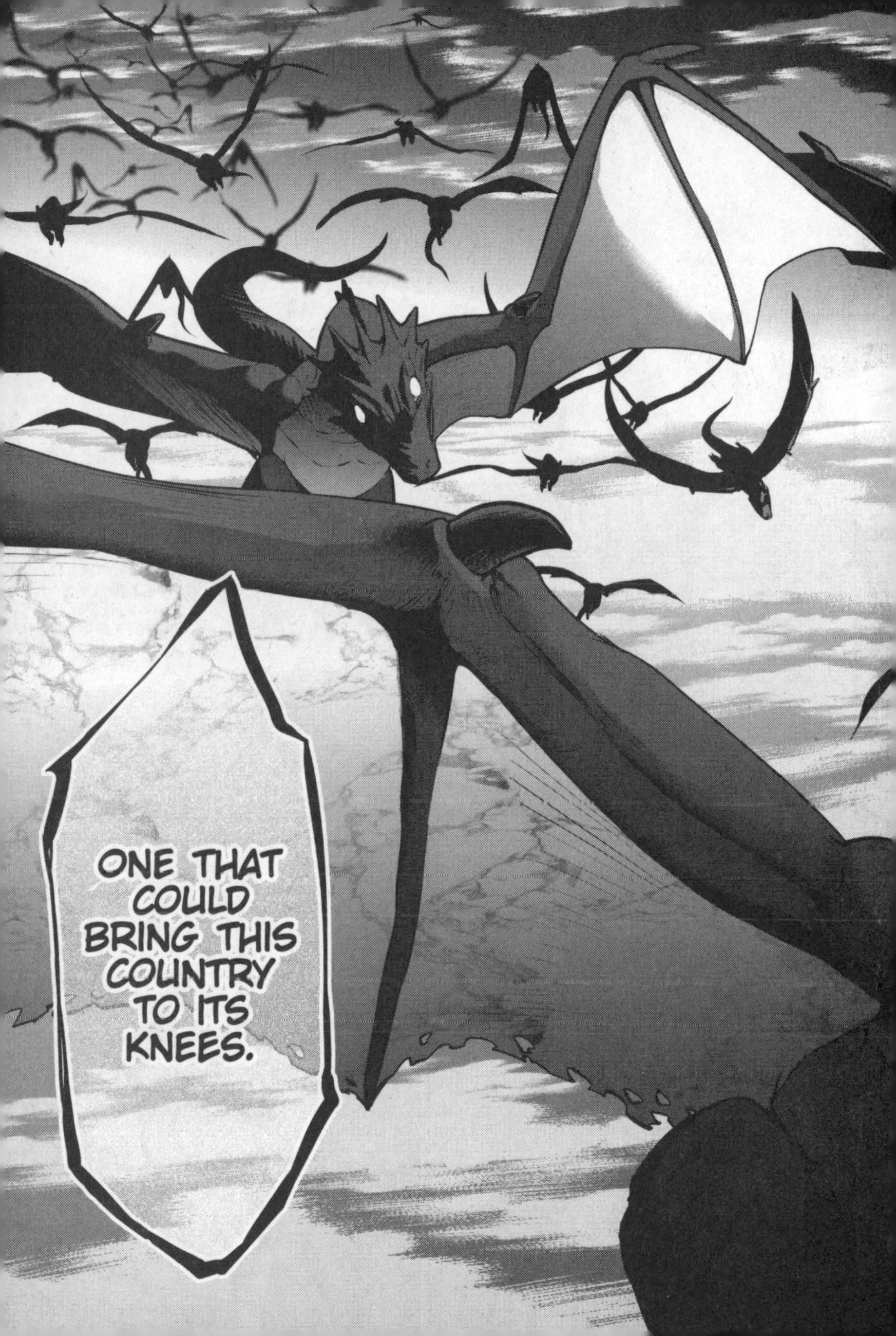
ONE THAT COULD BRING THIS COUNTRY TO ITS KNEES.

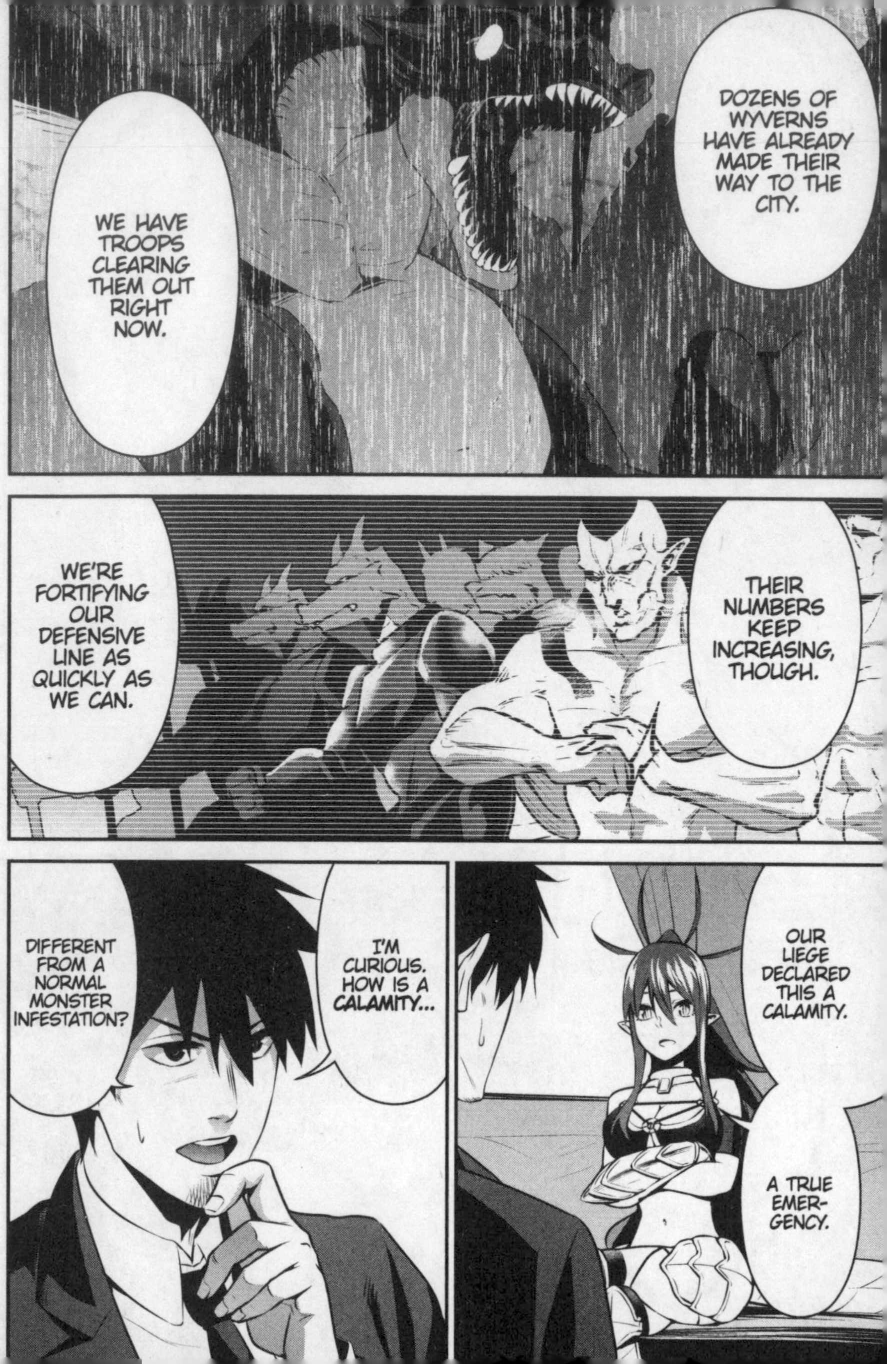
DOZENS OF WYVERNS HAVE ALREADY MADE THEIR WAY TO THE CITY.
WE HAVE TROOPS CLEARING THEM OUT RIGHT NOW.
THEIR NUMBERS KEEP INCREASING, THOUGH.
WE'RE FORTIFYING OUR DEFENSIVE LINE AS QUICKLY AS WE CAN.
OUR LIEGE DECLARED THIS A CALAMITY.
A TRUE EMERGENCY.
I'M CURIOUS. HOW IS A CALAMITY...
DIFFERENT FROM A NORMAL MONSTER INFESTATION?

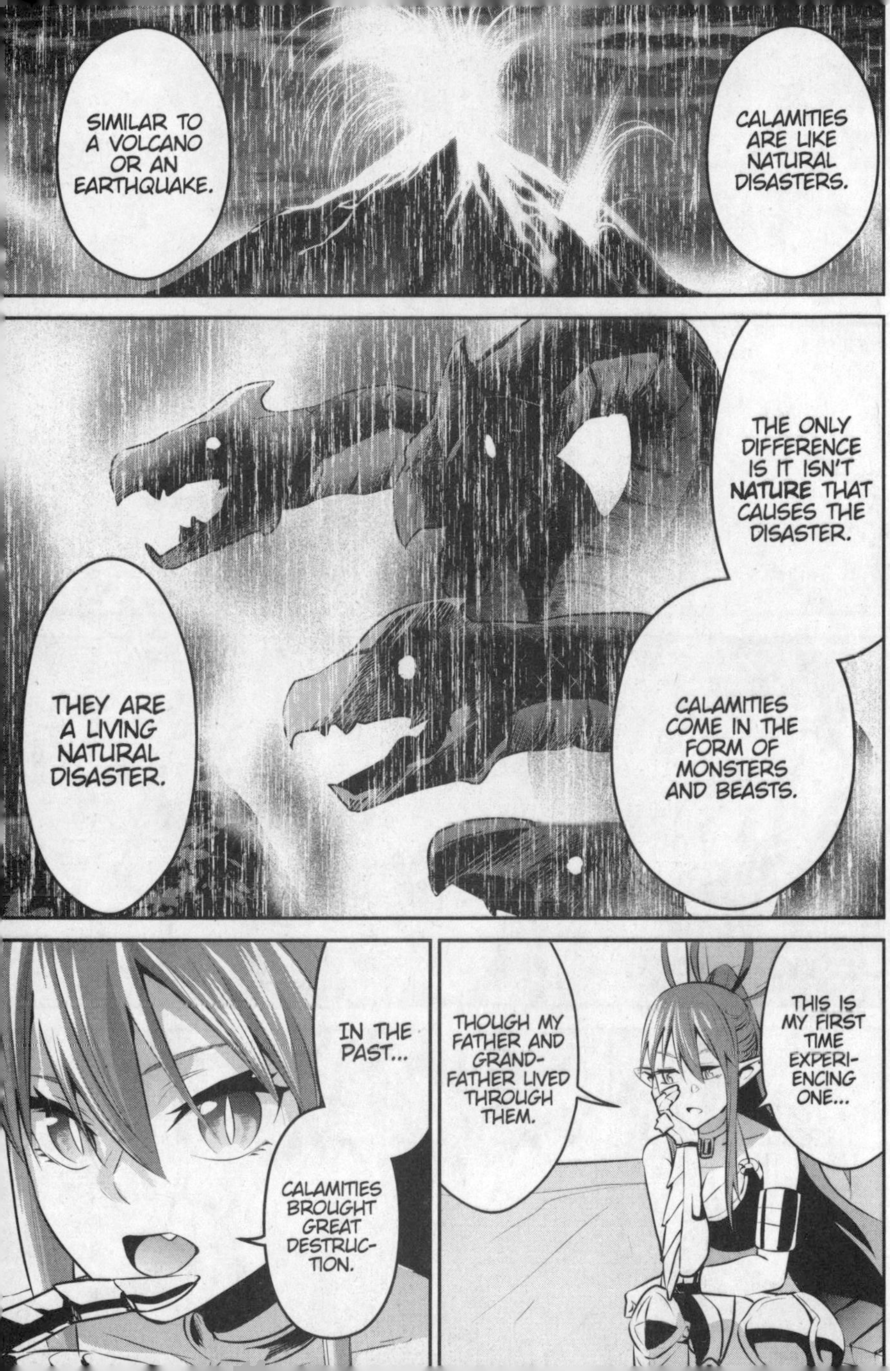
CALAMITIES ARE LIKE NATURAL DISASTERS.
SIMILAR TO A VOLCANO OR AN EARTHQUAKE.
THE ONLY DIFFERENCE IS IT ISN'T **NATURE** THAT CAUSES THE DISASTER.
CALAMITIES COME IN THE FORM OF MONSTERS AND BEASTS.
THEY ARE A LIVING NATURAL DISASTER.
THIS IS MY FIRST TIME EXPERI-ENCING ONE...
THOUGH MY FATHER AND GRAND-FATHER LIVED THROUGH THEM.
IN THE PAST...
CALAMITIES BROUGHT GREAT DESTRUC-TION.

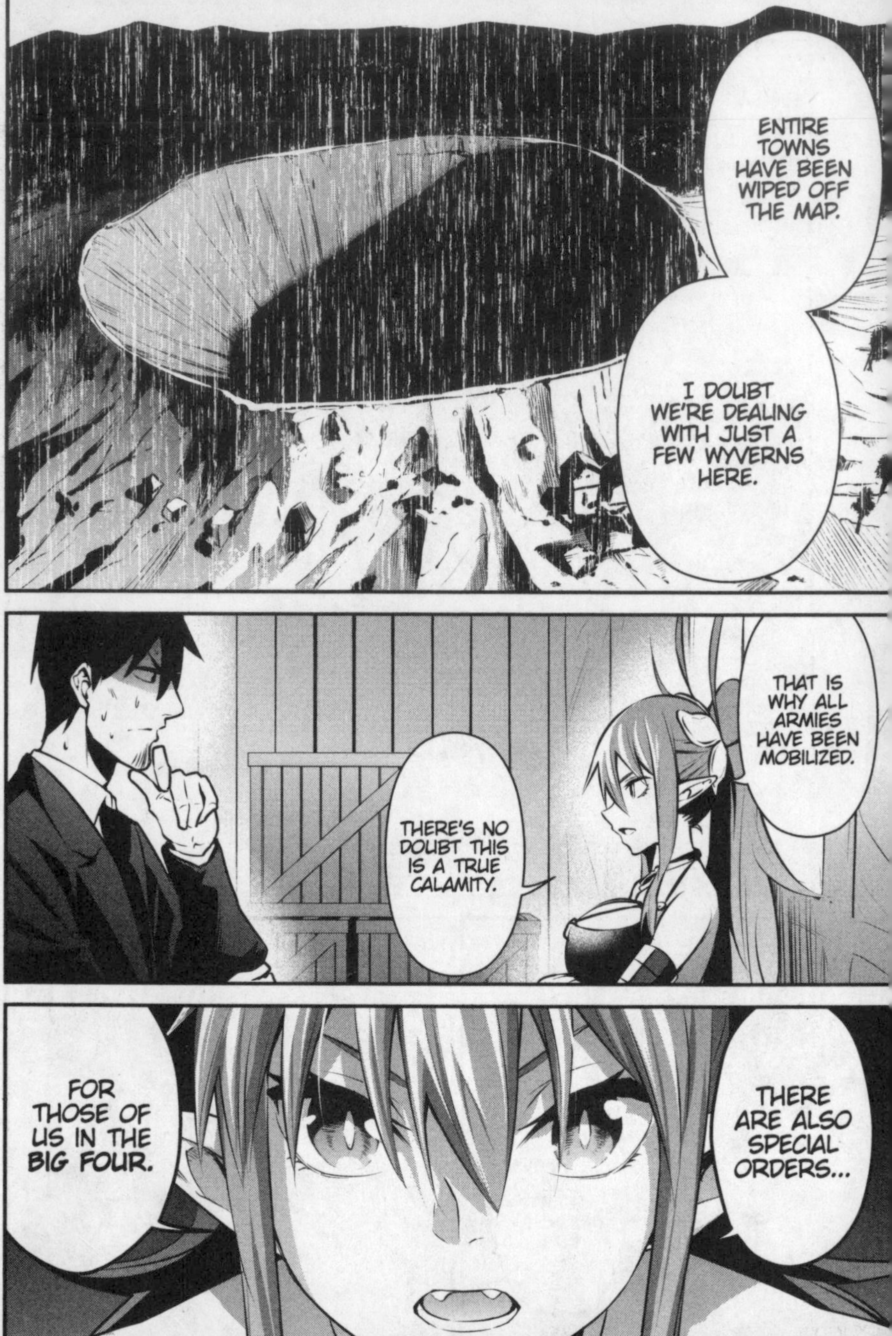
ENTIRE TOWNS HAVE BEEN WIPED OFF THE MAP.
I DOUBT WE'RE DEALING WITH JUST A FEW WYVERNS HERE.
THAT IS WHY ALL ARMIES HAVE BEEN MOBILIZED.
THERE'S NO DOUBT THIS IS A TRUE CALAMITY.
THERE ARE ALSO SPECIAL ORDERS...
FOR THOSE OF US IN THE BIG FOUR.

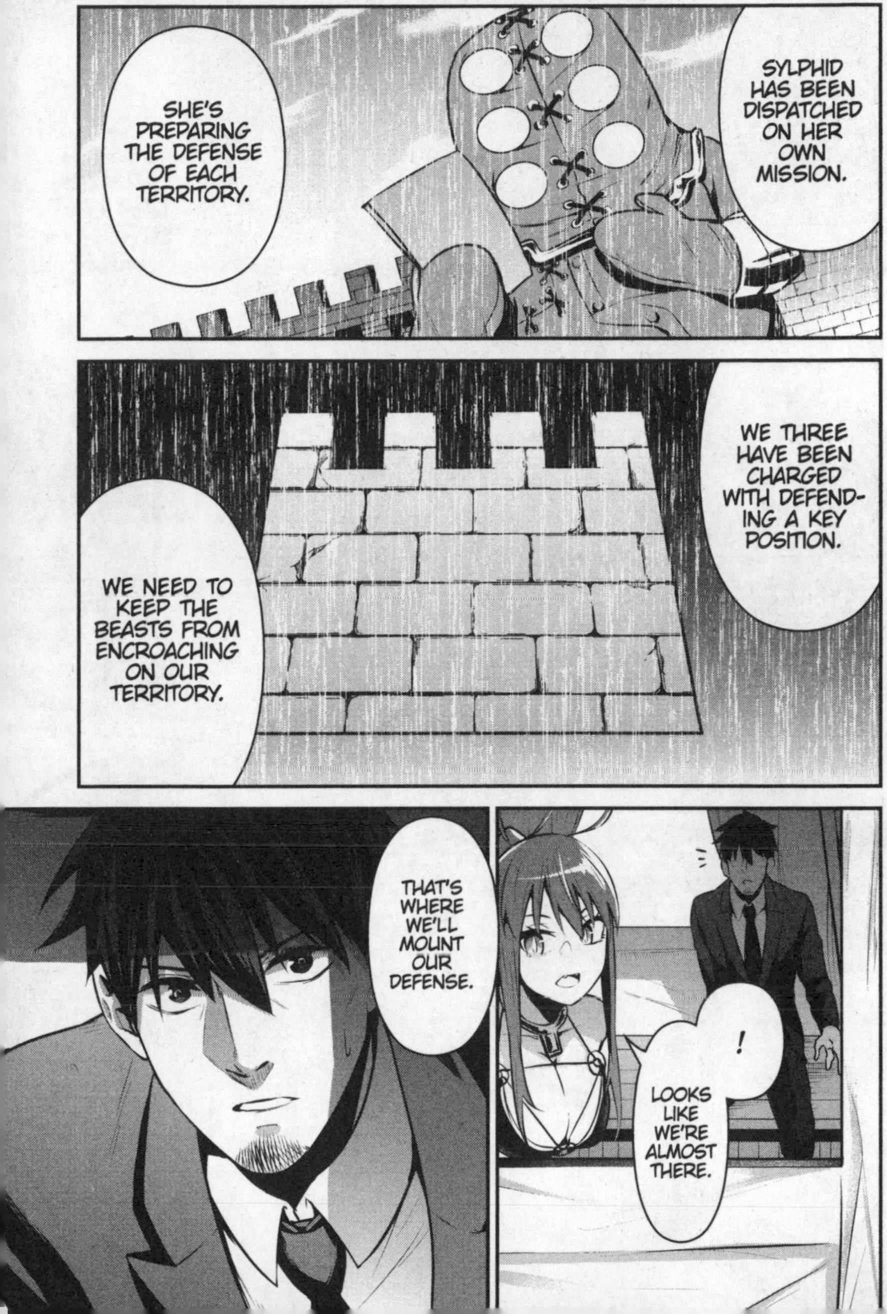
SYLPHID HAS BEEN DISPATCHED ON HER OWN MISSION.
SHE'S PREPARING THE DEFENSE OF EACH TERRITORY.
WE THREE HAVE BEEN CHARGED WITH DEFEND-ING A KEY POSITION.
WE NEED TO KEEP THE BEASTS FROM ENCROACHING ON OUR TERRITORY.
!
LOOKS LIKE WE'RE ALMOST THERE.
THAT'S WHERE WE'LL MOUNT OUR DEFENSE.

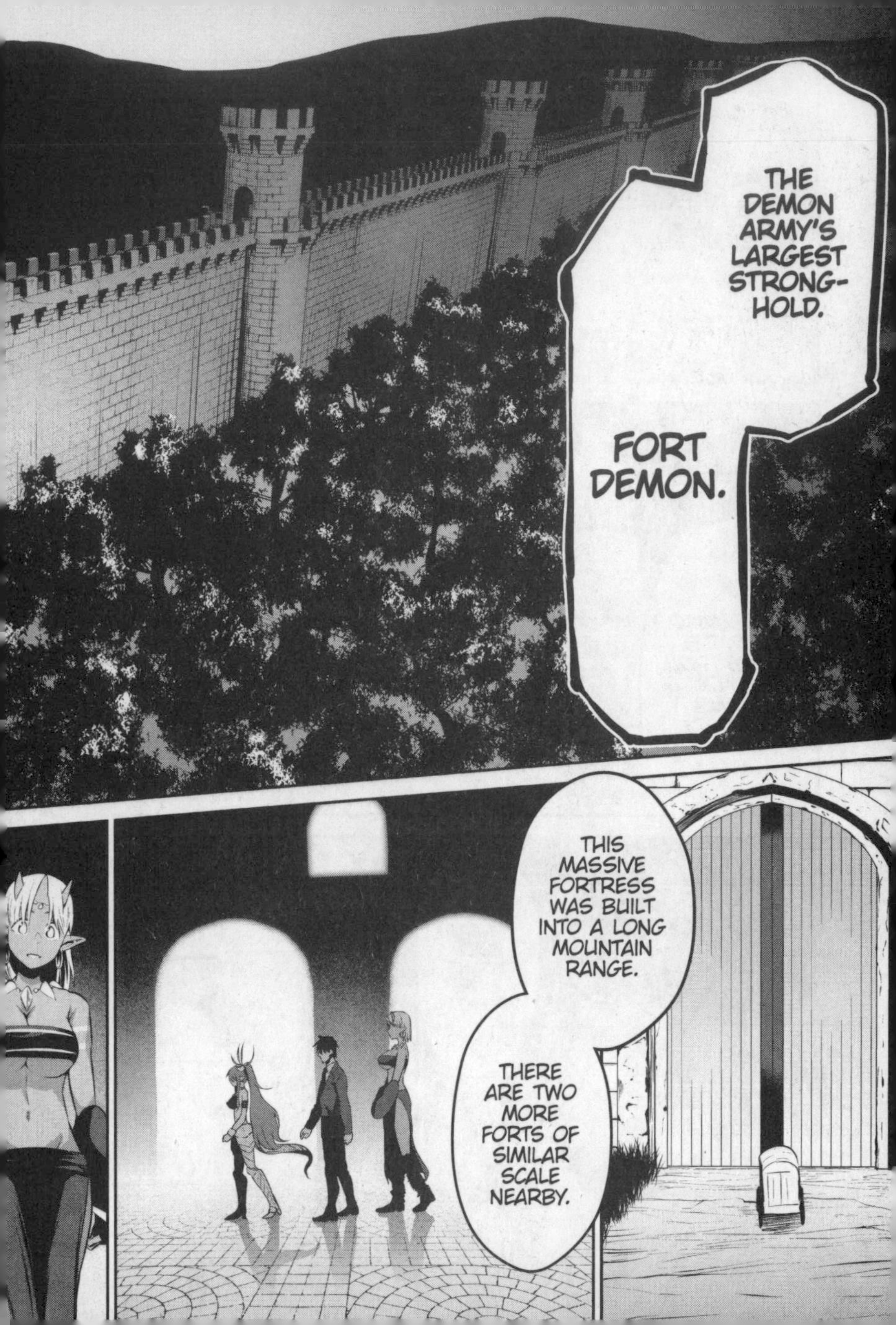
THE DEMON ARMY'S LARGEST STRONG-HOLD.
FORT DEMON.
THIS MASSIVE FORTRESS WAS BUILT INTO A LONG MOUNTAIN RANGE.
THERE ARE TWO MORE FORTS OF SIMILAR SCALE NEARBY.

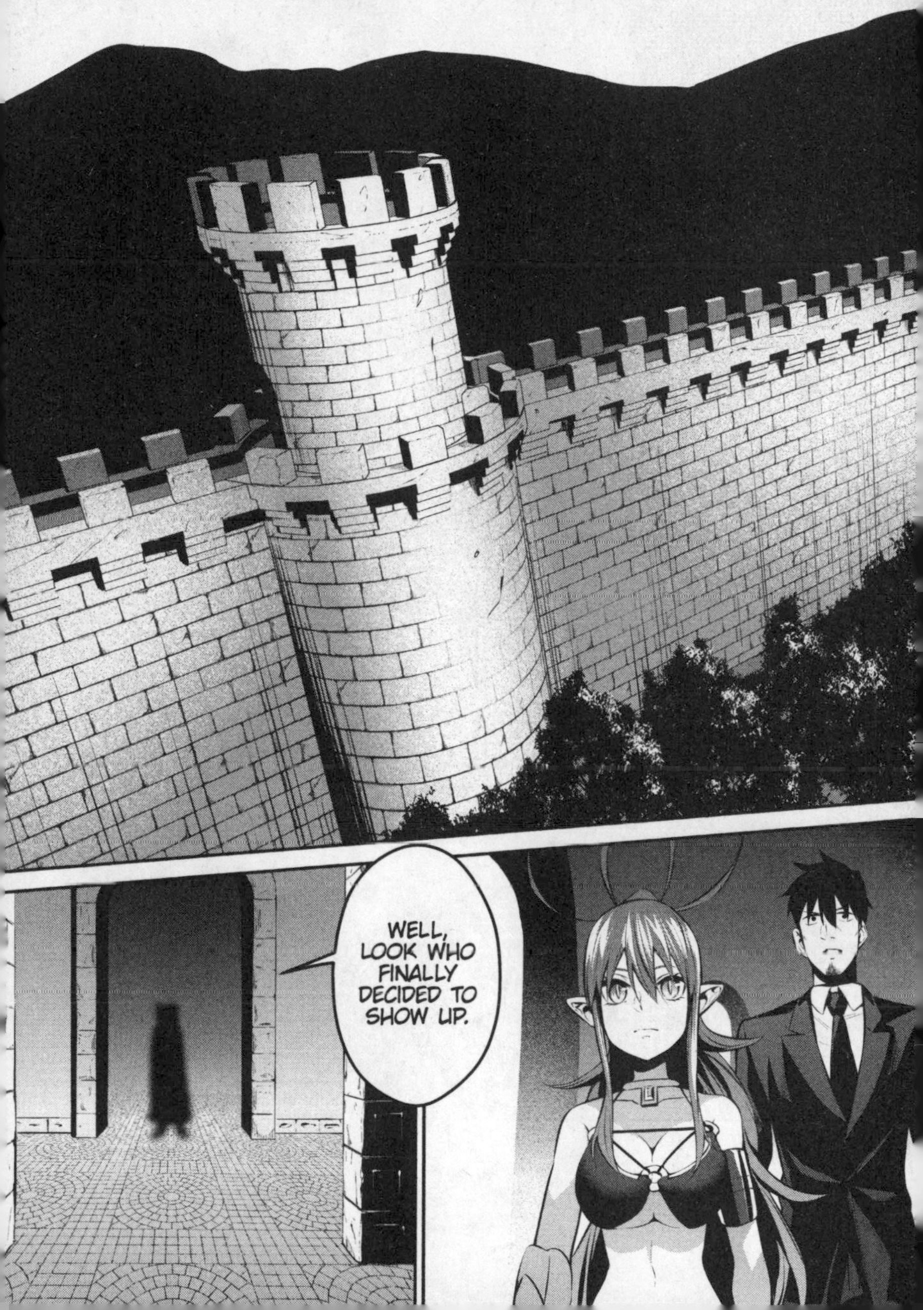
WELL, LOOK WHO FINALLY DECIDED TO SHOW UP.

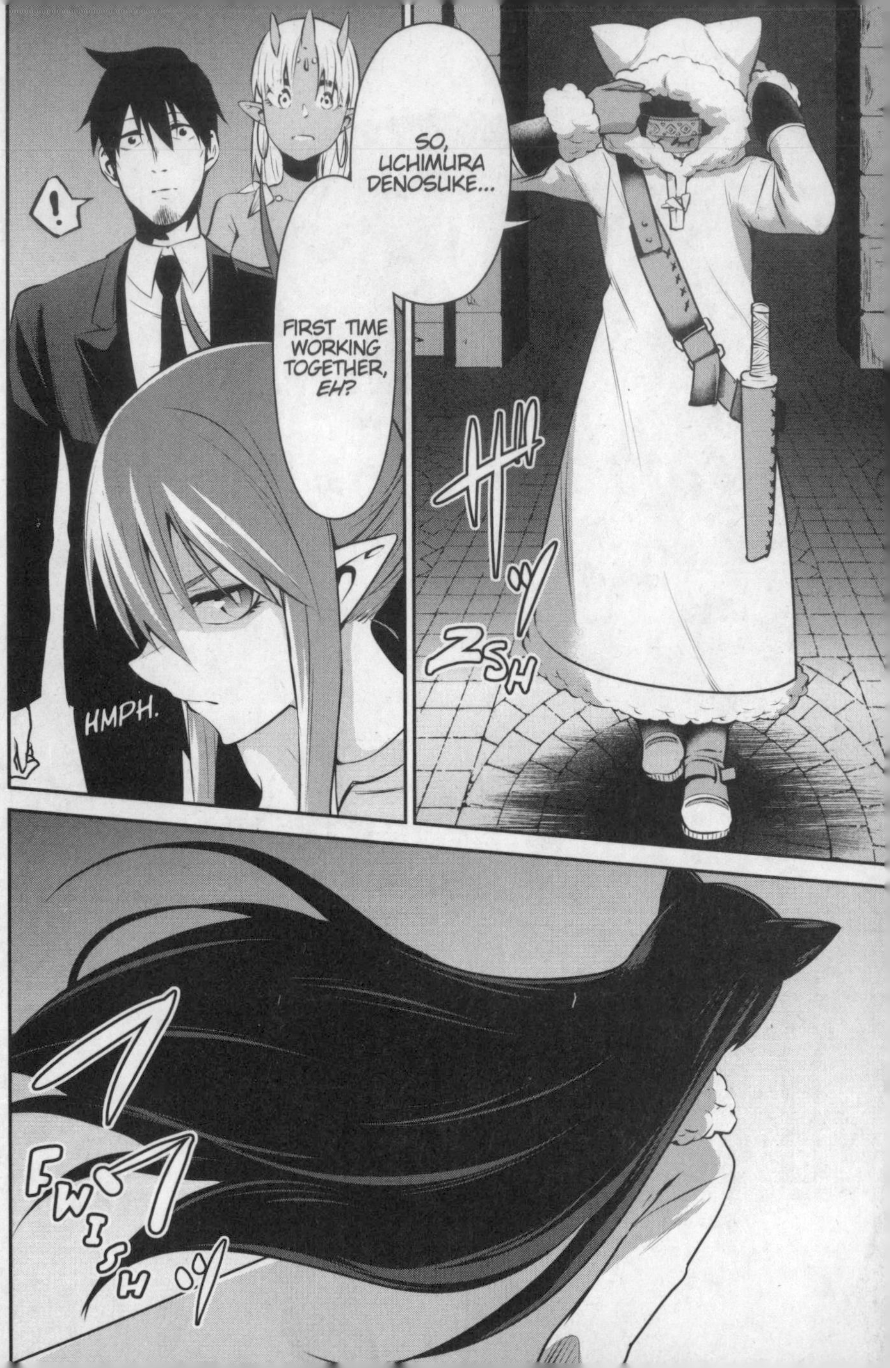
SO, UCHIMURA DENOSUKE...
FIRST TIME WORKING TOGETHER, EH?
ZSH
!
HMPH.
FWISH

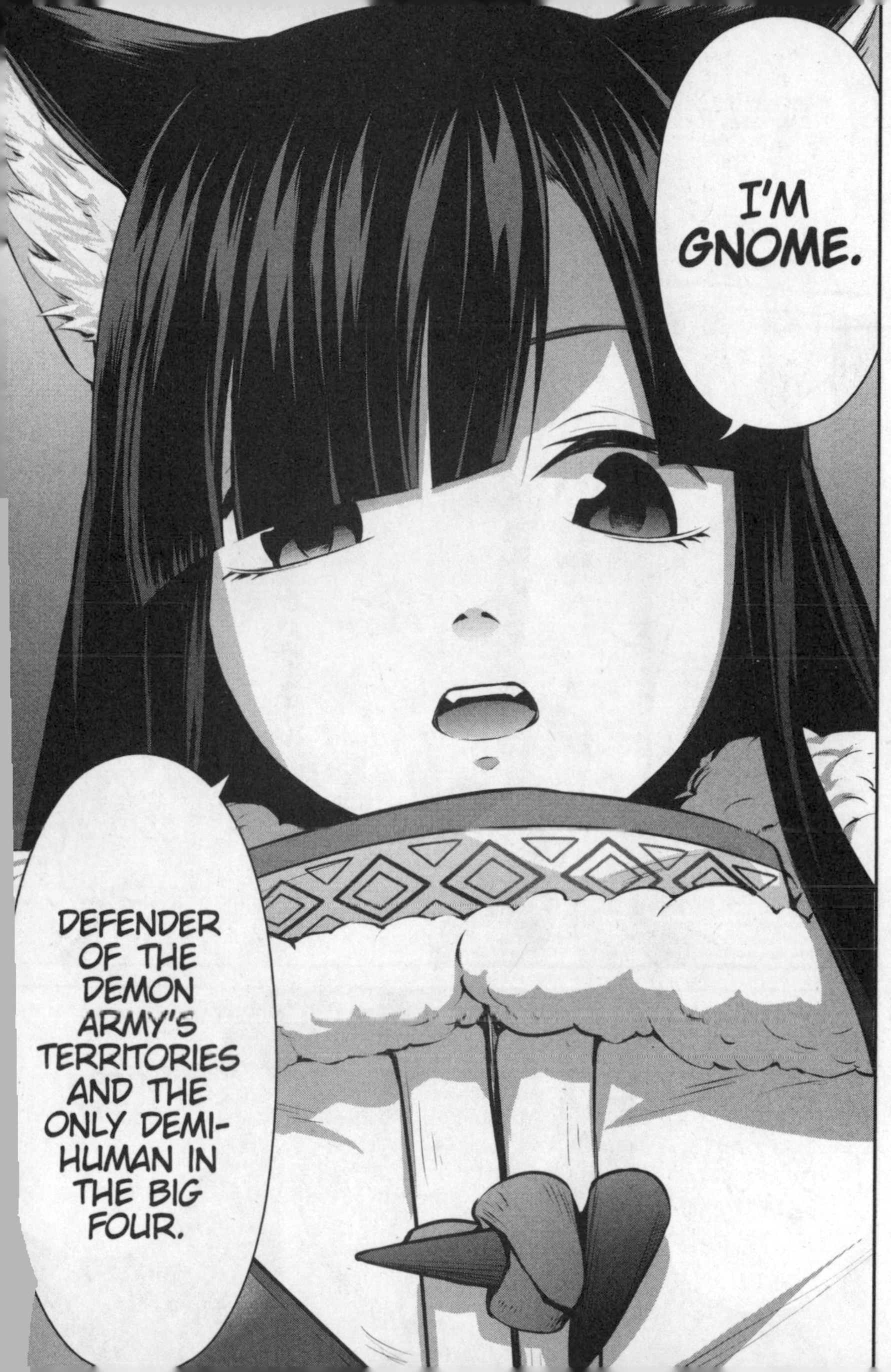
I'M GNOME.
DEFENDER OF THE DEMON ARMY'S TERRITORIES AND THE ONLY DEMI-HUMAN IN THE BIG FOUR.

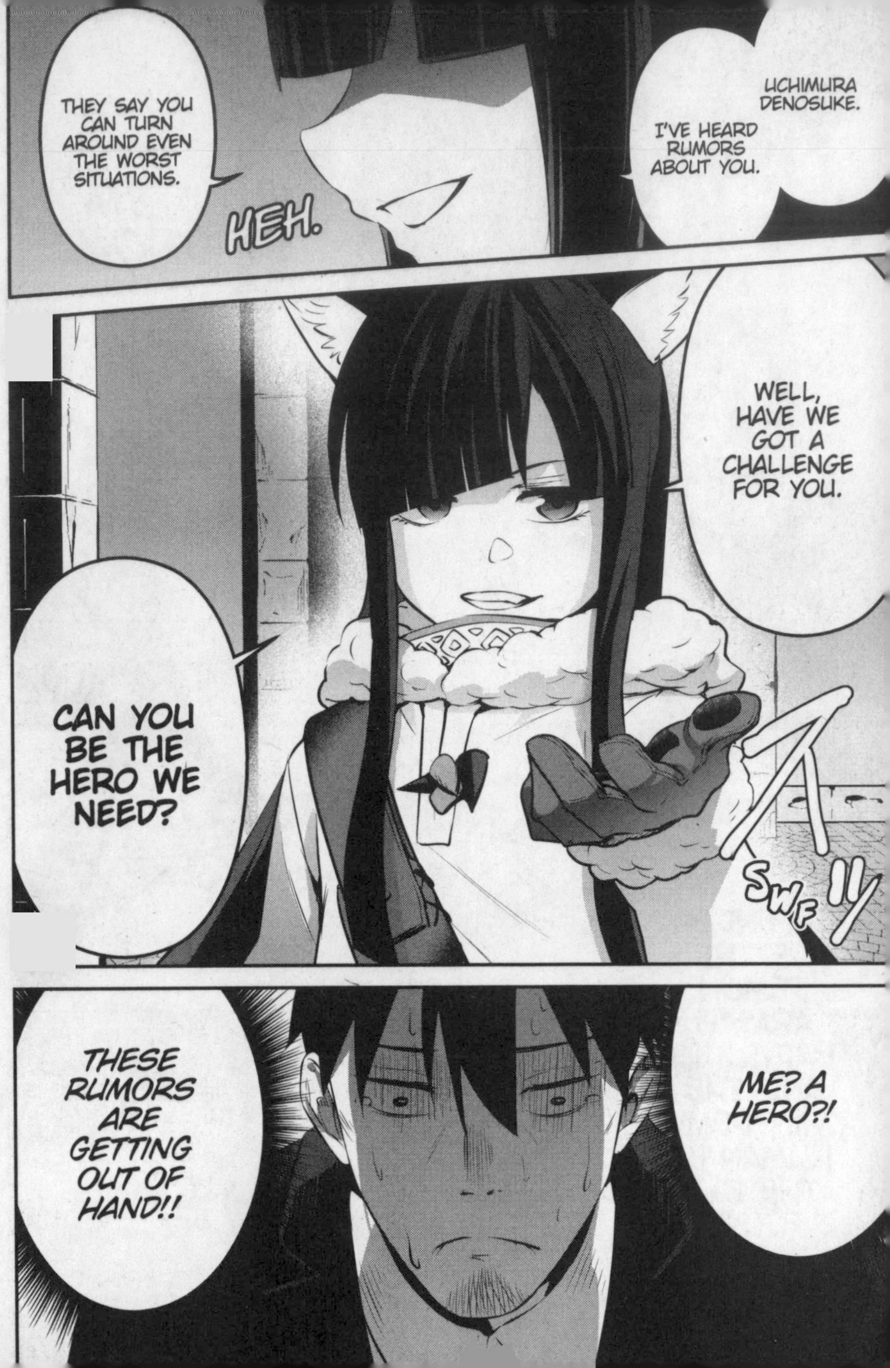
UCHIMURA DENOSUKE.
I'VE HEARD RUMORS ABOUT YOU.
THEY SAY YOU CAN TURN AROUND EVEN THE WORST SITUATIONS.
HEH.
WELL, HAVE WE GOT A CHALLENGE FOR YOU.
CAN YOU BE THE HERO WE NEED?
SWF
ME? A HERO?!
THESE RUMORS ARE GETTING OUT OF HAND!!

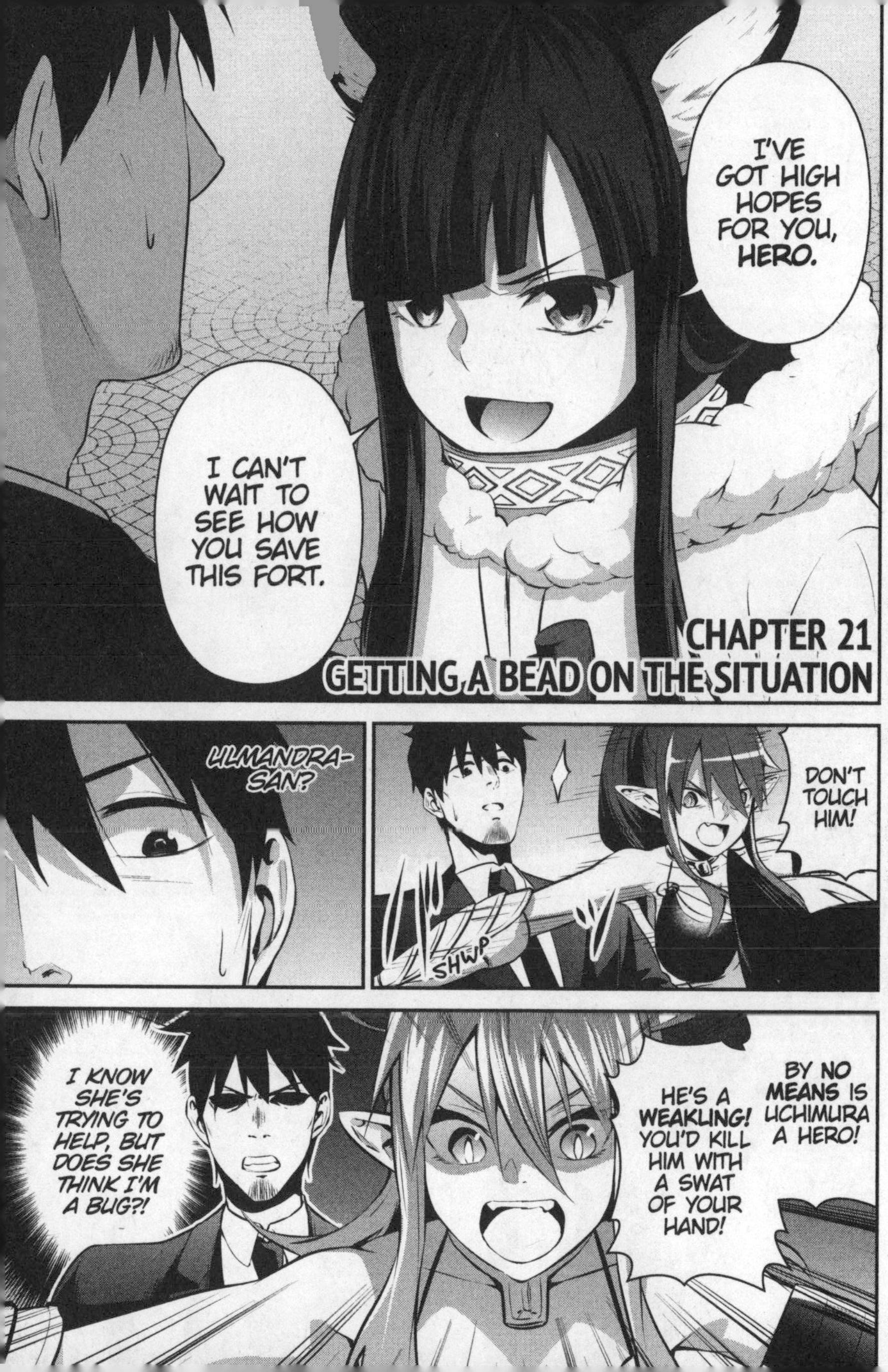
I'VE GOT HIGH HOPES FOR YOU, HERO.
I CAN'T WAIT TO SEE HOW YOU SAVE THIS FORT.
CHAPTER 21
GETTING A BEAD ON THE SITUATION
DON'T TOUCH HIM!
SHWP
ULMANDRA-SAN?
BY NO MEANS IS UCHIMURA A HERO!
HE'S A WEAKLING! YOU'D KILL HIM WITH A SWAT OF YOUR HAND!
I KNOW SHE'S TRYING TO HELP, BUT DOES SHE THINK I'M A BUG?!

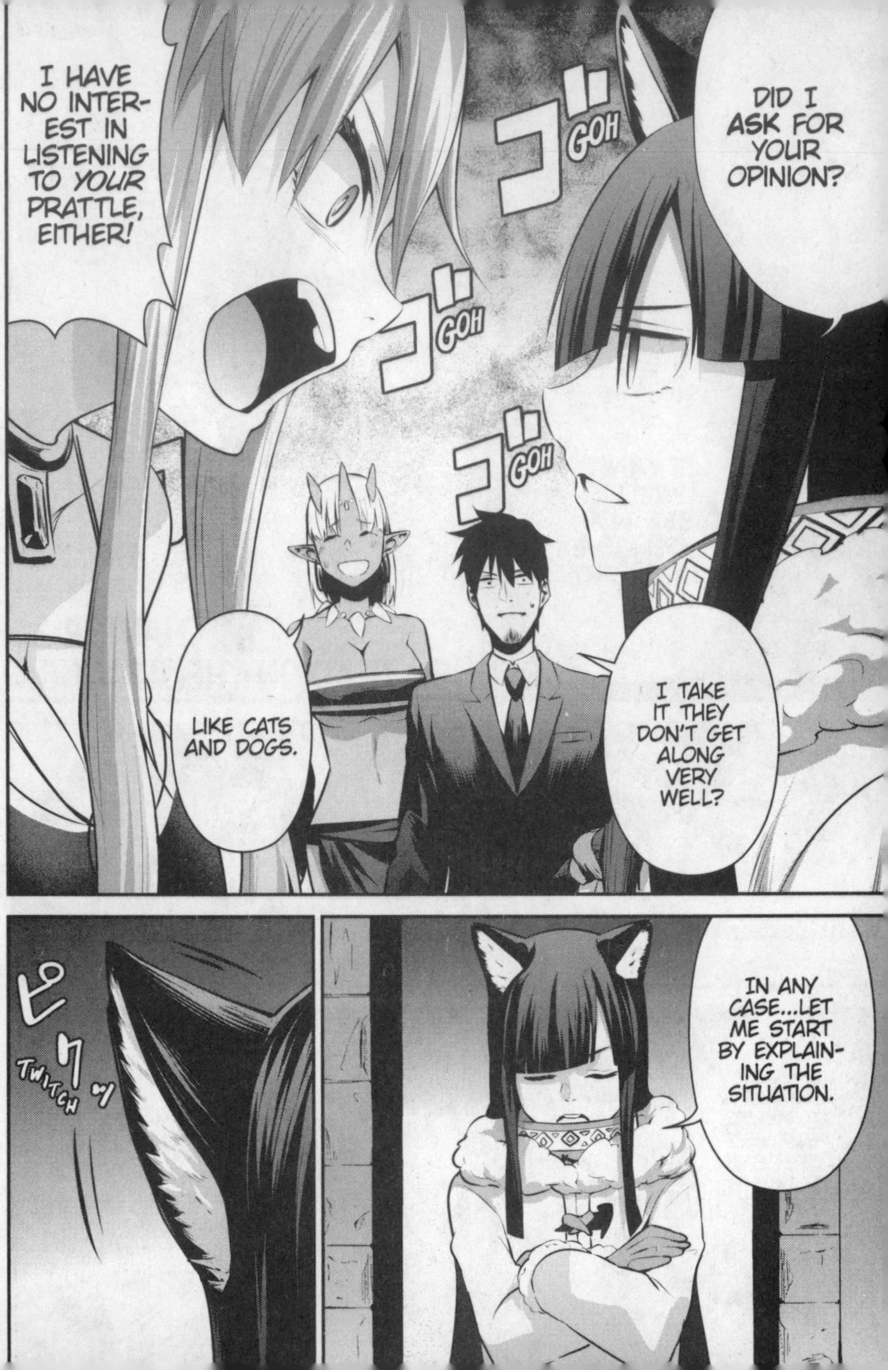
DID I ASK FOR YOUR OPINION?
I HAVE NO INTEREST IN LISTENING TO *YOUR* PRATTLE, EITHER!
GOH
GOH
GOH
I TAKE IT THEY DON'T GET ALONG VERY WELL?
LIKE CATS AND DOGS.
IN ANY CASE...LET ME START BY EXPLAINING THE SITUATION.
TWITCH

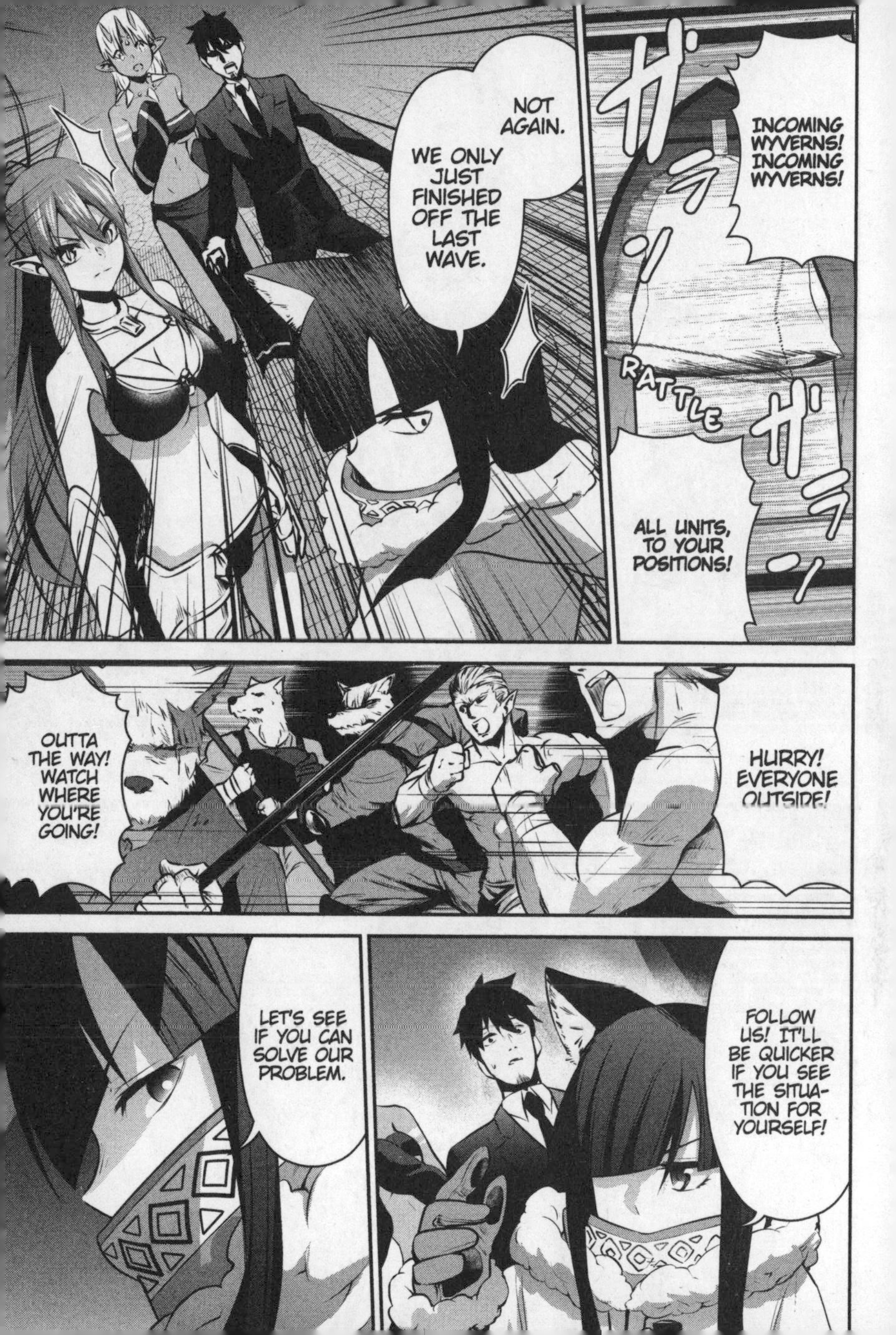
INCOMING WYVERNS! INCOMING WYVERNS!
RATTLE
ALL UNITS, TO YOUR POSITIONS!
NOT AGAIN.
WE ONLY JUST FINISHED OFF THE LAST WAVE.
HURRY! EVERYONE OUTSIDE!
OUTTA THE WAY! WATCH WHERE YOU'RE GOING!
FOLLOW US! IT'LL BE QUICKER IF YOU SEE THE SITUA-TION FOR YOURSELF!
LET'S SEE IF YOU CAN SOLVE OUR PROBLEM.

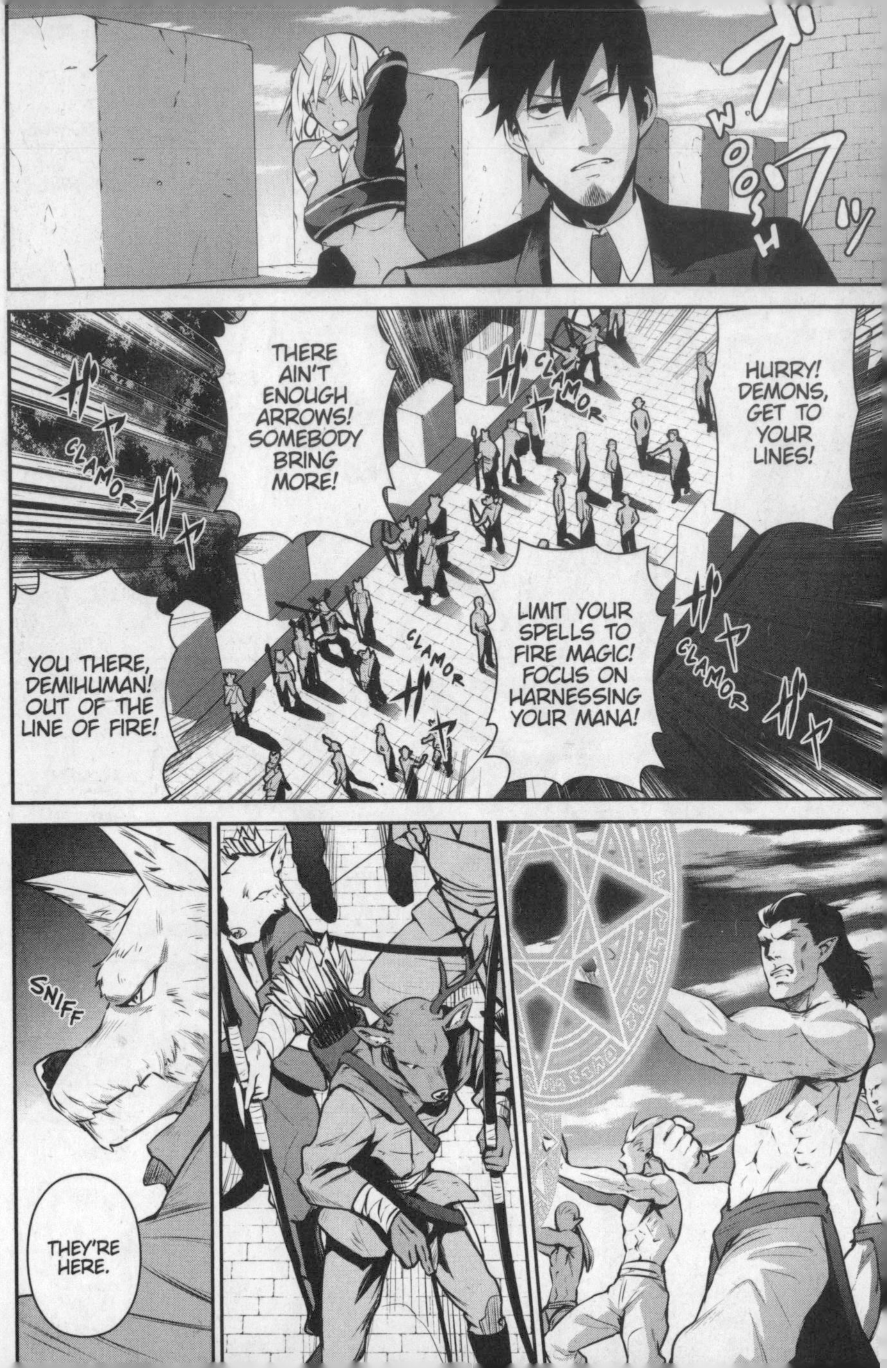
WOOSH
HURRY! DEMONS, GET TO YOUR LINES!
CLAMOR
THERE AIN'T ENOUGH ARROWS! SOMEBODY BRING MORE!
CLAMOR
CLAMOR
LIMIT YOUR SPELLS TO FIRE MAGIC! FOCUS ON HARNESSING YOUR MANA!
CLAMOR
YOU THERE, DEMIHUMAN! OUT OF THE LINE OF FIRE!
CLAMOR
SNIFF
THEY'RE HERE.

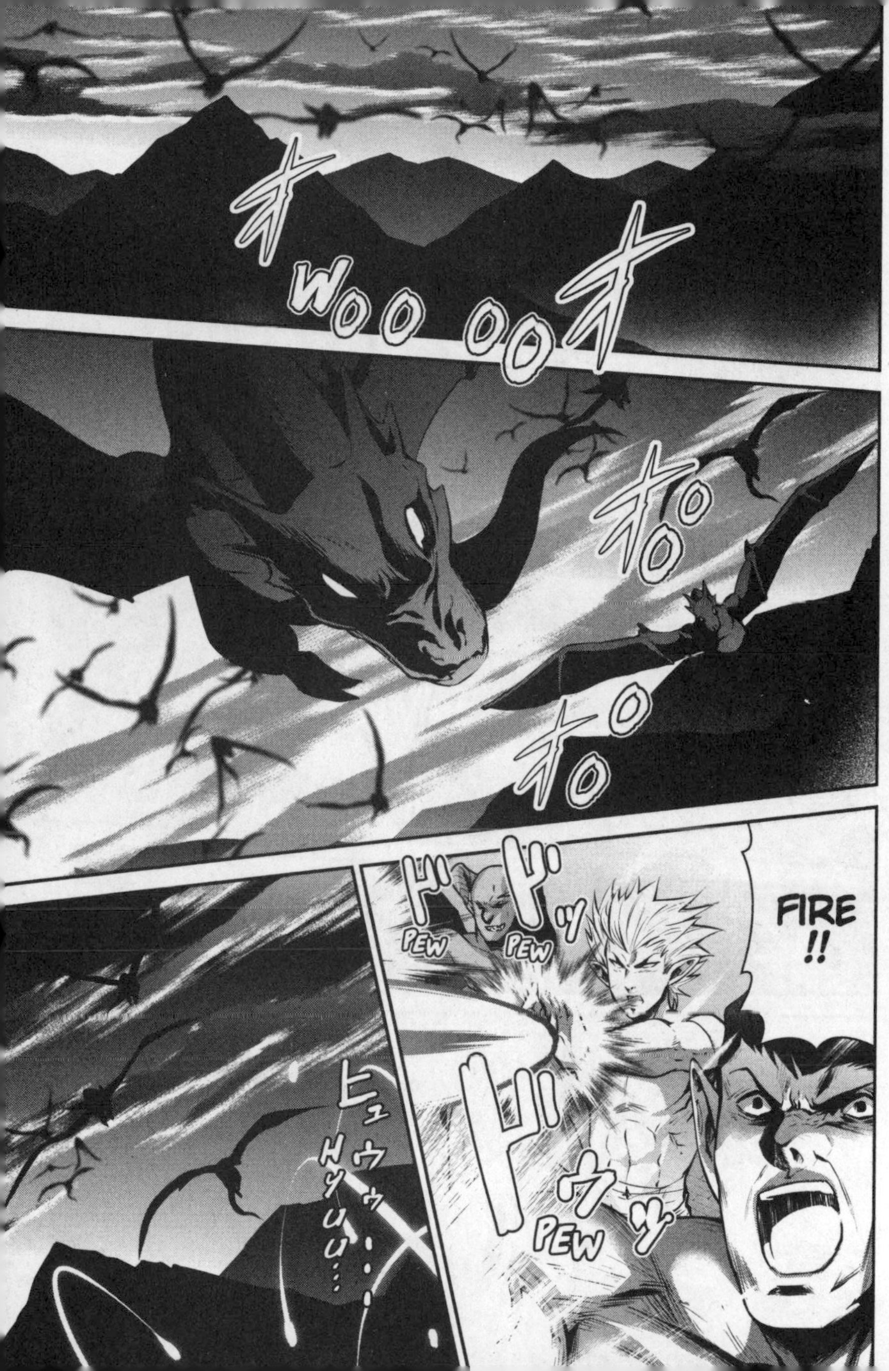
オ
WOO OO
オ
オ゜オ゜
オ゜オ゜
FIRE!!
ド
PEW
ドッ
PEW
ドゥッ
PEW
ヒュウゥ…
HYUUU…

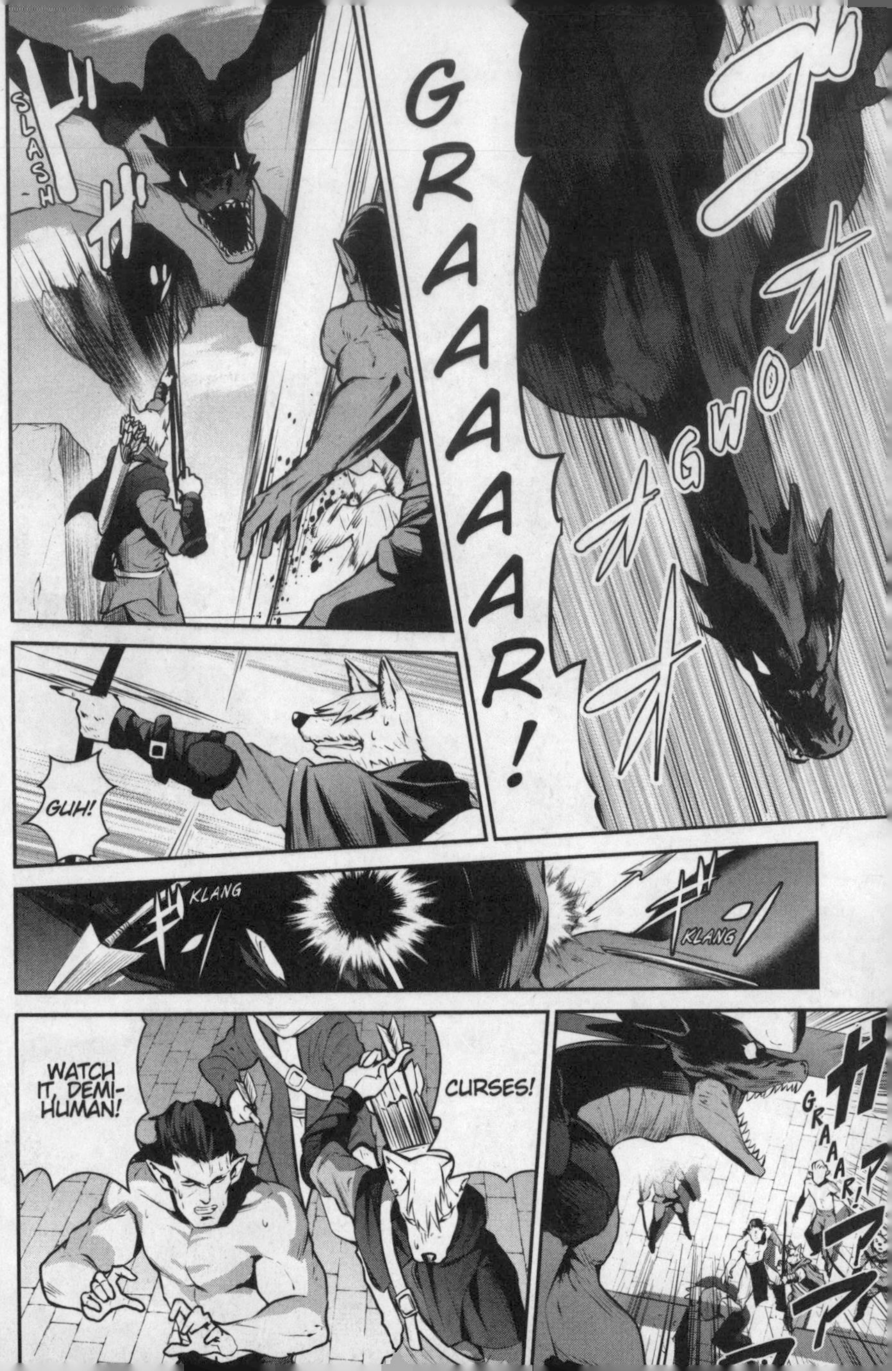
GWO
GRAAAAAR!
SLASH
GUH!
KLANG
KLANG
GRAAAR!
CURSES!
WATCH IT, DEMI-HUMAN!

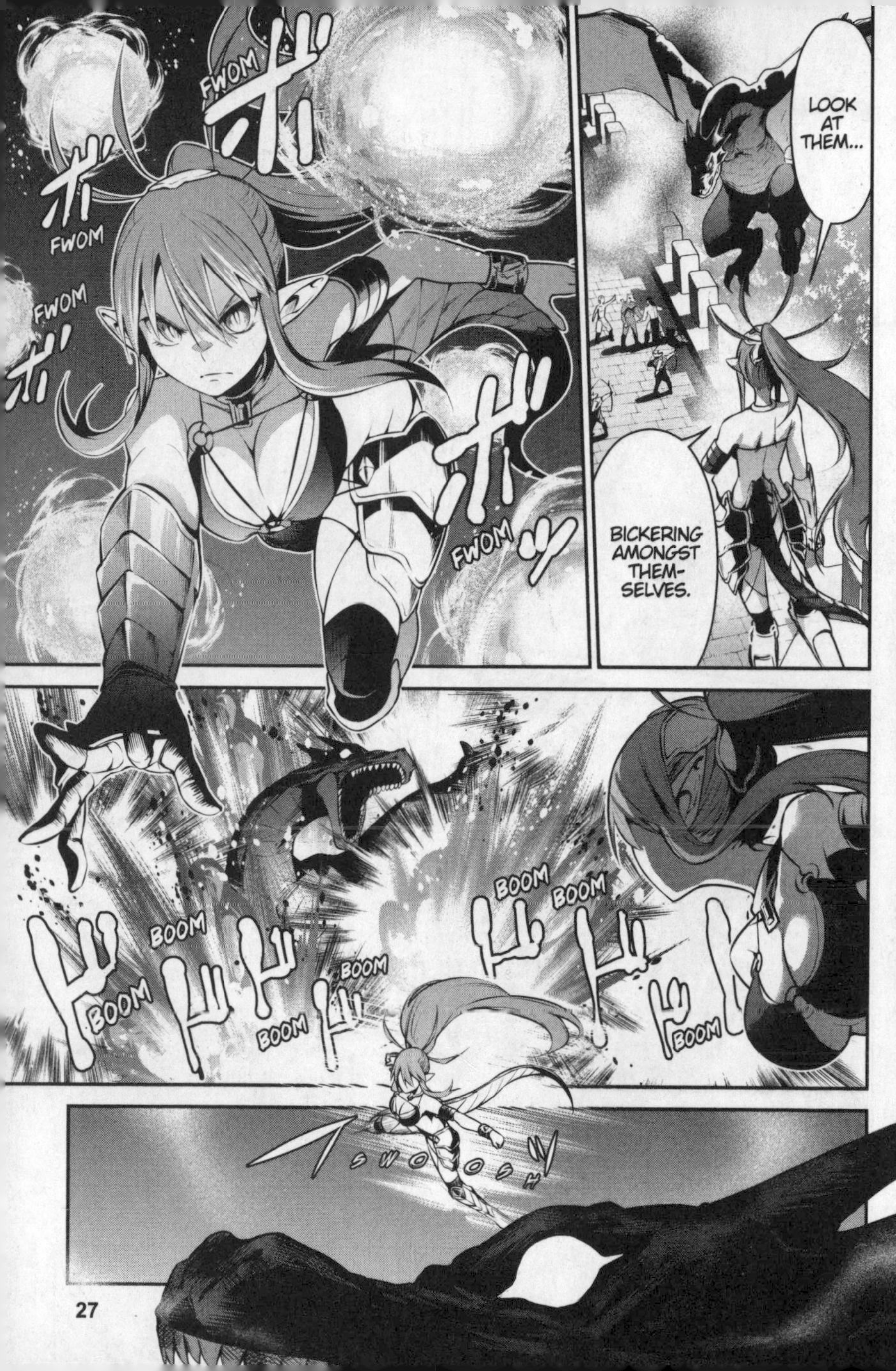
LOOK AT THEM...
BICKERING AMONGST THEM-SELVES.
FWOM
FWOM
FWOM
FWOM
BOOM
BOOM
BOOM
BOOM
BOOM
BOOM
BOOM
SWOOSH

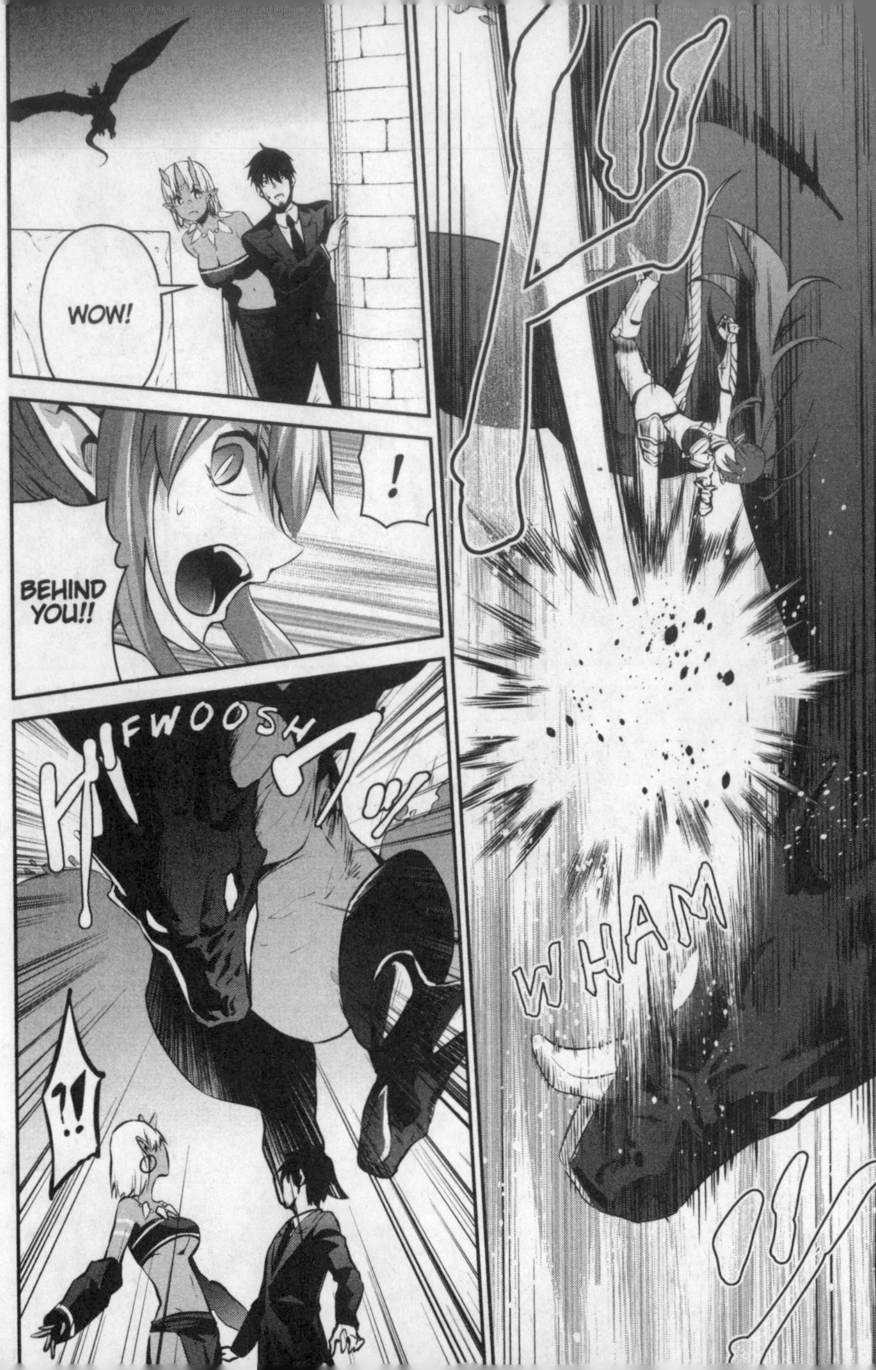
WHAM
WOW!
!
BEHIND YOU!!
FWOOSH
?!!

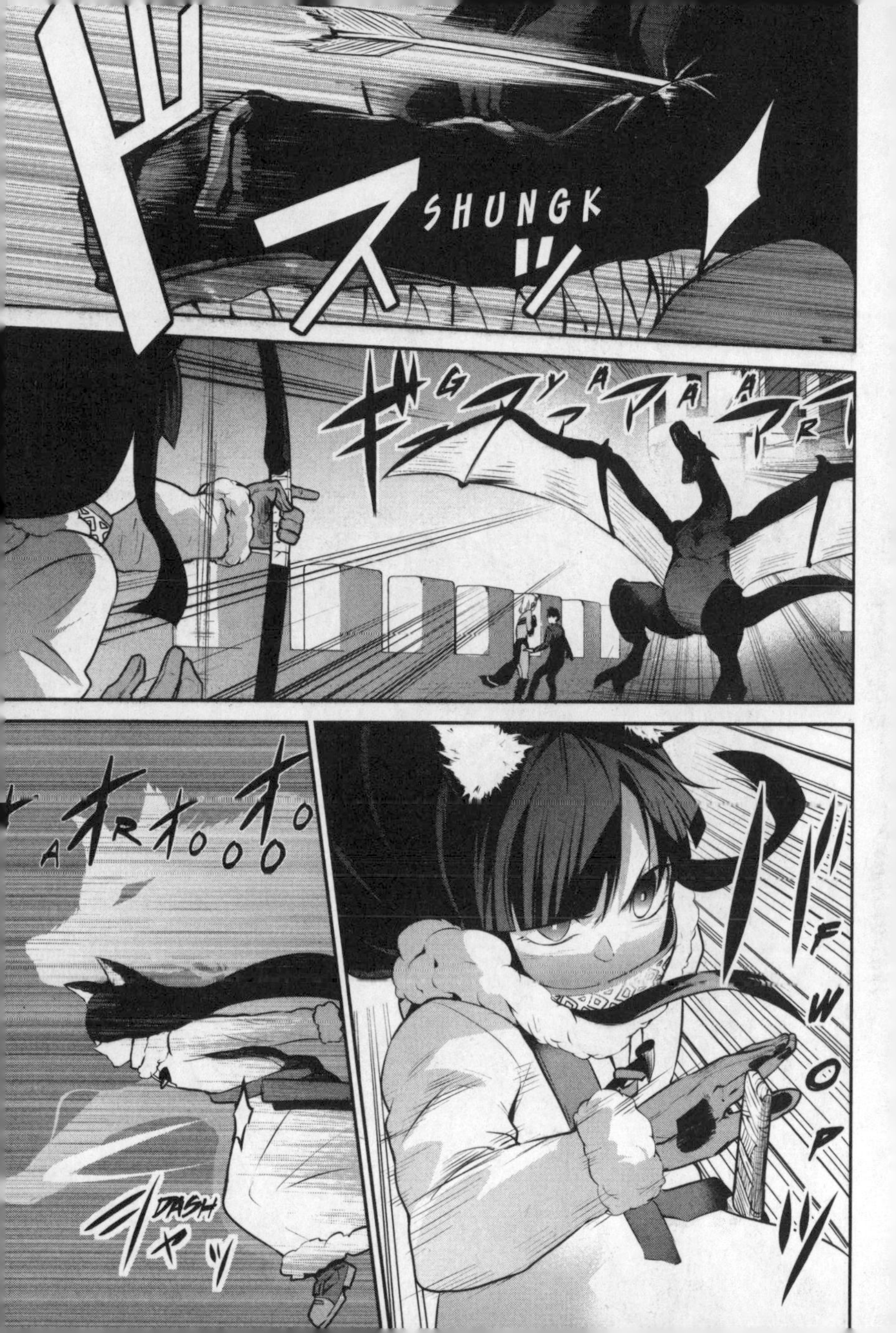
SHUNGK
GYAAAR
FWOOP
AROOOOO
DASH

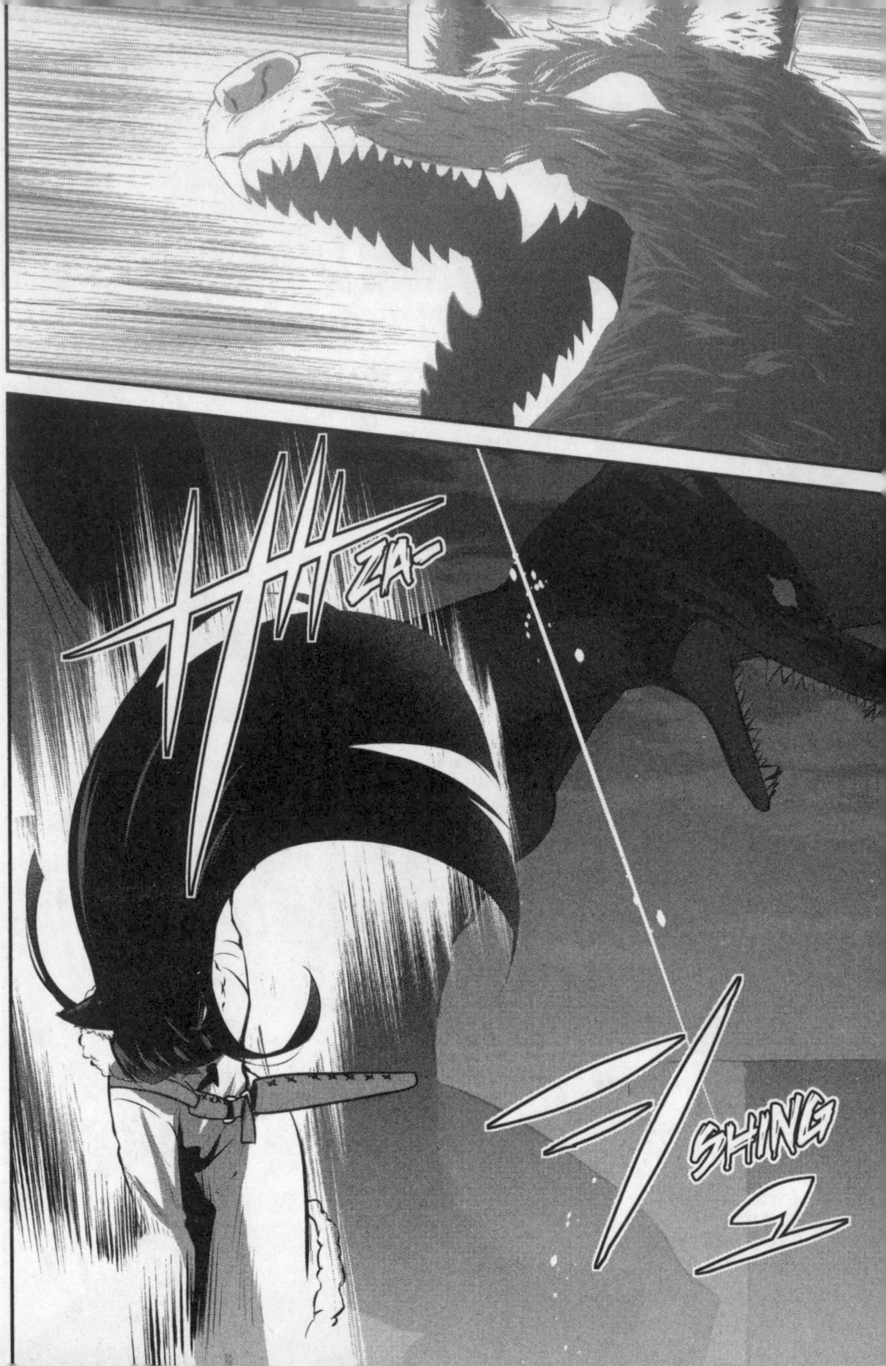
ZA-
SHING

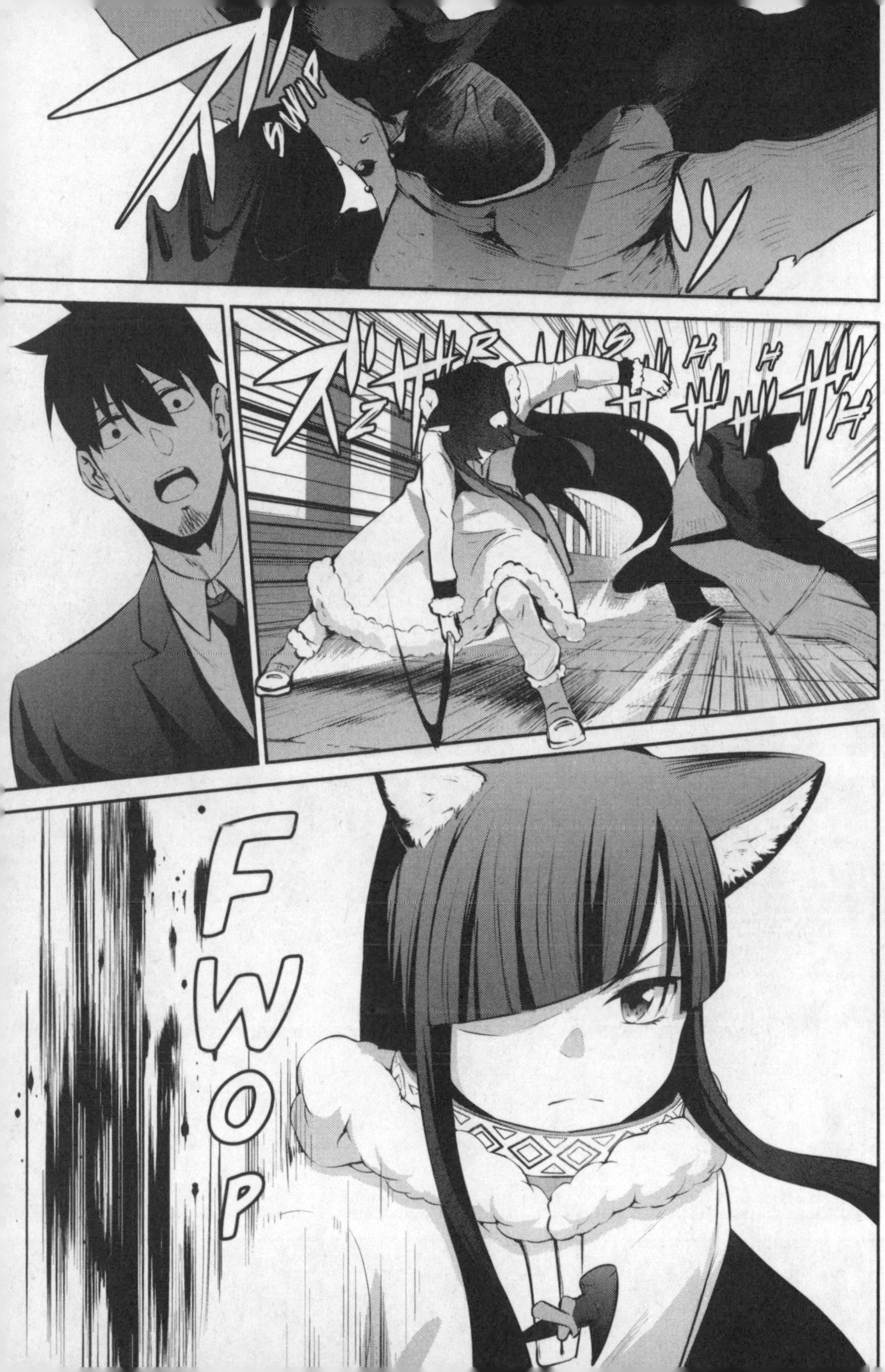
SWIP
ZR
SHHH
FWOP

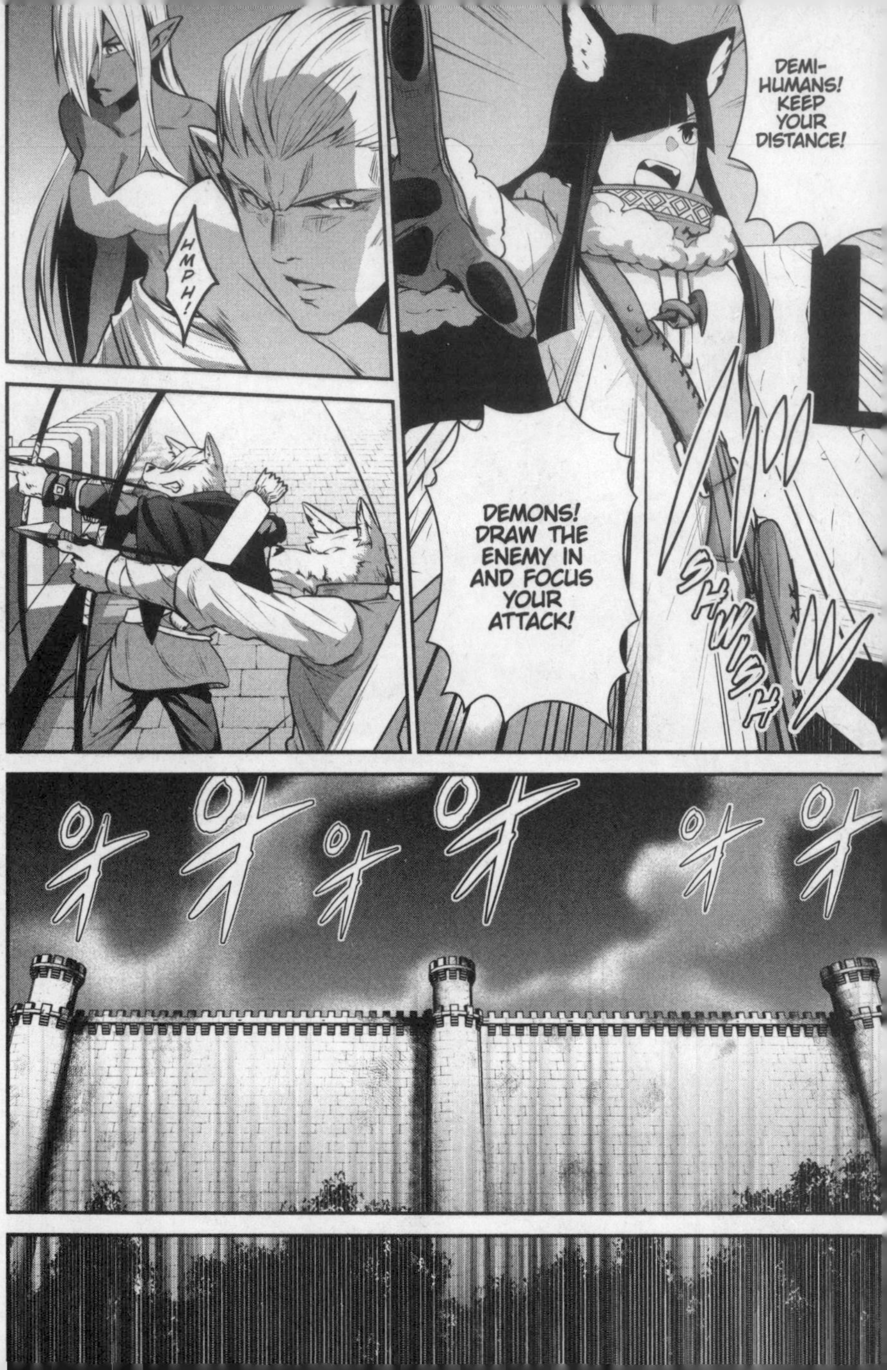
DEMI-HUMANS! KEEP YOUR DISTANCE!
DEMONS! DRAW THE ENEMY IN AND FOCUS YOUR ATTACK!
SHWISH
HMPH!

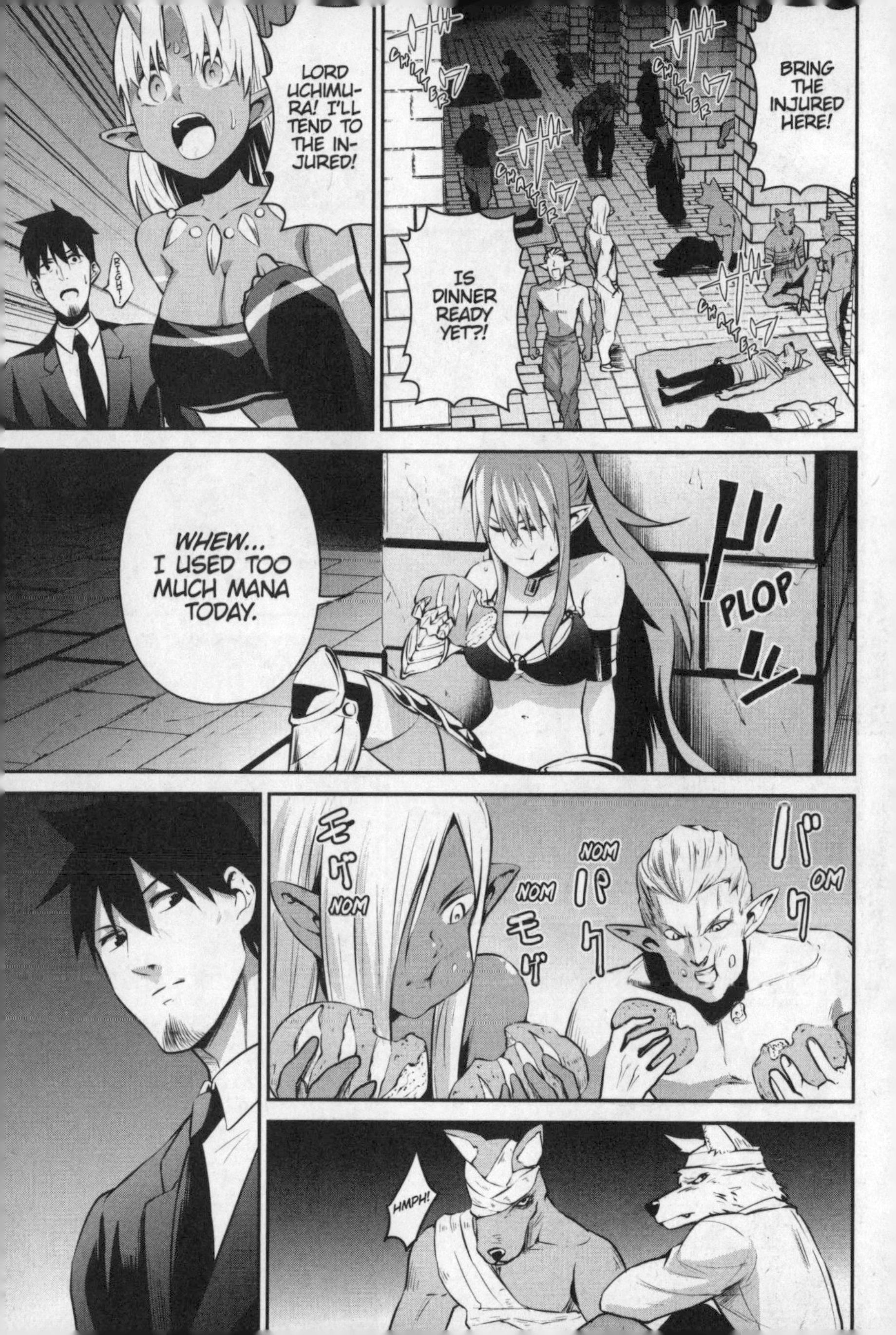
CHITTER
CHITTER
BRING THE INJURED HERE!
CHATTER
IS DINNER READY YET?!
CHATTER
LORD UCHIMURA! I'LL TEND TO THE INJURED!
RIGHT!
PLOP
WHEW... I USED TOO MUCH MANA TODAY.
OM
NOM
NOM
NOM
HMPH!

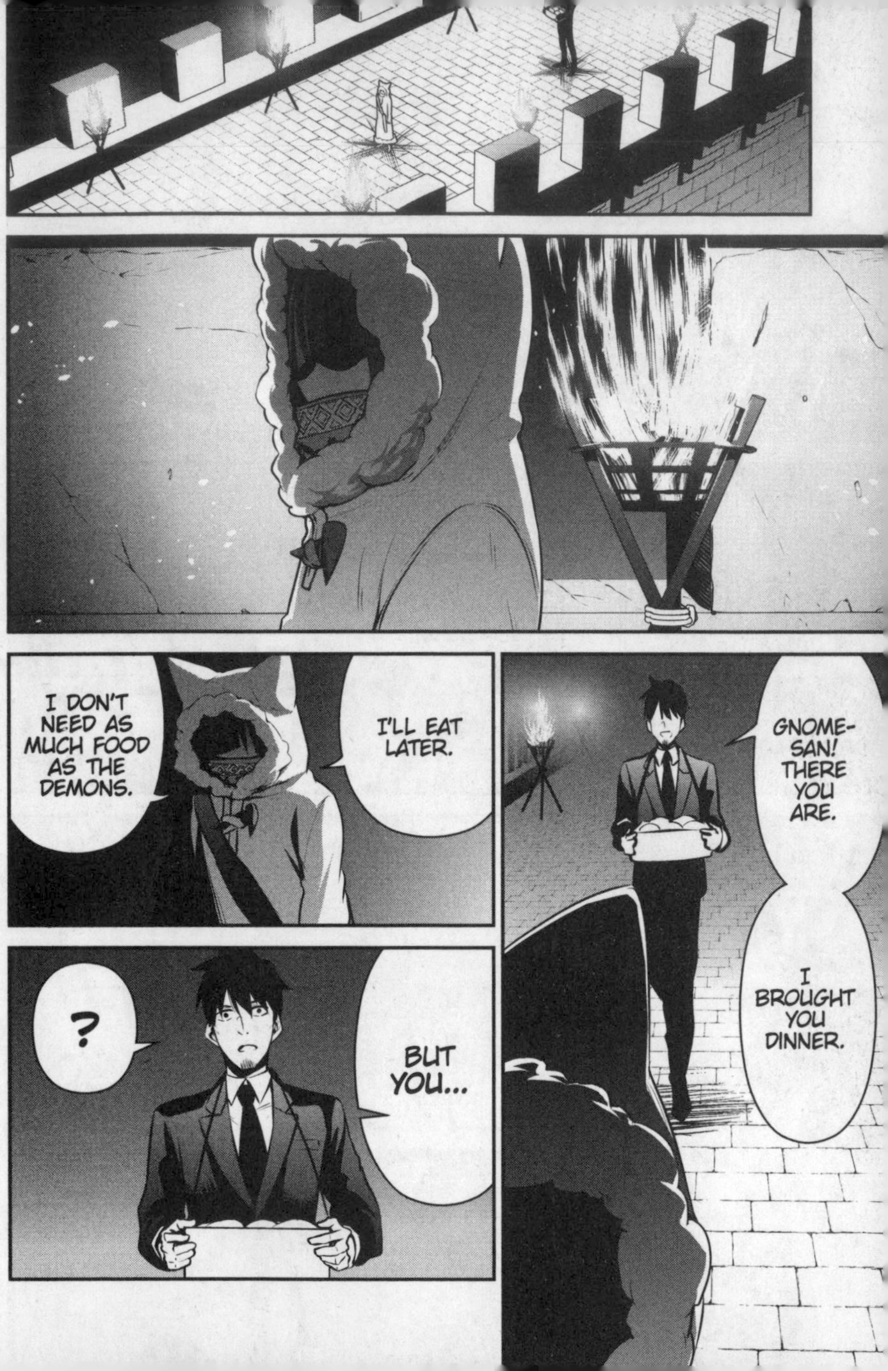
GNOME-SAN! THERE YOU ARE.
I BROUGHT YOU DINNER.
I'LL EAT LATER.
I DON'T NEED AS MUCH FOOD AS THE DEMONS.
BUT YOU...
?

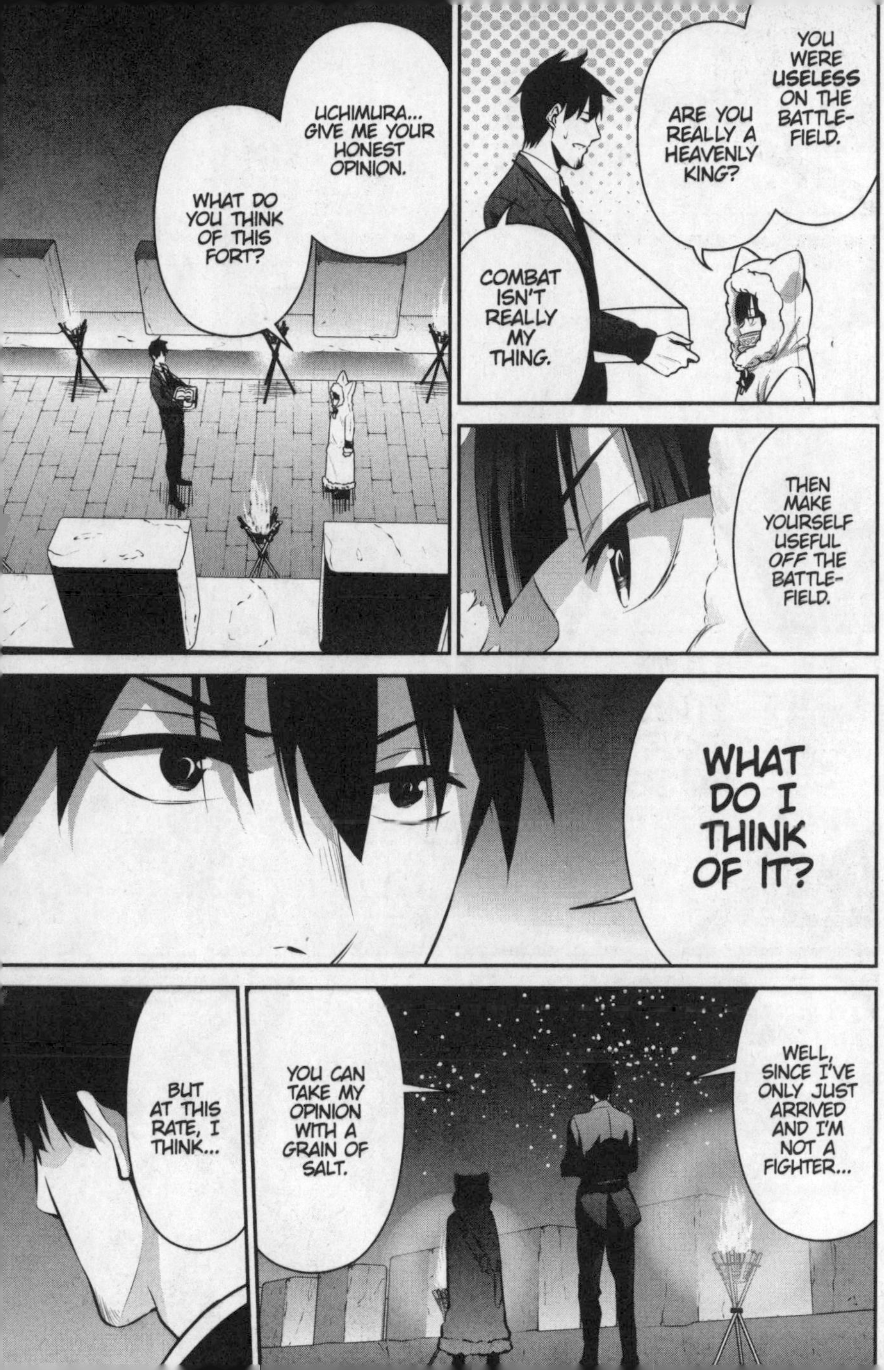
YOU WERE USELESS ON THE BATTLE-FIELD.
ARE YOU REALLY A HEAVENLY KING?
COMBAT ISN'T REALLY MY THING.
THEN MAKE YOURSELF USEFUL *OFF* THE BATTLE-FIELD.
UCHIMURA... GIVE ME YOUR HONEST OPINION.
WHAT DO YOU THINK OF THIS FORT?
WHAT DO I THINK OF IT?
WELL, SINCE I'VE ONLY JUST ARRIVED AND I'M NOT A FIGHTER...
YOU CAN TAKE MY OPINION WITH A GRAIN OF SALT.
BUT AT THIS RATE, I THINK...

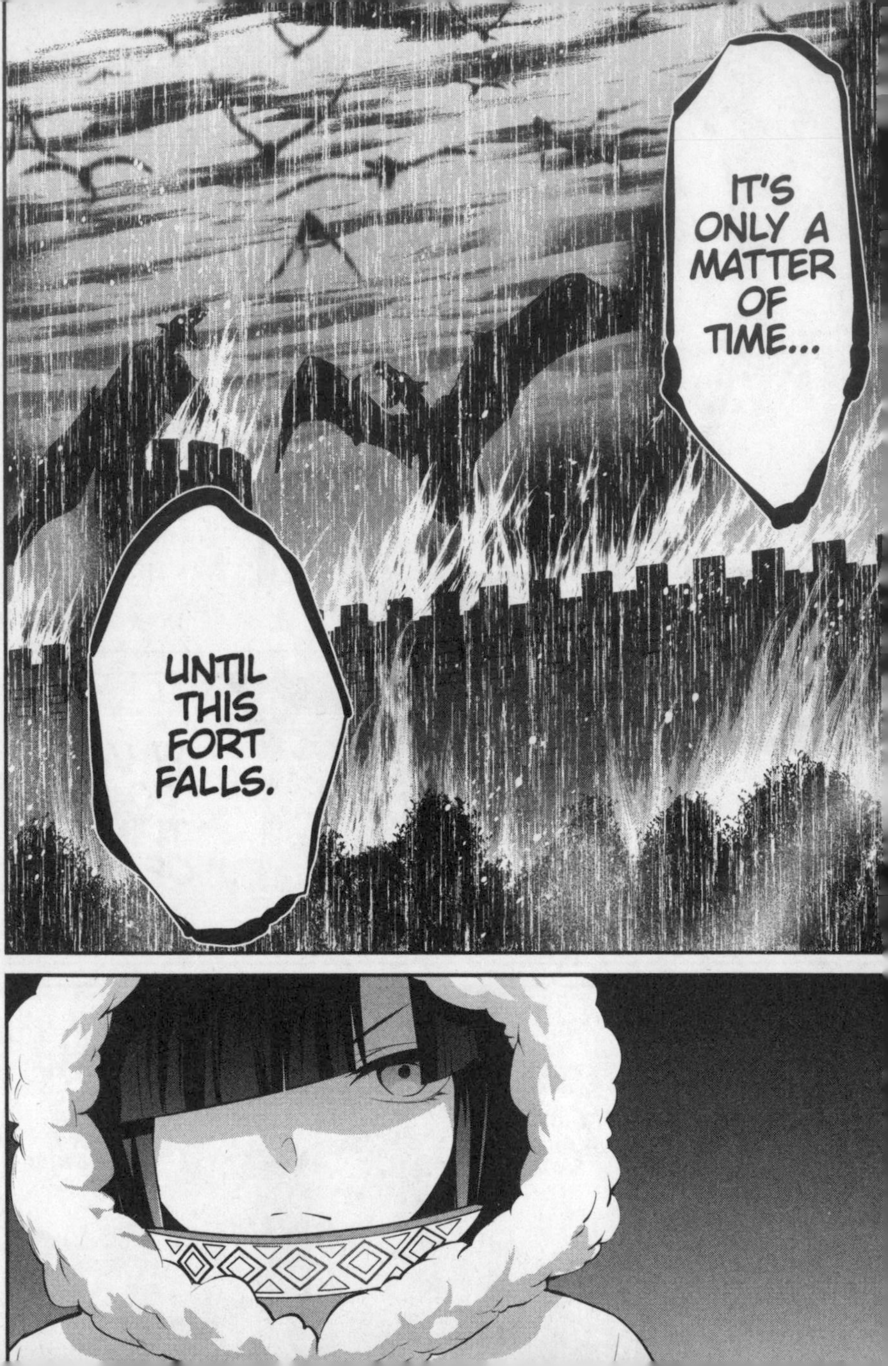
IT'S ONLY A MATTER OF TIME...
UNTIL THIS FORT FALLS.

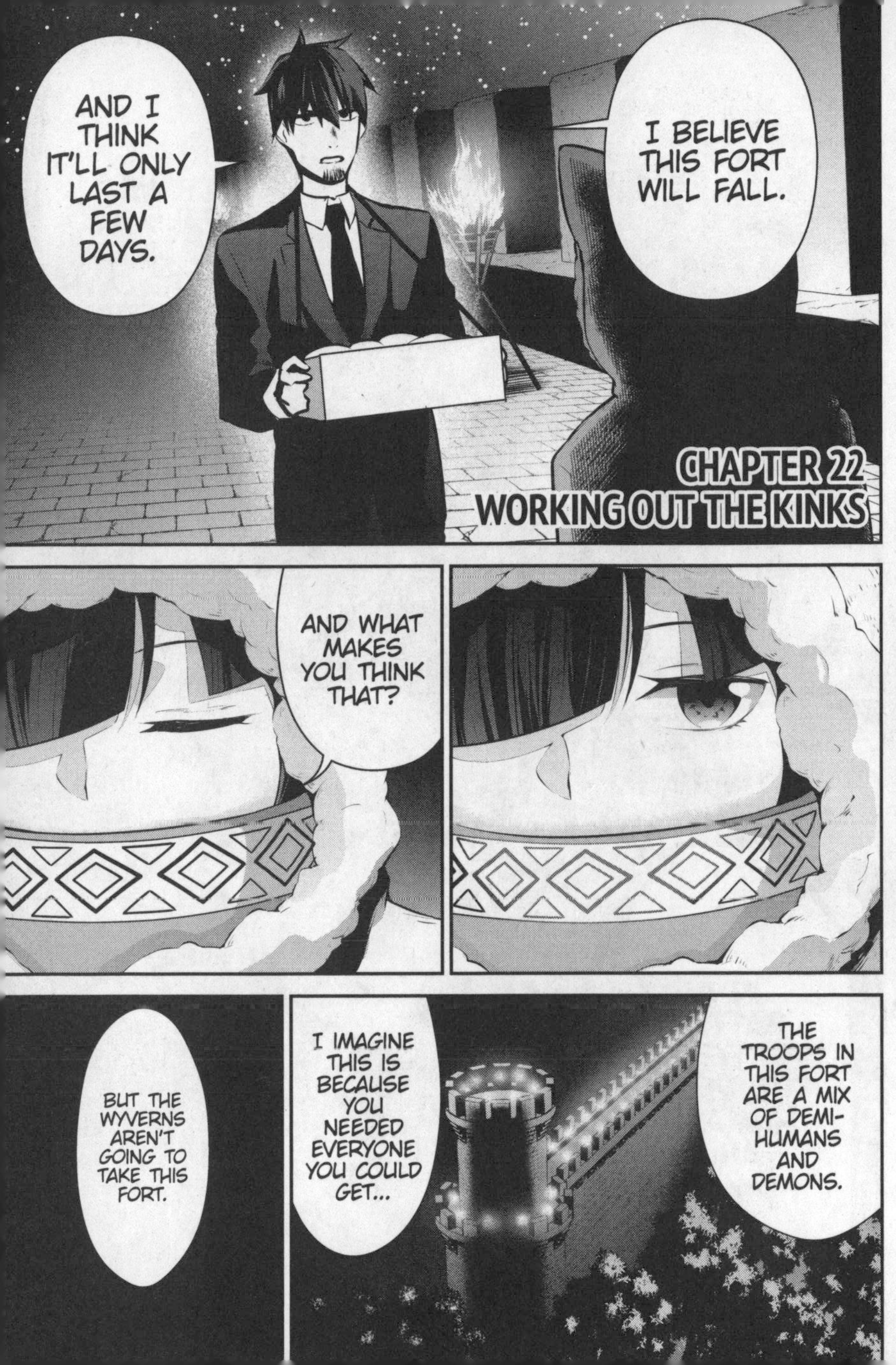
I BELIEVE THIS FORT WILL FALL.
AND I THINK IT'LL ONLY LAST A FEW DAYS.
CHAPTER 22
WORKING OUT THE KINKS
AND WHAT MAKES YOU THINK THAT?
THE TROOPS IN THIS FORT ARE A MIX OF DEMI-HUMANS AND DEMONS.
I IMAGINE THIS IS BECAUSE YOU NEEDED EVERYONE YOU COULD GET...
BUT THE WYVERNS AREN'T GOING TO TAKE THIS FORT.

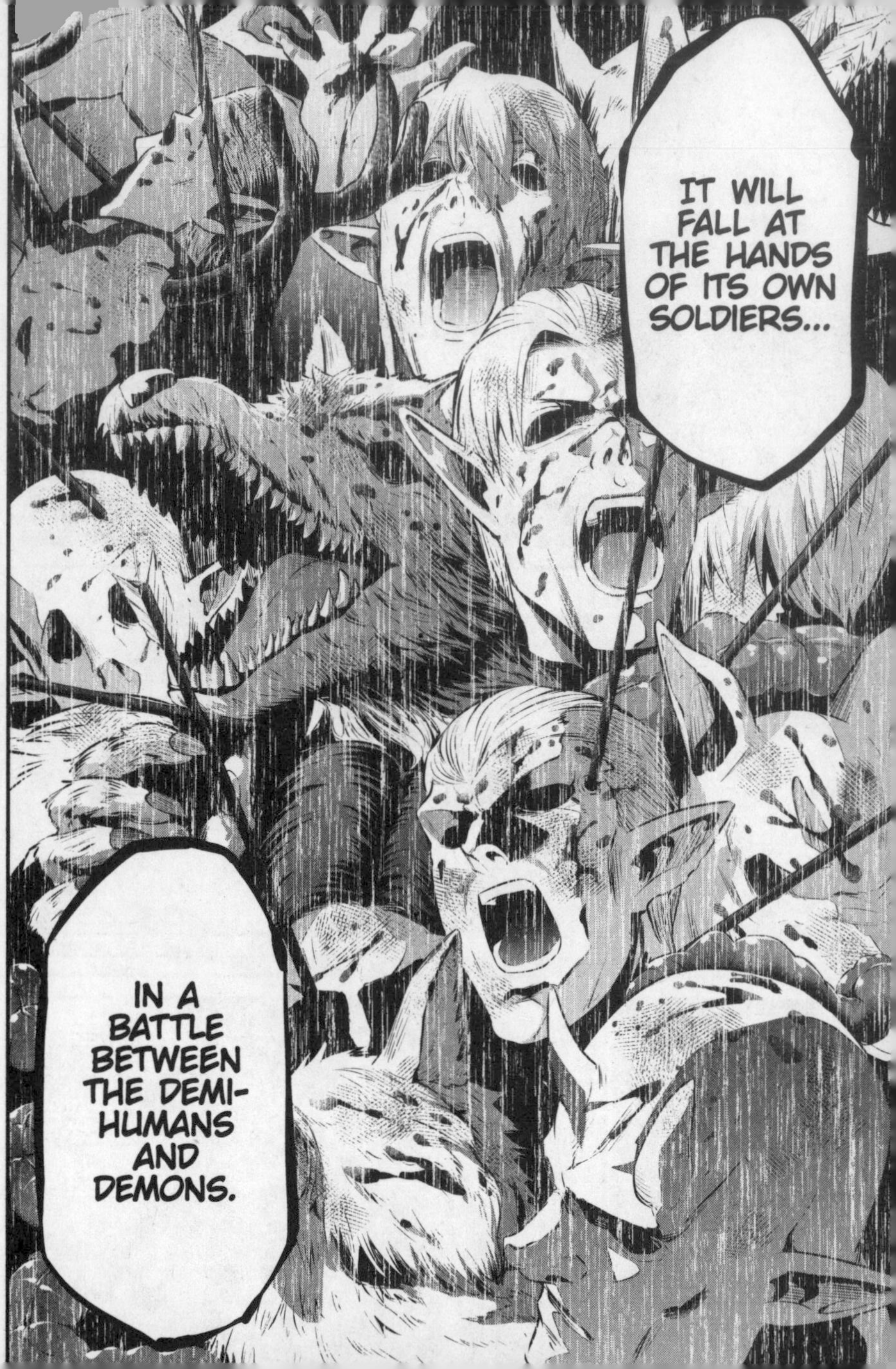
IT WILL FALL AT THE HANDS OF ITS OWN SOLDIERS...
IN A BATTLE BETWEEN THE DEMI-HUMANS AND DEMONS.

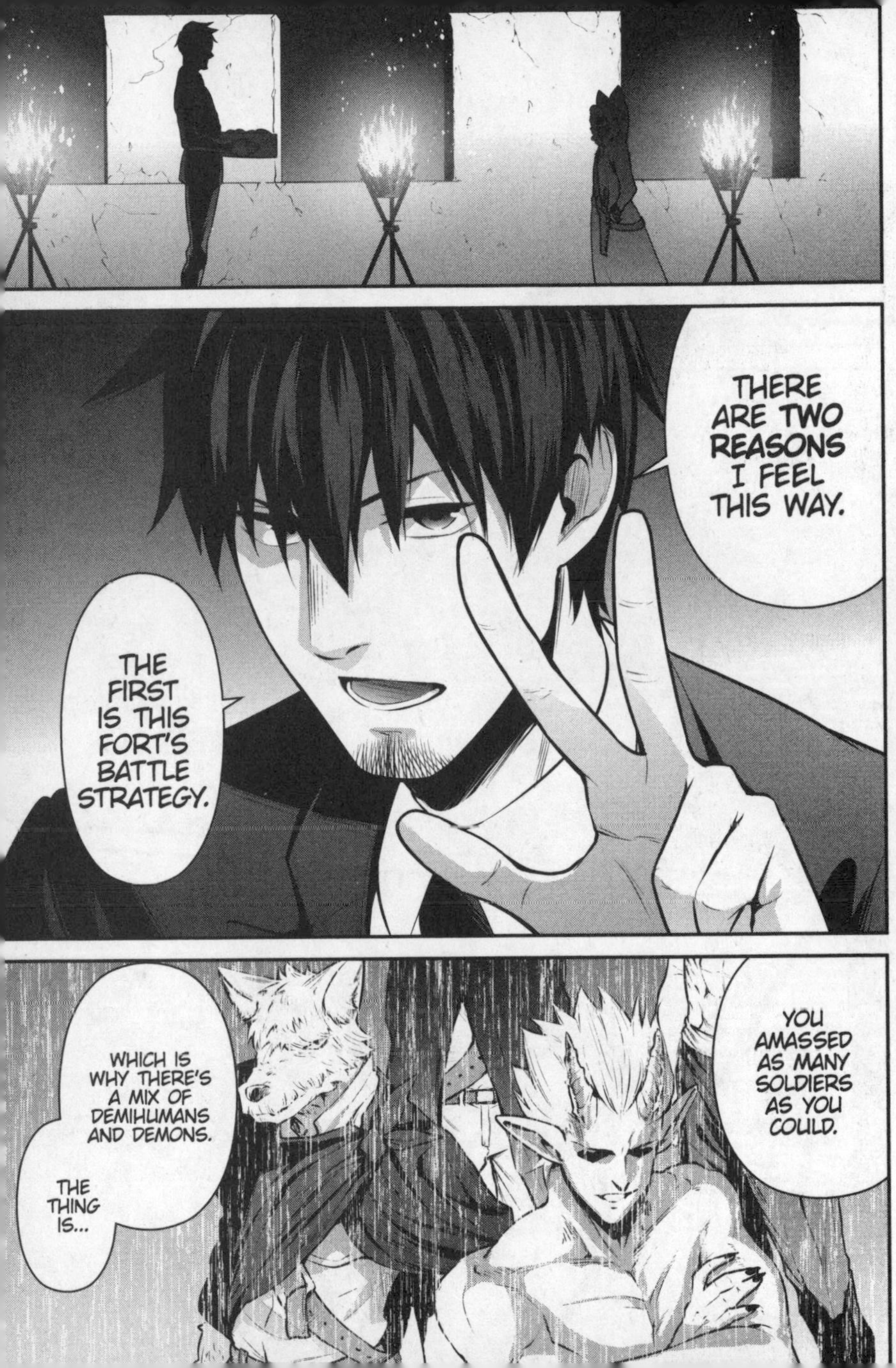
THERE ARE TWO REASONS I FEEL THIS WAY.
THE FIRST IS THIS FORT'S BATTLE STRATEGY.
YOU AMASSED AS MANY SOLDIERS AS YOU COULD.
WHICH IS WHY THERE'S A MIX OF DEMIHUMANS AND DEMONS.
THE THING IS...

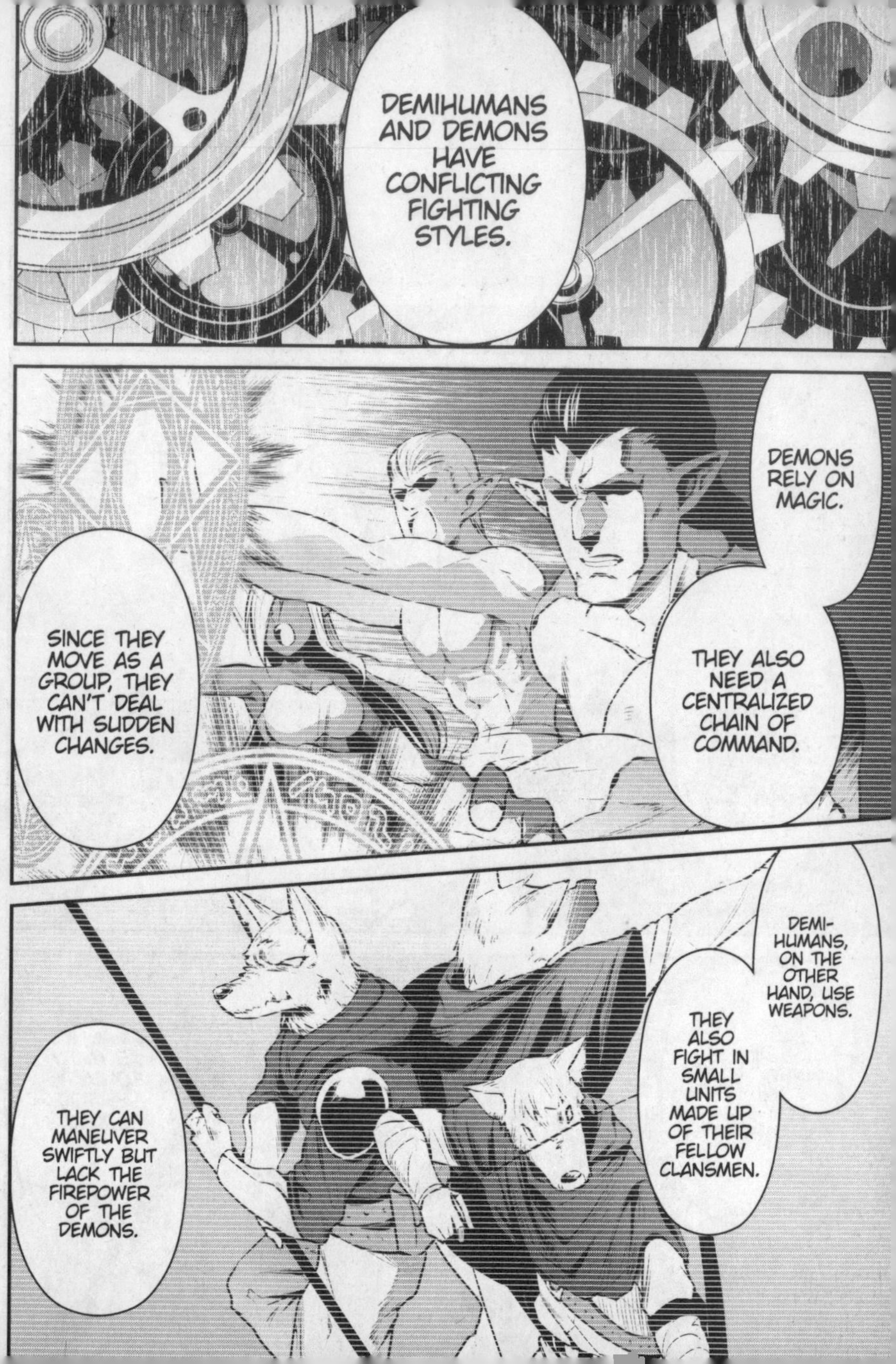
DEMIHUMANS AND DEMONS HAVE CONFLICTING FIGHTING STYLES.
DEMONS RELY ON MAGIC.
THEY ALSO NEED A CENTRALIZED CHAIN OF COMMAND.
SINCE THEY MOVE AS A GROUP, THEY CAN'T DEAL WITH SUDDEN CHANGES.
DEMI-HUMANS, ON THE OTHER HAND, USE WEAPONS.
THEY ALSO FIGHT IN SMALL UNITS MADE UP OF THEIR FELLOW CLANSMEN.
THEY CAN MANEUVER SWIFTLY BUT LACK THE FIREPOWER OF THE DEMONS.

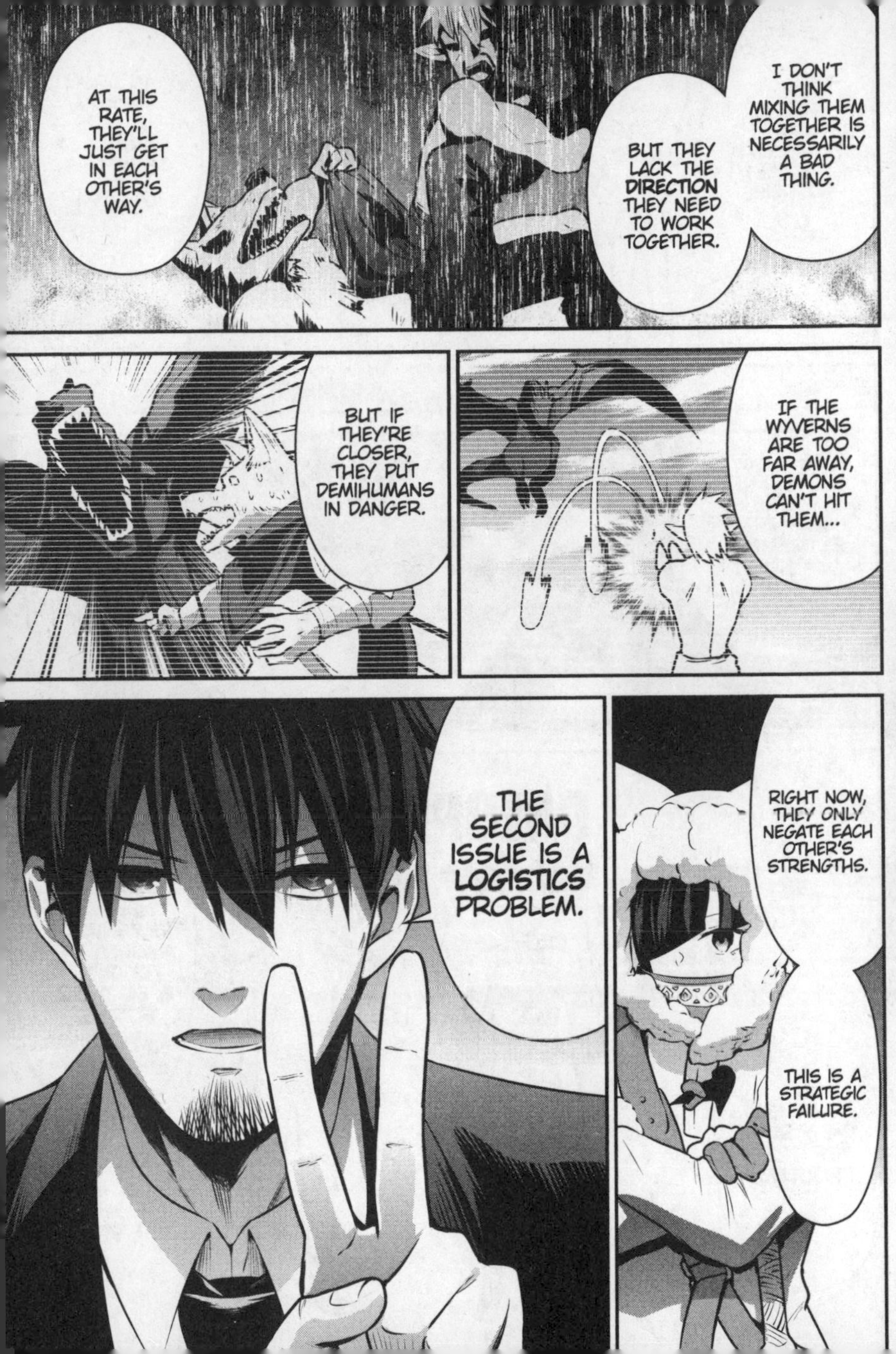
I DON'T THINK MIXING THEM TOGETHER IS NECESSARILY A BAD THING.
BUT THEY LACK THE **DIRECTION** THEY NEED TO WORK TOGETHER.
AT THIS RATE, THEY'LL JUST GET IN EACH OTHER'S WAY.
IF THE WYVERNS ARE TOO FAR AWAY, DEMONS CAN'T HIT THEM...
BUT IF THEY'RE CLOSER, THEY PUT DEMIHUMANS IN DANGER.
RIGHT NOW, THEY ONLY NEGATE EACH OTHER'S STRENGTHS.
THIS IS A STRATEGIC FAILURE.
THE SECOND ISSUE IS A LOGISTICS PROBLEM.

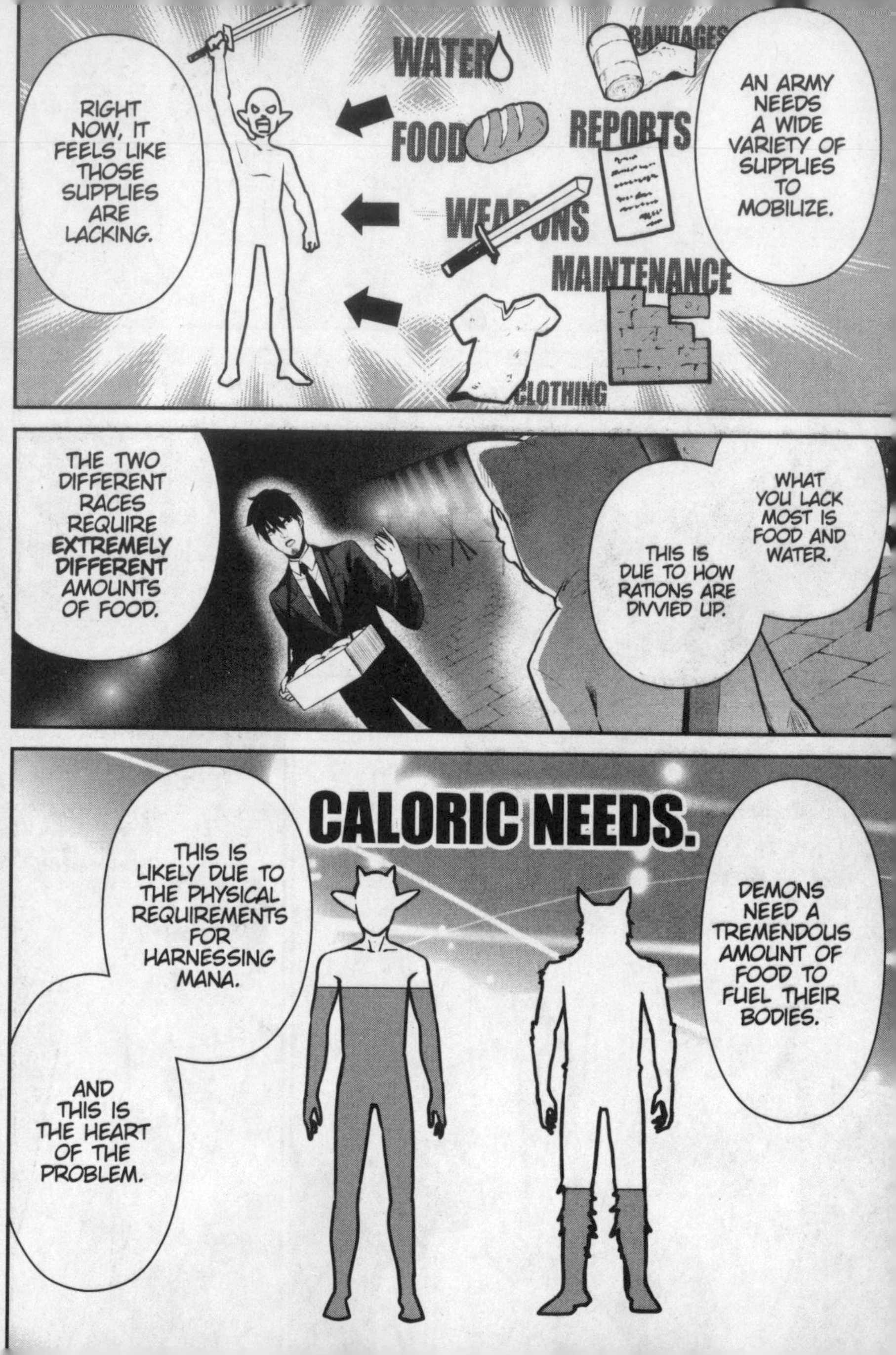
AN ARMY NEEDS A WIDE VARIETY OF SUPPLIES TO MOBILIZE.
BANDAGES
WATER
REPORTS
FOOD
WEAPONS
MAINTENANCE
CLOTHING
RIGHT NOW, IT FEELS LIKE THOSE SUPPLIES ARE LACKING.
WHAT YOU LACK MOST IS FOOD AND WATER.
THIS IS DUE TO HOW RATIONS ARE DIVVIED UP.
THE TWO DIFFERENT RACES REQUIRE EXTREMELY DIFFERENT AMOUNTS OF FOOD.
DEMONS NEED A TREMENDOUS AMOUNT OF FOOD TO FUEL THEIR BODIES.
CALORIC NEEDS.
THIS IS LIKELY DUE TO THE PHYSICAL REQUIREMENTS FOR HARNESSING MANA.
AND THIS IS THE HEART OF THE PROBLEM.

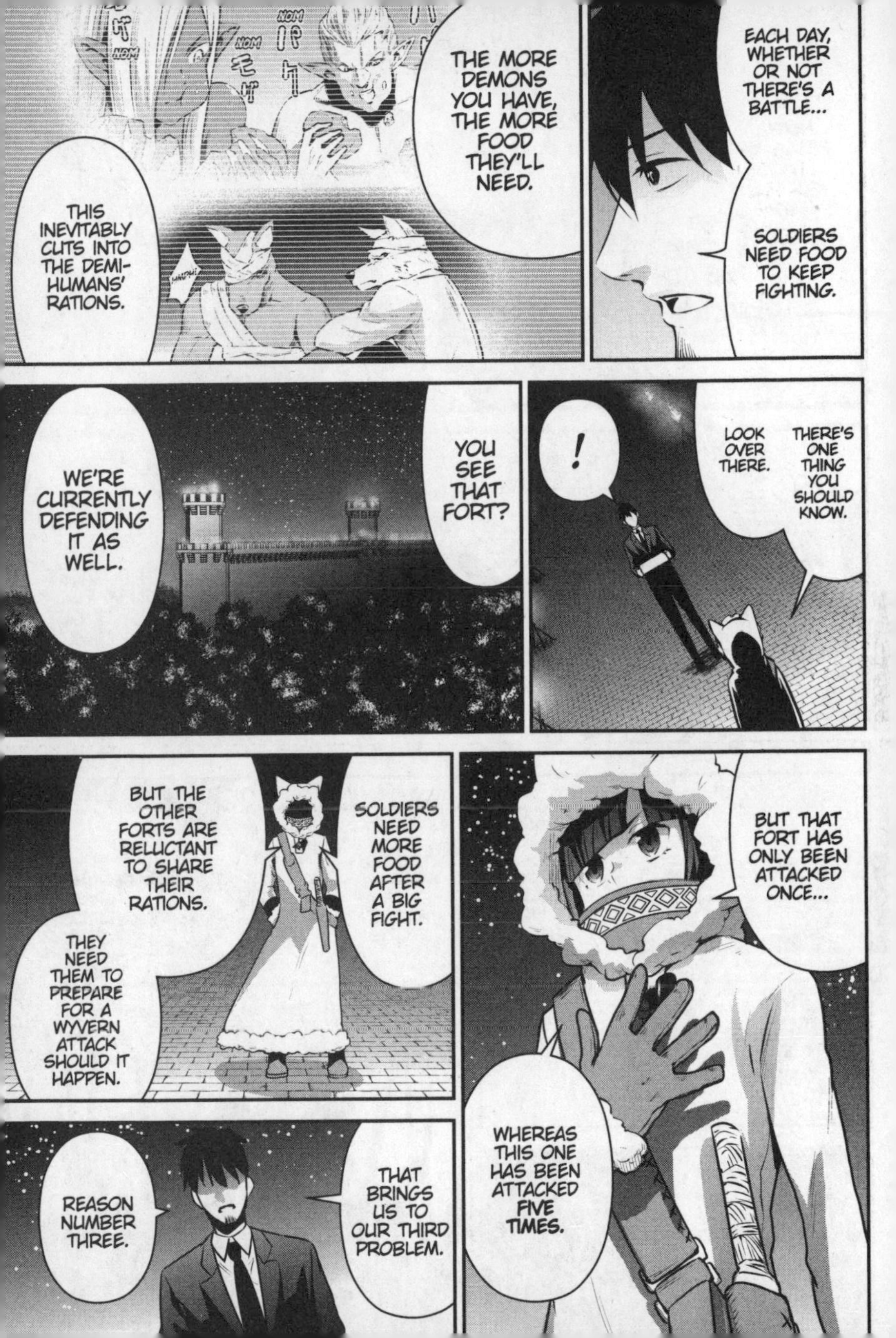
EACH DAY, WHETHER OR NOT THERE'S A BATTLE...
SOLDIERS NEED FOOD TO KEEP FIGHTING.
NOM
NOM
NOM
THE MORE DEMONS YOU HAVE, THE MORE FOOD THEY'LL NEED.
HAPH!
THIS INEVITABLY CUTS INTO THE DEMI-HUMANS' RATIONS.
THERE'S ONE THING YOU SHOULD KNOW.
LOOK OVER THERE.
!
YOU SEE THAT FORT?
WE'RE CURRENTLY DEFENDING IT AS WELL.
BUT THAT FORT HAS ONLY BEEN ATTACKED ONCE...
WHEREAS THIS ONE HAS BEEN ATTACKED FIVE TIMES.
SOLDIERS NEED MORE FOOD AFTER A BIG FIGHT.
BUT THE OTHER FORTS ARE RELUCTANT TO SHARE THEIR RATIONS.
THEY NEED THEM TO PREPARE FOR A WYVERN ATTACK SHOULD IT HAPPEN.
THAT BRINGS US TO OUR THIRD PROBLEM.
REASON NUMBER THREE.

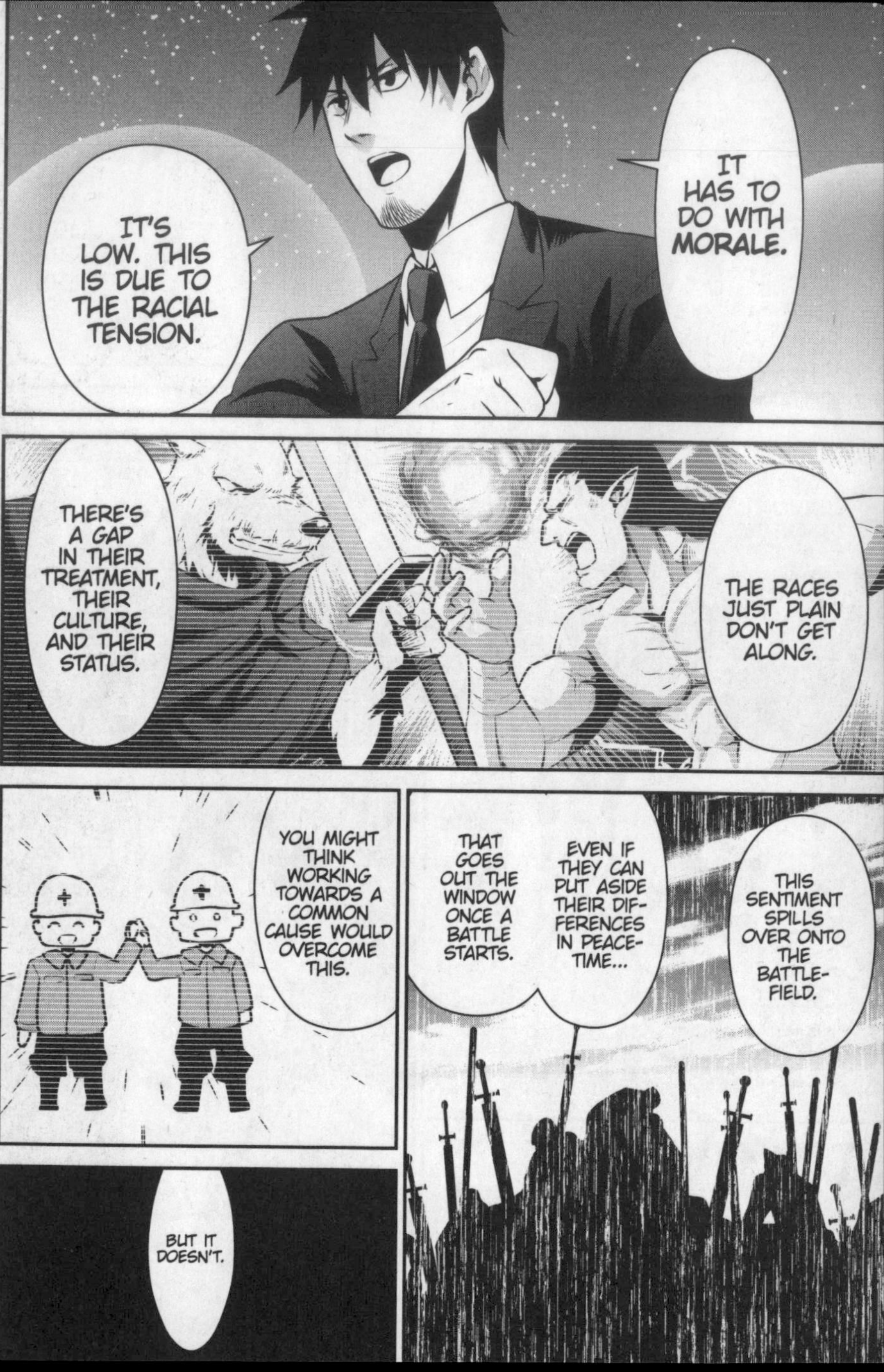
IT HAS TO DO WITH MORALE.
IT'S LOW. THIS IS DUE TO THE RACIAL TENSION.
THE RACES JUST PLAIN DON'T GET ALONG.
THERE'S A GAP IN THEIR TREATMENT, THEIR CULTURE, AND THEIR STATUS.
THIS SENTIMENT SPILLS OVER ONTO THE BATTLEFIELD.
EVEN IF THEY CAN PUT ASIDE THEIR DIFFERENCES IN PEACETIME...
THAT GOES OUT THE WINDOW ONCE A BATTLE STARTS.
YOU MIGHT THINK WORKING TOWARDS A COMMON CAUSE WOULD OVERCOME THIS.
BUT IT DOESN'T.

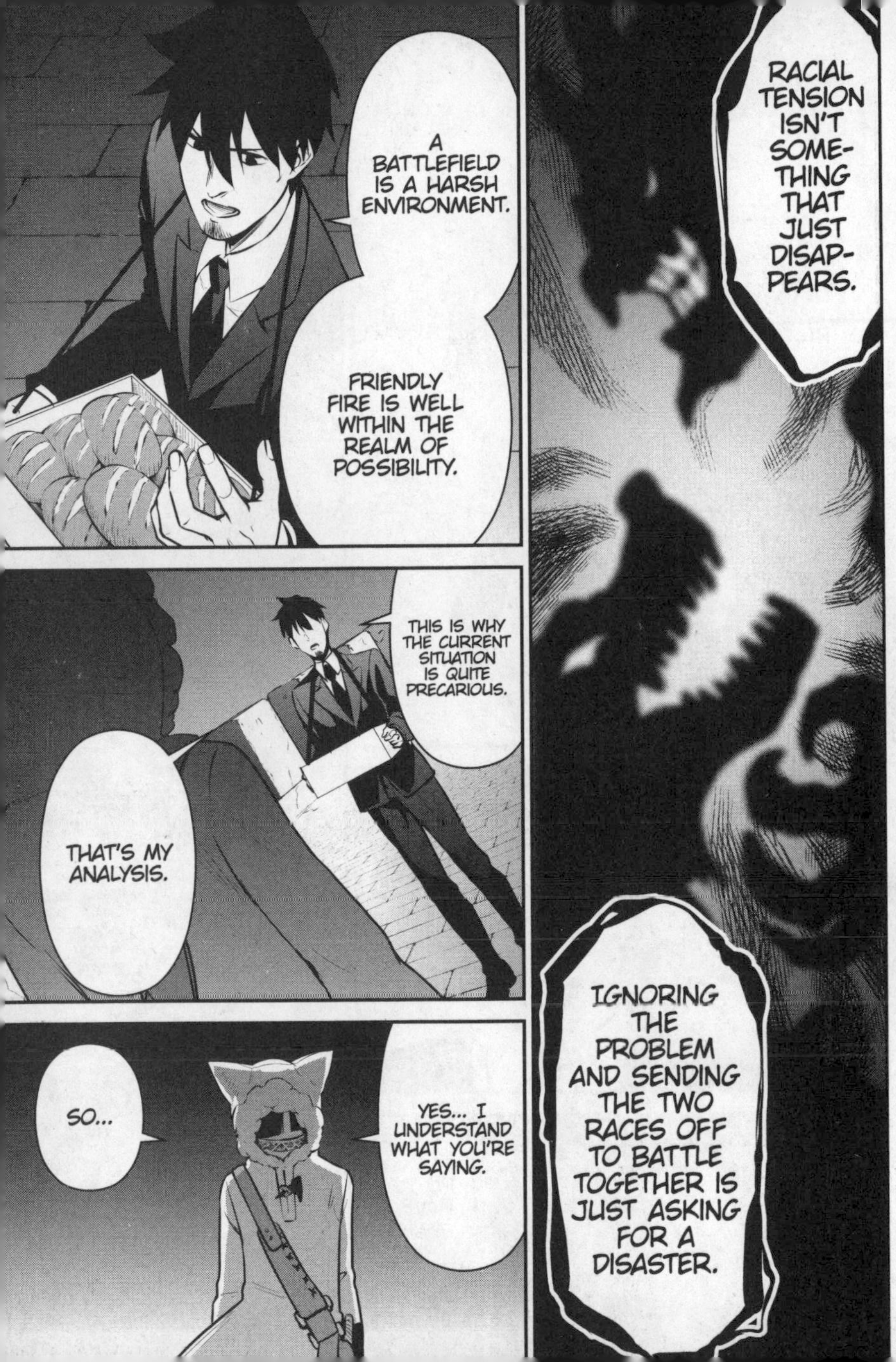
RACIAL TENSION ISN'T SOMETHING THAT JUST DISAPPEARS.
IGNORING THE PROBLEM AND SENDING THE TWO RACES OFF TO BATTLE TOGETHER IS JUST ASKING FOR A DISASTER.
A BATTLEFIELD IS A HARSH ENVIRONMENT.
FRIENDLY FIRE IS WELL WITHIN THE REALM OF POSSIBILITY.
THIS IS WHY THE CURRENT SITUATION IS QUITE PRECARIOUS.
THAT'S MY ANALYSIS.
YES... I UNDERSTAND WHAT YOU'RE SAYING.
SO...

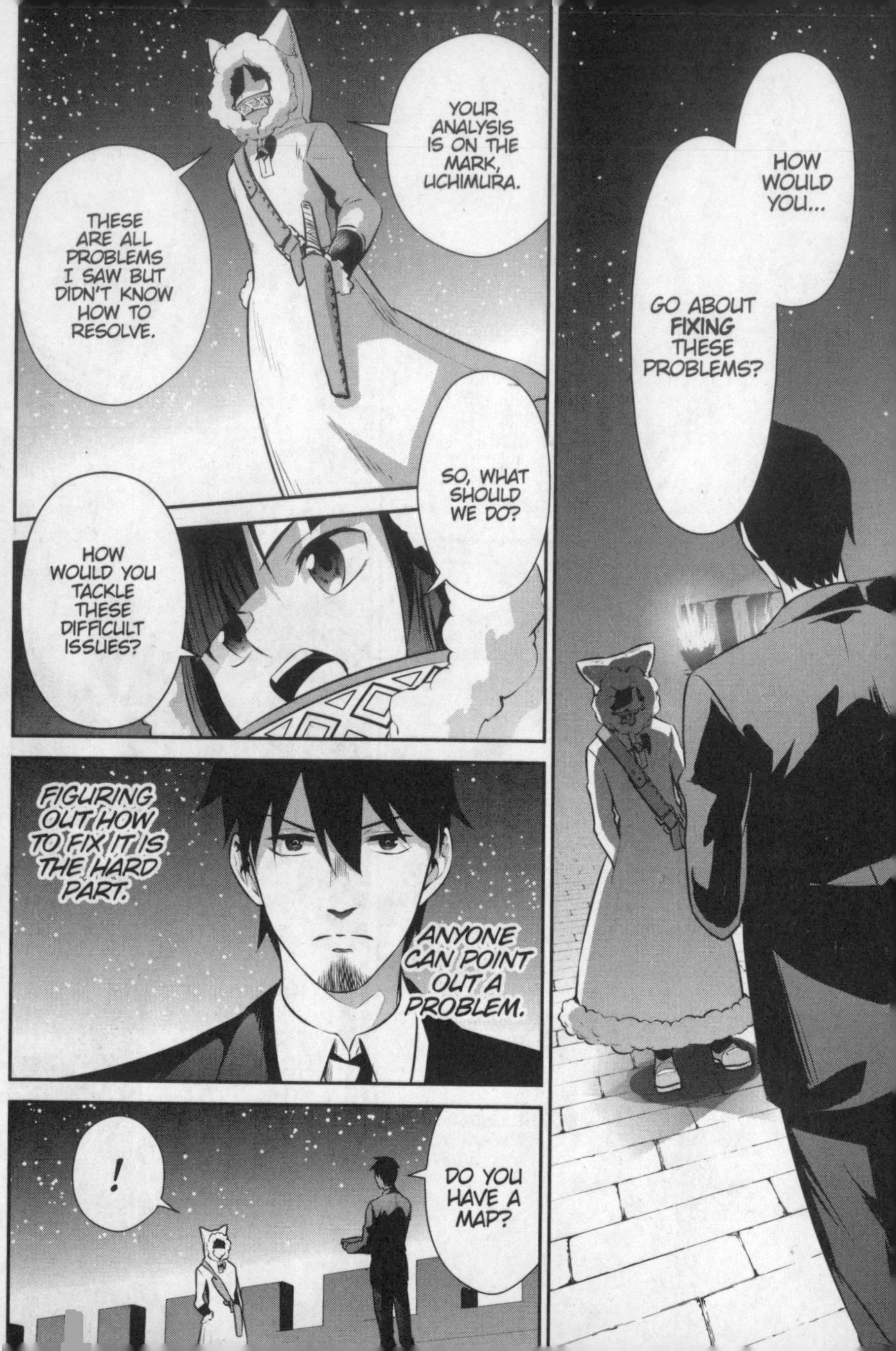
HOW WOULD YOU...
GO ABOUT FIXING THESE PROBLEMS?
YOUR ANALYSIS IS ON THE MARK, UCHIMURA.
THESE ARE ALL PROBLEMS I SAW BUT DIDN'T KNOW HOW TO RESOLVE.
SO, WHAT SHOULD WE DO?
HOW WOULD YOU TACKLE THESE DIFFICULT ISSUES?
ANYONE CAN POINT OUT A PROBLEM.
FIGURING OUT HOW TO FIX IT IS THE HARD PART.
DO YOU HAVE A MAP?
!

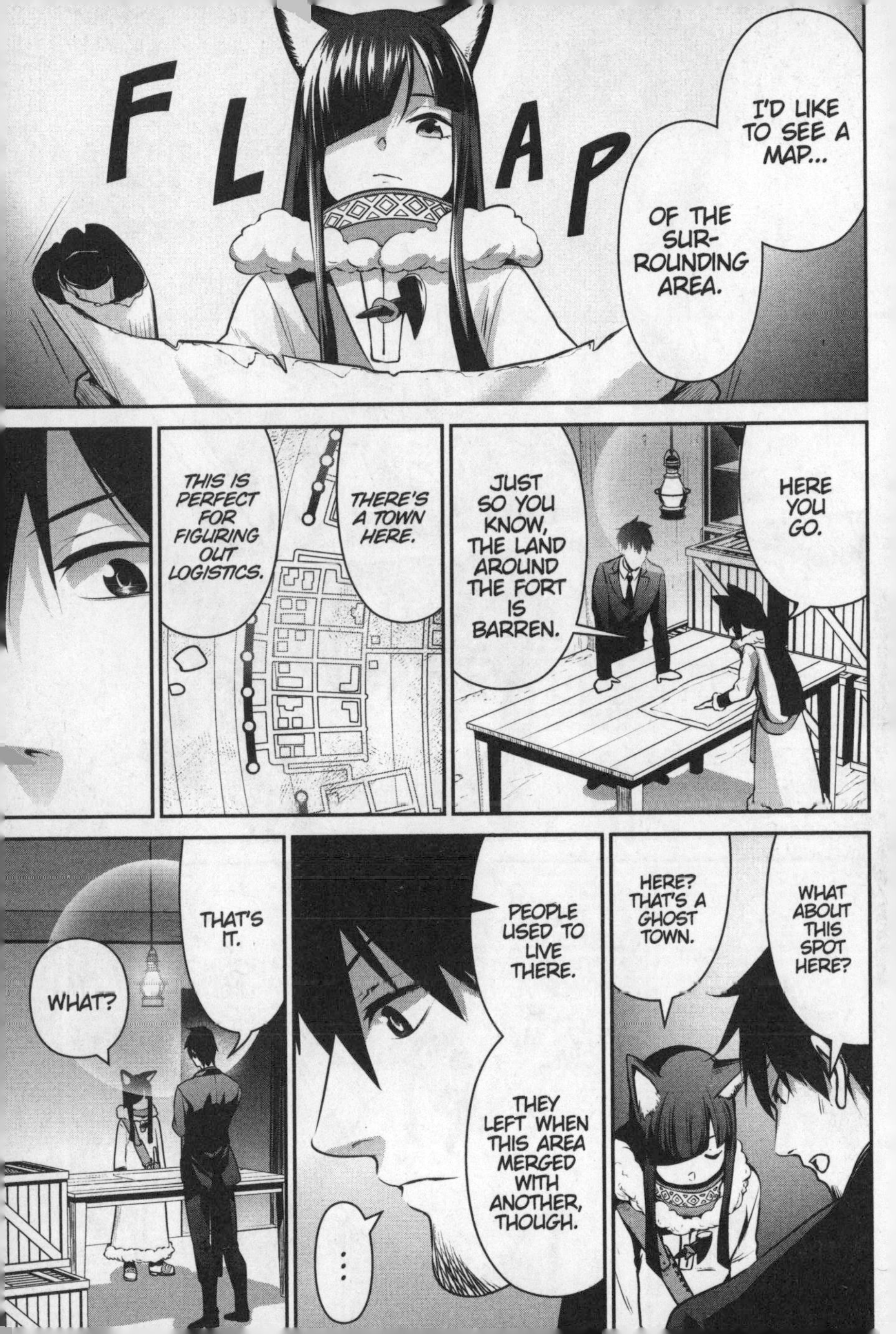
I'D LIKE TO SEE A MAP...
OF THE SUR-ROUNDING AREA.
FLAP
HERE YOU GO.
JUST SO YOU KNOW, THE LAND AROUND THE FORT IS BARREN.
THERE'S A TOWN HERE.
THIS IS PERFECT FOR FIGURING OUT LOGISTICS.
WHAT ABOUT THIS SPOT HERE?
HERE? THAT'S A GHOST TOWN.
PEOPLE USED TO LIVE THERE.
THEY LEFT WHEN THIS AREA MERGED WITH ANOTHER, THOUGH.
...
THAT'S IT.
WHAT?

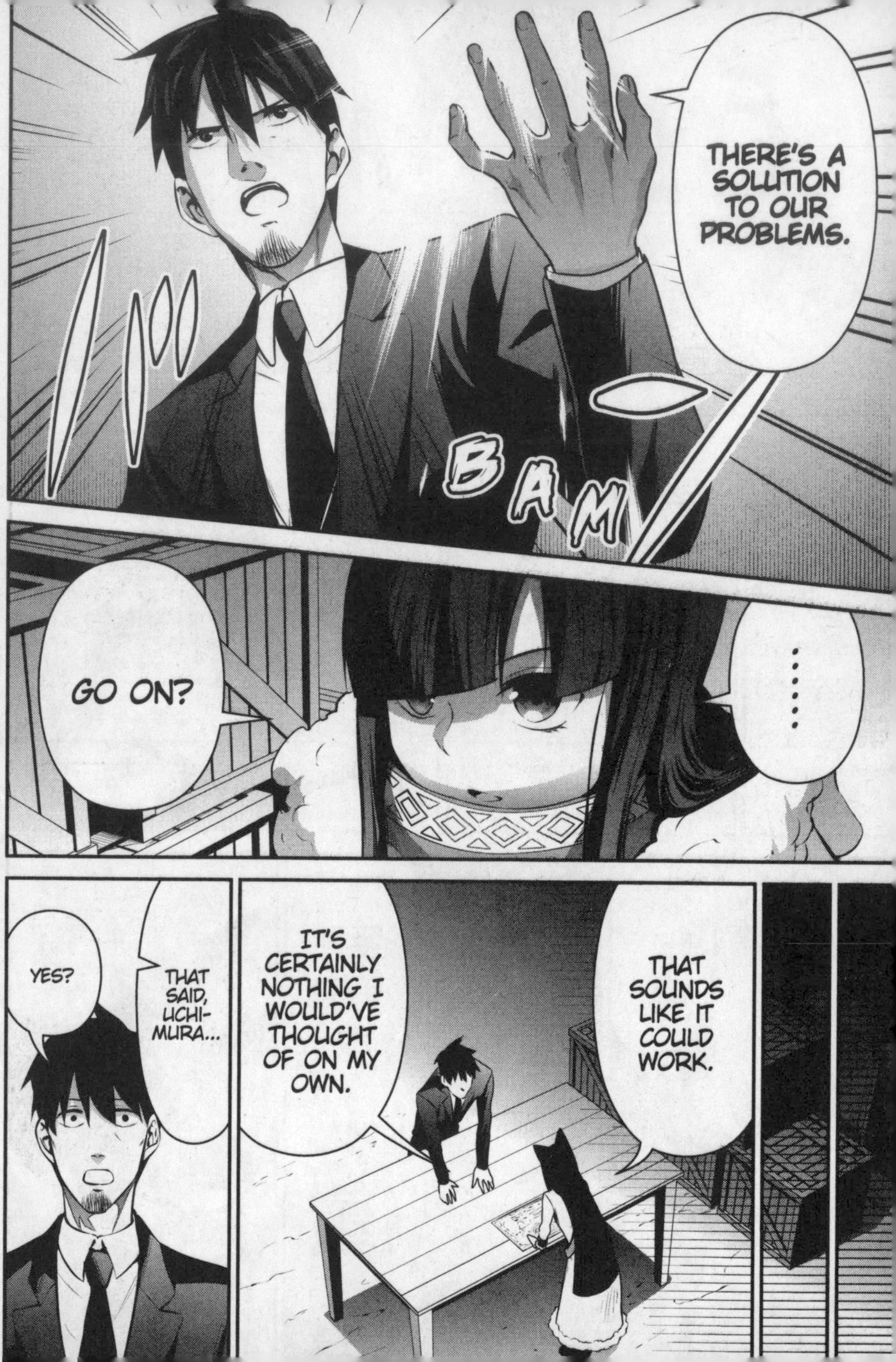
THERE'S A SOLUTION TO OUR PROBLEMS.
BAM
......
GO ON?
THAT SOUNDS LIKE IT COULD WORK.
IT'S CERTAINLY NOTHING I WOULD'VE THOUGHT OF ON MY OWN.
THAT SAID, UCHI-MURA...
YES?

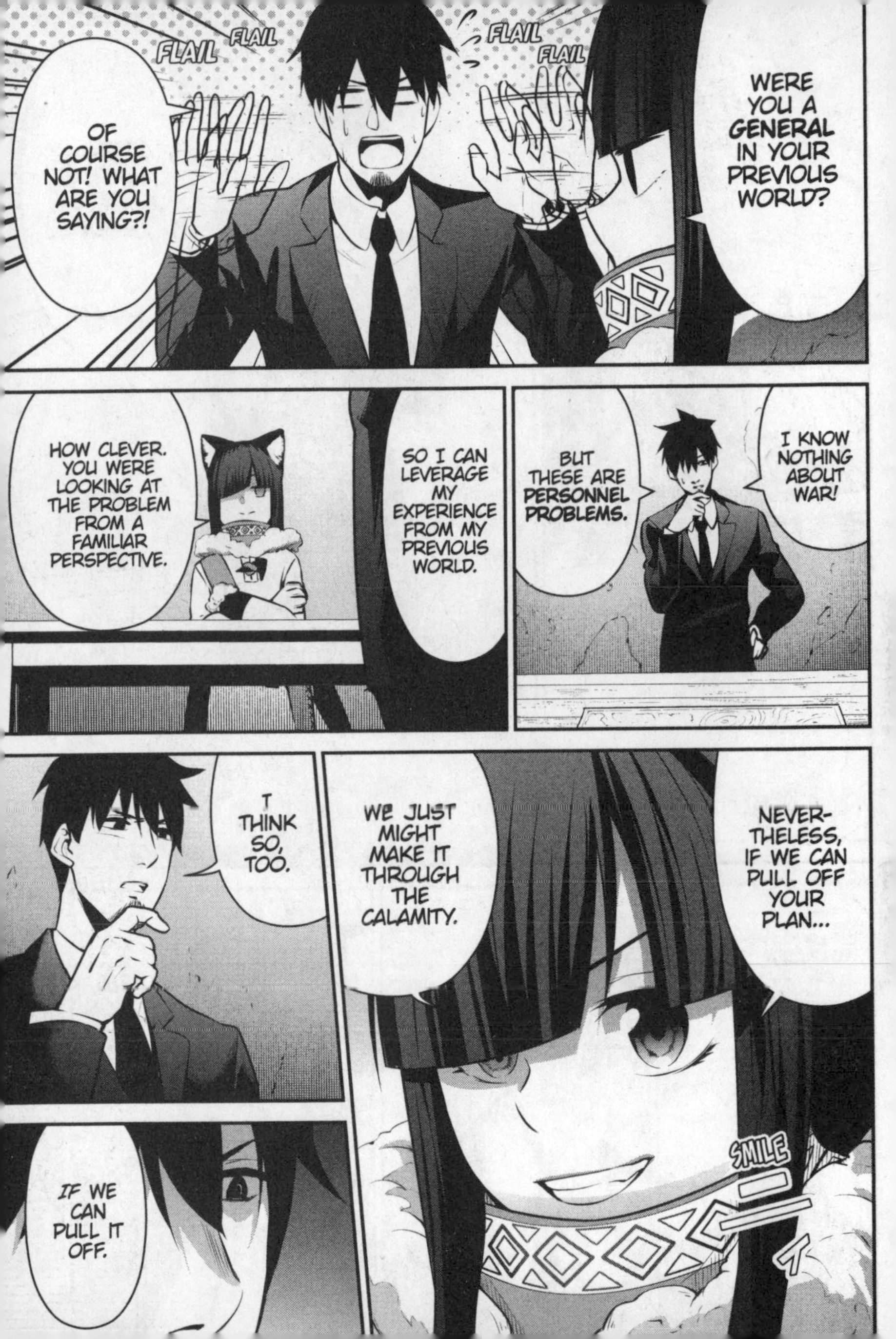
WERE YOU A GENERAL IN YOUR PREVIOUS WORLD?
FLAIL
FLAIL
FLAIL
FLAIL
OF COURSE NOT! WHAT ARE YOU SAYING?!
I KNOW NOTHING ABOUT WAR!
BUT THESE ARE PERSONNEL PROBLEMS.
SO I CAN LEVERAGE MY EXPERIENCE FROM MY PREVIOUS WORLD.
HOW CLEVER. YOU WERE LOOKING AT THE PROBLEM FROM A FAMILIAR PERSPECTIVE.
NEVERTHELESS, IF WE CAN PULL OFF YOUR PLAN...
WE JUST MIGHT MAKE IT THROUGH THE CALAMITY.
SMILE
I THINK SO, TOO.
IF WE CAN PULL IT OFF.

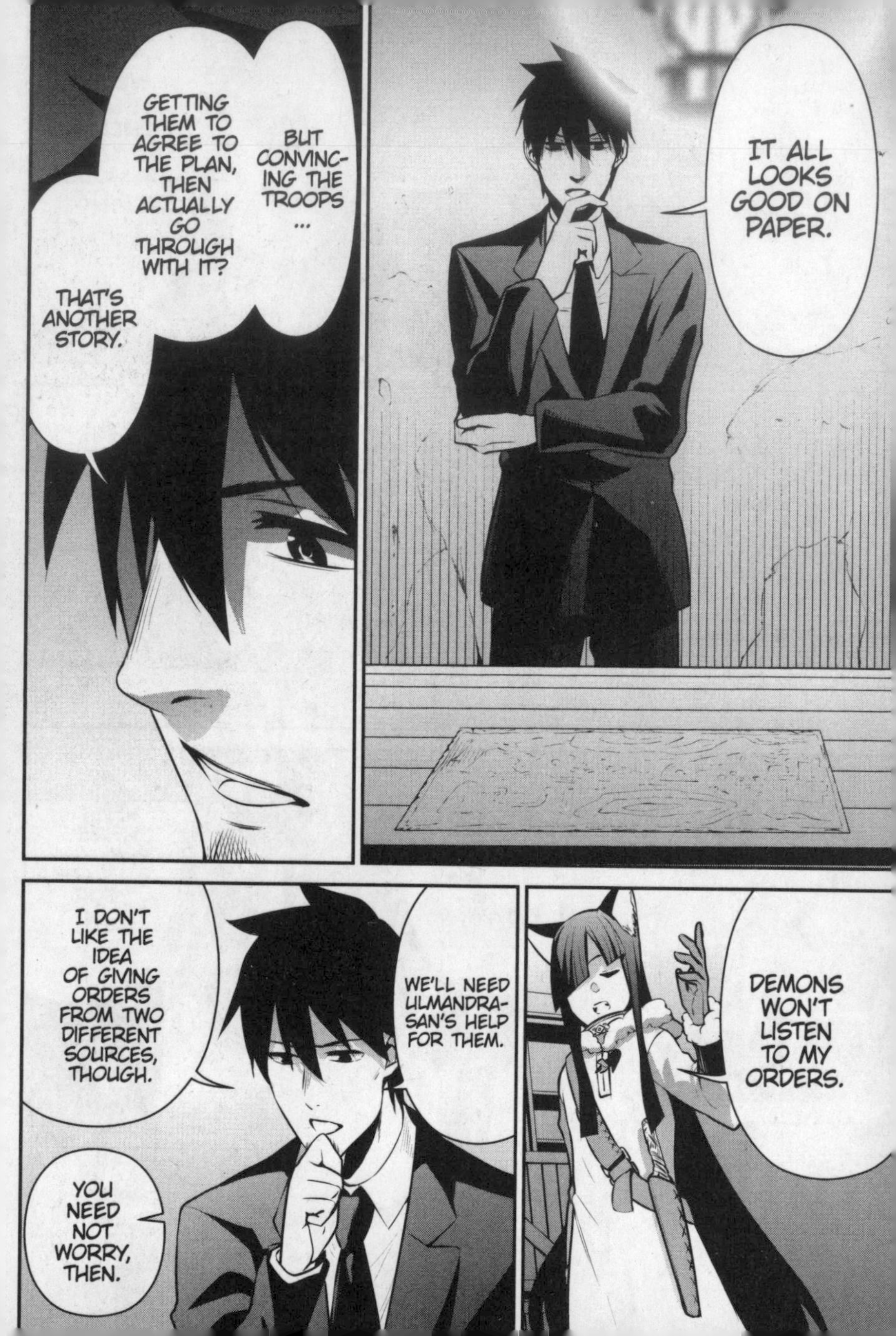
IT ALL LOOKS GOOD ON PAPER.
BUT CONVINCING THE TROOPS...
GETTING THEM TO AGREE TO THE PLAN, THEN ACTUALLY GO THROUGH WITH IT?
THAT'S ANOTHER STORY.
DEMONS WON'T LISTEN TO MY ORDERS.
WE'LL NEED ULMANDRA-SAN'S HELP FOR THEM.
I DON'T LIKE THE IDEA OF GIVING ORDERS FROM TWO DIFFERENT SOURCES, THOUGH.
YOU NEED NOT WORRY, THEN.

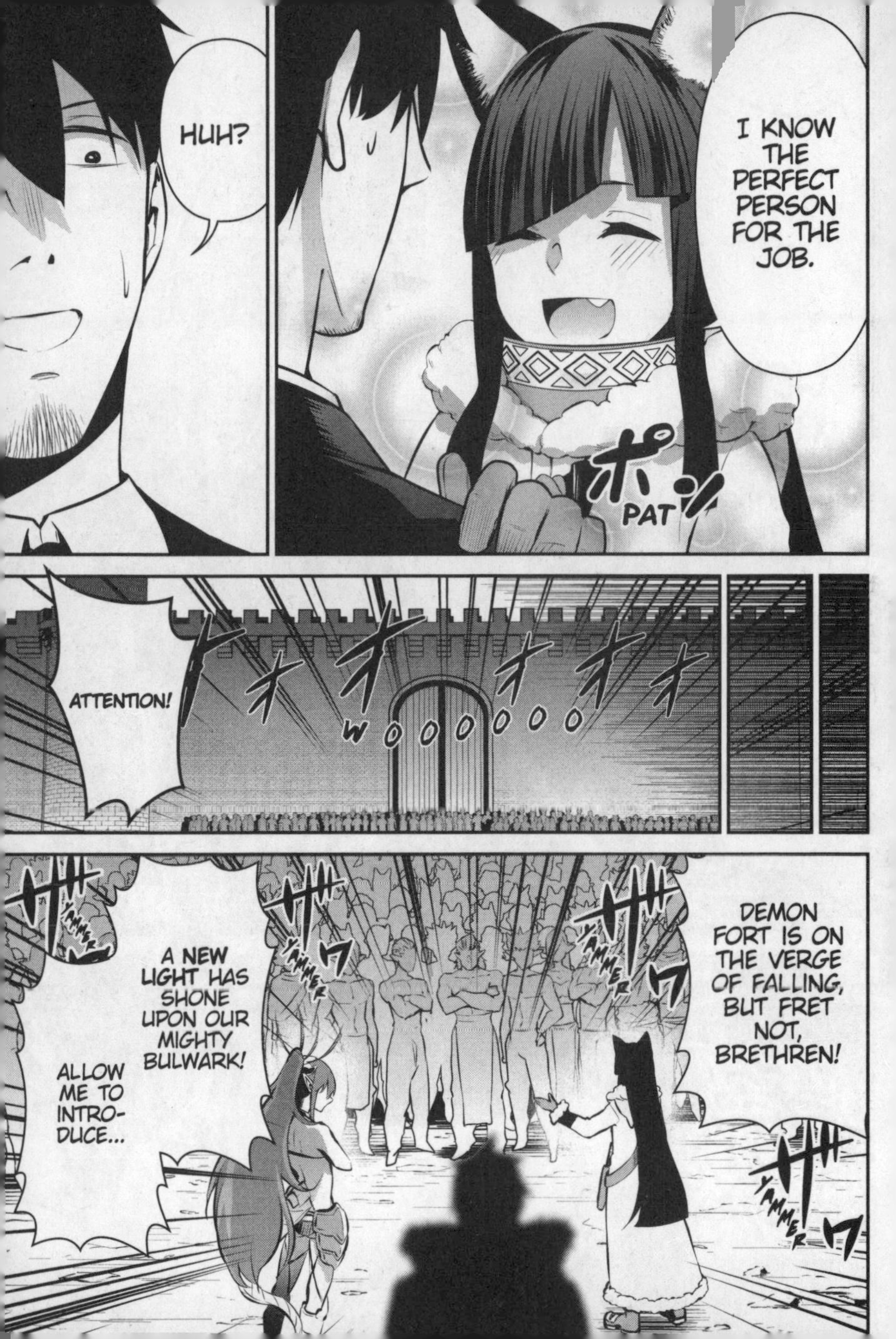
I KNOW THE PERFECT PERSON FOR THE JOB.
PAT
HUH?
ATTENTION!
WOOOOOO
DEMON FORT IS ON THE VERGE OF FALLING, BUT FRET NOT, BRETHREN!
YAMMER
YAMMER
A NEW LIGHT HAS SHONE UPON OUR MIGHTY BULWARK!
ALLOW ME TO INTRODUCE...
YAMMER
YAMMER

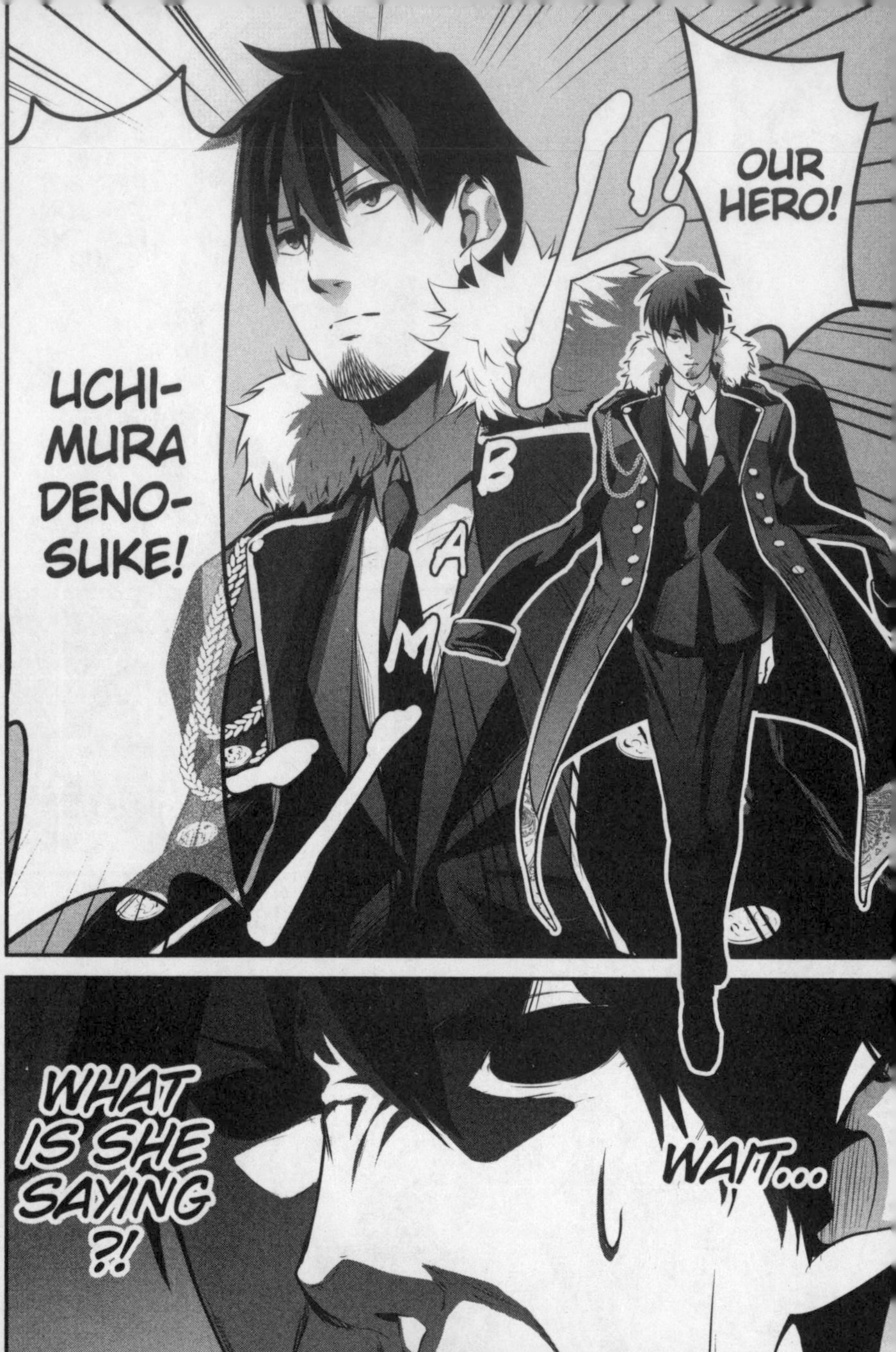
OUR HERO!
UCHIMURA DENOSUKE!
BAM
WAIT...
WHAT IS SHE SAYING ?!

HEAD HUNTED TO ANOTHER WORLD

FROM SALARYMAN TO BIG FOUR!

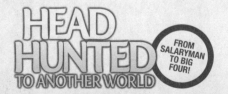

HEAD HUNTED TO ANOTHER WORLD

FROM SALARYMAN TO BIG FOUR!

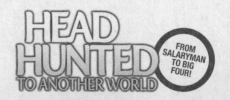

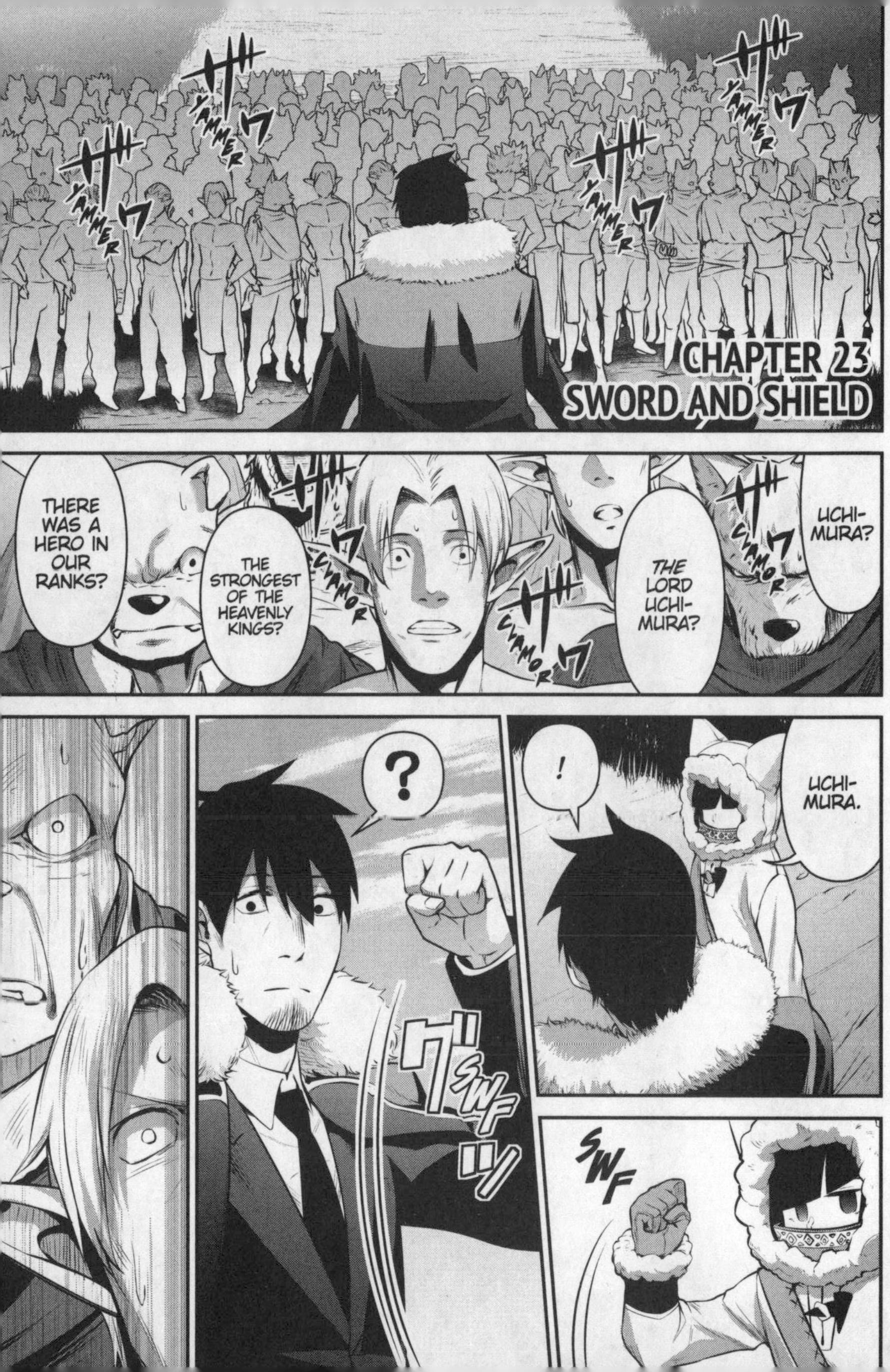

YAMMER
YAMMER
YAMMER
YAMMER
CHAPTER 23
SWORD AND SHIELD
UCHI-MURA?
CLAMOR
THE LORD UCHI-MURA?
CLAMOR
CLAMOR
THE STRONGEST OF THE HEAVENLY KINGS?
THERE WAS A HERO IN OUR RANKS?
UCHI-MURA.
!
SWF
?
SWF

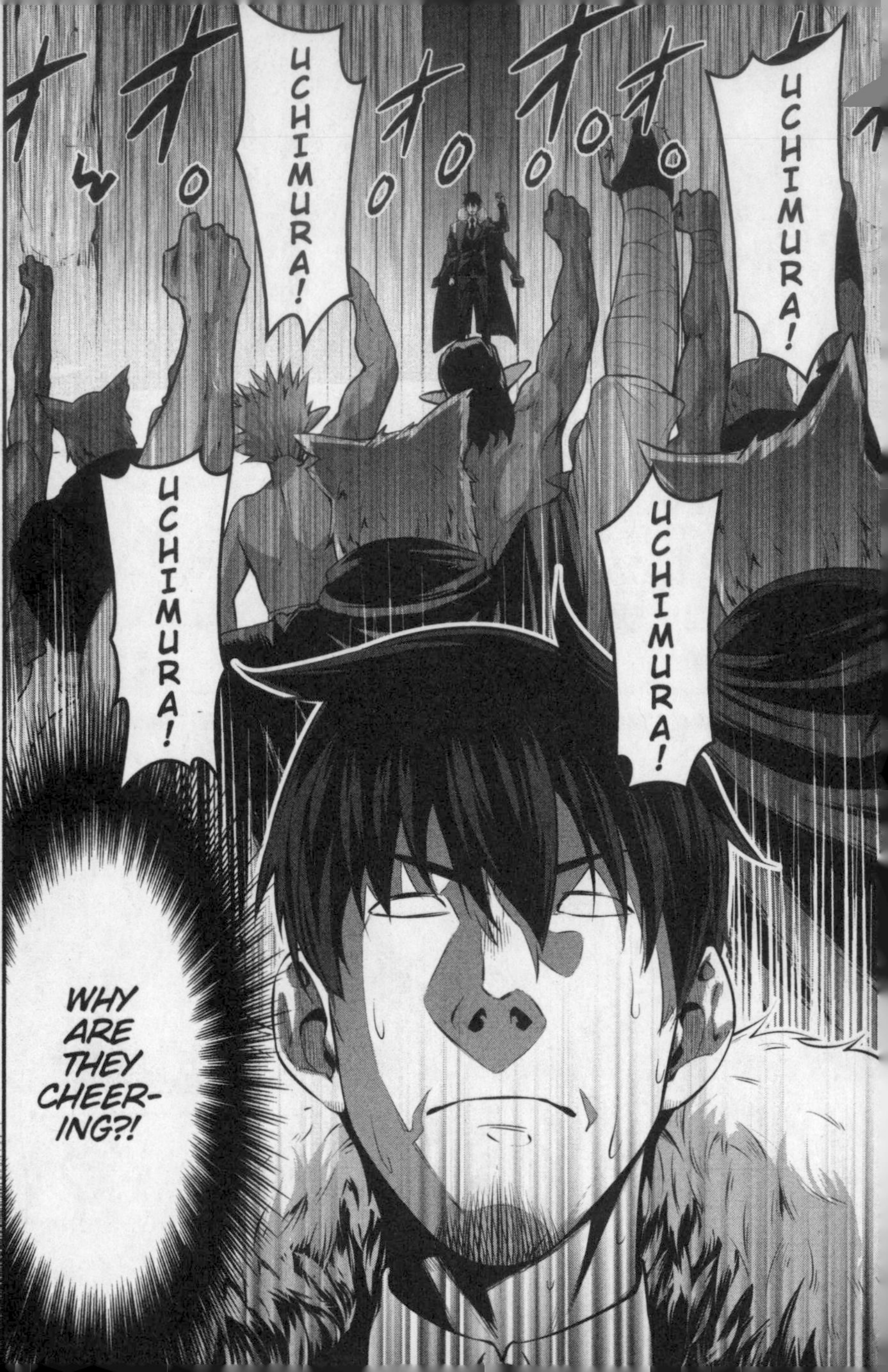
UCHIMURA!
UCHIMURA!
UCHIMURA!
UCHIMURA!
WHY ARE THEY CHEER-ING?!

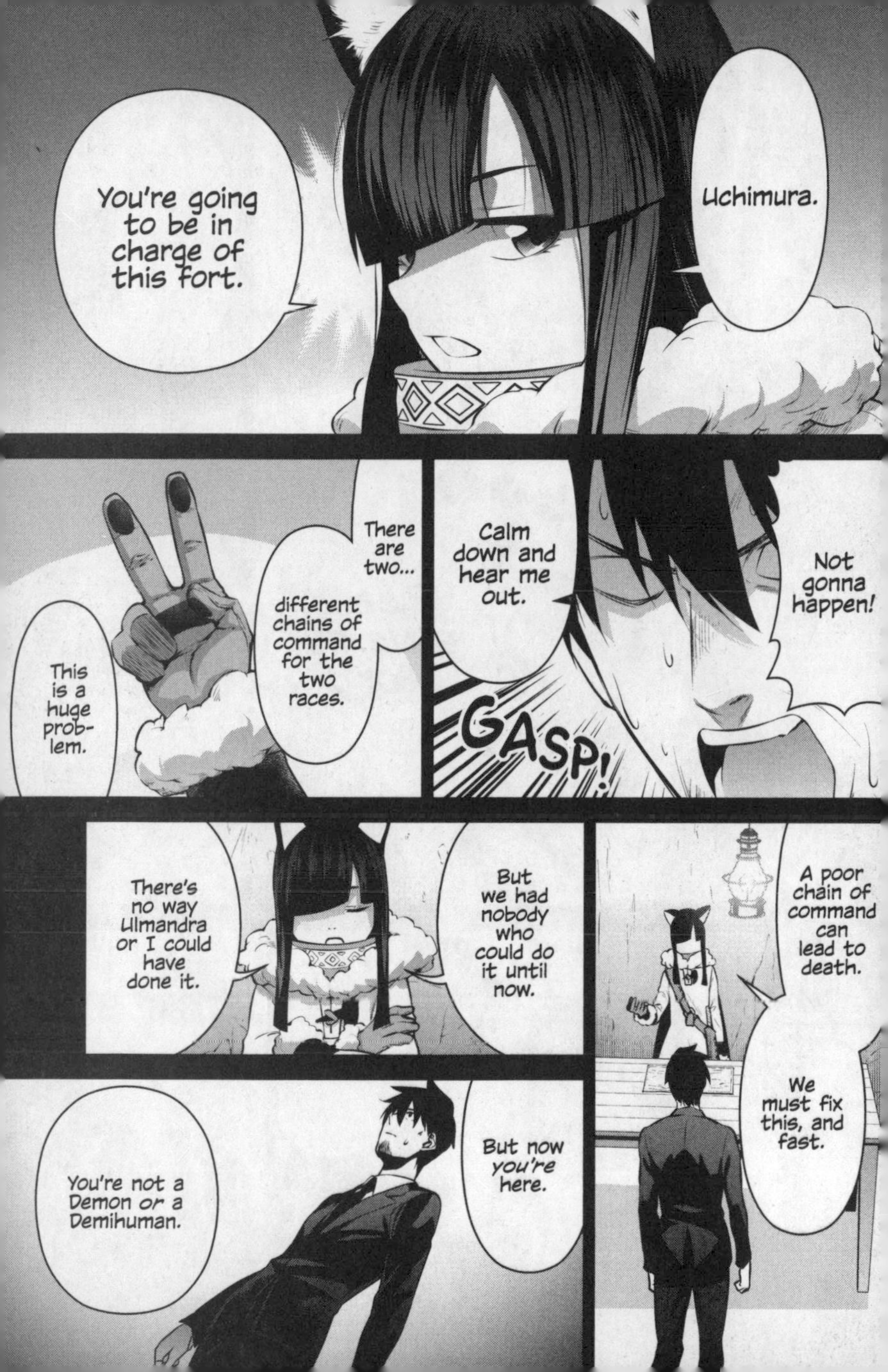
Uchimura.
You're going to be in charge of this fort.
Not gonna happen!
GASP!
Calm down and hear me out.
There are two...
different chains of command for the two races.
This is a huge prob-lem.
A poor chain of command can lead to death.
We must fix this, and fast.
But we had nobody who could do it until now.
There's no way Ulmandra or I could have done it.
But now *you're* here.
You're not a Demon *or* a Demihuman.

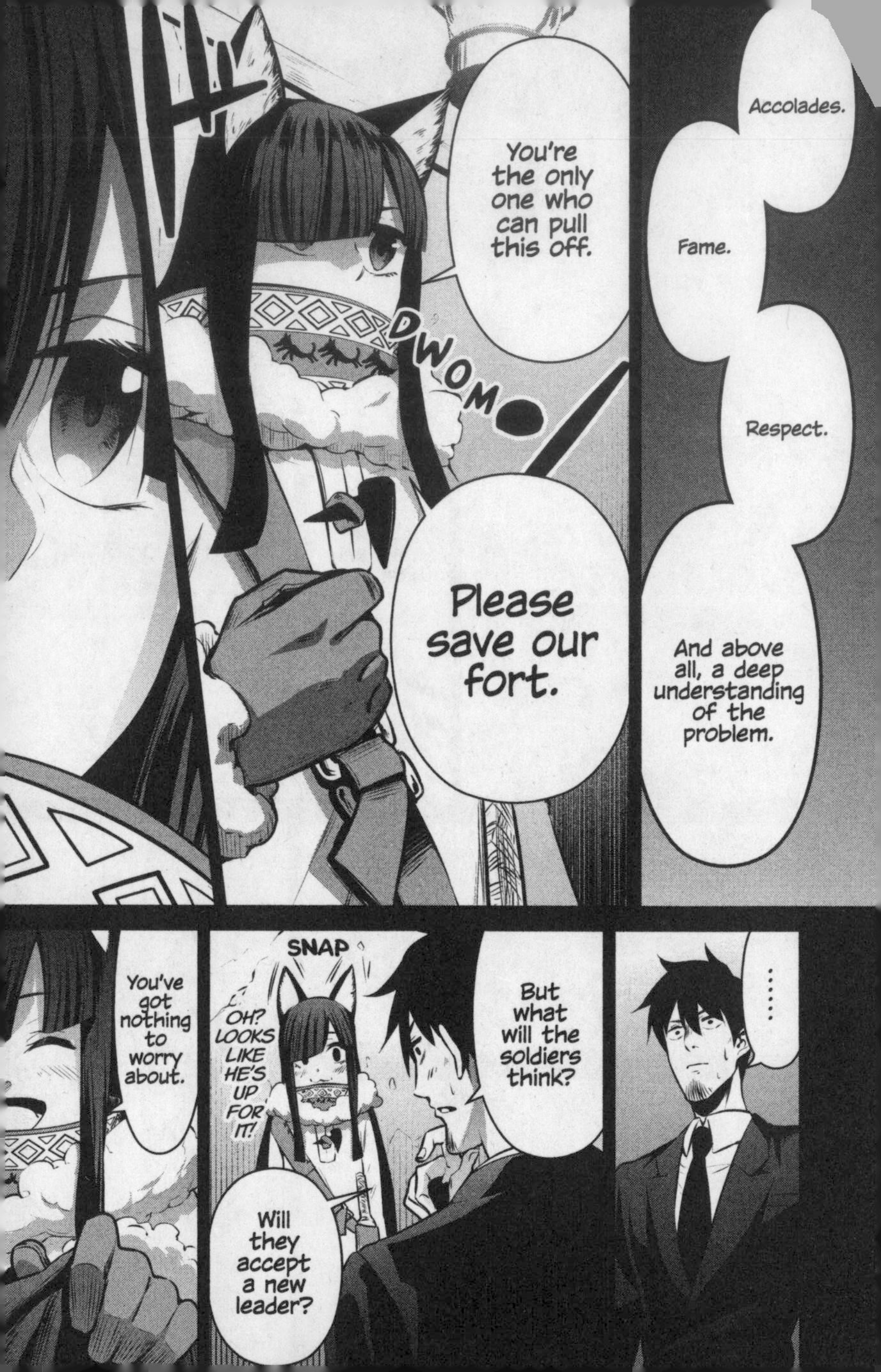
Accolades.
Fame.
Respect.
And above all, a deep understanding of the problem.
You're the only one who can pull this off.
DWOM
Please save our fort.
......
But what will the soldiers think?
SNAP
OH? LOOKS LIKE HE'S UP FOR IT!
Will they accept a new leader?
You've got nothing to worry about.

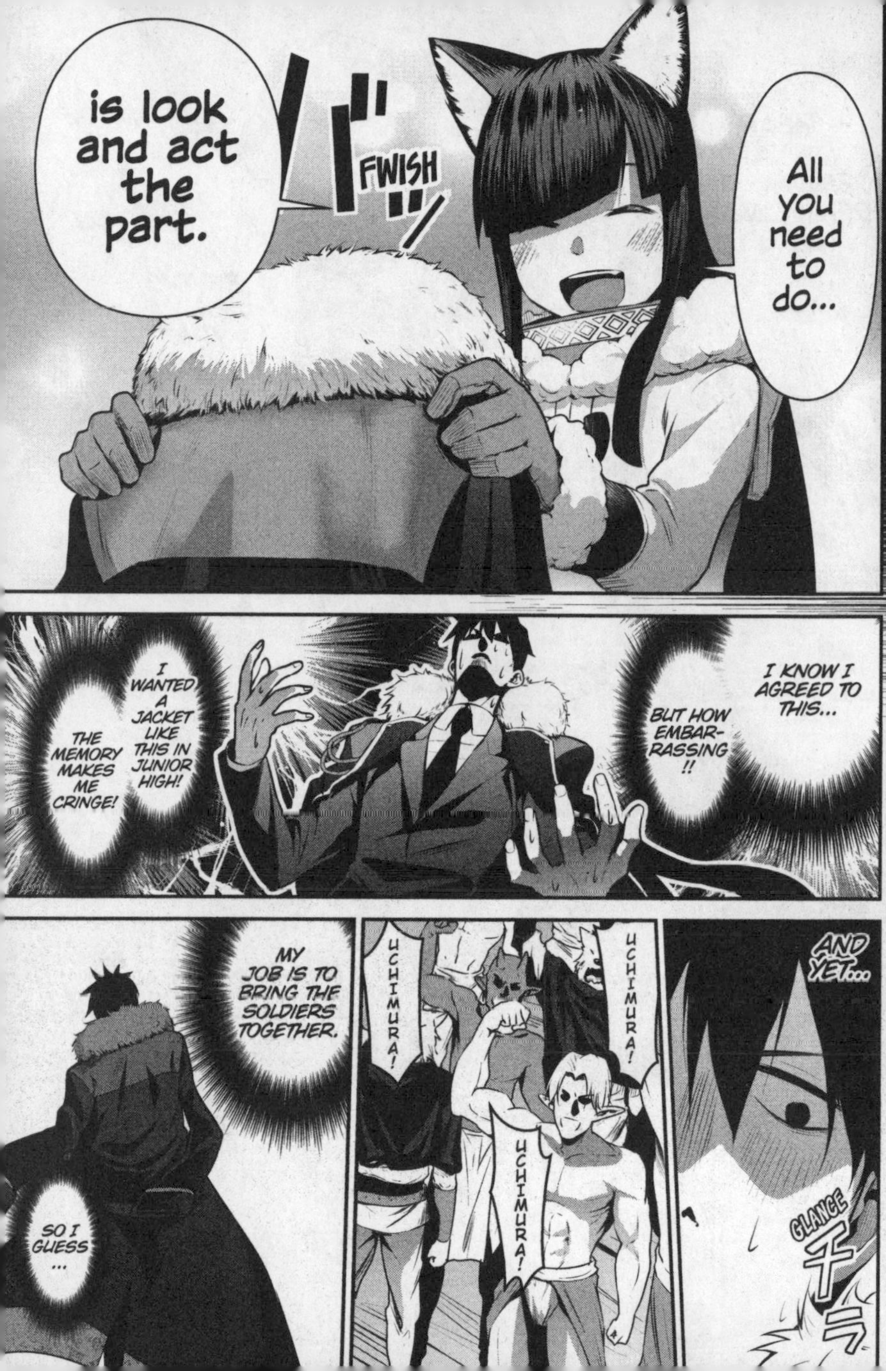
All you need to do...
is look and act the part.
FWISH
I KNOW I AGREED TO THIS...
BUT HOW EMBARRASSING !!
I WANTED A JACKET LIKE THIS IN JUNIOR HIGH!
THE MEMORY MAKES ME CRINGE!
AND YET...
GLANCE
UCHIMURA!
UCHIMURA!
UCHIMURA!
MY JOB IS TO BRING THE SOLDIERS TOGETHER.
SO I GUESS ...

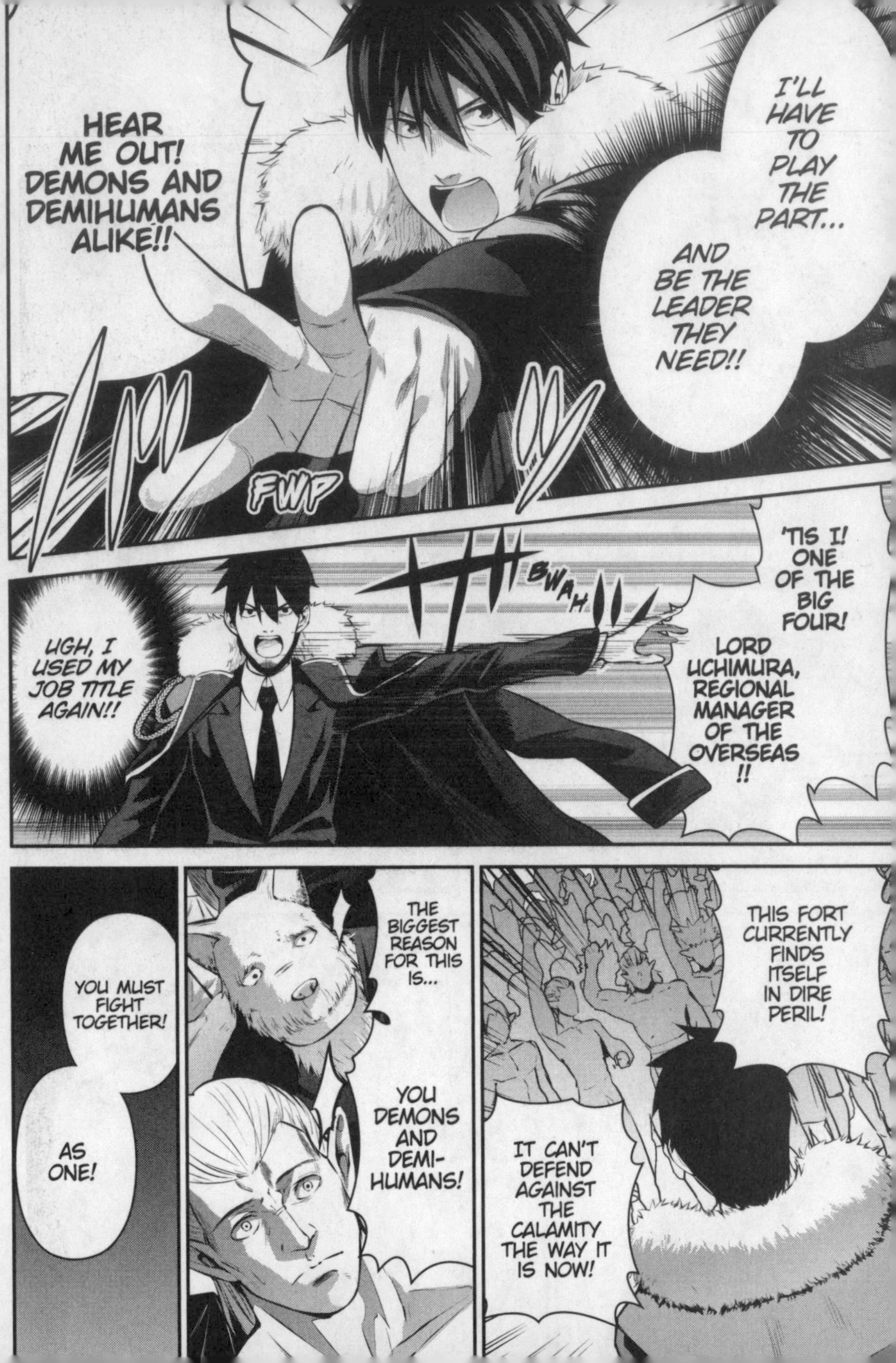
I'LL HAVE TO PLAY THE PART...
AND BE THE LEADER THEY NEED!!
HEAR ME OUT! DEMONS AND DEMIHUMANS ALIKE!!
FWIP
'TIS I! ONE OF THE BIG FOUR!
LORD UCHIMURA, REGIONAL MANAGER OF THE OVERSEAS!!
BWAH
UGH, I USED MY JOB TITLE AGAIN!!
THIS FORT CURRENTLY FINDS ITSELF IN DIRE PERIL!
IT CAN'T DEFEND AGAINST THE CALAMITY THE WAY IT IS NOW!
THE BIGGEST REASON FOR THIS IS...
YOU DEMONS AND DEMI-HUMANS!
YOU MUST FIGHT TOGETHER!
AS ONE!

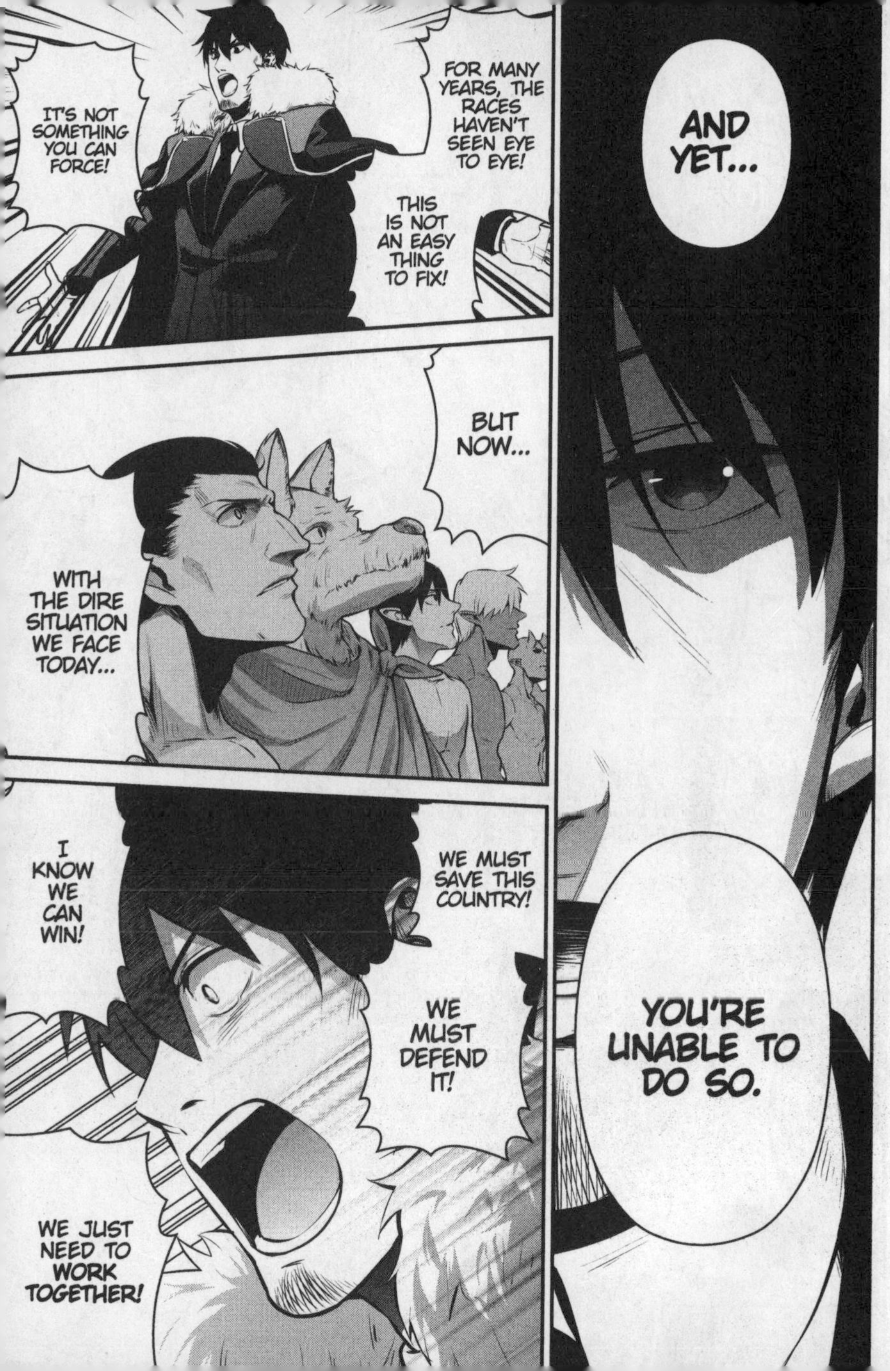
AND YET...
YOU'RE UNABLE TO DO SO.
FOR MANY YEARS, THE RACES HAVEN'T SEEN EYE TO EYE!
THIS IS NOT AN EASY THING TO FIX!
IT'S NOT SOMETHING YOU CAN FORCE!
BUT NOW...
WITH THE DIRE SITUATION WE FACE TODAY...
WE MUST SAVE THIS COUNTRY!
I KNOW WE CAN WIN!
WE MUST DEFEND IT!
WE JUST NEED TO WORK TOGETHER!

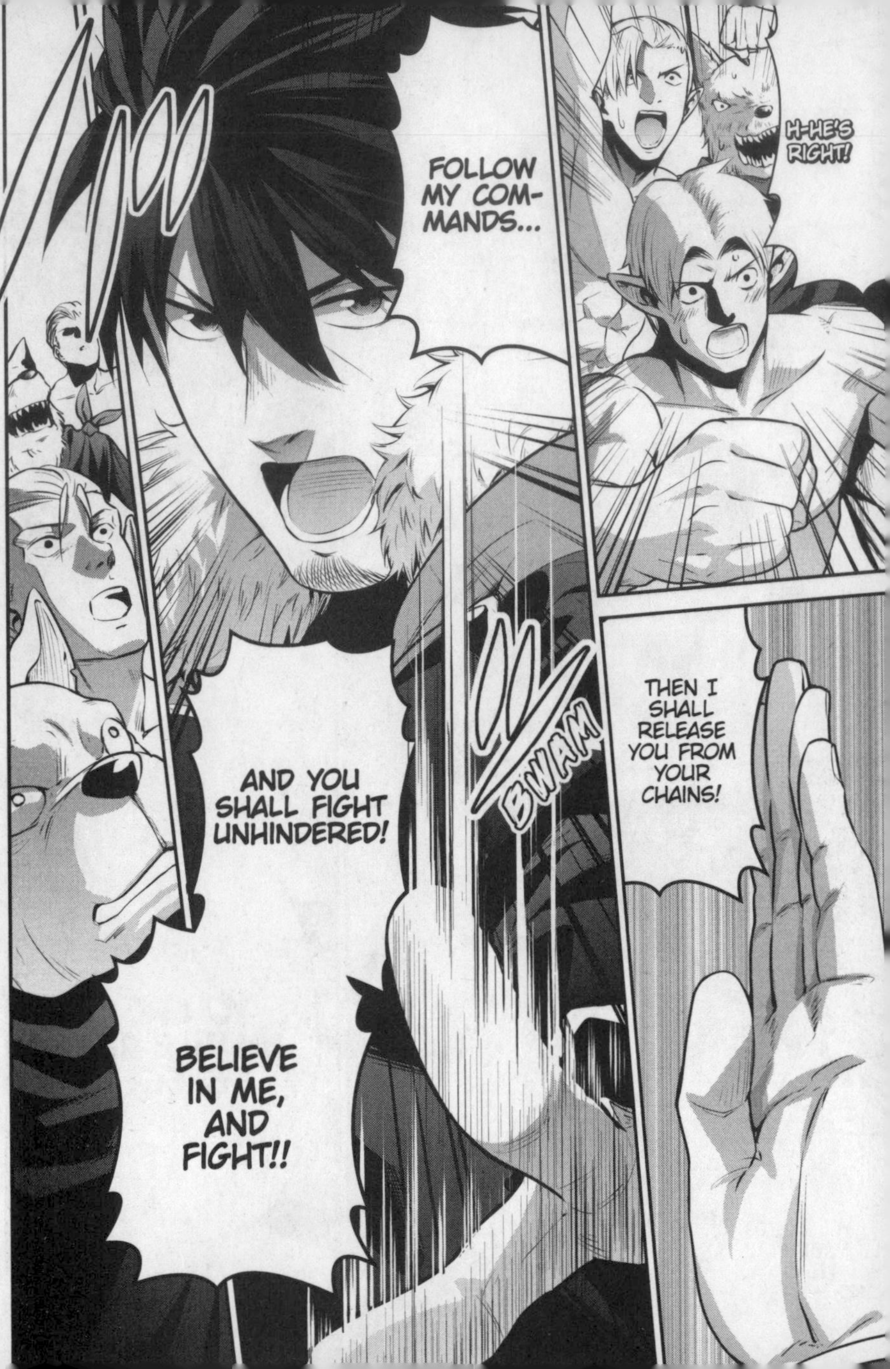
H-HE'S RIGHT!
THEN I SHALL RELEASE YOU FROM YOUR CHAINS!
FOLLOW MY COMMANDS...
BWAM
AND YOU SHALL FIGHT UNHINDERED!
BELIEVE IN ME, AND FIGHT!!

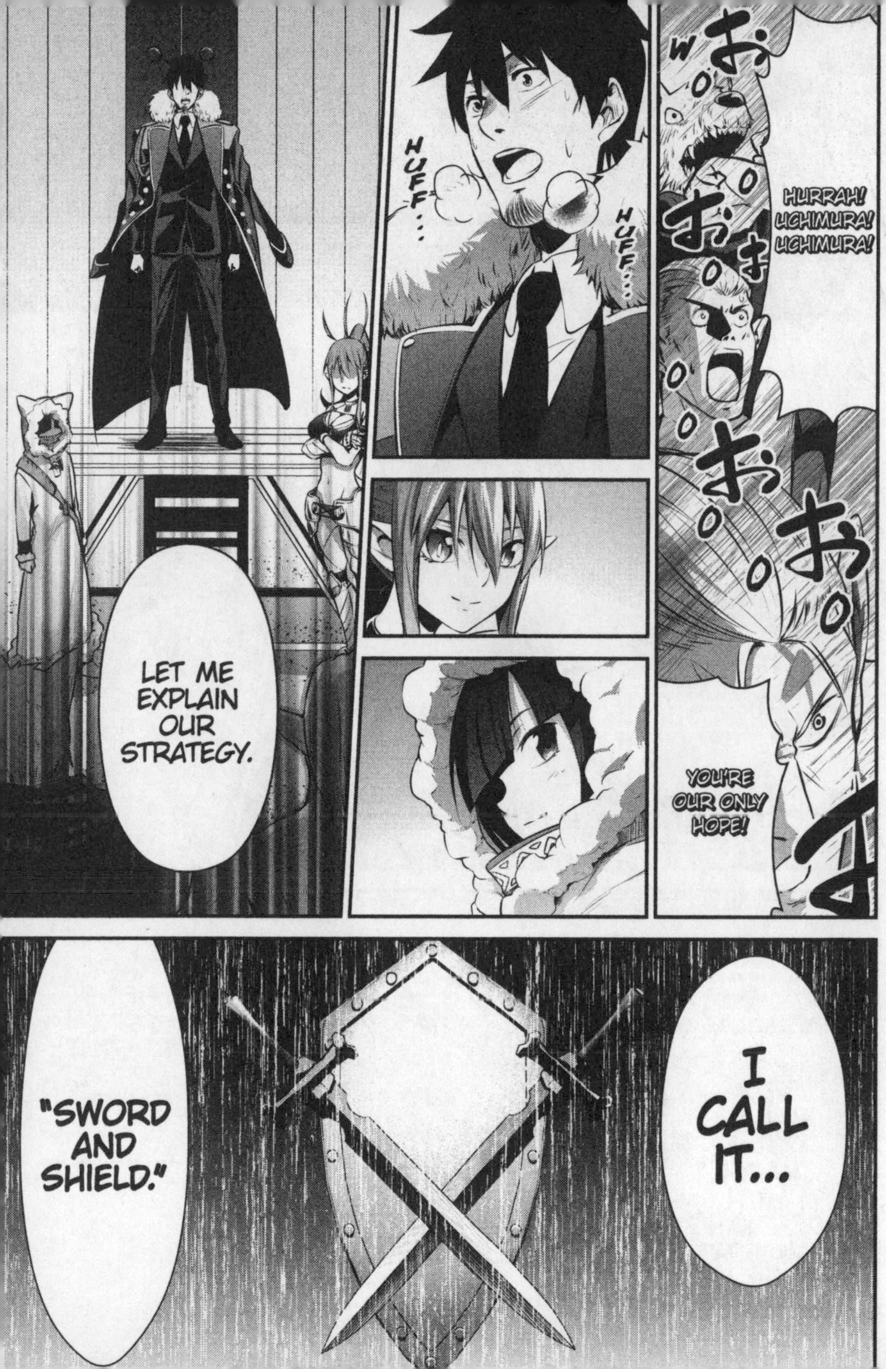
HURRAH! UCHIMURA! UCHIMURA!
YOU'RE OUR ONLY HOPE!
HUFF...
HUFF...
LET ME EXPLAIN OUR STRATEGY.
I CALL IT...
"SWORD AND SHIELD."

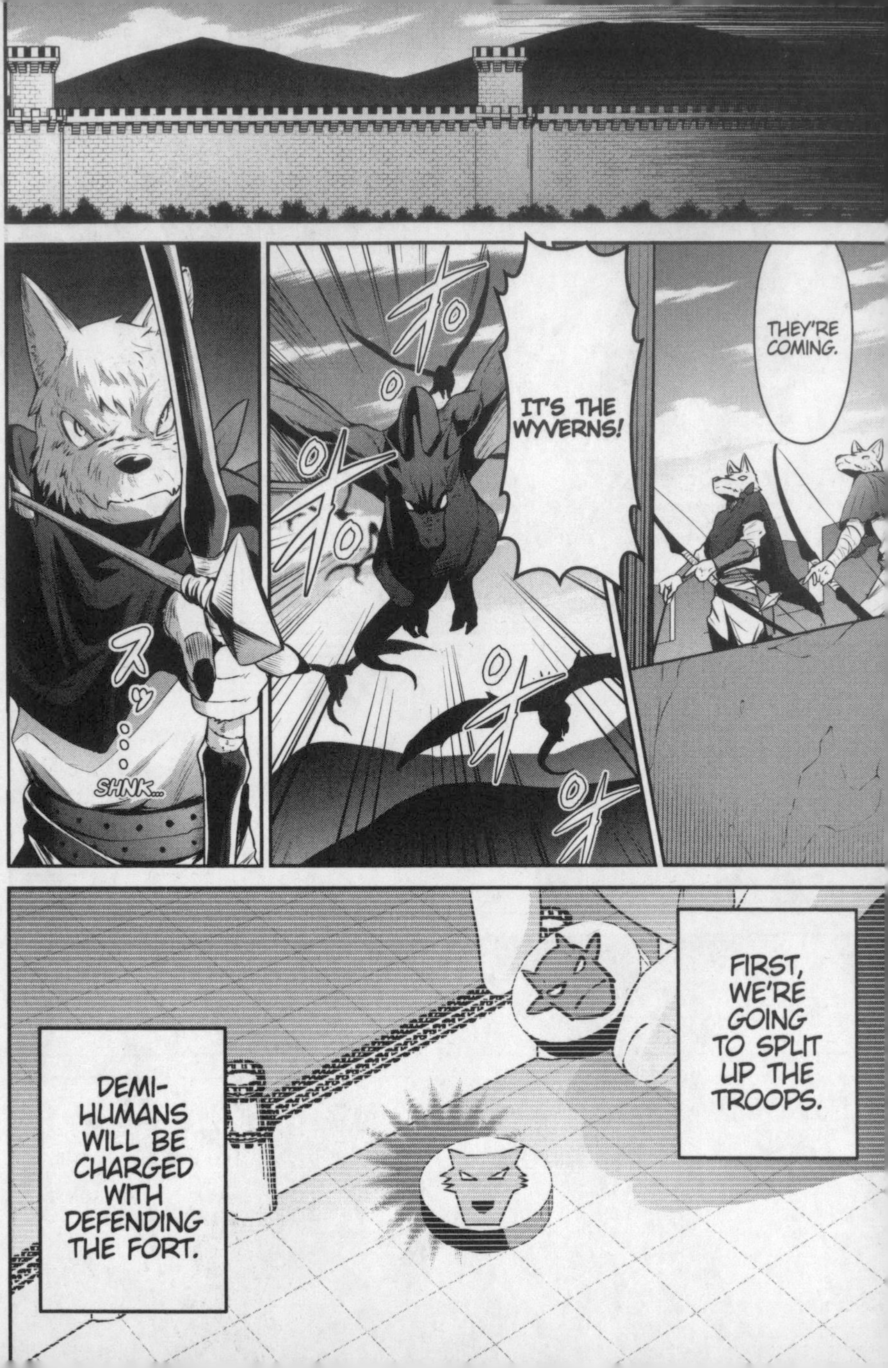
THEY'RE COMING.
IT'S THE WYVERNS!
SHNK...
FIRST, WE'RE GOING TO SPLIT UP THE TROOPS.
DEMI-HUMANS WILL BE CHARGED WITH DEFENDING THE FORT.

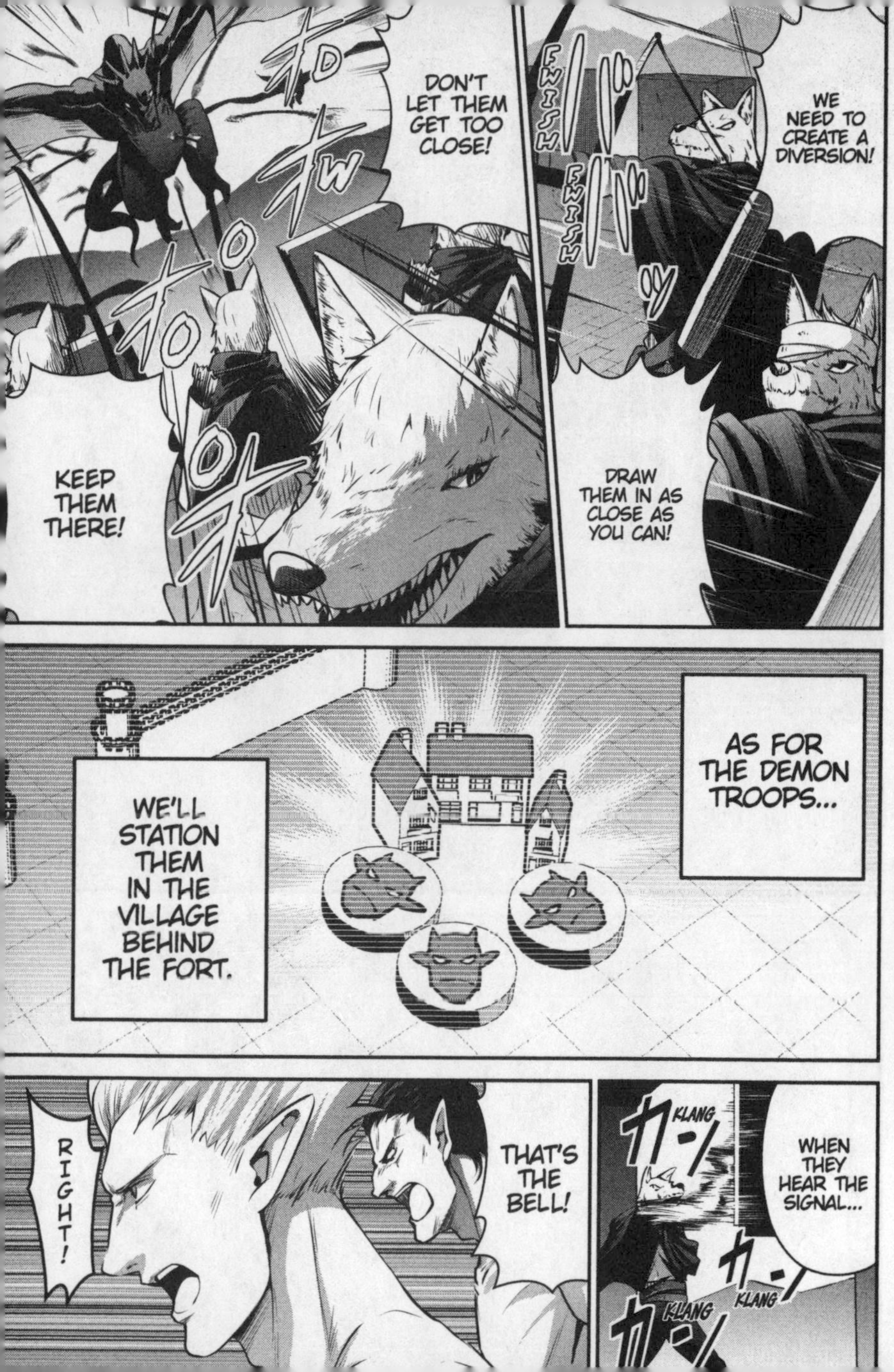
WE NEED TO CREATE A DIVERSION!
FWISH
FWISH
DRAW THEM IN AS CLOSE AS YOU CAN!
DON'T LET THEM GET TOO CLOSE!
KEEP THEM THERE!
AS FOR THE DEMON TROOPS...
WE'LL STATION THEM IN THE VILLAGE BEHIND THE FORT.
WHEN THEY HEAR THE SIGNAL...
KLANG
KLANG
KLANG
KLANG
THAT'S THE BELL!
RIGHT!

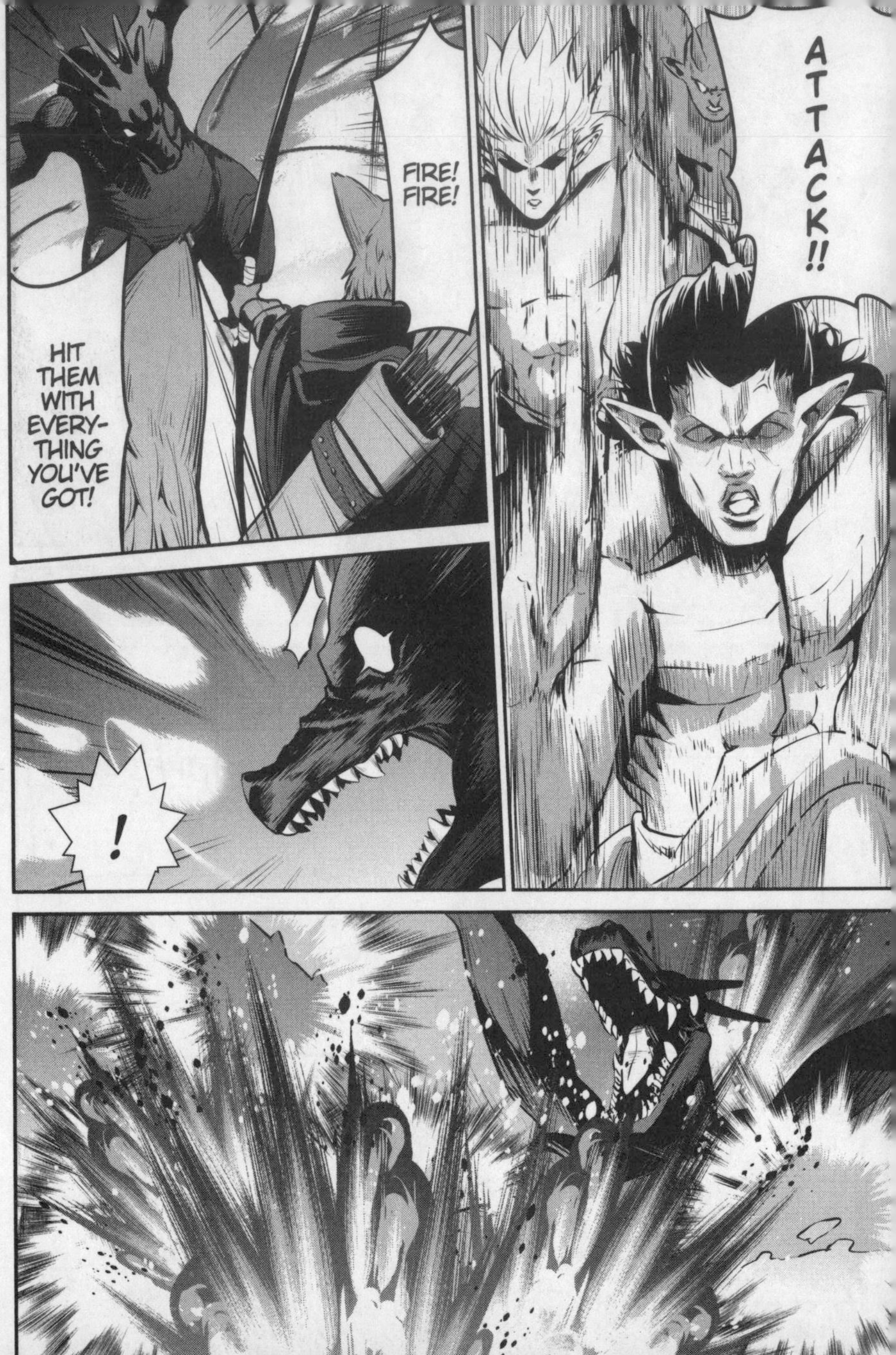
ATTACK!!
FIRE! FIRE!
HIT THEM WITH EVERYTHING YOU'VE GOT!
!

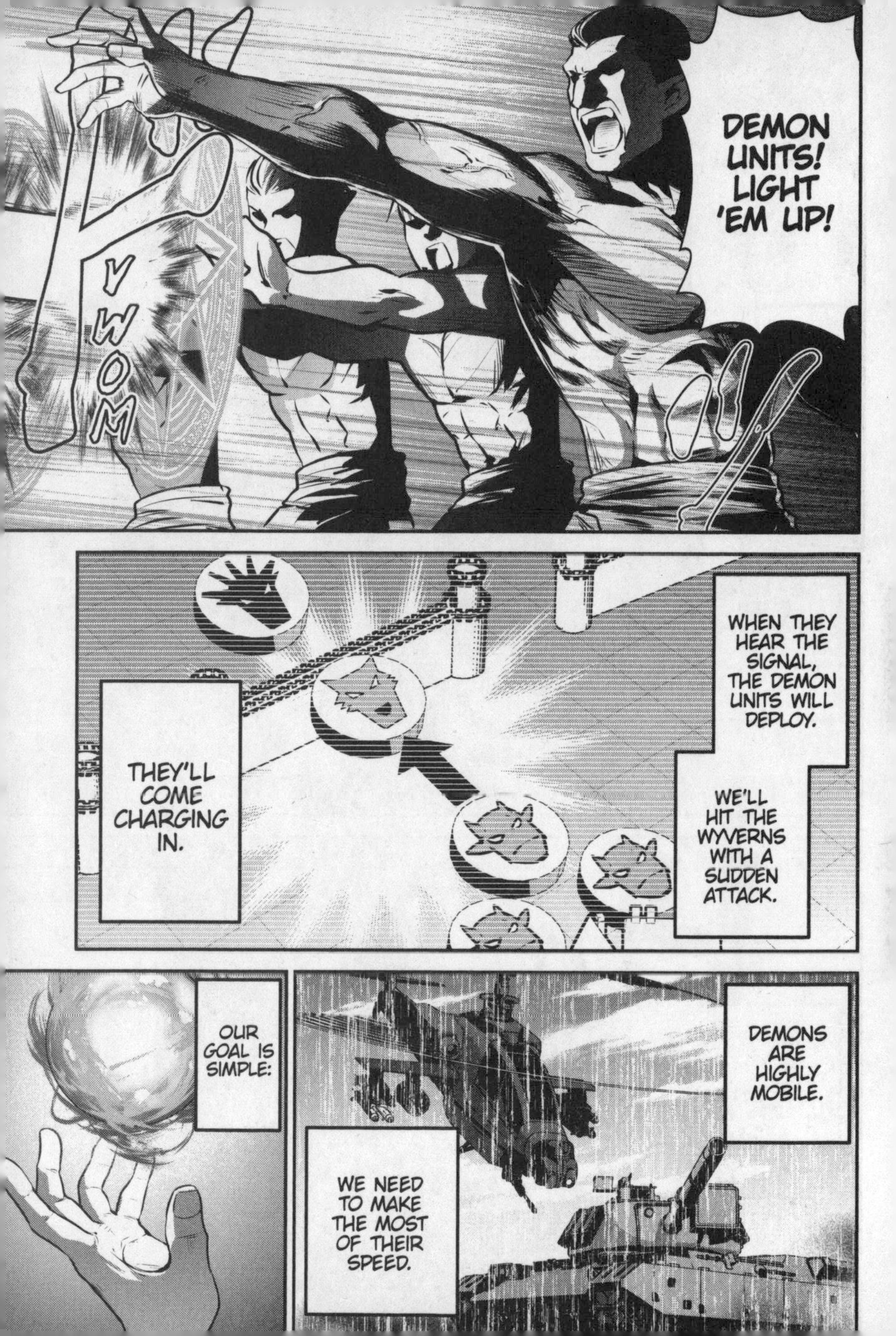
DEMON UNITS! LIGHT 'EM UP!
VWOM
WHEN THEY HEAR THE SIGNAL, THE DEMON UNITS WILL DEPLOY.
WE'LL HIT THE WYVERNS WITH A SUDDEN ATTACK.
THEY'LL COME CHARGING IN.
DEMONS ARE HIGHLY MOBILE.
WE NEED TO MAKE THE MOST OF THEIR SPEED.
OUR GOAL IS SIMPLE:

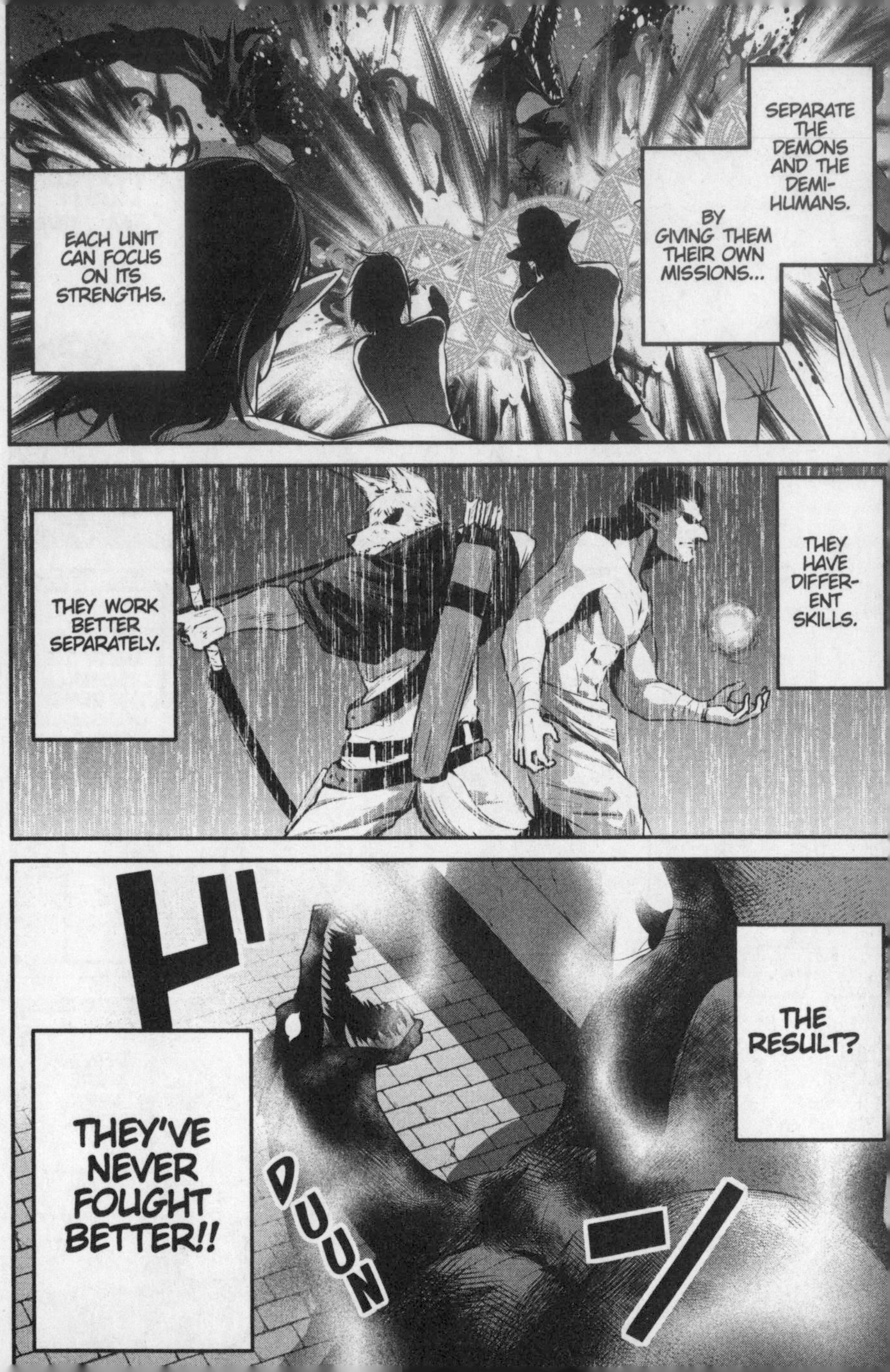
SEPARATE THE DEMONS AND THE DEMI-HUMANS.
BY GIVING THEM THEIR OWN MISSIONS...
EACH UNIT CAN FOCUS ON ITS STRENGTHS.
THEY HAVE DIFFER-ENT SKILLS.
THEY WORK BETTER SEPARATELY.
THE RESULT?
THEY'VE NEVER FOUGHT BETTER!!
DUUN

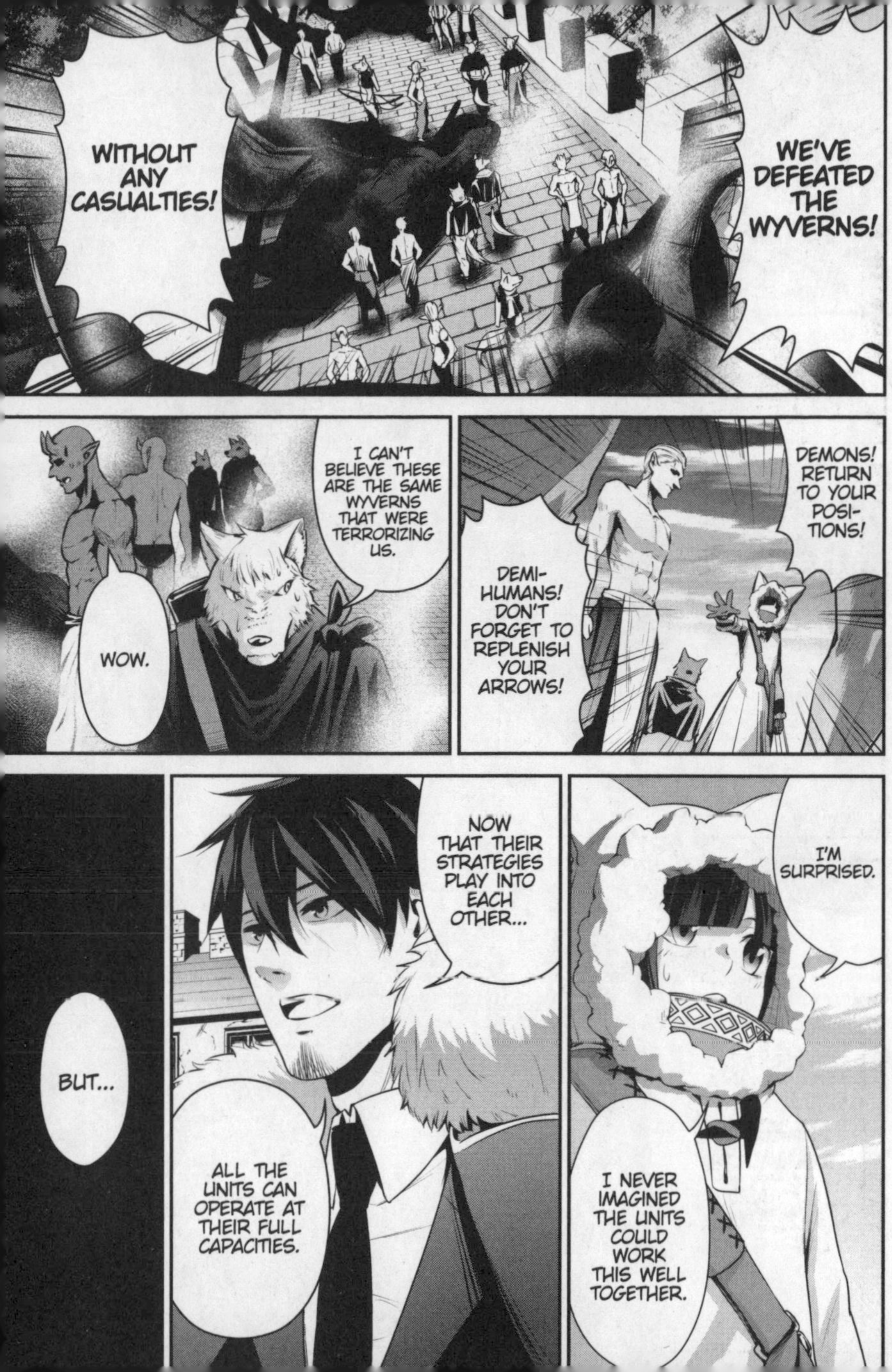
WE'VE DEFEATED THE WYVERNS!
WITHOUT ANY CASUALTIES!
DEMONS! RETURN TO YOUR POSI- TIONS!
DEMI- HUMANS! DON'T FORGET TO REPLENISH YOUR ARROWS!
I CAN'T BELIEVE THESE ARE THE SAME WYVERNS THAT WERE TERRORIZING US.
WOW.
I'M SURPRISED.
I NEVER IMAGINED THE UNITS COULD WORK THIS WELL TOGETHER.
NOW THAT THEIR STRATEGIES PLAY INTO EACH OTHER...
ALL THE UNITS CAN OPERATE AT THEIR FULL CAPACITIES.
BUT...

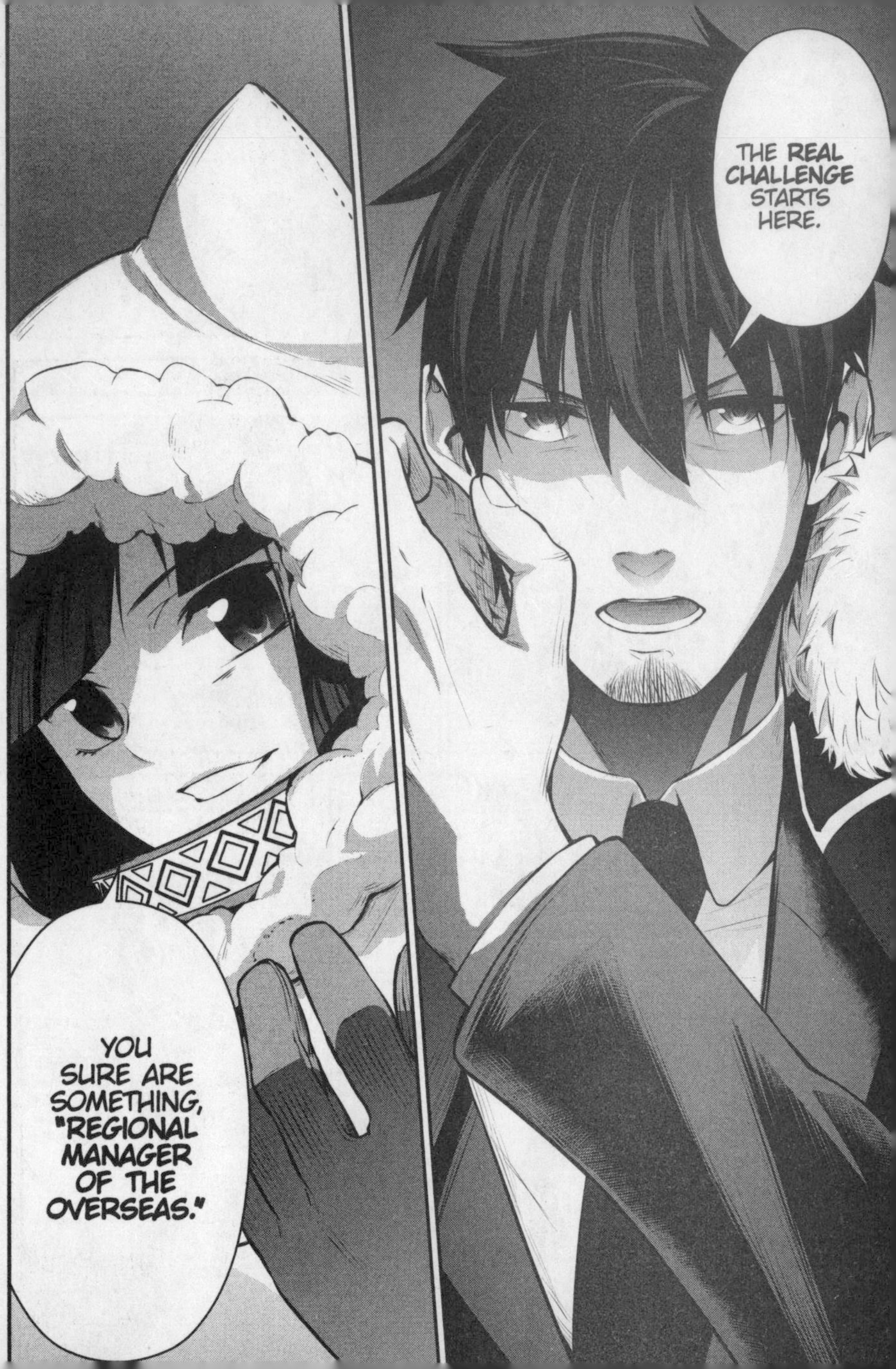
THE REAL CHALLENGE STARTS HERE.
YOU SURE ARE SOMETHING, "REGIONAL MANAGER OF THE OVERSEAS."

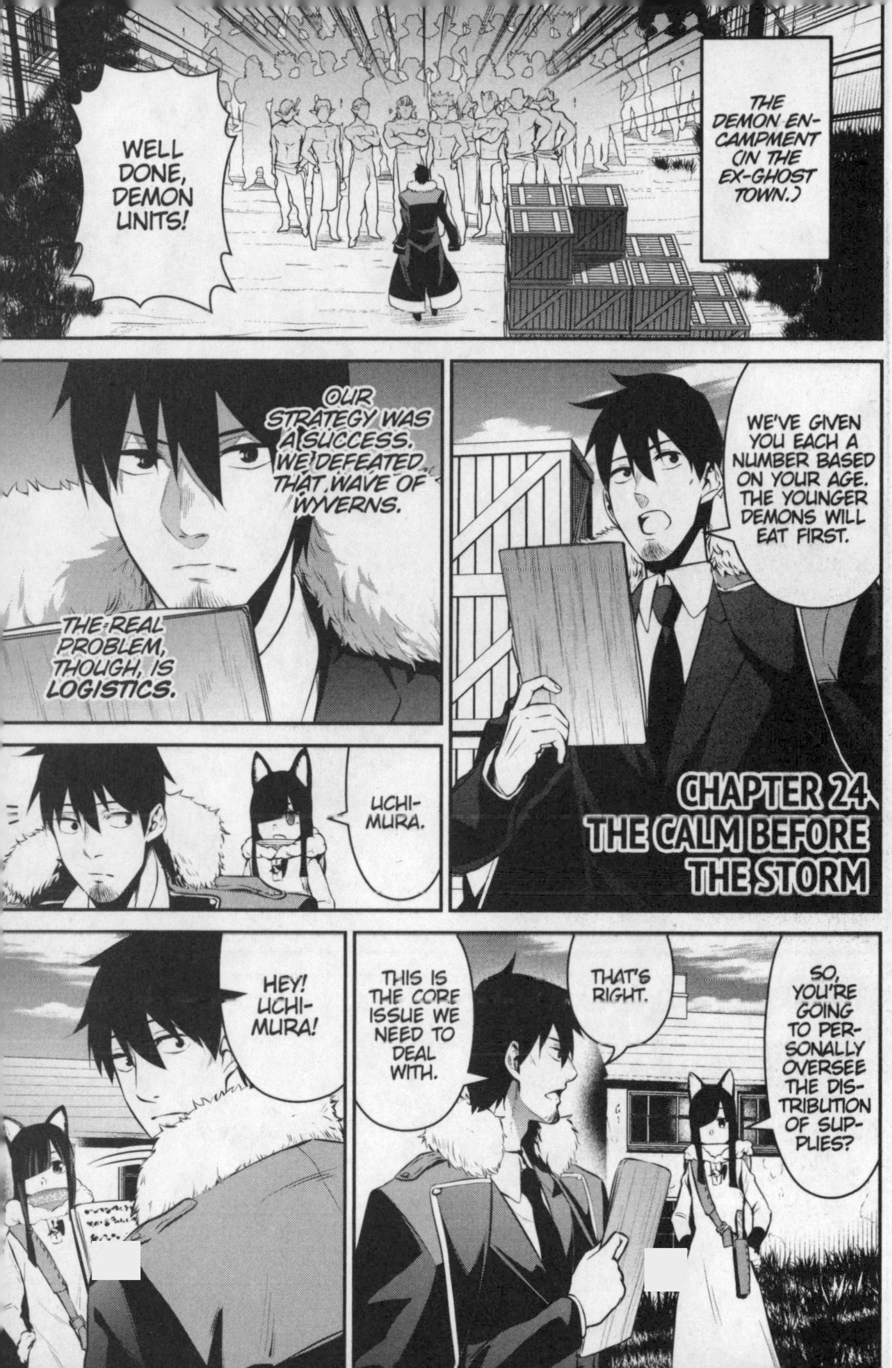
THE DEMON ENCAMPMENT (IN THE EX-GHOST TOWN.)
WELL DONE, DEMON UNITS!
WE'VE GIVEN YOU EACH A NUMBER BASED ON YOUR AGE. THE YOUNGER DEMONS WILL EAT FIRST.
CHAPTER 24 THE CALM BEFORE THE STORM
OUR STRATEGY WAS A SUCCESS. WE DEFEATED THAT WAVE OF WYVERNS.
THE REAL PROBLEM, THOUGH, IS LOGISTICS.
UCHIMURA.
SO, YOU'RE GOING TO PERSONALLY OVERSEE THE DISTRIBUTION OF SUPPLIES?
THAT'S RIGHT.
THIS IS THE CORE ISSUE WE NEED TO DEAL WITH.
HEY! UCHIMURA!

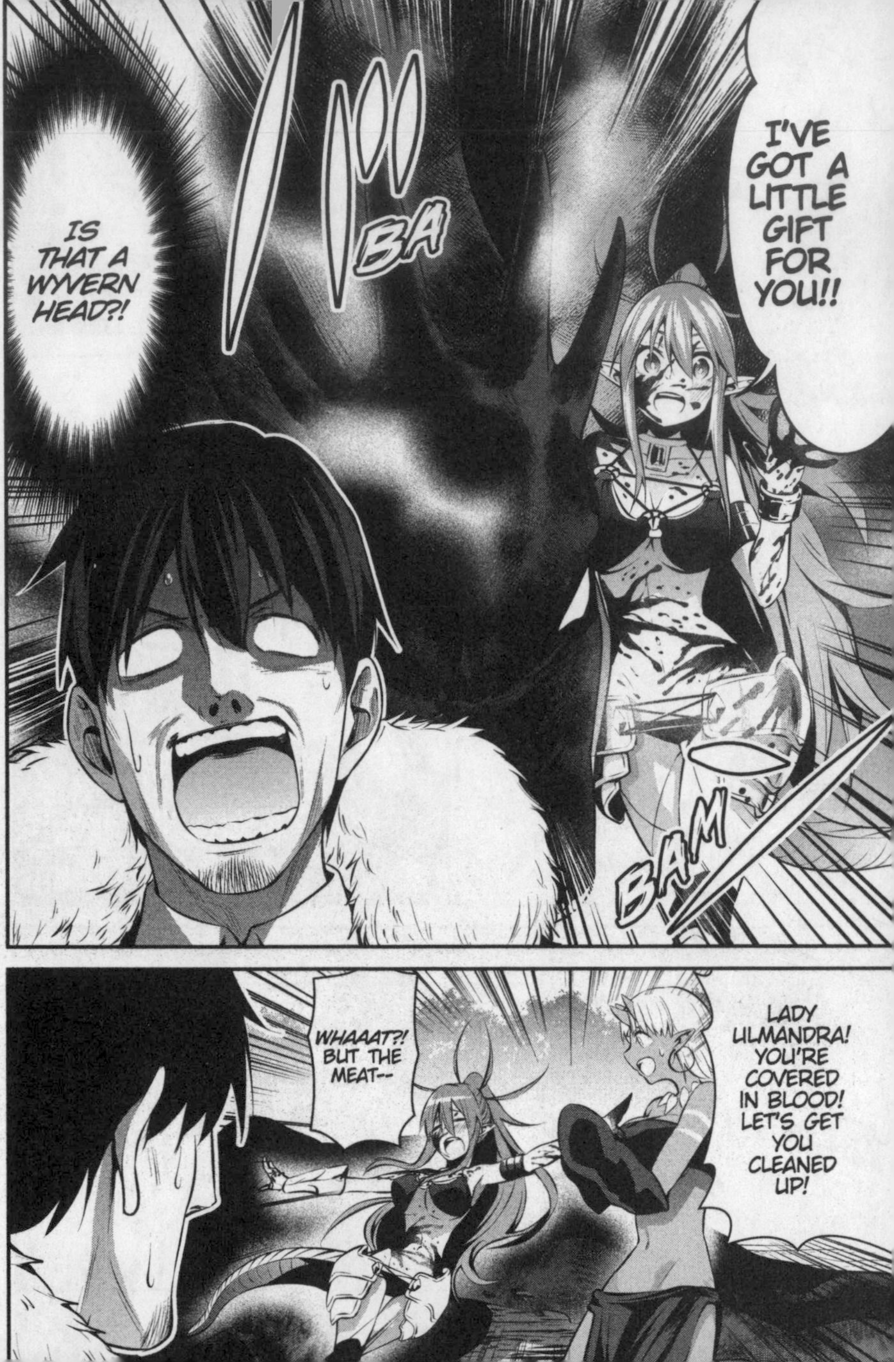
I'VE GOT A LITTLE GIFT FOR YOU!!
BA
IS THAT A WYVERN HEAD?!
BAM
LADY ULMANDRA! YOU'RE COVERED IN BLOOD! LET'S GET YOU CLEANED UP!
WHAAAT?! BUT THE MEAT--

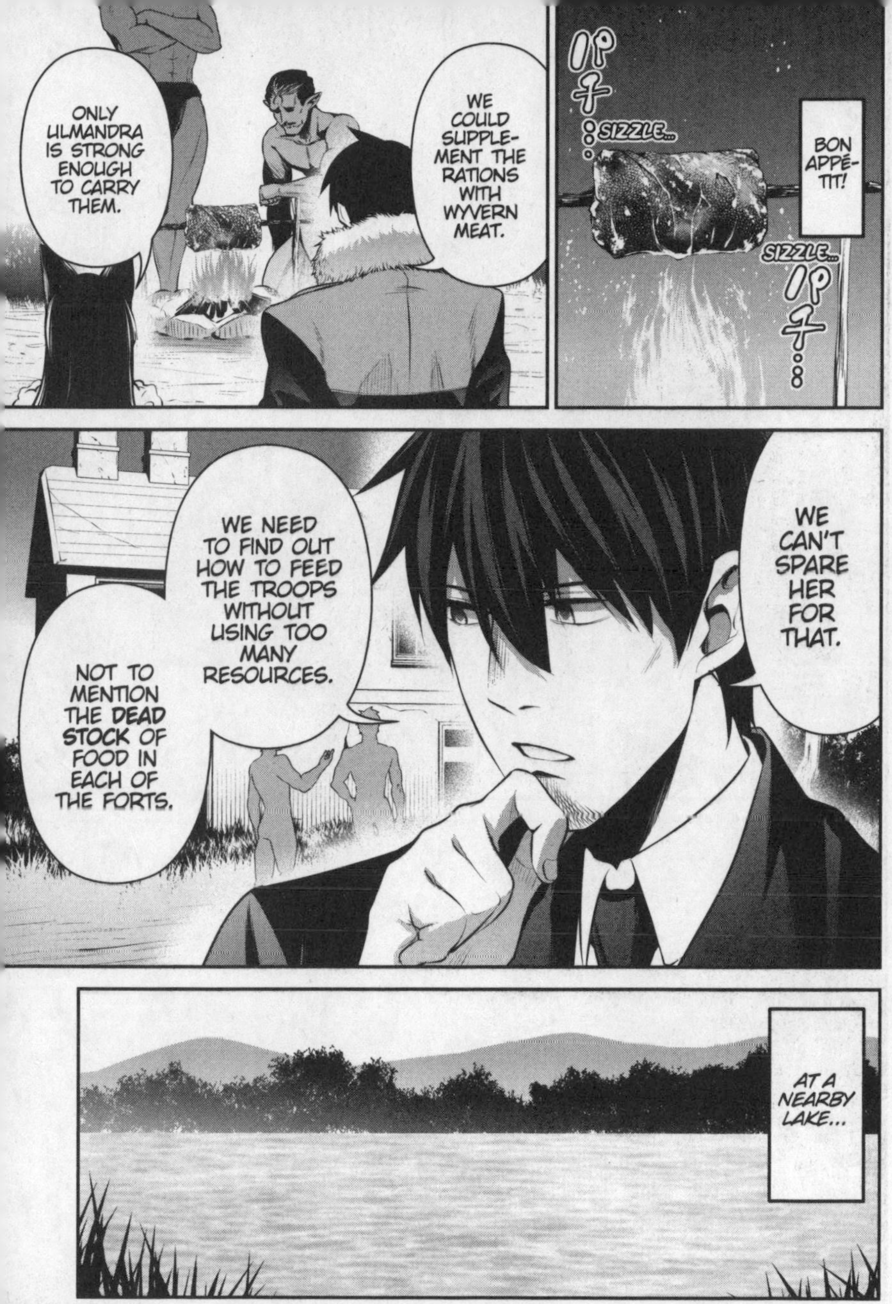
BON APPÉ-TIT!
パチ… SIZZLE…
SIZZLE… パチ…
WE COULD SUPPLE-MENT THE RATIONS WITH WYVERN MEAT.
ONLY ULMANDRA IS STRONG ENOUGH TO CARRY THEM.
WE CAN'T SPARE HER FOR THAT.
WE NEED TO FIND OUT HOW TO FEED THE TROOPS WITHOUT USING TOO MANY RESOURCES.
NOT TO MENTION THE DEAD STOCK OF FOOD IN EACH OF THE FORTS.
AT A NEARBY LAKE…

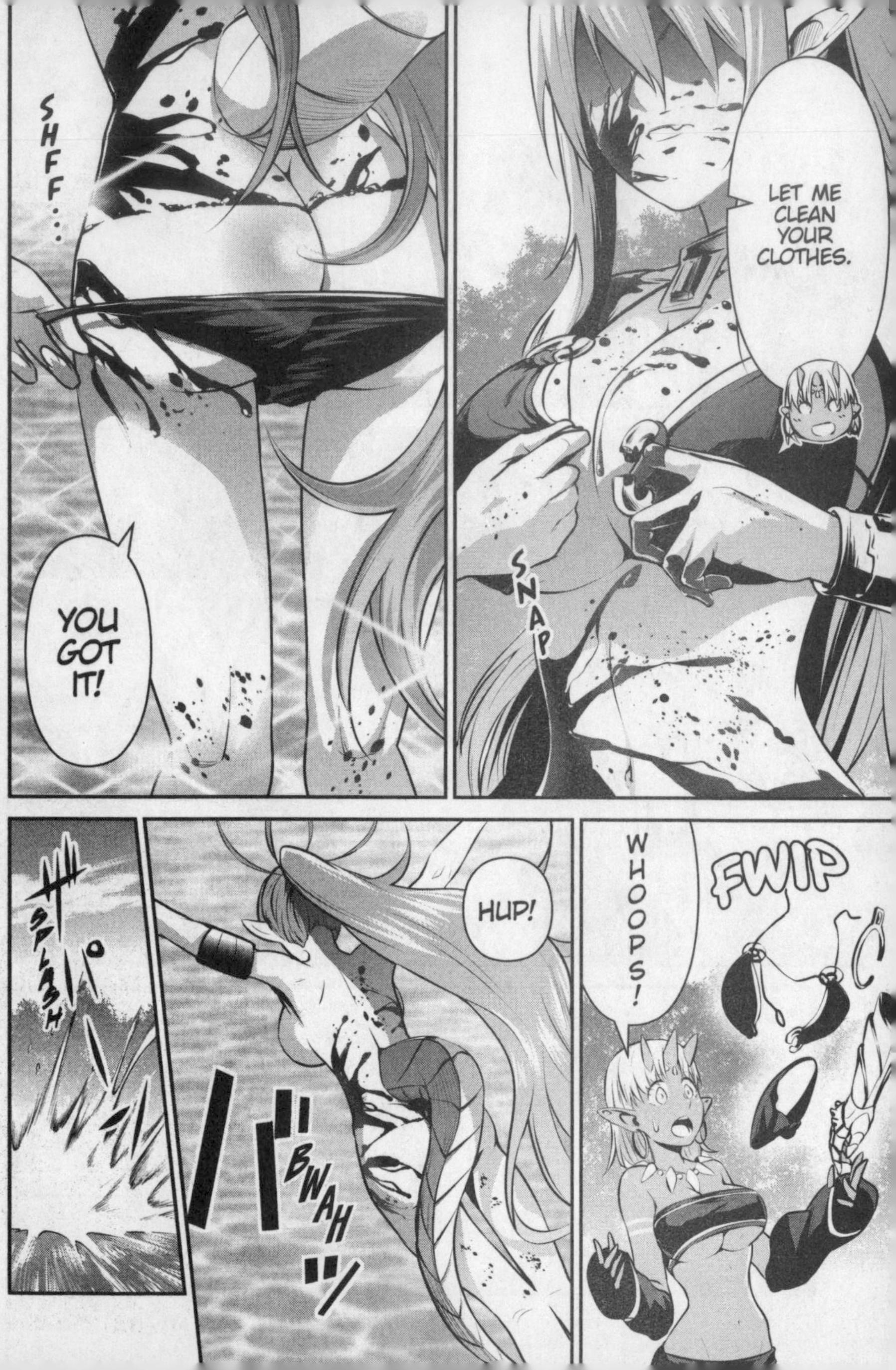
LET ME CLEAN YOUR CLOTHES.
SNAP
SHFF...
YOU GOT IT!
WHOOPS!
FWIP
HUP!
BWAH
SPLASH

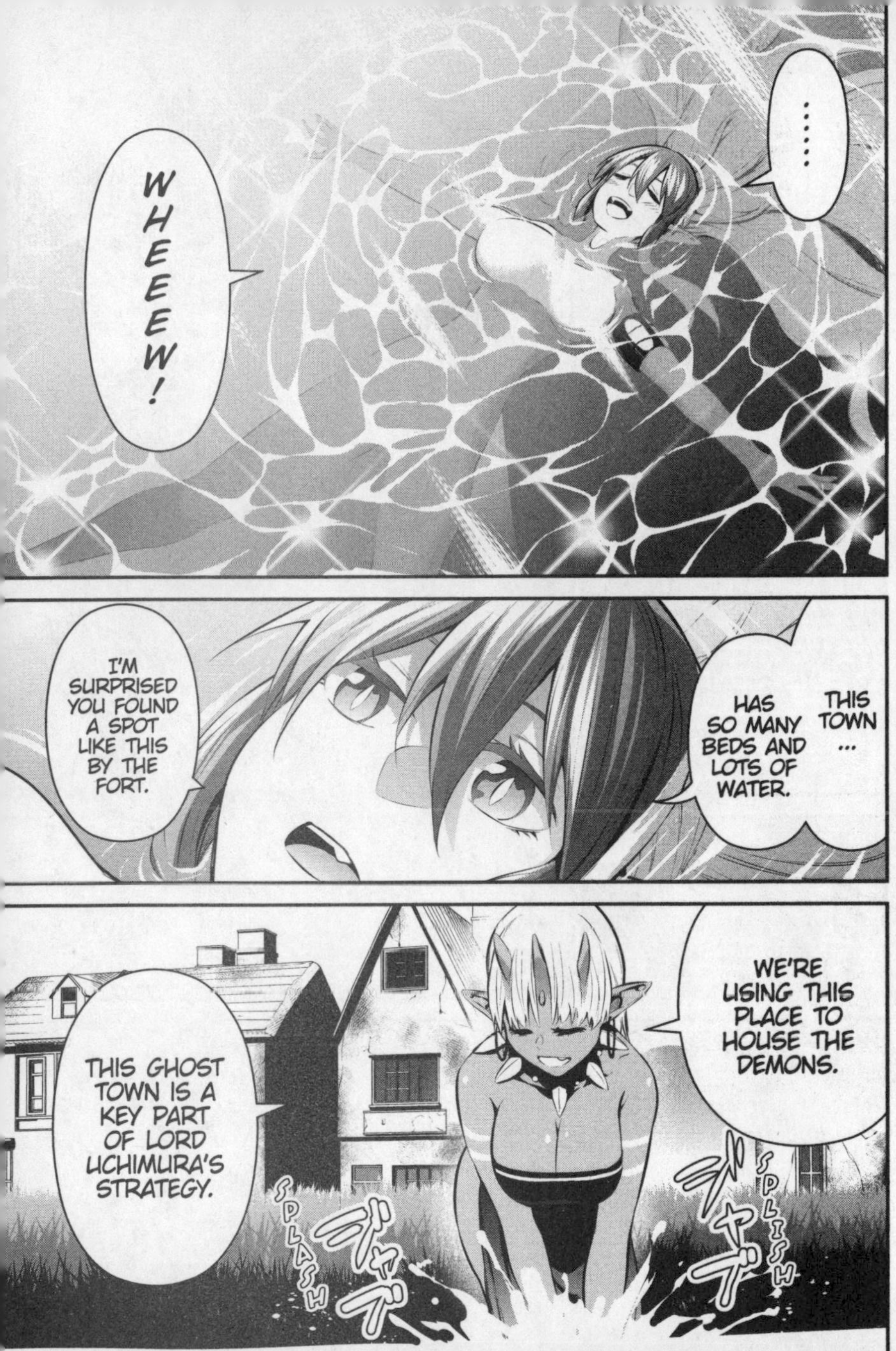
......
WHEEEEW!
THIS TOWN...
HAS SO MANY BEDS AND LOTS OF WATER.
I'M SURPRISED YOU FOUND A SPOT LIKE THIS BY THE FORT.
WE'RE USING THIS PLACE TO HOUSE THE DEMONS.
SPLISH
THIS GHOST TOWN IS A KEY PART OF LORD UCHIMURA'S STRATEGY.
SPLASH

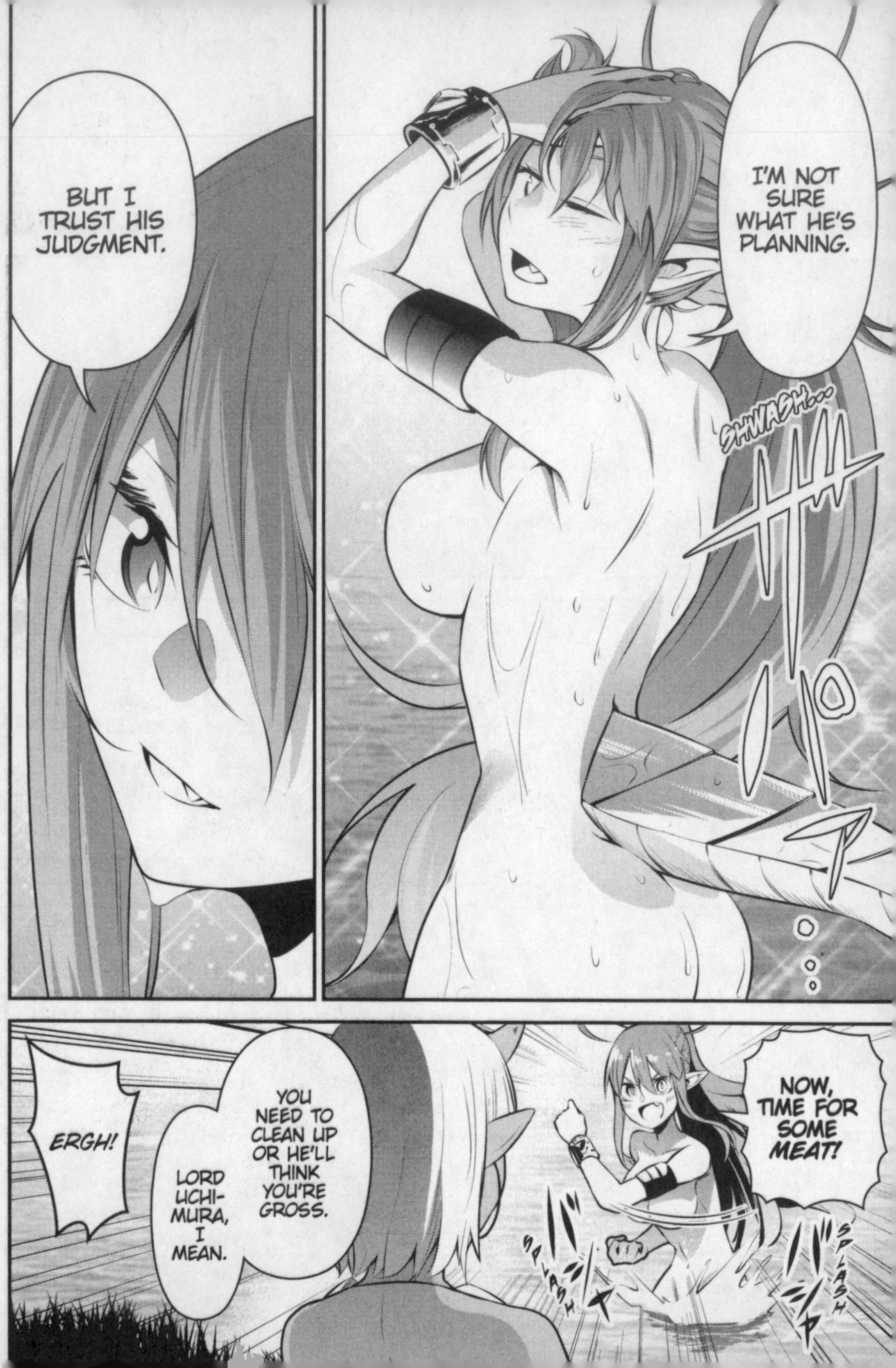
I'M NOT SURE WHAT HE'S PLANNING.
SHWASH...
BUT I TRUST HIS JUDGMENT.
NOW, TIME FOR SOME MEAT!
SPLASH
SPLASH
YOU NEED TO CLEAN UP OR HE'LL THINK YOU'RE GROSS.
LORD UCHIMURA, I MEAN.
ERGH!

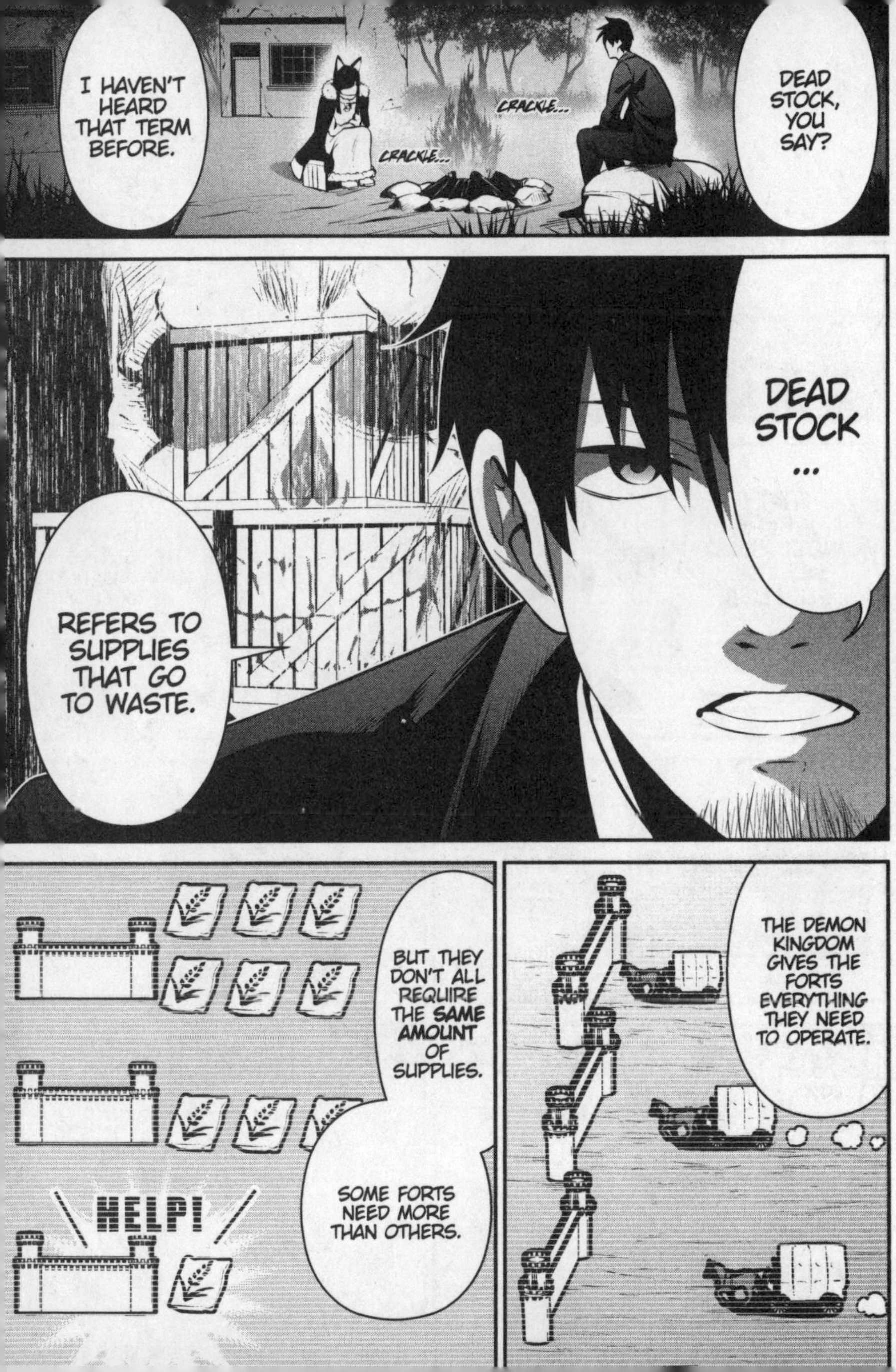
DEAD STOCK, YOU SAY?
CRACKLE...
CRACKLE...
I HAVEN'T HEARD THAT TERM BEFORE.
DEAD STOCK ...
REFERS TO SUPPLIES THAT GO TO WASTE.
THE DEMON KINGDOM GIVES THE FORTS EVERYTHING THEY NEED TO OPERATE.
BUT THEY DON'T ALL REQUIRE THE SAME AMOUNT OF SUPPLIES.
HELP!
SOME FORTS NEED MORE THAN OTHERS.

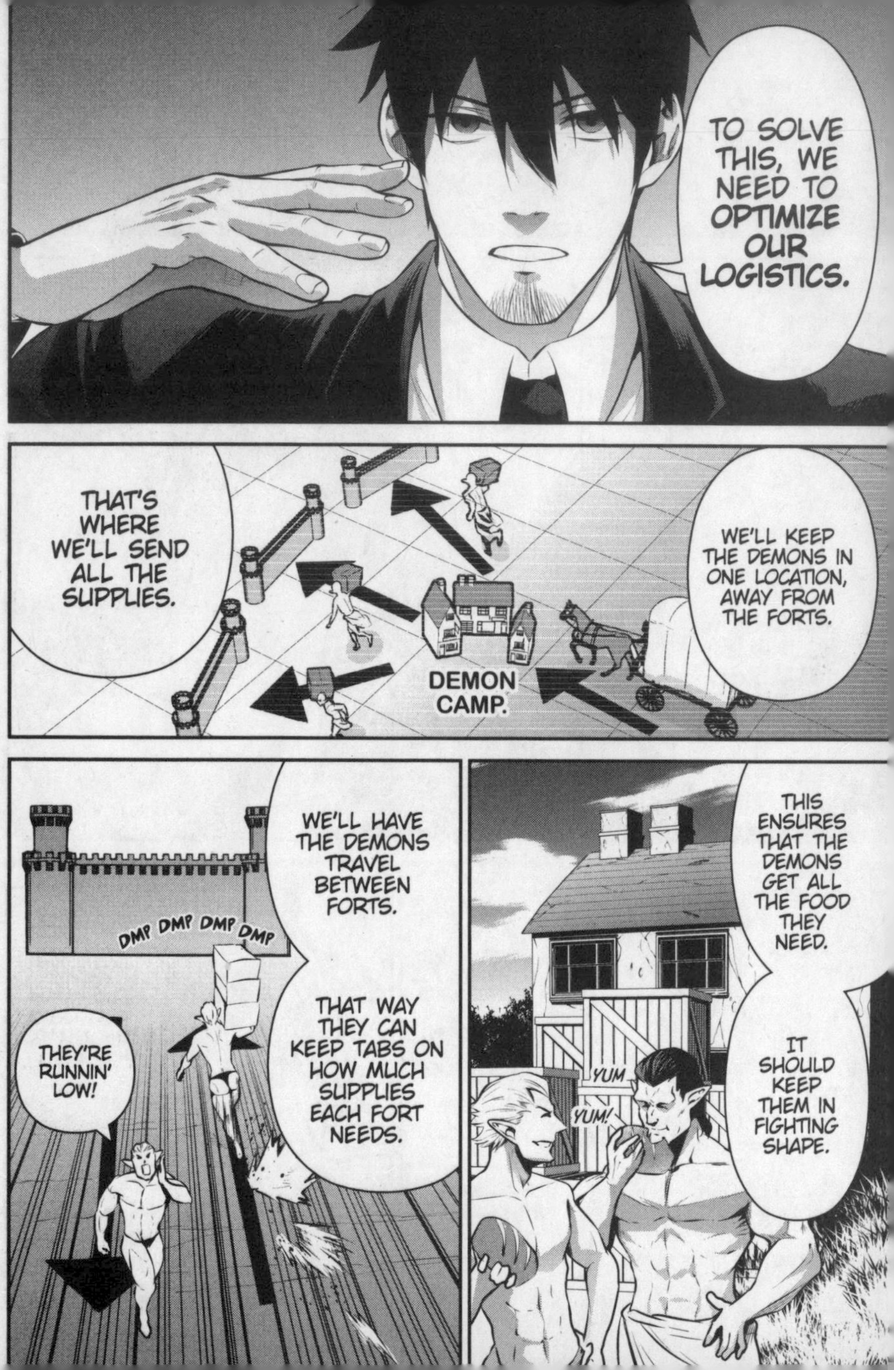
TO SOLVE THIS, WE NEED TO OPTIMIZE OUR LOGISTICS.
WE'LL KEEP THE DEMONS IN ONE LOCATION, AWAY FROM THE FORTS.
THAT'S WHERE WE'LL SEND ALL THE SUPPLIES.
DEMON CAMP.
THIS ENSURES THAT THE DEMONS GET ALL THE FOOD THEY NEED.
IT SHOULD KEEP THEM IN FIGHTING SHAPE.
YUM
YUM!
WE'LL HAVE THE DEMONS TRAVEL BETWEEN FORTS.
THAT WAY THEY CAN KEEP TABS ON HOW MUCH SUPPLIES EACH FORT NEEDS.
DMP DMP DMP DMP
THEY'RE RUNNIN' LOW!

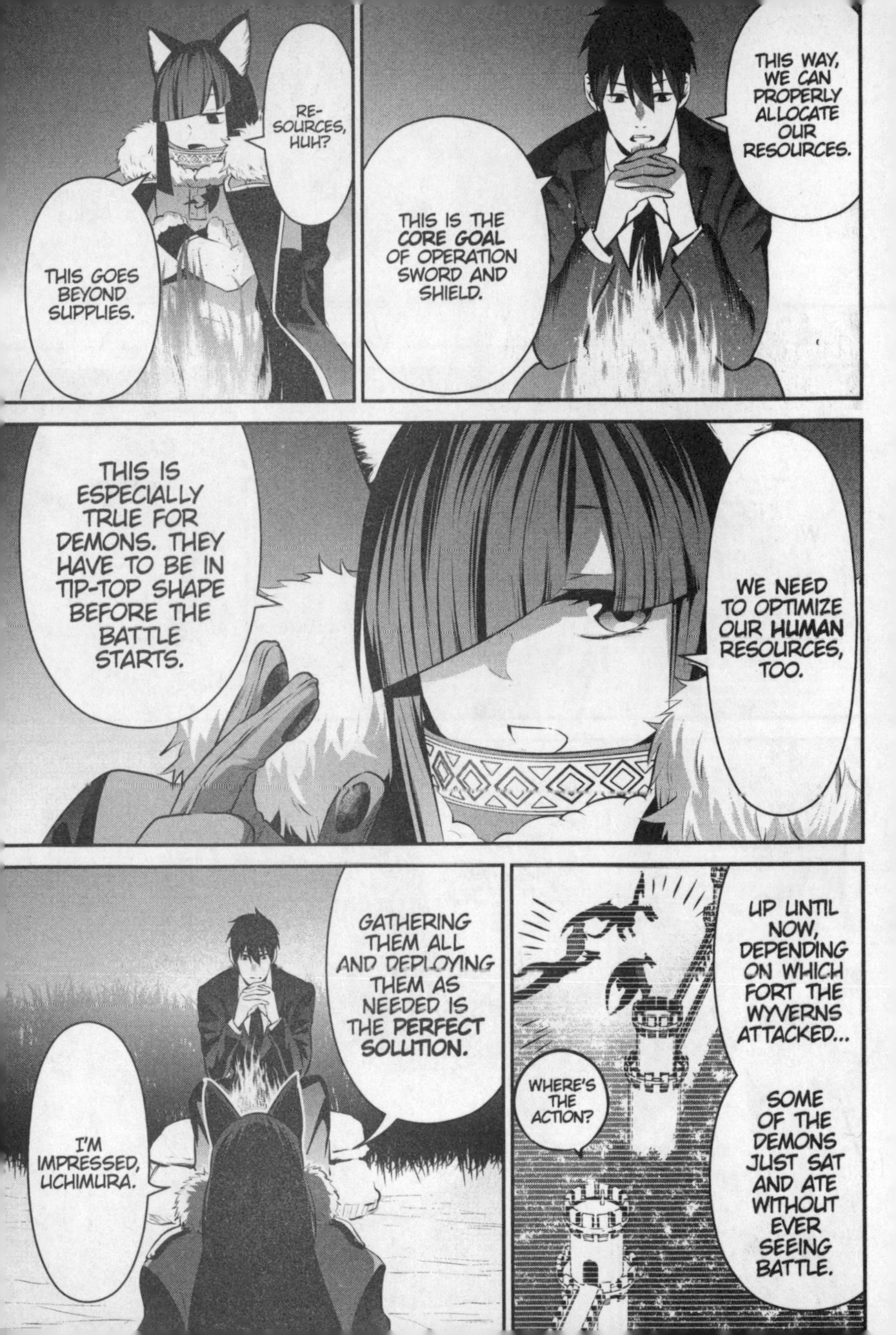
THIS WAY, WE CAN PROPERLY ALLOCATE OUR RESOURCES.
THIS IS THE CORE GOAL OF OPERATION SWORD AND SHIELD.
RE-SOURCES, HUH?
THIS GOES BEYOND SUPPLIES.
WE NEED TO OPTIMIZE OUR HUMAN RESOURCES, TOO.
THIS IS ESPECIALLY TRUE FOR DEMONS. THEY HAVE TO BE IN TIP-TOP SHAPE BEFORE THE BATTLE STARTS.
UP UNTIL NOW, DEPENDING ON WHICH FORT THE WYVERNS ATTACKED...
SOME OF THE DEMONS JUST SAT AND ATE WITHOUT EVER SEEING BATTLE.
WHERE'S THE ACTION?
GATHERING THEM ALL AND DEPLOYING THEM AS NEEDED IS THE PERFECT SOLUTION.
I'M IMPRESSED, UCHIMURA.

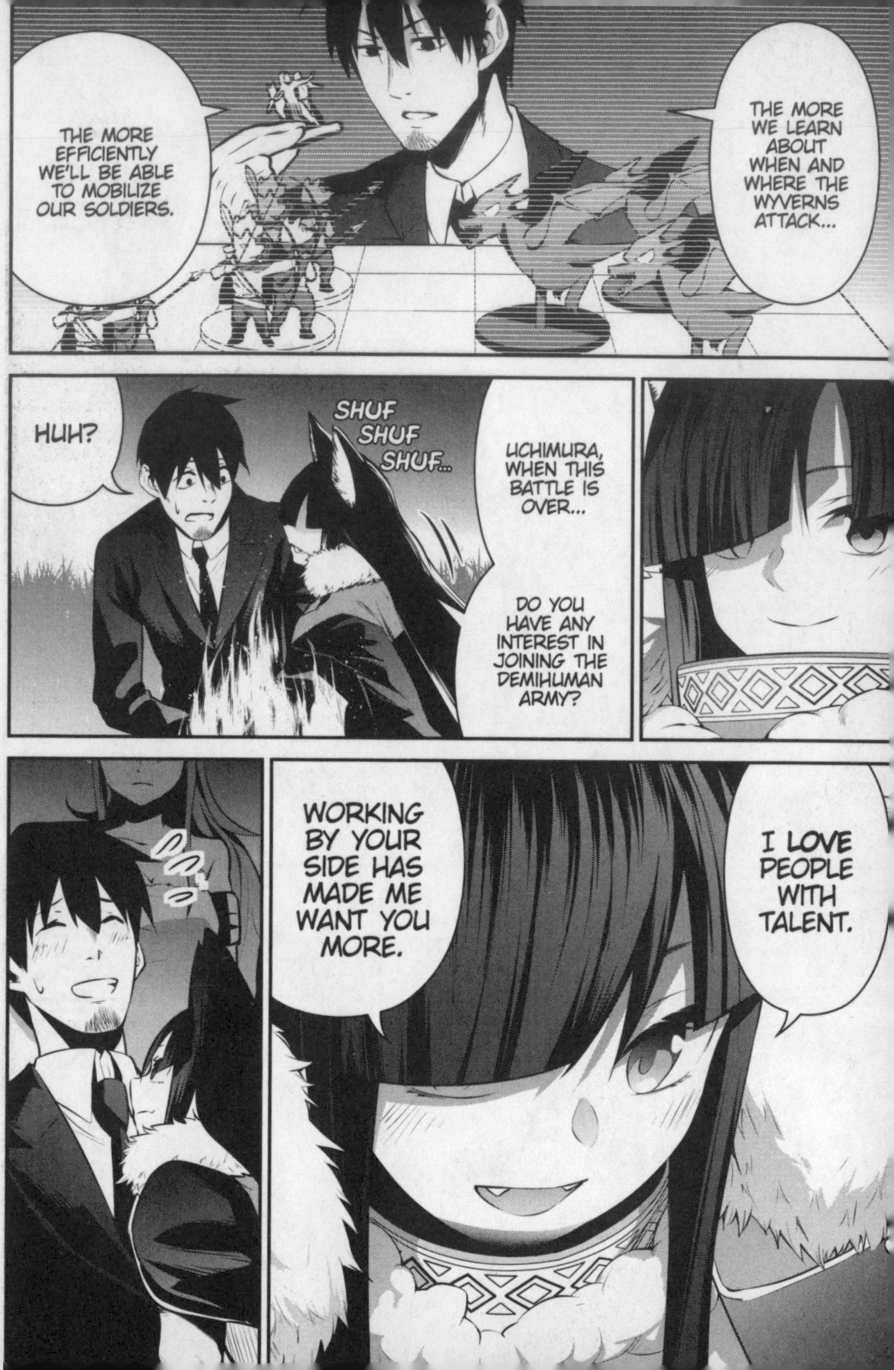
THE MORE WE LEARN ABOUT WHEN AND WHERE THE WYVERNS ATTACK...
THE MORE EFFICIENTLY WE'LL BE ABLE TO MOBILIZE OUR SOLDIERS.
UCHIMURA, WHEN THIS BATTLE IS OVER...
DO YOU HAVE ANY INTEREST IN JOINING THE DEMIHUMAN ARMY?
SHUF SHUF SHUF...
HUH?
I LOVE PEOPLE WITH TALENT.
WORKING BY YOUR SIDE HAS MADE ME WANT YOU MORE.

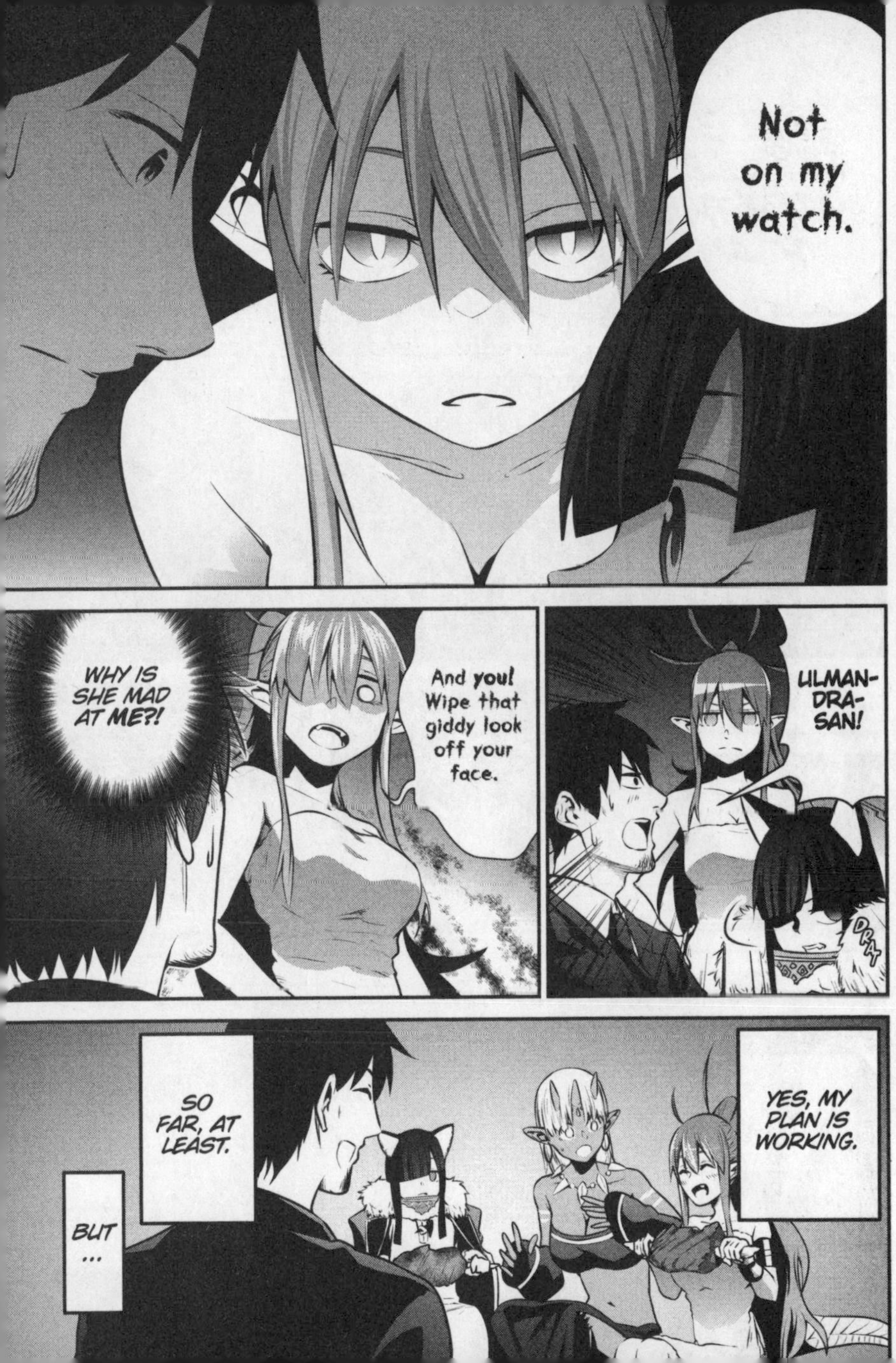
Not on my watch.
ULMAN-DRA-SAN!
DRAT
And you! Wipe that giddy look off your face.
WHY IS SHE MAD AT ME?!
YES, MY PLAN IS WORKING.
SO FAR, AT LEAST.
BUT ...

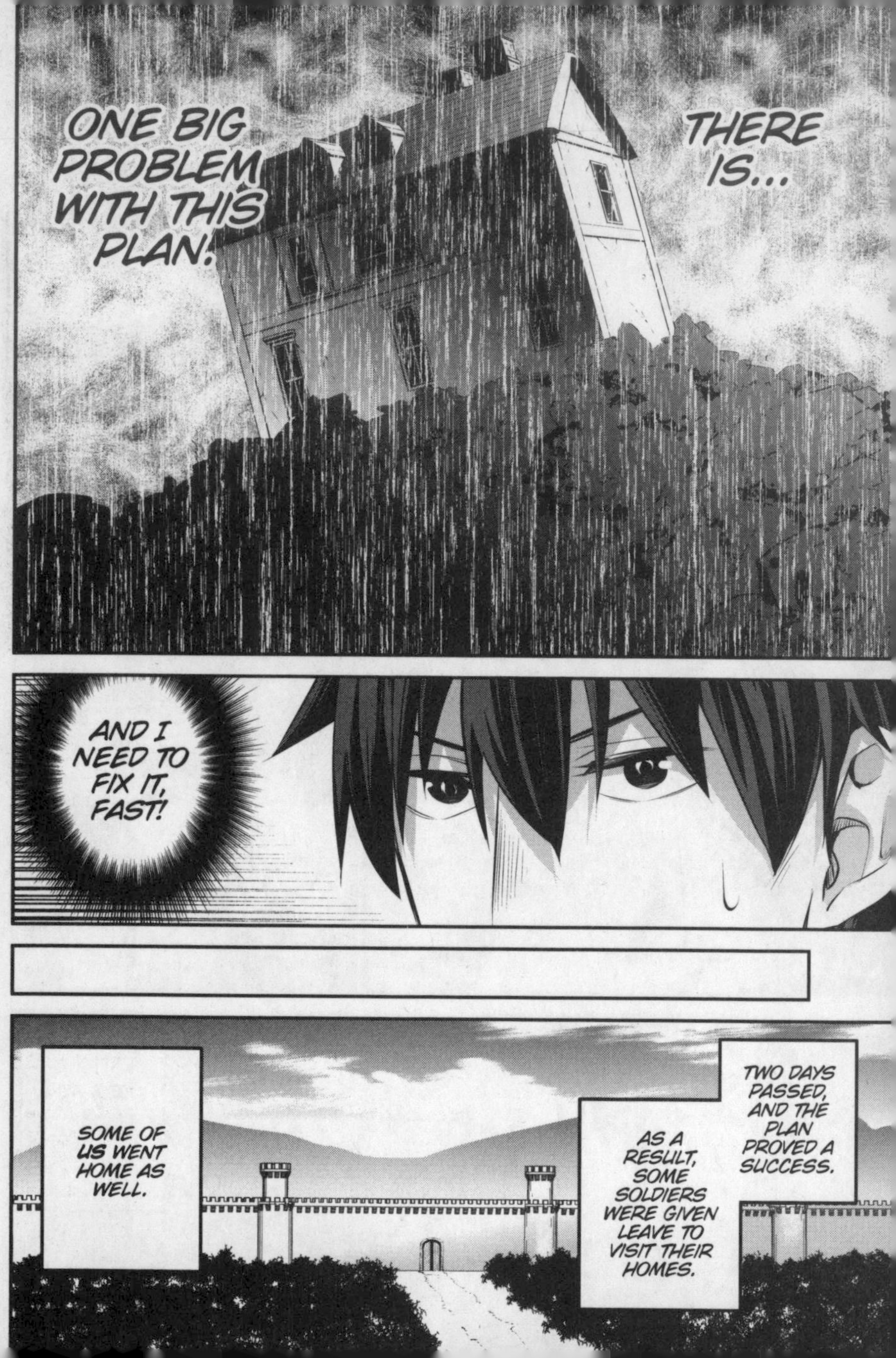
THERE IS...
ONE BIG PROBLEM WITH THIS PLAN!
AND I NEED TO FIX IT, FAST!
TWO DAYS PASSED, AND THE PLAN PROVED A SUCCESS.
AS A RESULT, SOME SOLDIERS WERE GIVEN LEAVE TO VISIT THEIR HOMES.
SOME OF US WENT HOME AS WELL.

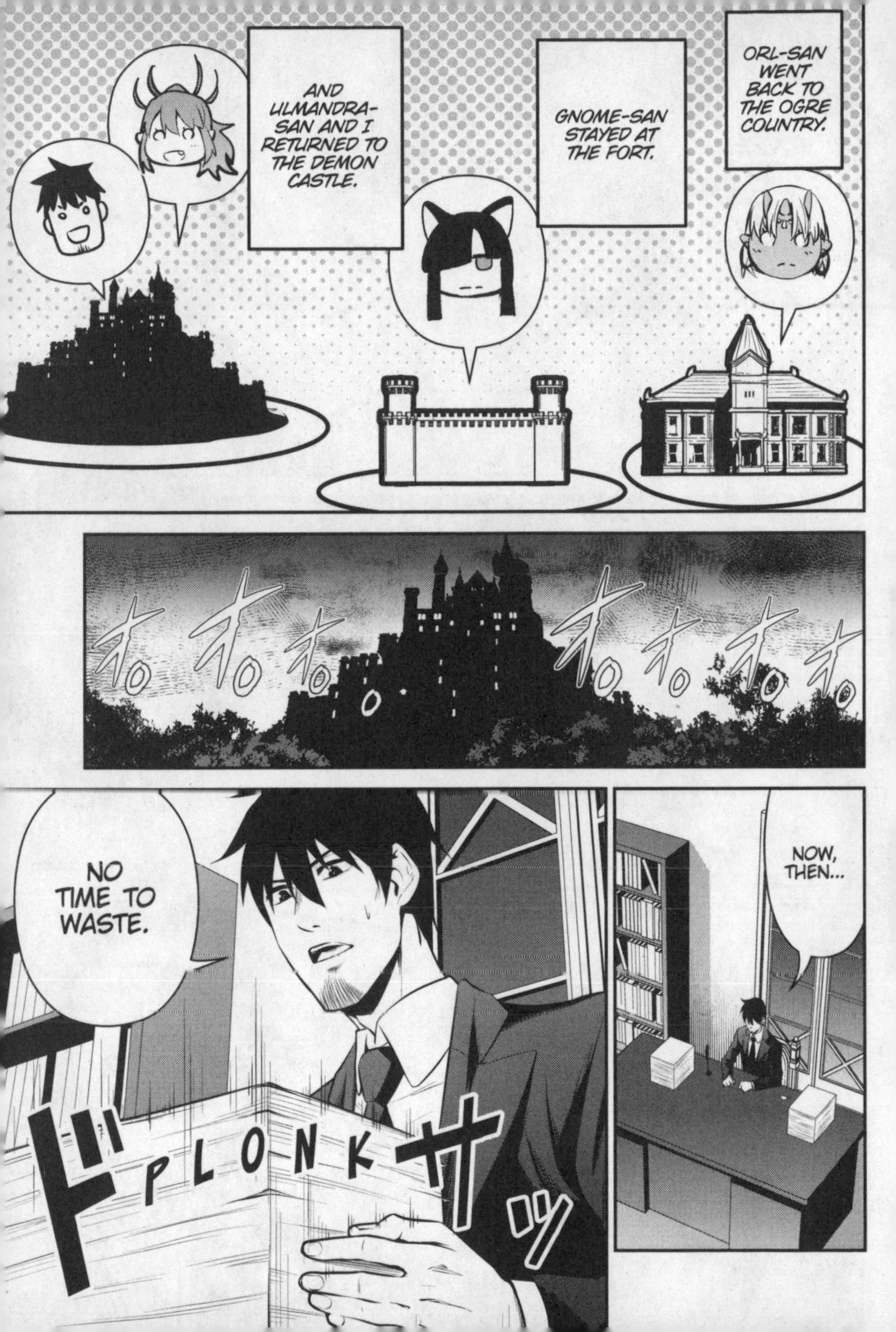
ORL-SAN WENT BACK TO THE OGRE COUNTRY.
GNOME-SAN STAYED AT THE FORT.
AND ULMANDRA-SAN AND I RETURNED TO THE DEMON CASTLE.
NOW, THEN...
NO TIME TO WASTE.
PLONK

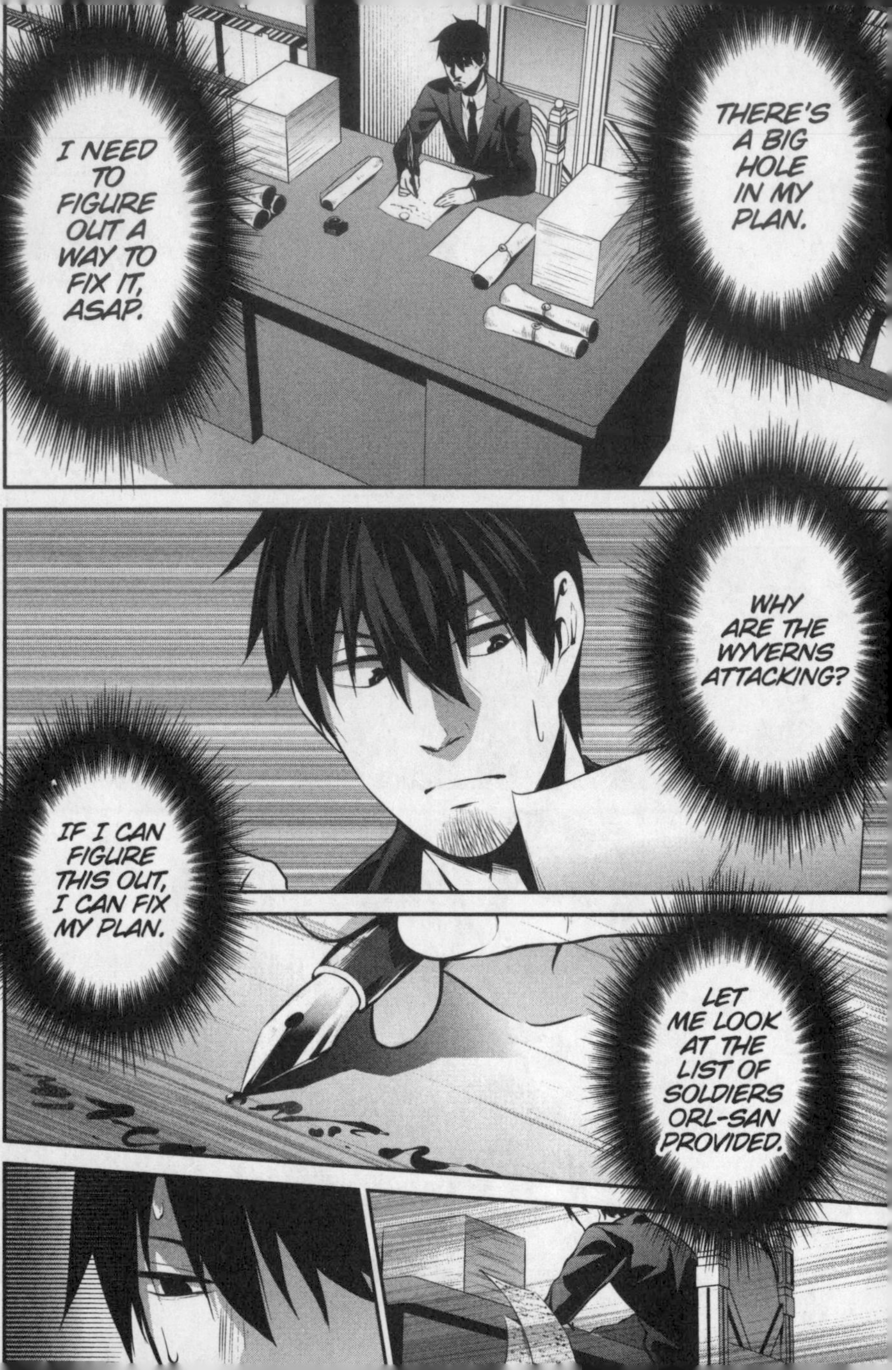
THERE'S A BIG HOLE IN MY PLAN.
I NEED TO FIGURE OUT A WAY TO FIX IT, ASAP.
WHY ARE THE WYVERNS ATTACKING?
IF I CAN FIGURE THIS OUT, I CAN FIX MY PLAN.
LET ME LOOK AT THE LIST OF SOLDIERS ORL-SAN PROVIDED.

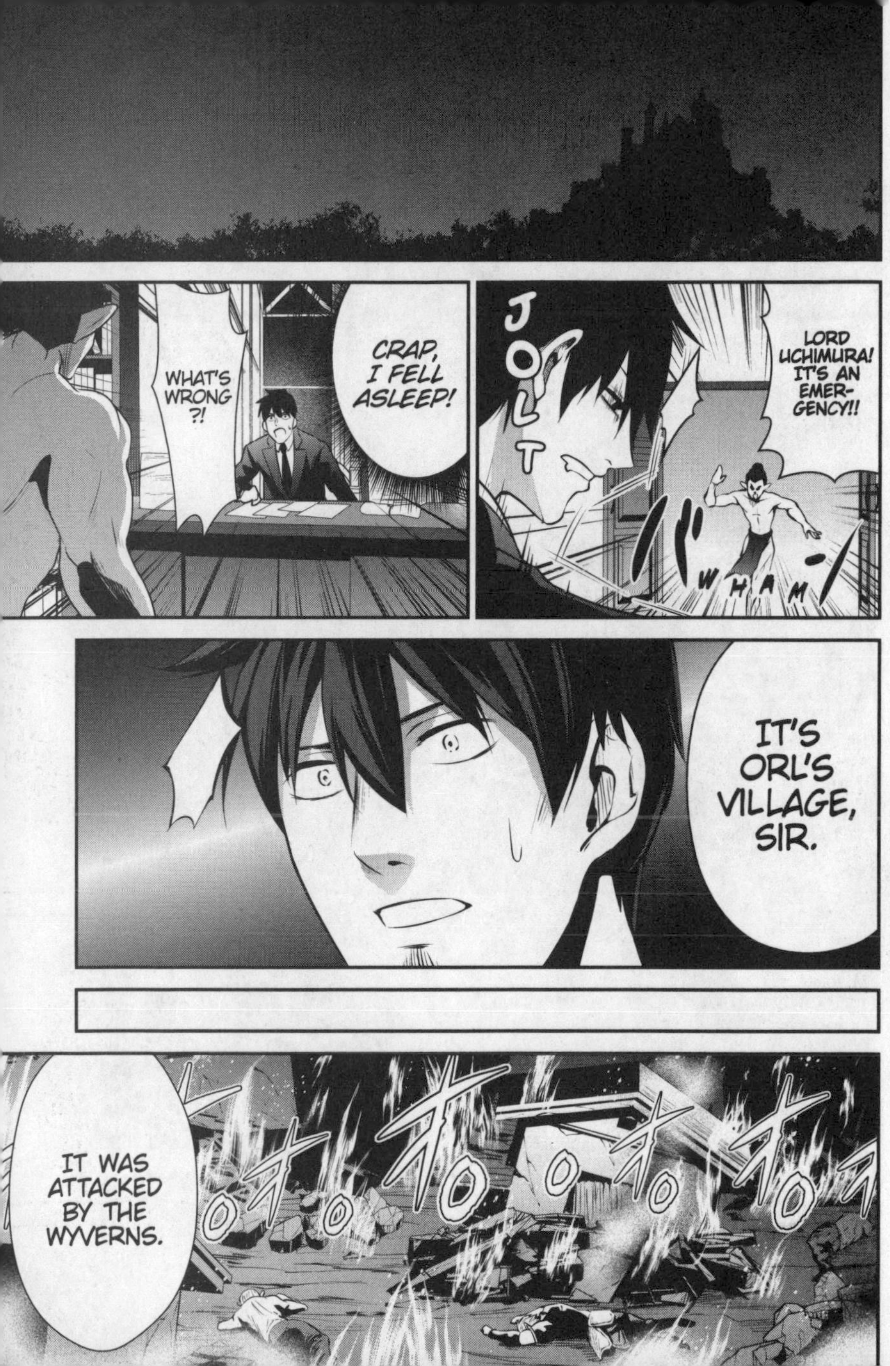
LORD UCHIMURA! IT'S AN EMERGENCY!!
JOLT
WHAM
CRAP, I FELL ASLEEP!
WHAT'S WRONG?!
IT'S ORL'S VILLAGE, SIR.
IT WAS ATTACKED BY THE WYVERNS.

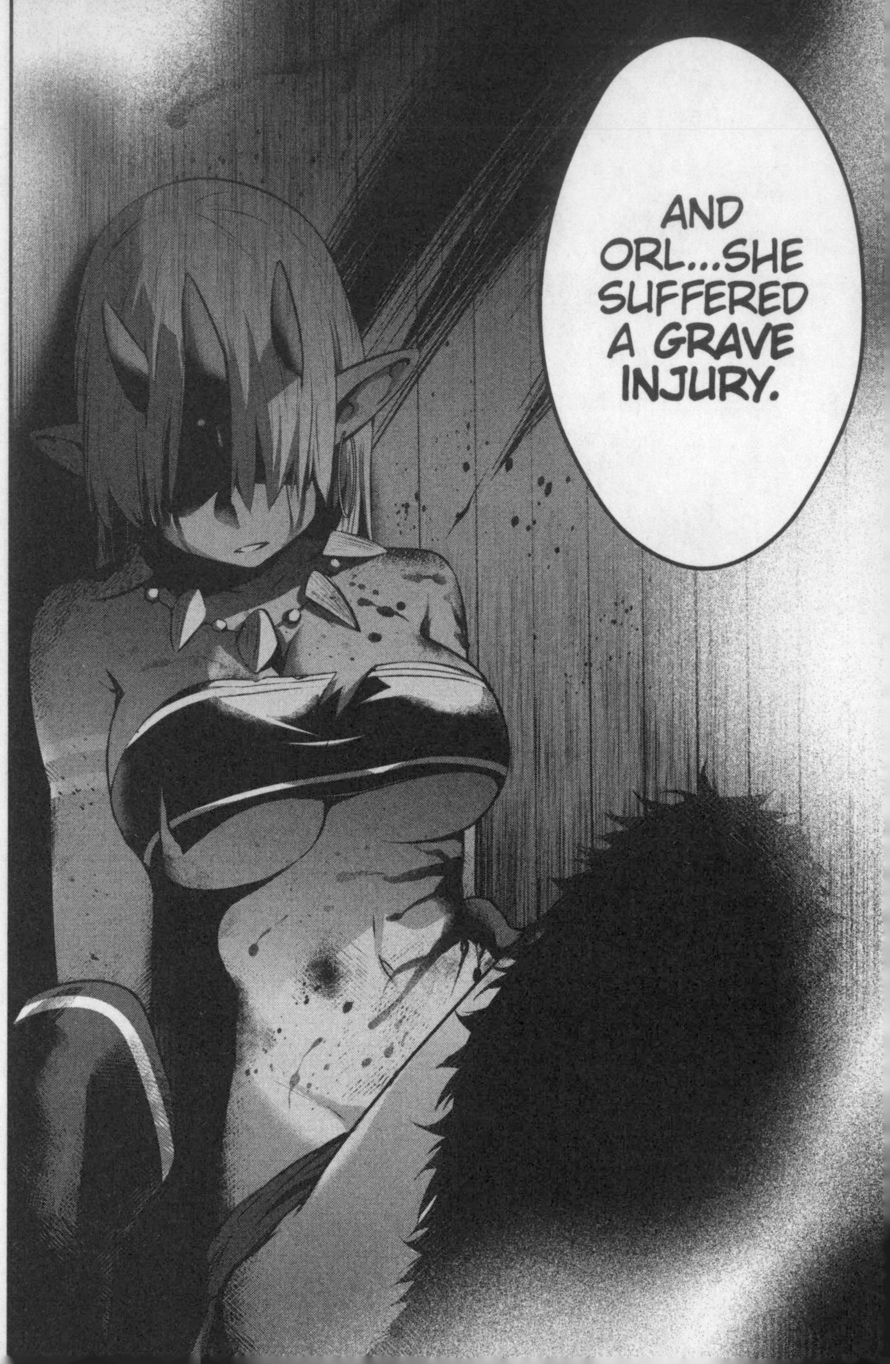
AND ORL...SHE SUFFERED A GRAVE INJURY.

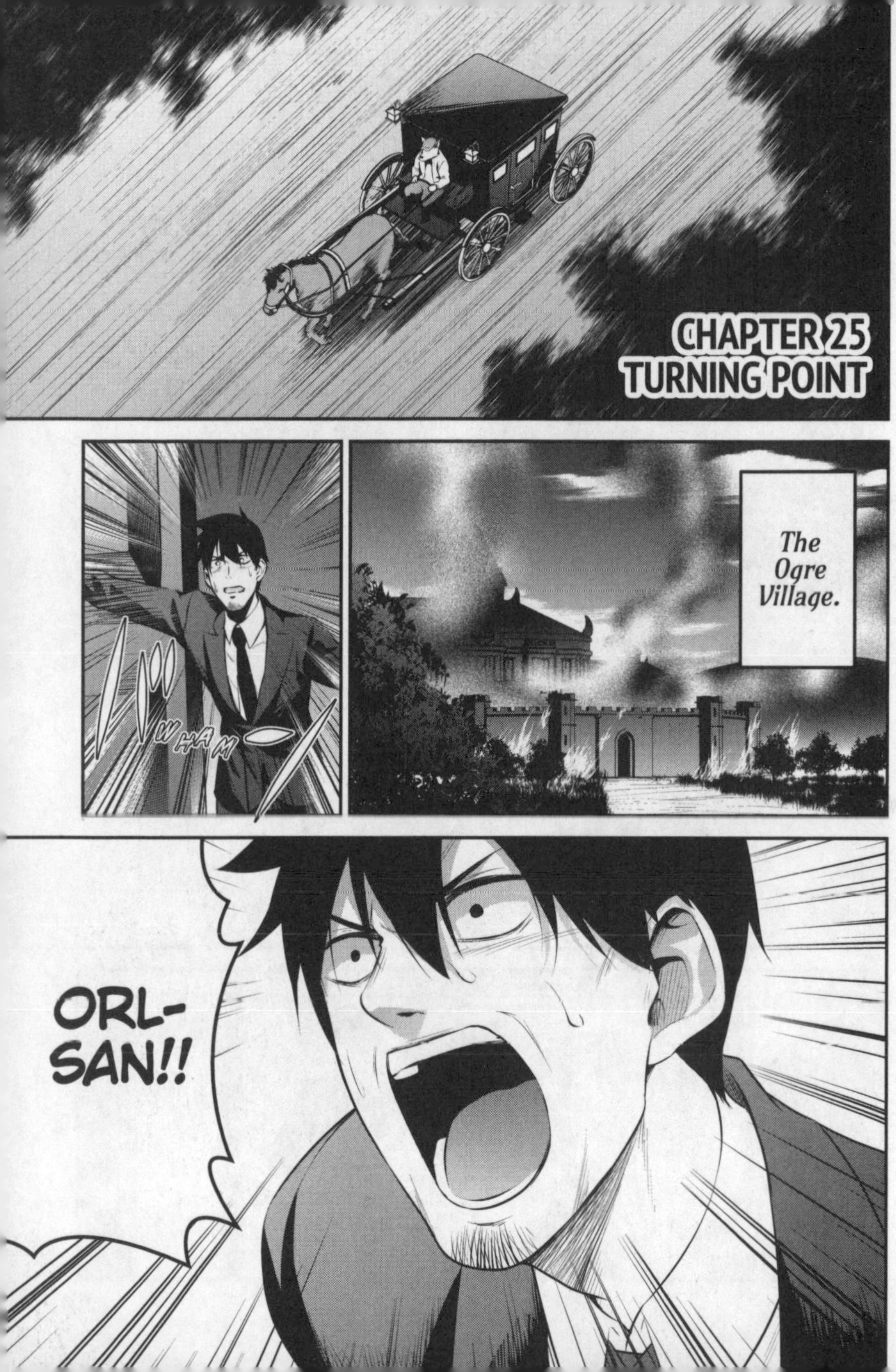
CHAPTER 25
TURNING POINT
The Ogre Village.
WHAM
ORL-SAN!!

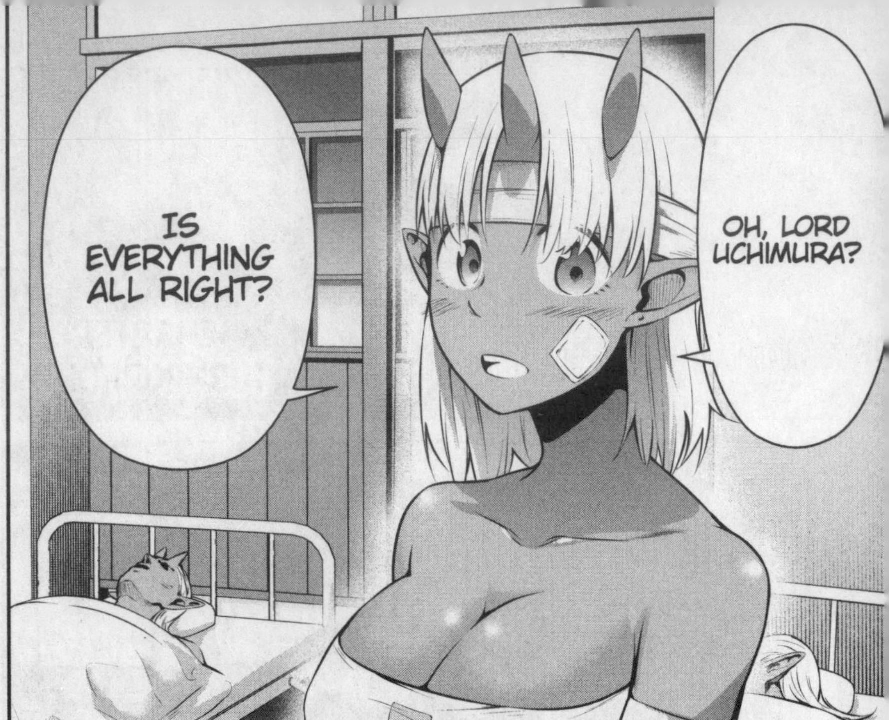
OH, LORD UCHIMURA?
IS EVERYTHING ALL RIGHT?

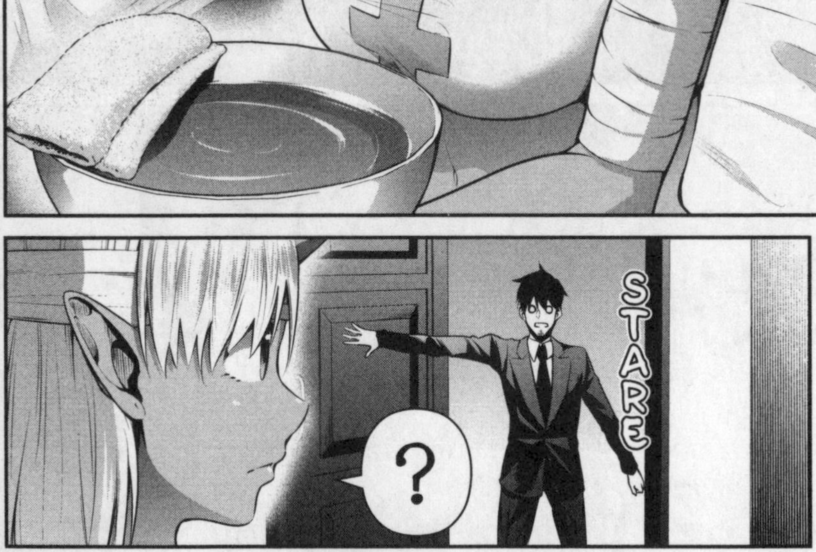
STARE
?

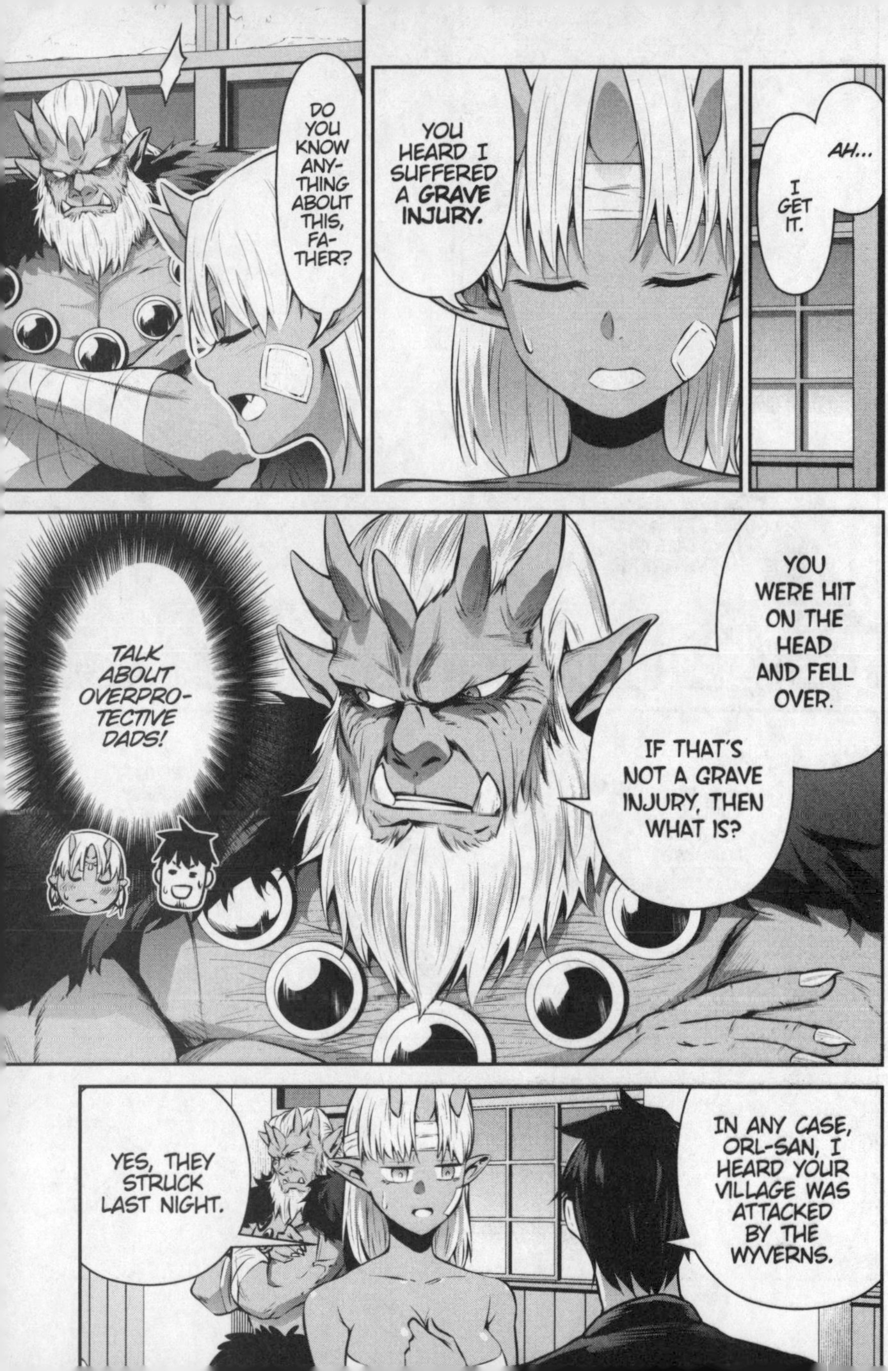
AH... I GET IT.
YOU HEARD I SUFFERED A GRAVE INJURY.
DO YOU KNOW ANYTHING ABOUT THIS, FATHER?
YOU WERE HIT ON THE HEAD AND FELL OVER.
IF THAT'S NOT A GRAVE INJURY, THEN WHAT IS?
TALK ABOUT OVERPROTECTIVE DADS!
IN ANY CASE, ORL-SAN, I HEARD YOUR VILLAGE WAS ATTACKED BY THE WYVERNS.
YES, THEY STRUCK LAST NIGHT.

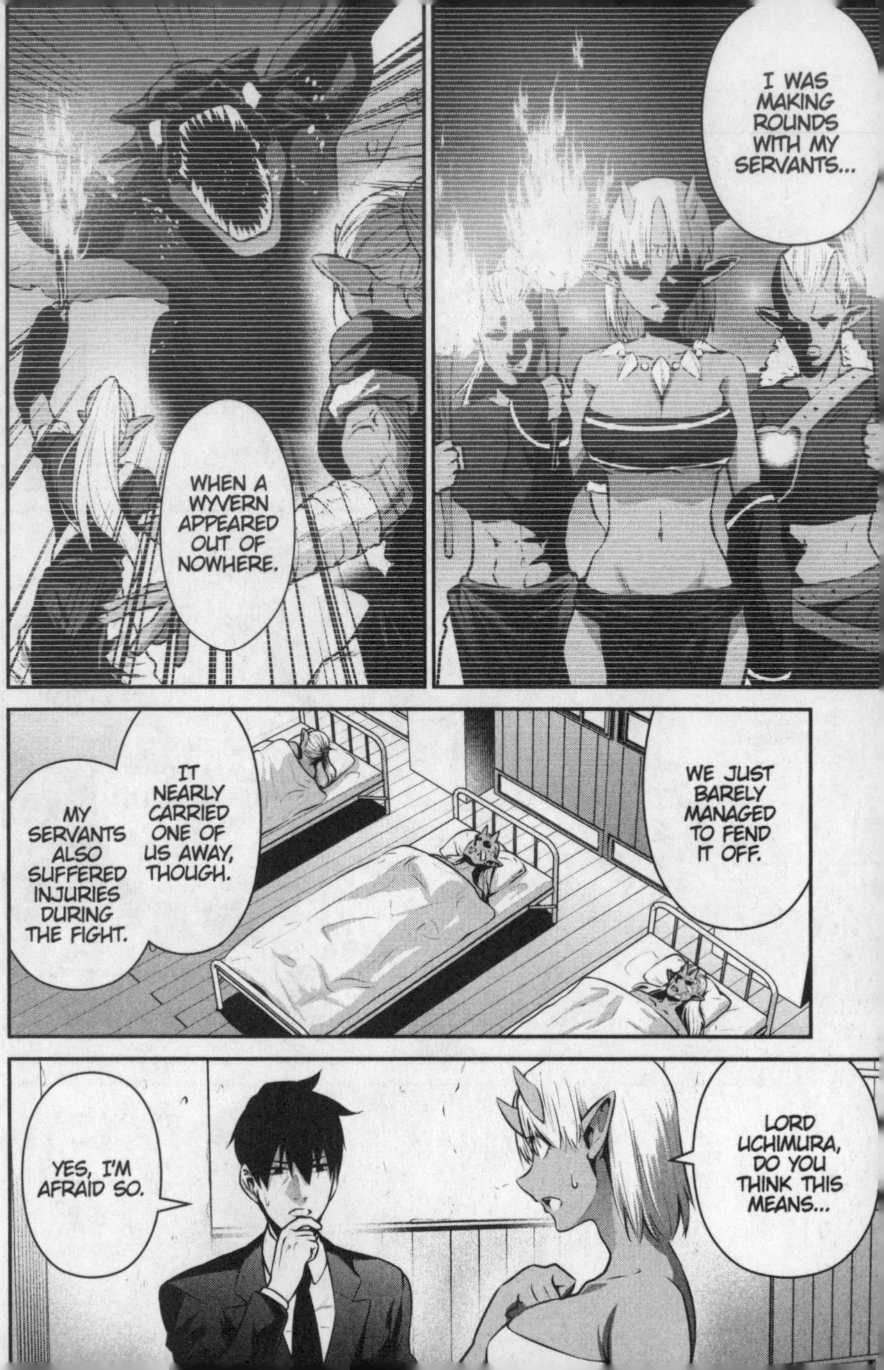
I WAS MAKING ROUNDS WITH MY SERVANTS...
WHEN A WYVERN APPEARED OUT OF NOWHERE.
WE JUST BARELY MANAGED TO FEND IT OFF.
IT NEARLY CARRIED ONE OF US AWAY, THOUGH.
MY SERVANTS ALSO SUFFERED INJURIES DURING THE FIGHT.
LORD UCHIMURA, DO YOU THINK THIS MEANS...
YES, I'M AFRAID SO.

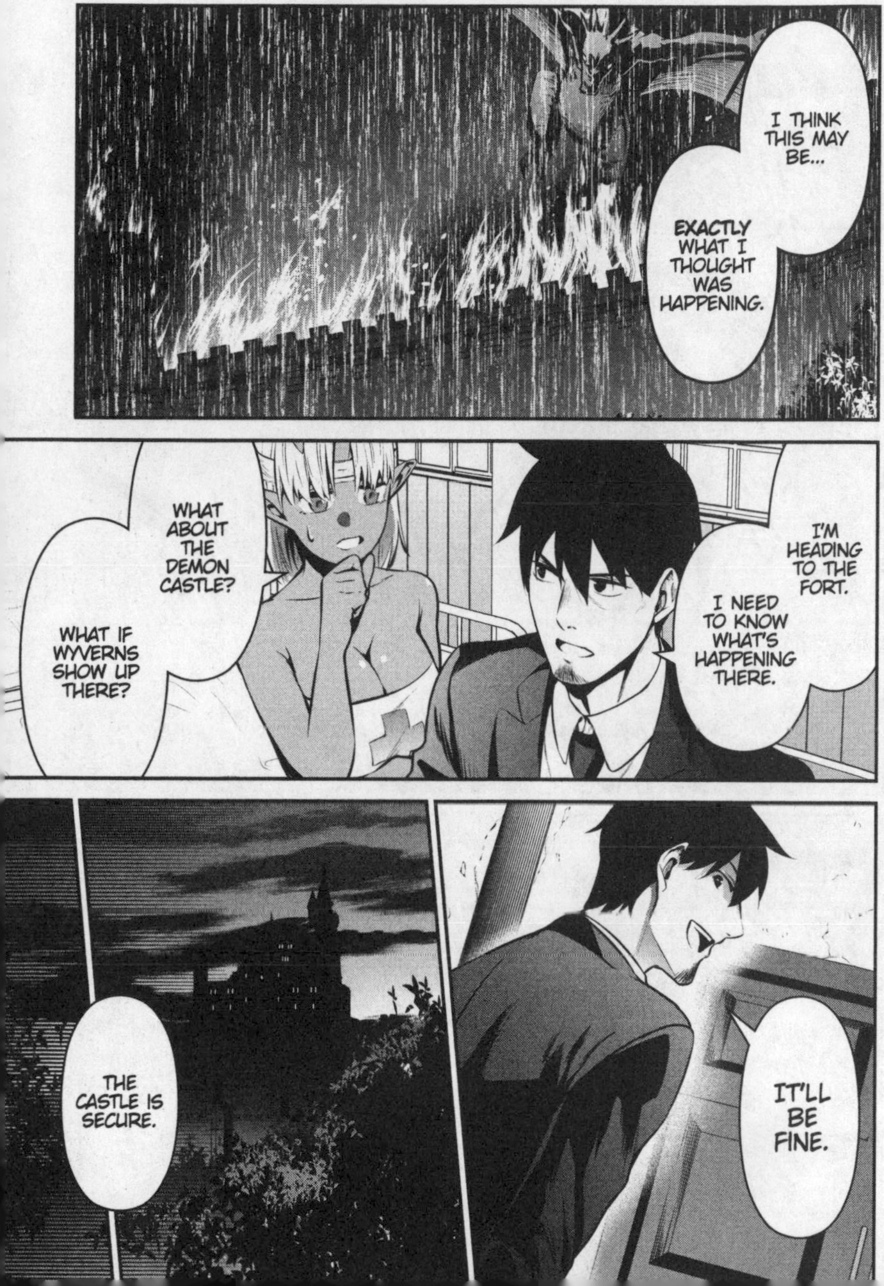

I THINK THIS MAY BE...
EXACTLY WHAT I THOUGHT WAS HAPPENING.
I'M HEADING TO THE FORT.
I NEED TO KNOW WHAT'S HAPPENING THERE.
WHAT ABOUT THE DEMON CASTLE?
WHAT IF WYVERNS SHOW UP THERE?
IT'LL BE FINE.
THE CASTLE IS SECURE.

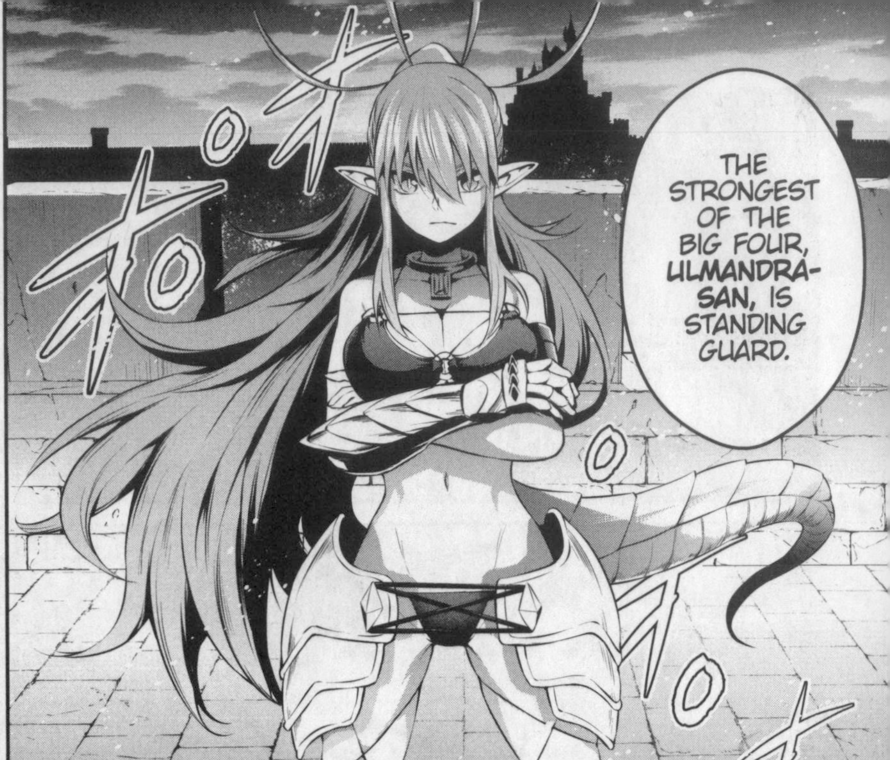
THE STRONGEST OF THE BIG FOUR, ULMANDRA-SAN, IS STANDING GUARD.
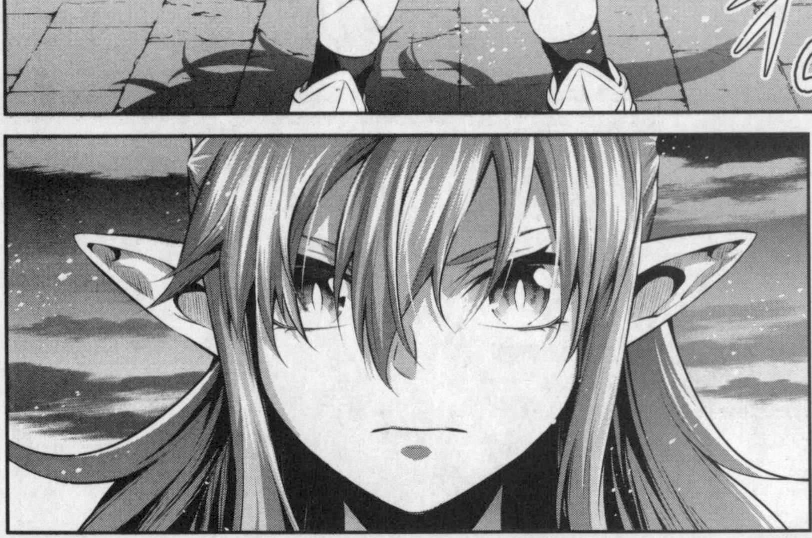

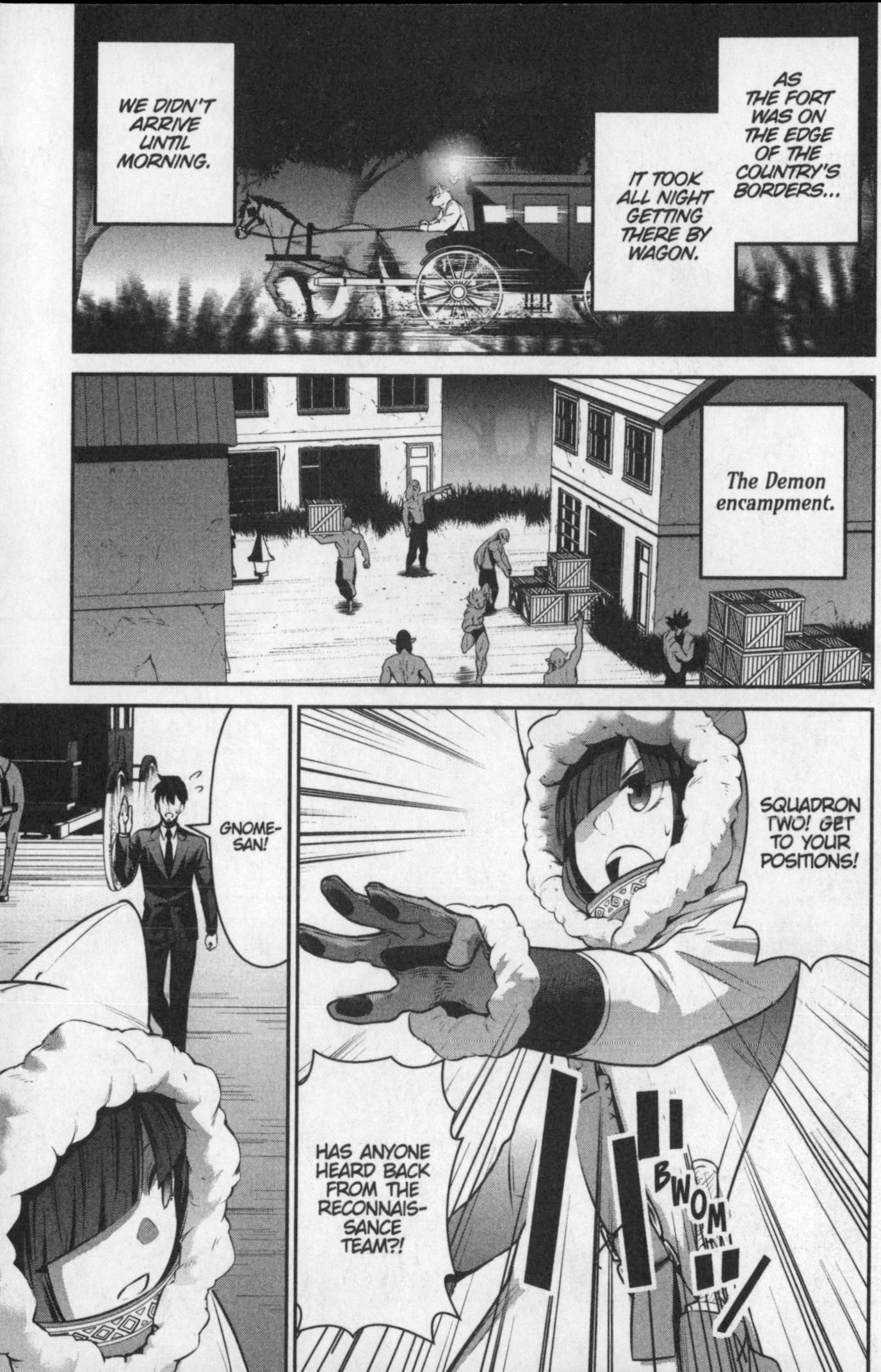
AS THE FORT WAS ON THE EDGE OF THE COUNTRY'S BORDERS...
IT TOOK ALL NIGHT GETTING THERE BY WAGON.
WE DIDN'T ARRIVE UNTIL MORNING.
The Demon encampment.
SQUADRON TWO! GET TO YOUR POSITIONS!
BWOM!!
HAS ANYONE HEARD BACK FROM THE RECONNAIS-SANCE TEAM?!
GNOME-SAN!

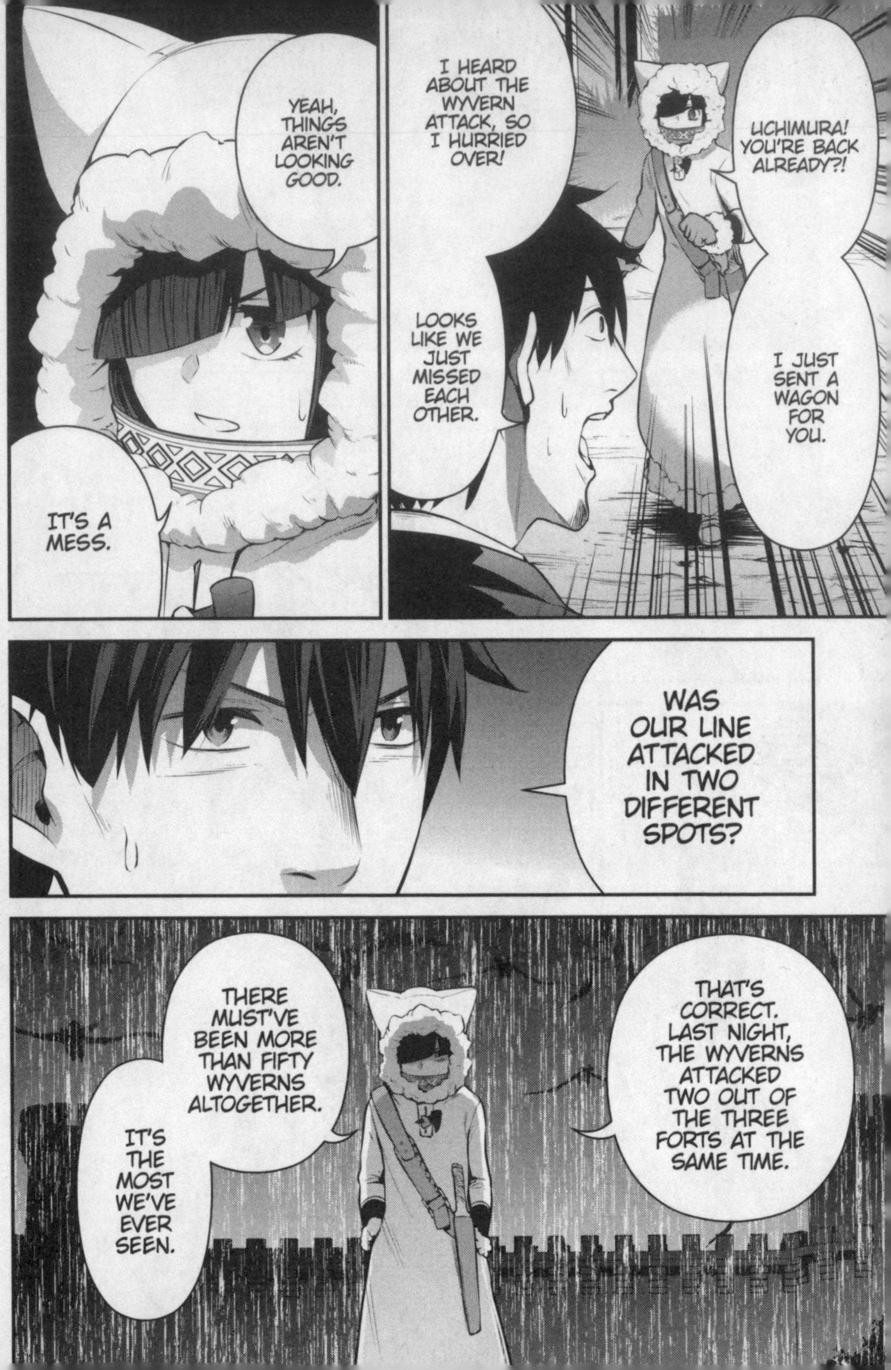
UCHIMURA! YOU'RE BACK ALREADY?!
I JUST SENT A WAGON FOR YOU.
I HEARD ABOUT THE WYVERN ATTACK, SO I HURRIED OVER!
LOOKS LIKE WE JUST MISSED EACH OTHER.
YEAH, THINGS AREN'T LOOKING GOOD.
IT'S A MESS.
WAS OUR LINE ATTACKED IN TWO DIFFERENT SPOTS?
THAT'S CORRECT. LAST NIGHT, THE WYVERNS ATTACKED TWO OUT OF THE THREE FORTS AT THE SAME TIME.
THERE MUST'VE BEEN MORE THAN FIFTY WYVERNS ALTOGETHER.
IT'S THE MOST WE'VE EVER SEEN.

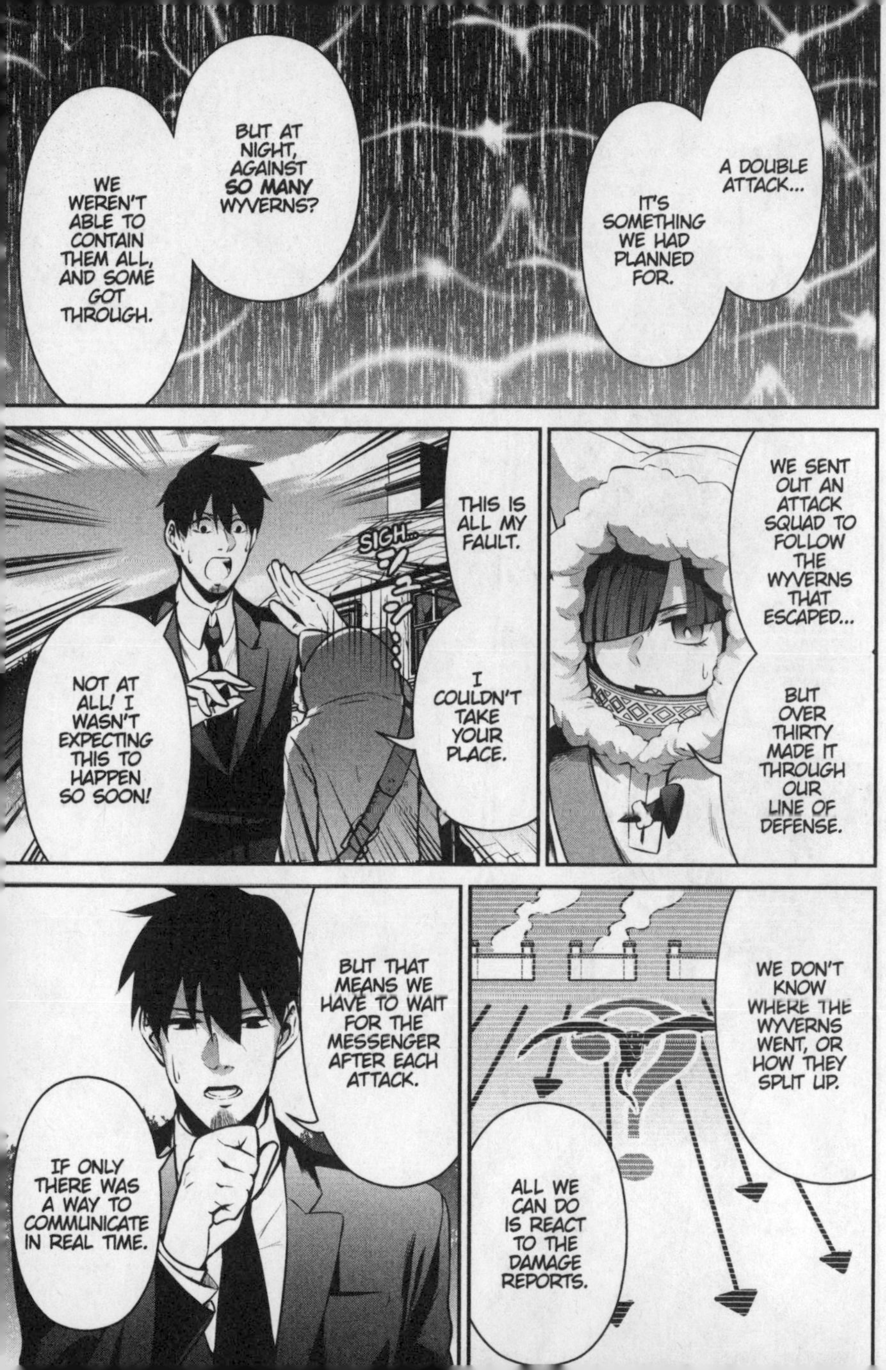
A DOUBLE ATTACK...
IT'S SOMETHING WE HAD PLANNED FOR.
BUT AT NIGHT, AGAINST SO MANY WYVERNS?
WE WEREN'T ABLE TO CONTAIN THEM ALL, AND SOME GOT THROUGH.
WE SENT OUT AN ATTACK SQUAD TO FOLLOW THE WYVERNS THAT ESCAPED...
BUT OVER THIRTY MADE IT THROUGH OUR LINE OF DEFENSE.
THIS IS ALL MY FAULT.
SIGH...
I COULDN'T TAKE YOUR PLACE.
NOT AT ALL! I WASN'T EXPECTING THIS TO HAPPEN SO SOON!
WE DON'T KNOW WHERE THE WYVERNS WENT, OR HOW THEY SPLIT UP.
ALL WE CAN DO IS REACT TO THE DAMAGE REPORTS.
BUT THAT MEANS WE HAVE TO WAIT FOR THE MESSENGER AFTER EACH ATTACK.
IF ONLY THERE WAS A WAY TO COMMUNICATE IN REAL TIME.

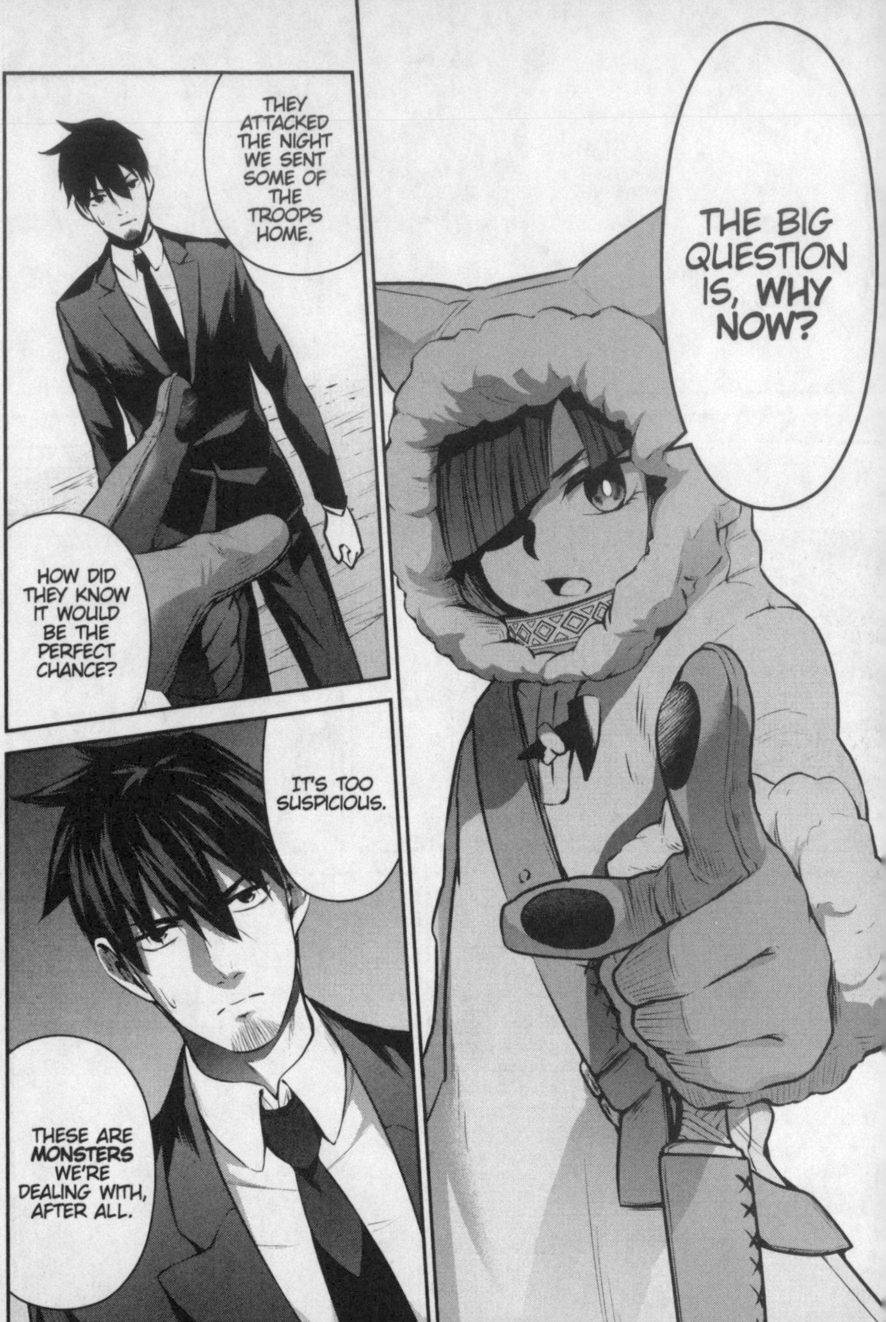
THE BIG QUESTION IS, WHY NOW?
THEY ATTACKED THE NIGHT WE SENT SOME OF THE TROOPS HOME.
HOW DID THEY KNOW IT WOULD BE THE PERFECT CHANCE?
IT'S TOO SUSPICIOUS.
THESE ARE **MONSTERS** WE'RE DEALING WITH, AFTER ALL.

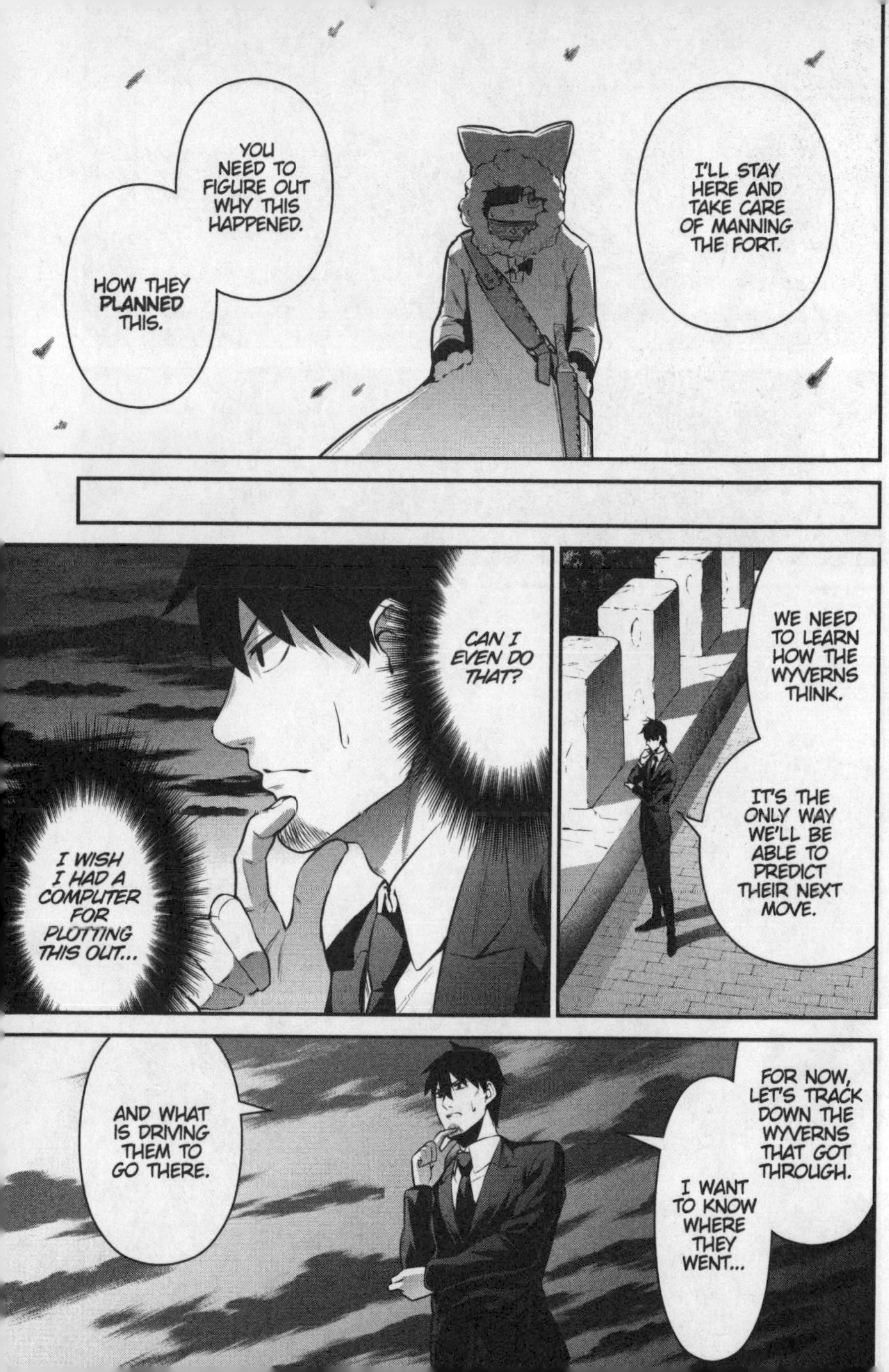
I'LL STAY HERE AND TAKE CARE OF MANNING THE FORT.
YOU NEED TO FIGURE OUT WHY THIS HAPPENED.
HOW THEY PLANNED THIS.
WE NEED TO LEARN HOW THE WYVERNS THINK.
IT'S THE ONLY WAY WE'LL BE ABLE TO PREDICT THEIR NEXT MOVE.
CAN I EVEN DO THAT?
I WISH I HAD A COMPUTER FOR PLOTTING THIS OUT...
FOR NOW, LET'S TRACK DOWN THE WYVERNS THAT GOT THROUGH.
I WANT TO KNOW WHERE THEY WENT...
AND WHAT IS DRIVING THEM TO GO THERE.

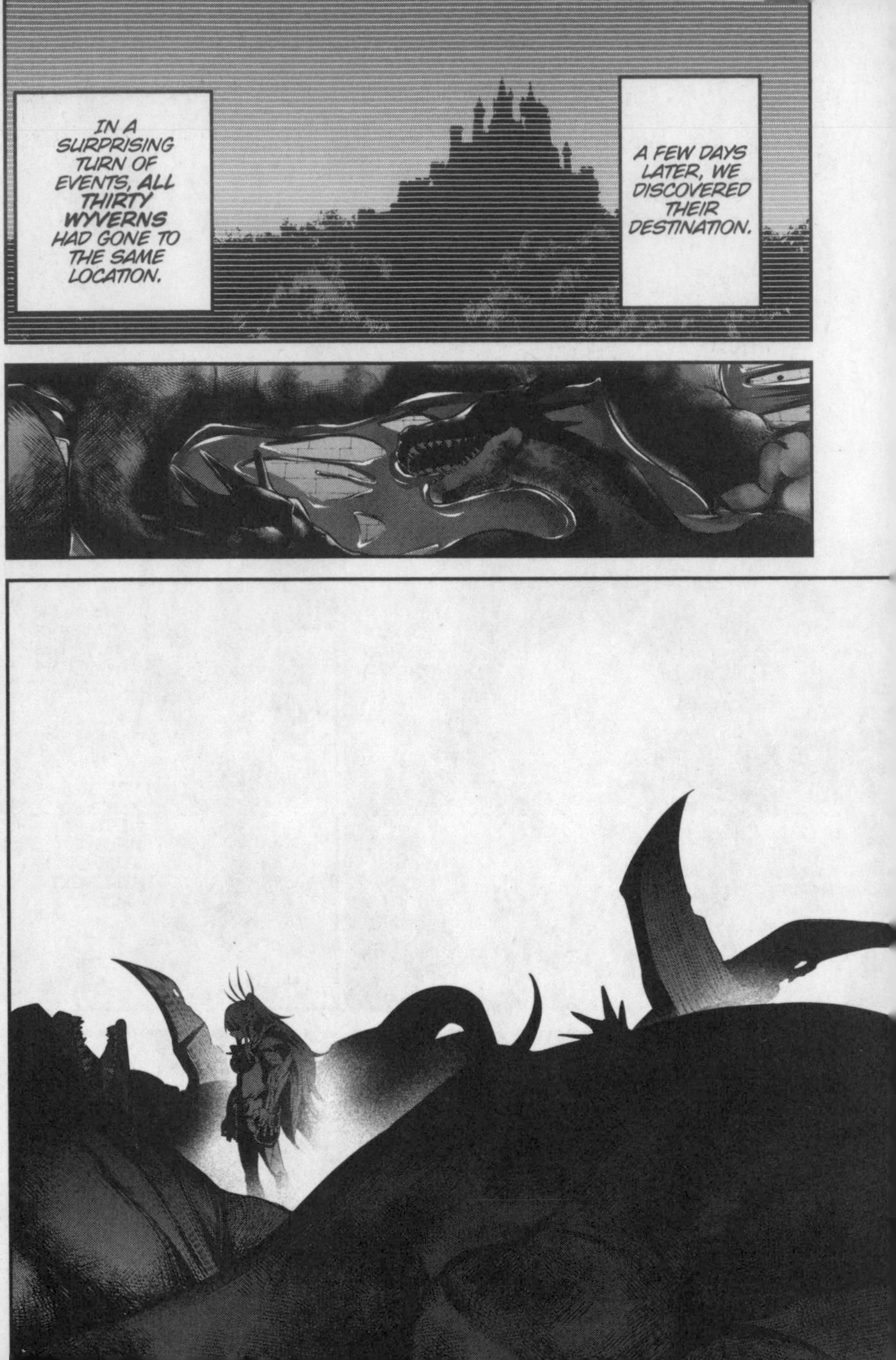
A FEW DAYS LATER, WE DISCOVERED THEIR DESTINATION.
IN A SURPRISING TURN OF EVENTS, ALL THIRTY WYVERNS HAD GONE TO THE SAME LOCATION.

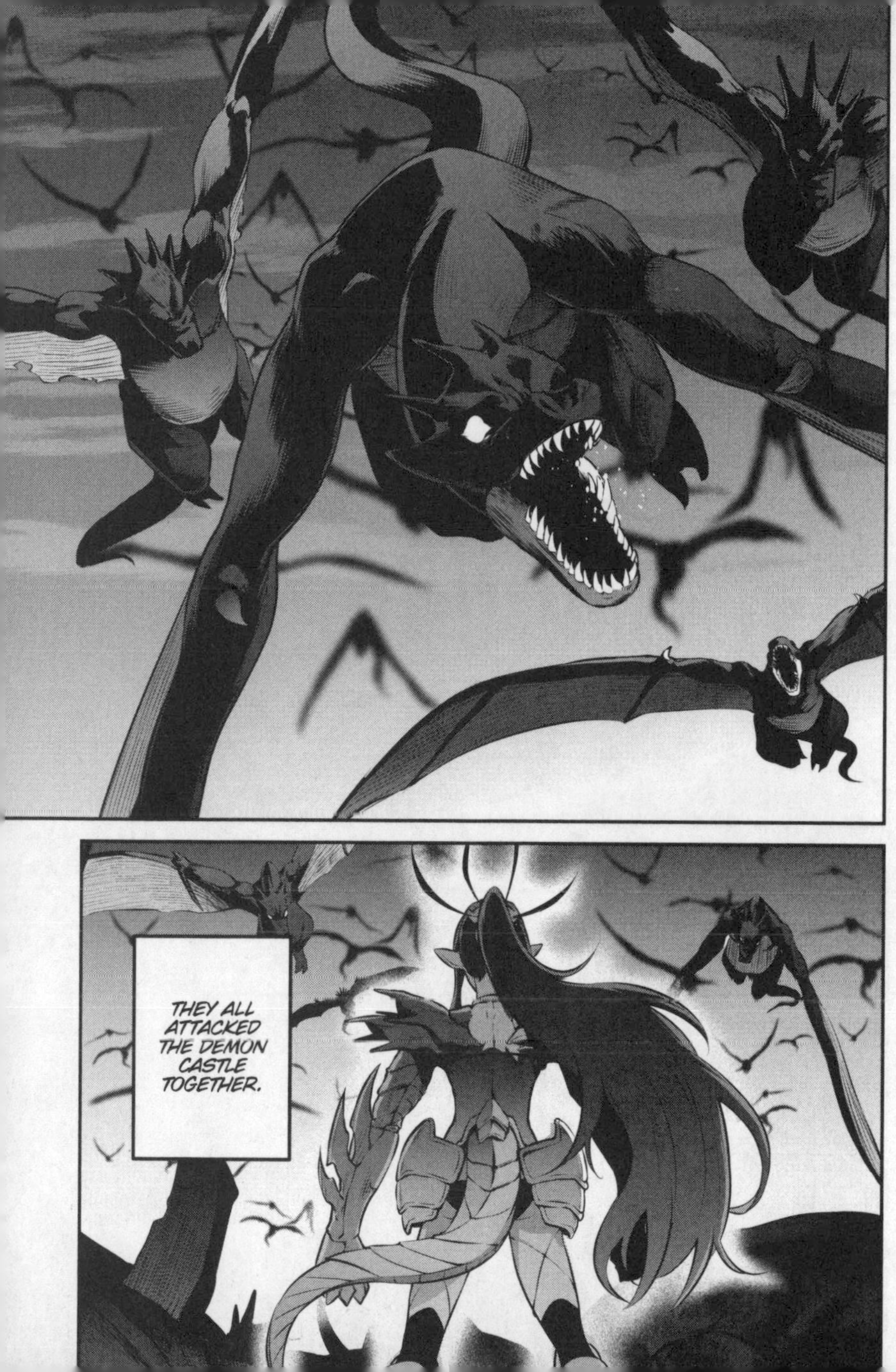
THEY ALL ATTACKED THE DEMON CASTLE TOGETHER.

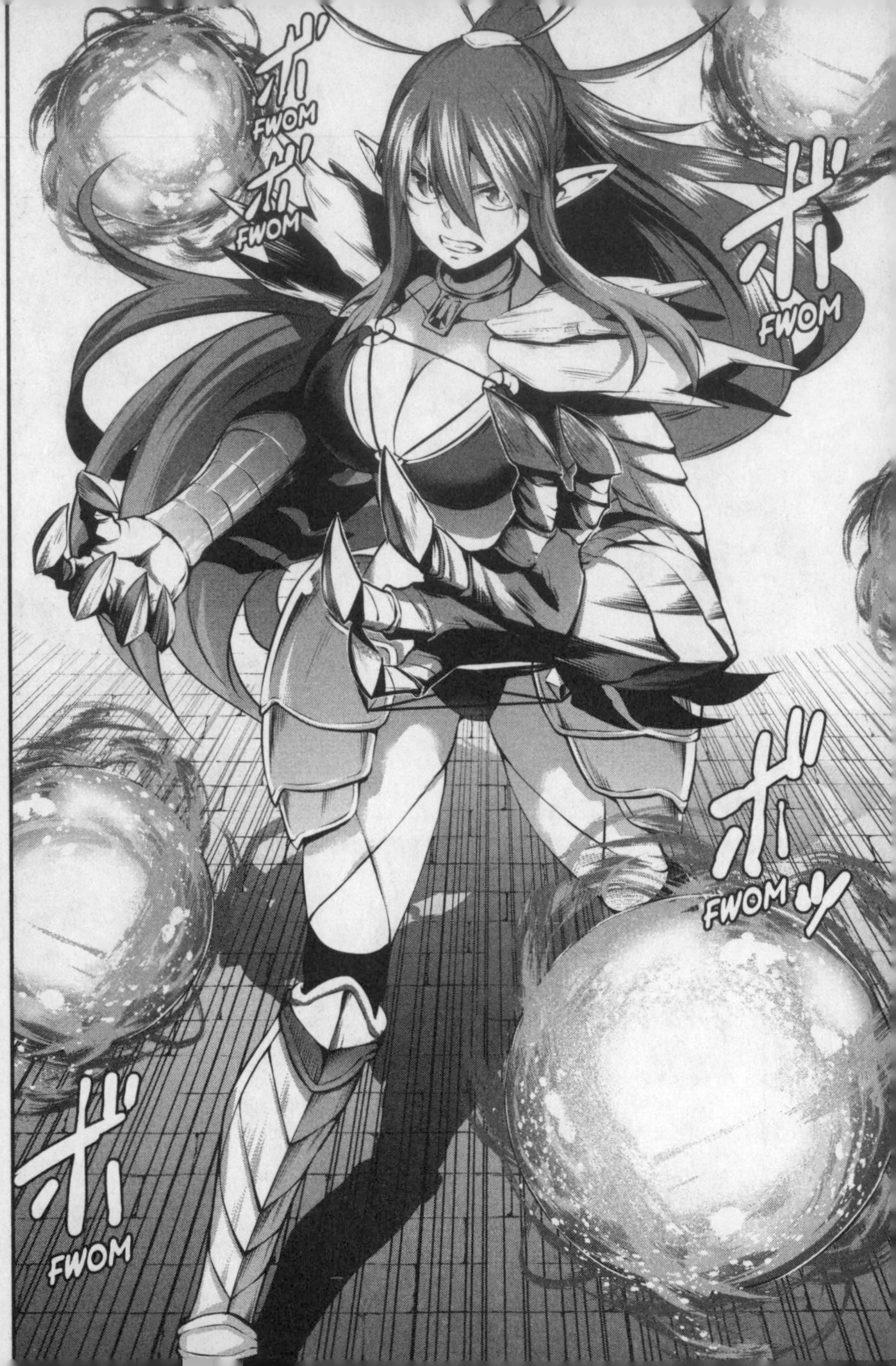
ザ
FWOM
ザ
FWOM
ザ
FWOM
ザ
FWOM
ザ
FWOM

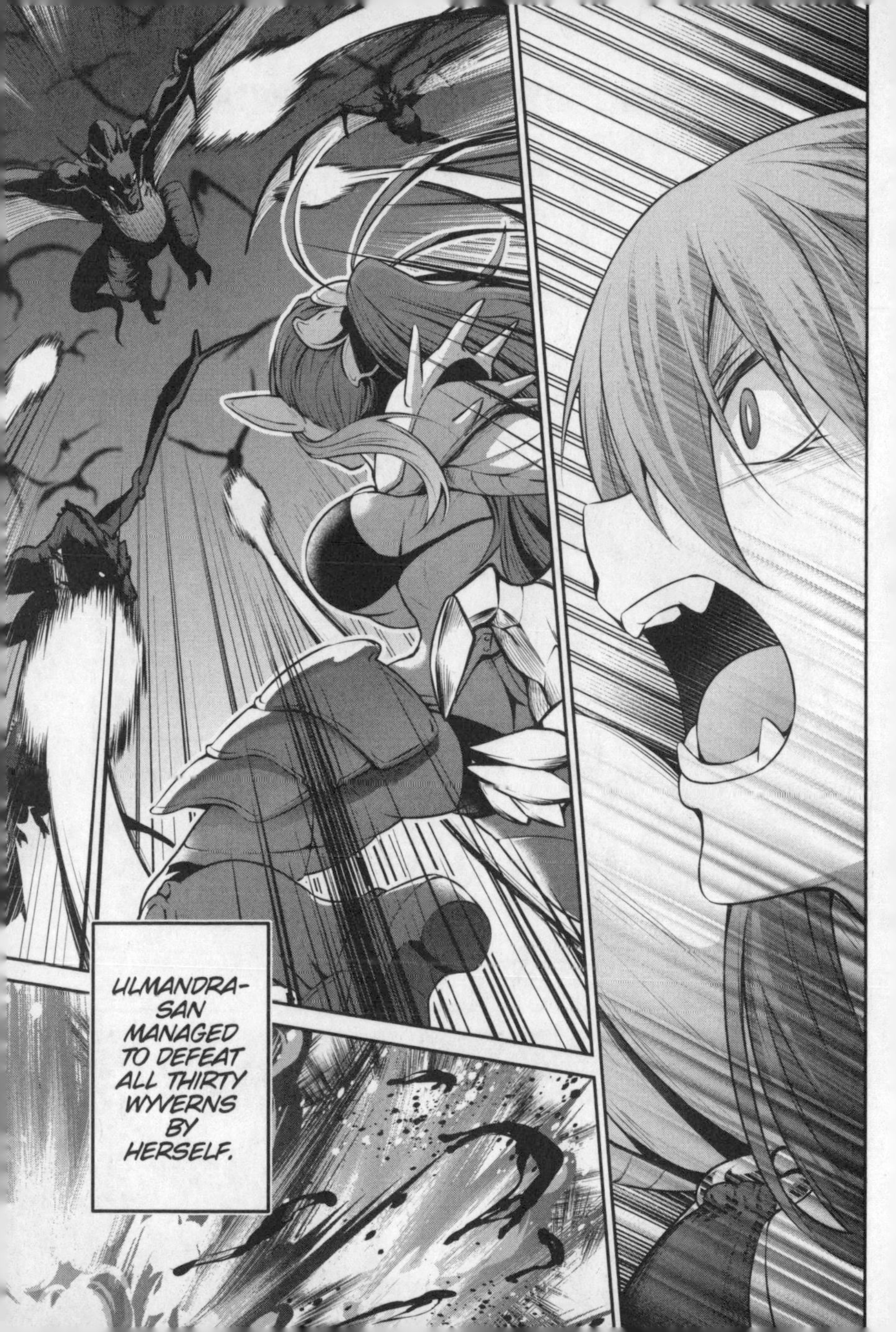
ULMANDRA-SAN MANAGED TO DEFEAT ALL THIRTY WYVERNS BY HERSELF.

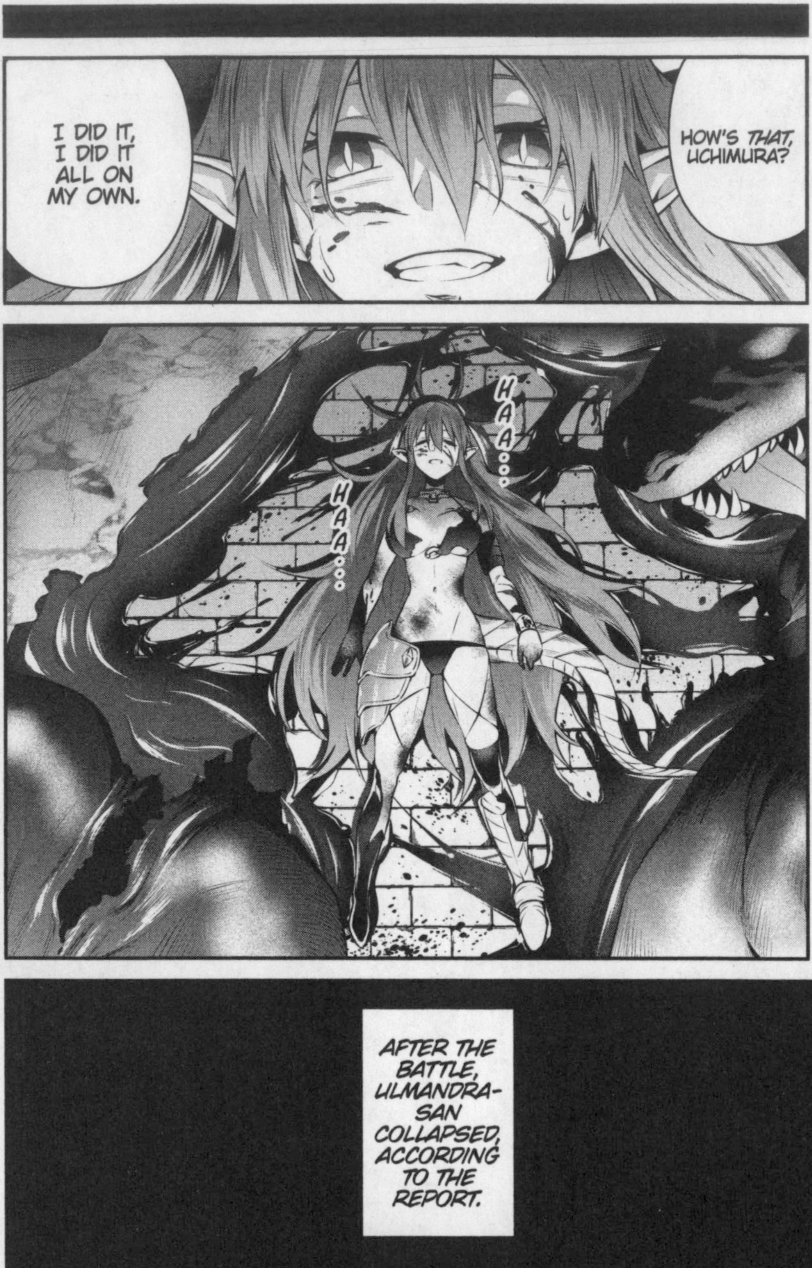
HOW'S *THAT*, UCHIMURA?
I DID IT, I DID IT ALL ON MY OWN.
HAAA...
HAAA...
AFTER THE BATTLE, ULMANDRA-SAN COLLAPSED, ACCORDING TO THE REPORT.

HEAD HUNTED TO ANOTHER WORLD

FROM SALARYMAN TO BIG FOUR!

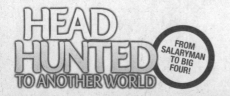

HEAD HUNTED TO ANOTHER WORLD

FROM SALARYMAN TO BIG FOUR!

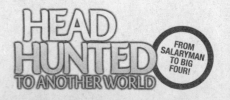

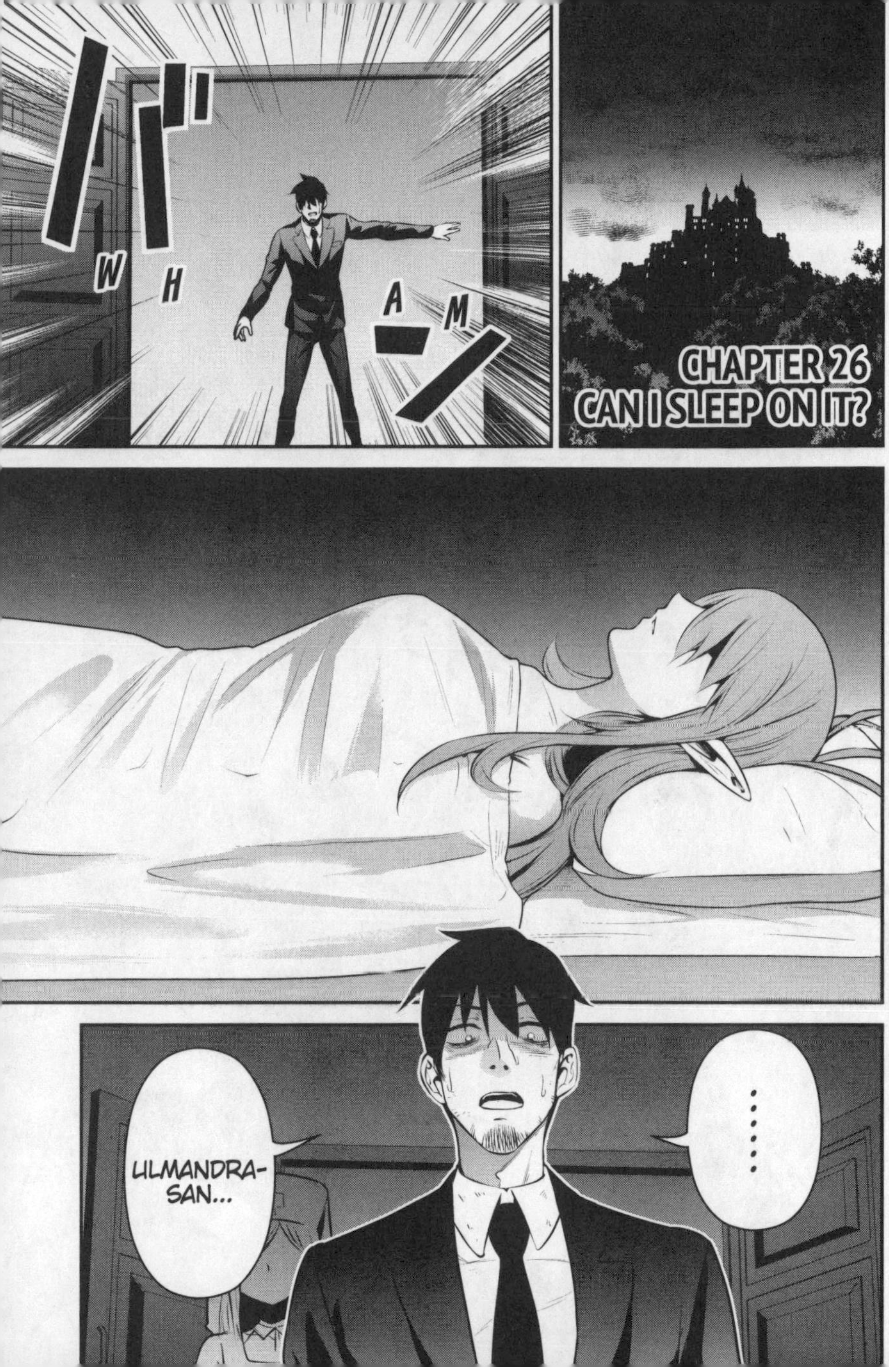
CHAPTER 26
CAN I SLEEP ON IT?
WHAM
......
ULMANDRA-SAN...

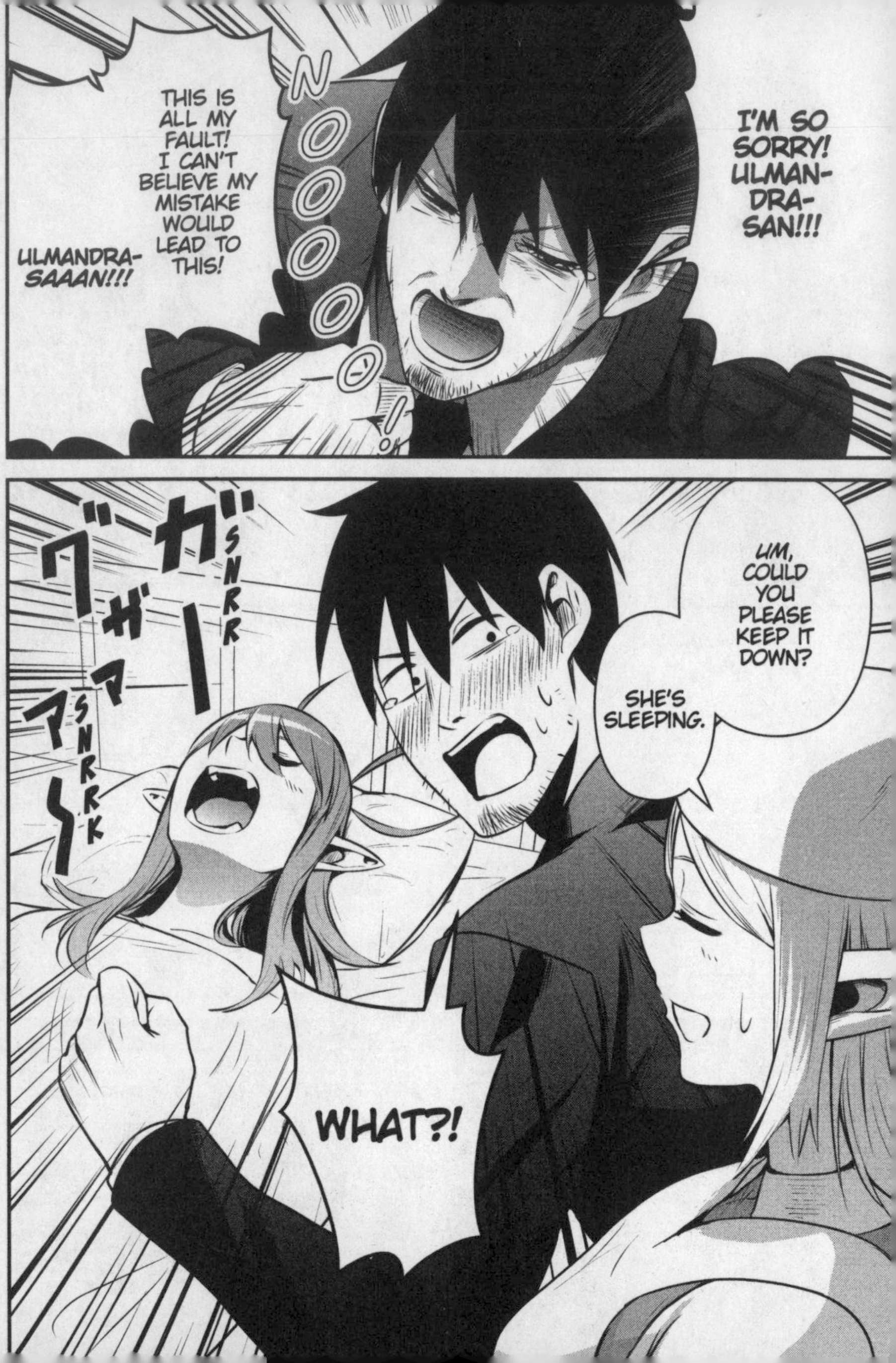
I'M SO SORRY! ULMAN-DRA-SAN!!!
NOOOOOOO-!!
THIS IS ALL MY FAULT! I CAN'T BELIEVE MY MISTAKE WOULD LEAD TO THIS!
ULMANDRA-SAAAN!!!
UM, COULD YOU PLEASE KEEP IT DOWN?
SHE'S SLEEPING.
ガー
SNRR
ヴザァア
SNRRK
WHAT?!

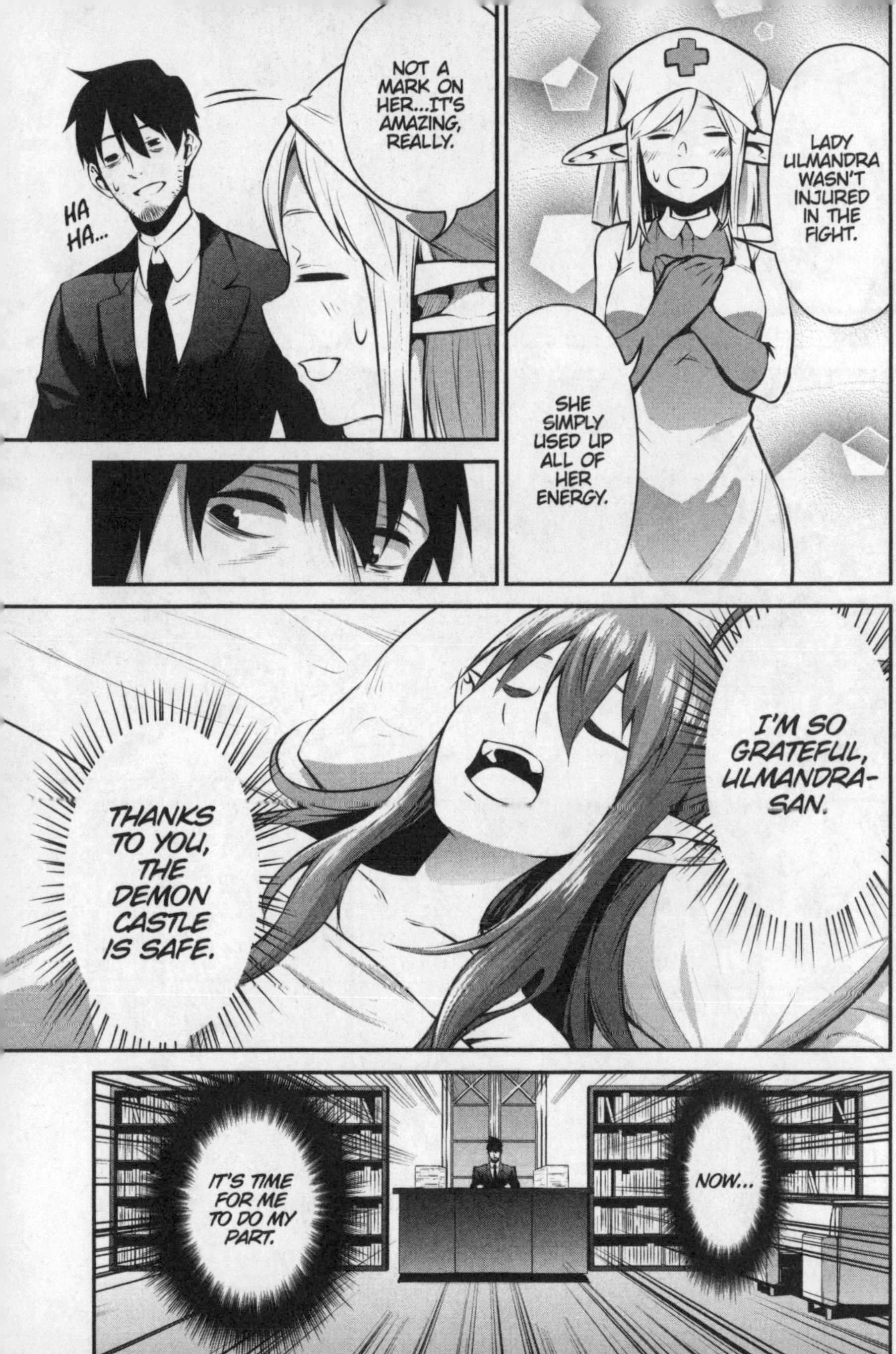
LADY ULMANDRA WASN'T INJURED IN THE FIGHT.
SHE SIMPLY USED UP ALL OF HER ENERGY.
NOT A MARK ON HER...IT'S AMAZING, REALLY.
HA HA...
I'M SO GRATEFUL, ULMANDRA-SAN.
THANKS TO YOU, THE DEMON CASTLE IS SAFE.
NOW...
IT'S TIME FOR ME TO DO MY PART.

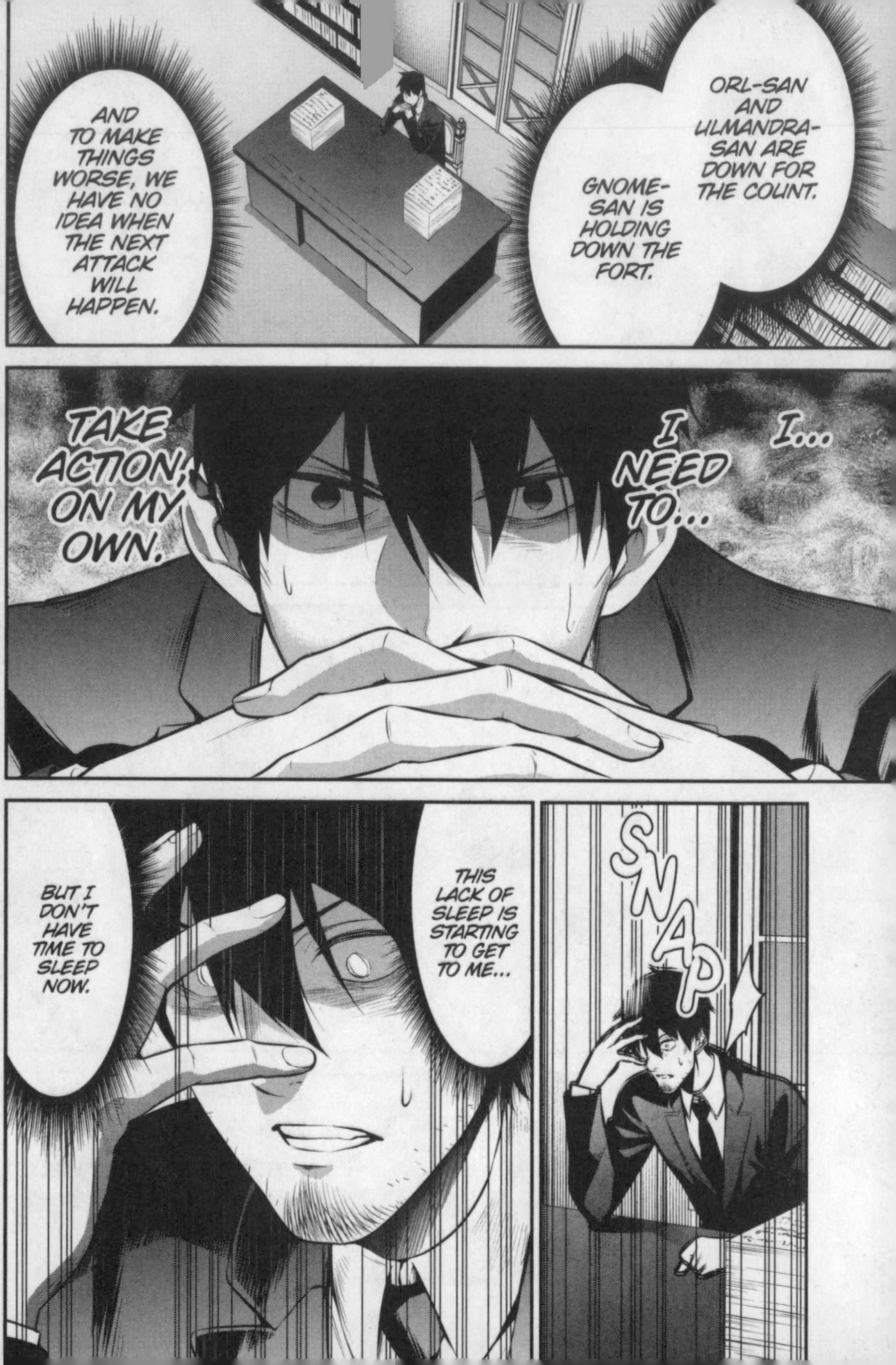
ORL-SAN AND ULMANDRA-SAN ARE DOWN FOR THE COUNT.
GNOME-SAN IS HOLDING DOWN THE FORT.
AND TO MAKE THINGS WORSE, WE HAVE NO IDEA WHEN THE NEXT ATTACK WILL HAPPEN.
I...
I NEED TO...
TAKE ACTION, ON MY OWN.
SNAP
THIS LACK OF SLEEP IS STARTING TO GET TO ME...
BUT I DON'T HAVE TIME TO SLEEP NOW.

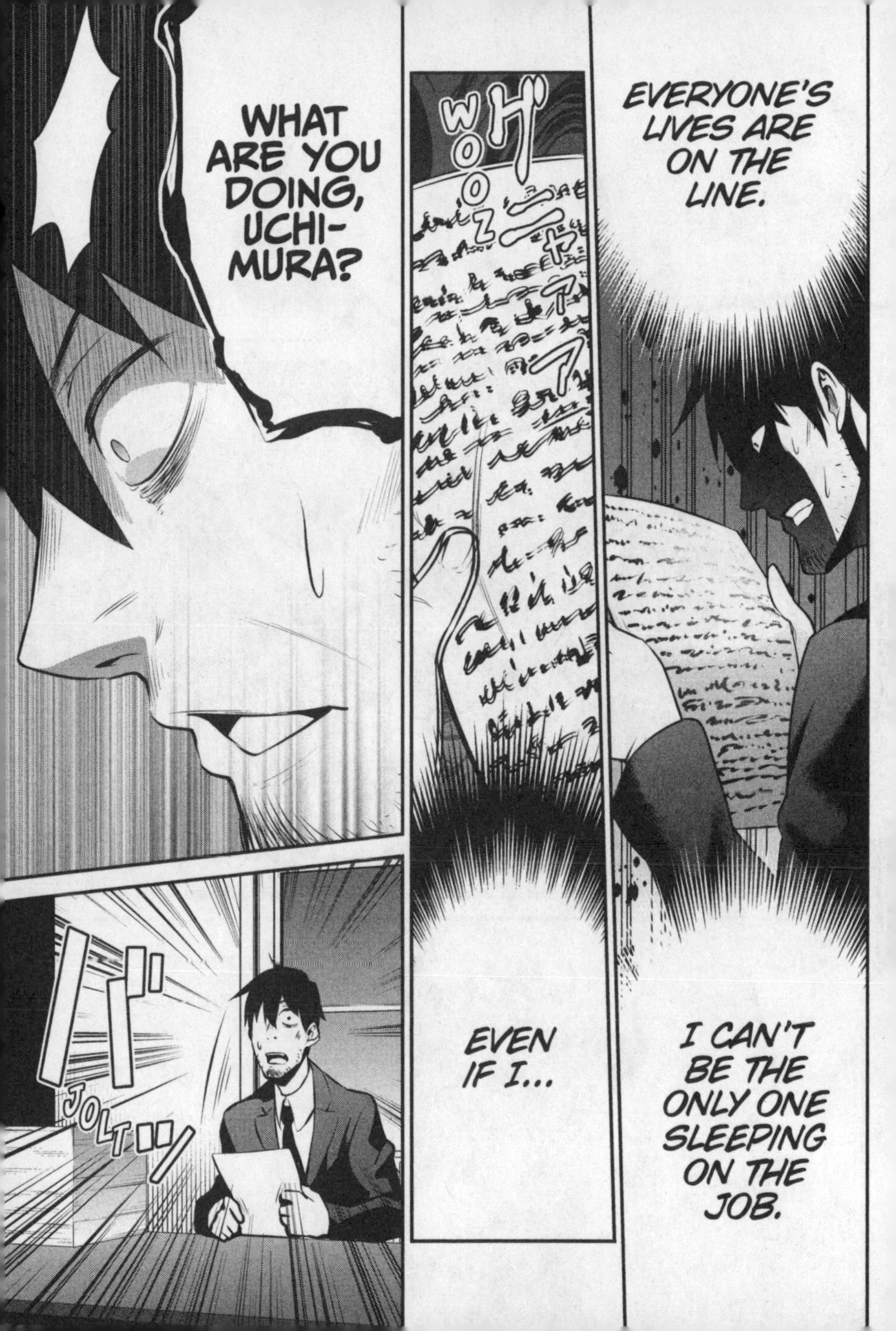
EVERYONE'S LIVES ARE ON THE LINE.
I CAN'T BE THE ONLY ONE SLEEPING ON THE JOB.
WOOZ
EVEN IF I...
WHAT ARE YOU DOING, UCHI-MURA?
JOLT!!

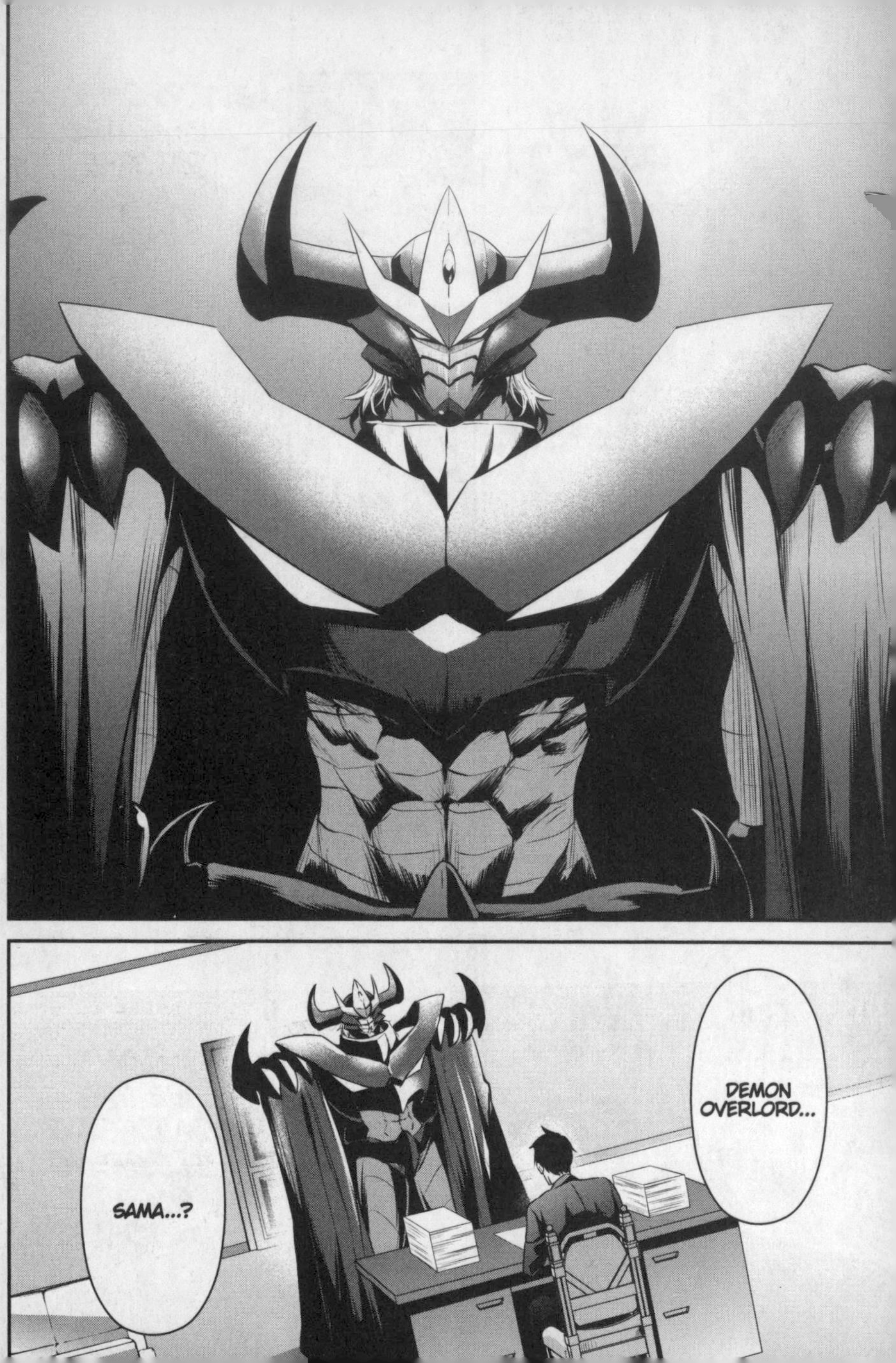
DEMON OVERLORD...
SAMA...?

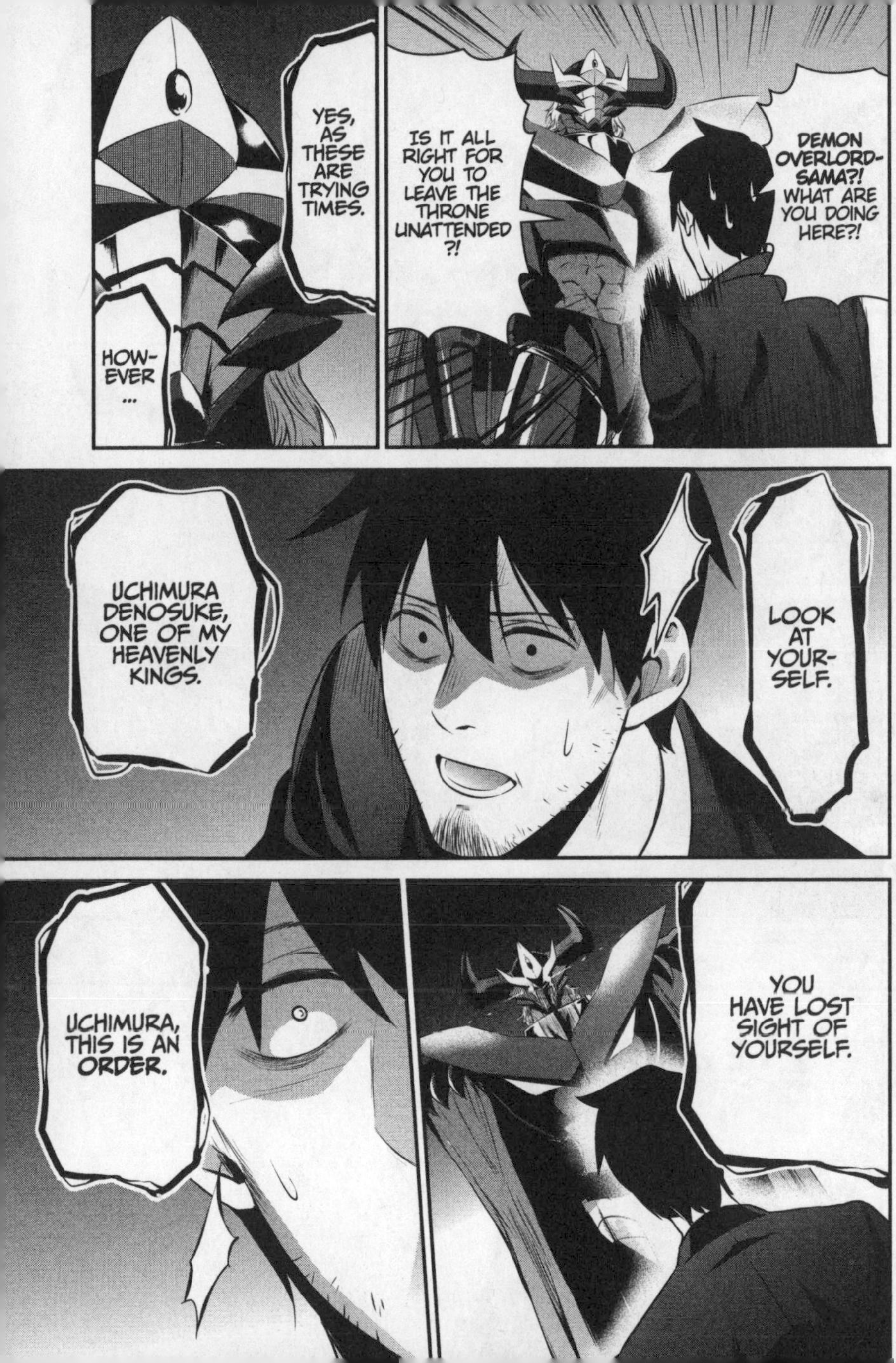
DEMON OVERLORD-SAMA?! WHAT ARE YOU DOING HERE?!
IS IT ALL RIGHT FOR YOU TO LEAVE THE THRONE UNATTENDED ?!
YES, AS THESE ARE TRYING TIMES.
HOWEVER ...
LOOK AT YOURSELF.
UCHIMURA DENOSUKE, ONE OF MY HEAVENLY KINGS.
YOU HAVE LOST SIGHT OF YOURSELF.
UCHIMURA, THIS IS AN ORDER.

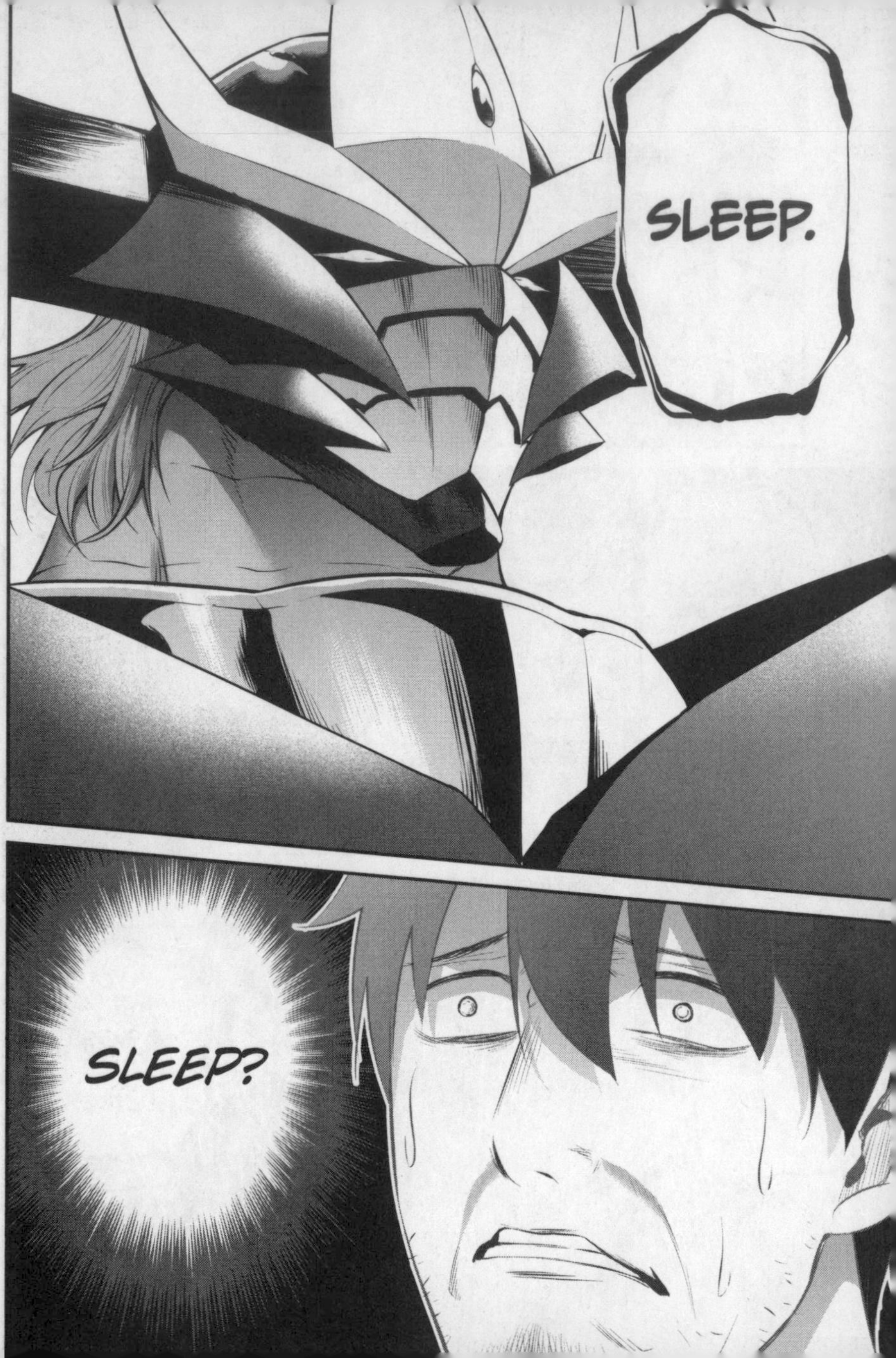
SLEEP.
SLEEP?

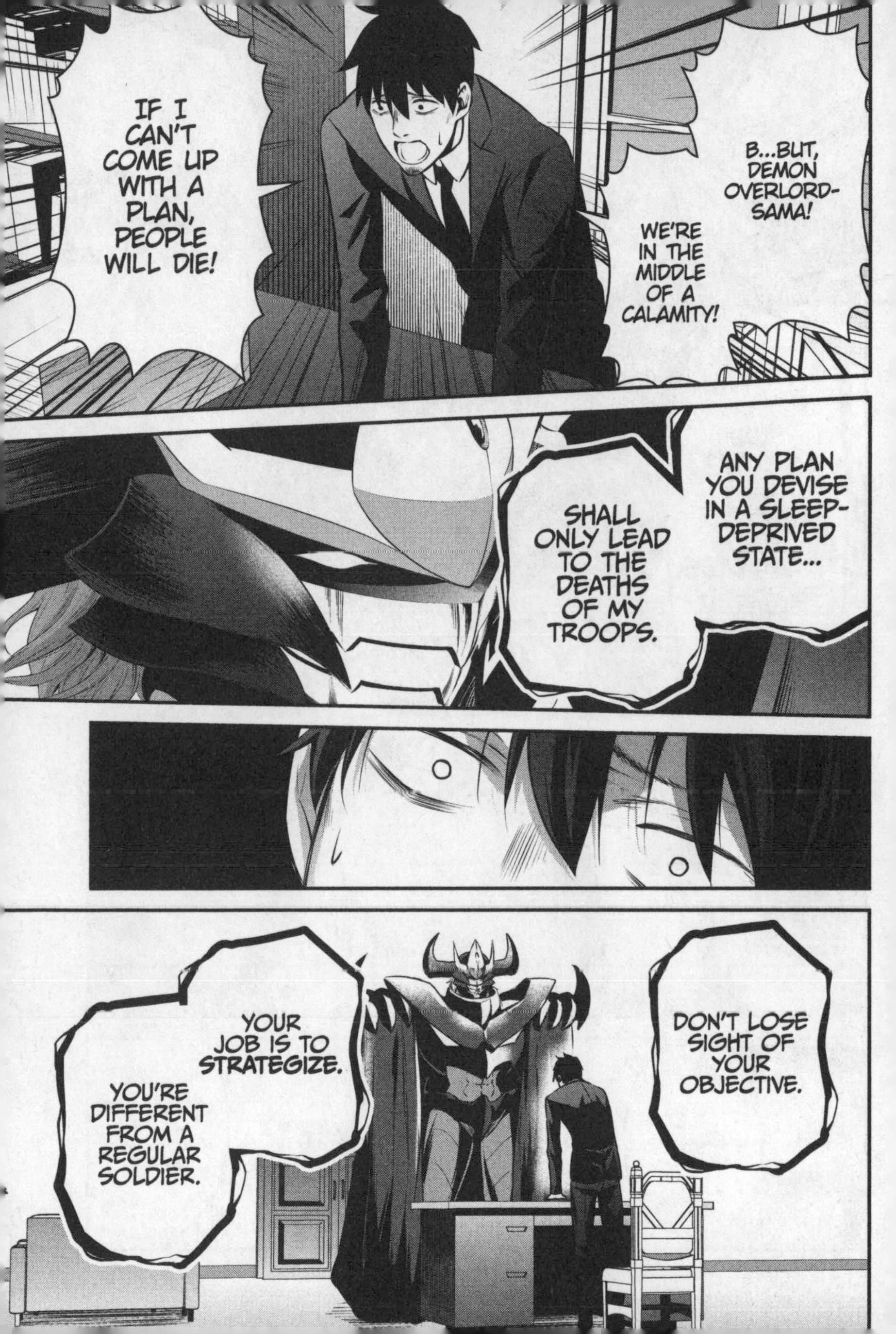
B...BUT, DEMON OVERLORD-SAMA!
WE'RE IN THE MIDDLE OF A CALAMITY!
IF I CAN'T COME UP WITH A PLAN, PEOPLE WILL DIE!
ANY PLAN YOU DEVISE IN A SLEEP-DEPRIVED STATE...
SHALL ONLY LEAD TO THE DEATHS OF MY TROOPS.
DON'T LOSE SIGHT OF YOUR OBJECTIVE.
YOUR JOB IS TO STRATEGIZE.
YOU'RE DIFFERENT FROM A REGULAR SOLDIER.

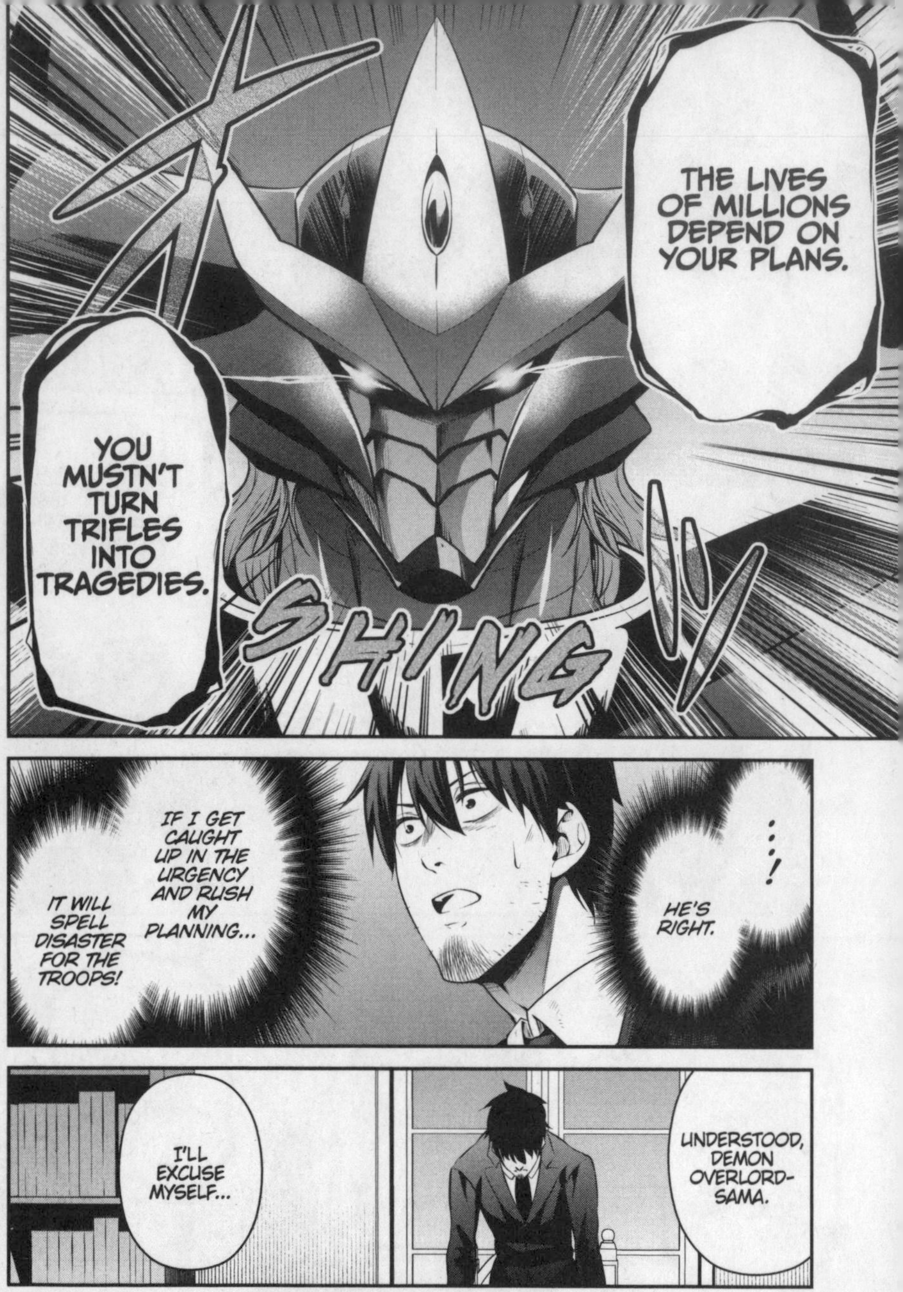
THE LIVES OF MILLIONS DEPEND ON YOUR PLANS.
YOU MUSTN'T TURN TRIFLES INTO TRAGEDIES.
SHING
...!
HE'S RIGHT.
IF I GET CAUGHT UP IN THE URGENCY AND RUSH MY PLANNING...
IT WILL SPELL DISASTER FOR THE TROOPS!
UNDERSTOOD, DEMON OVERLORD-SAMA.
I'LL EXCUSE MYSELF...

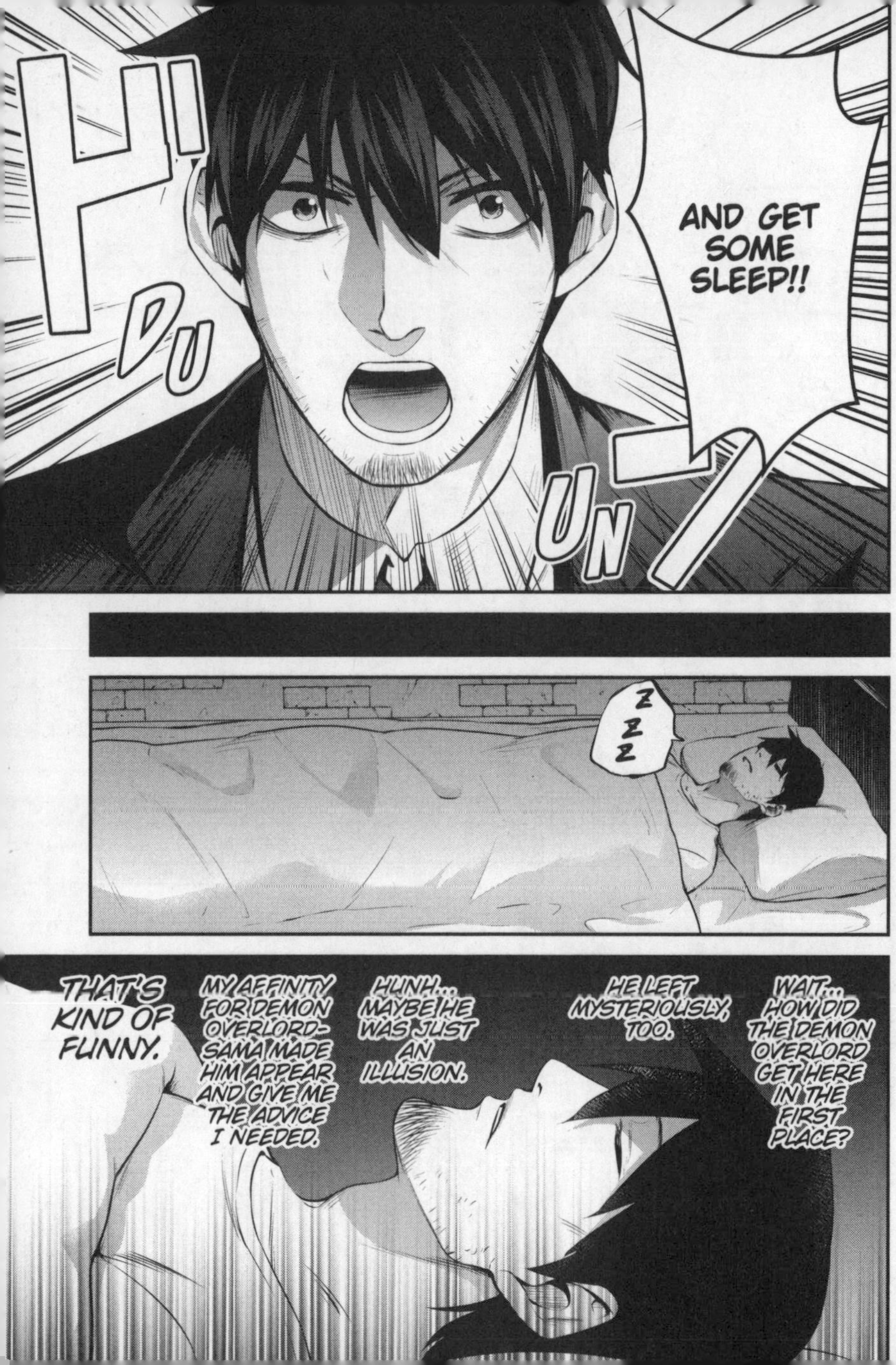
AND GET SOME SLEEP!!
DUUN
Z Z Z
WAIT... HOW DID THE DEMON OVERLORD GET HERE IN THE FIRST PLACE?
HE LEFT MYSTERIOUSLY, TOO.
HUNH... MAYBE HE WAS JUST AN ILLUSION.
MY AFFINITY FOR DEMON OVERLORD-SAMA MADE HIM APPEAR AND GIVE ME THE ADVICE I NEEDED.
THAT'S KIND OF FUNNY.

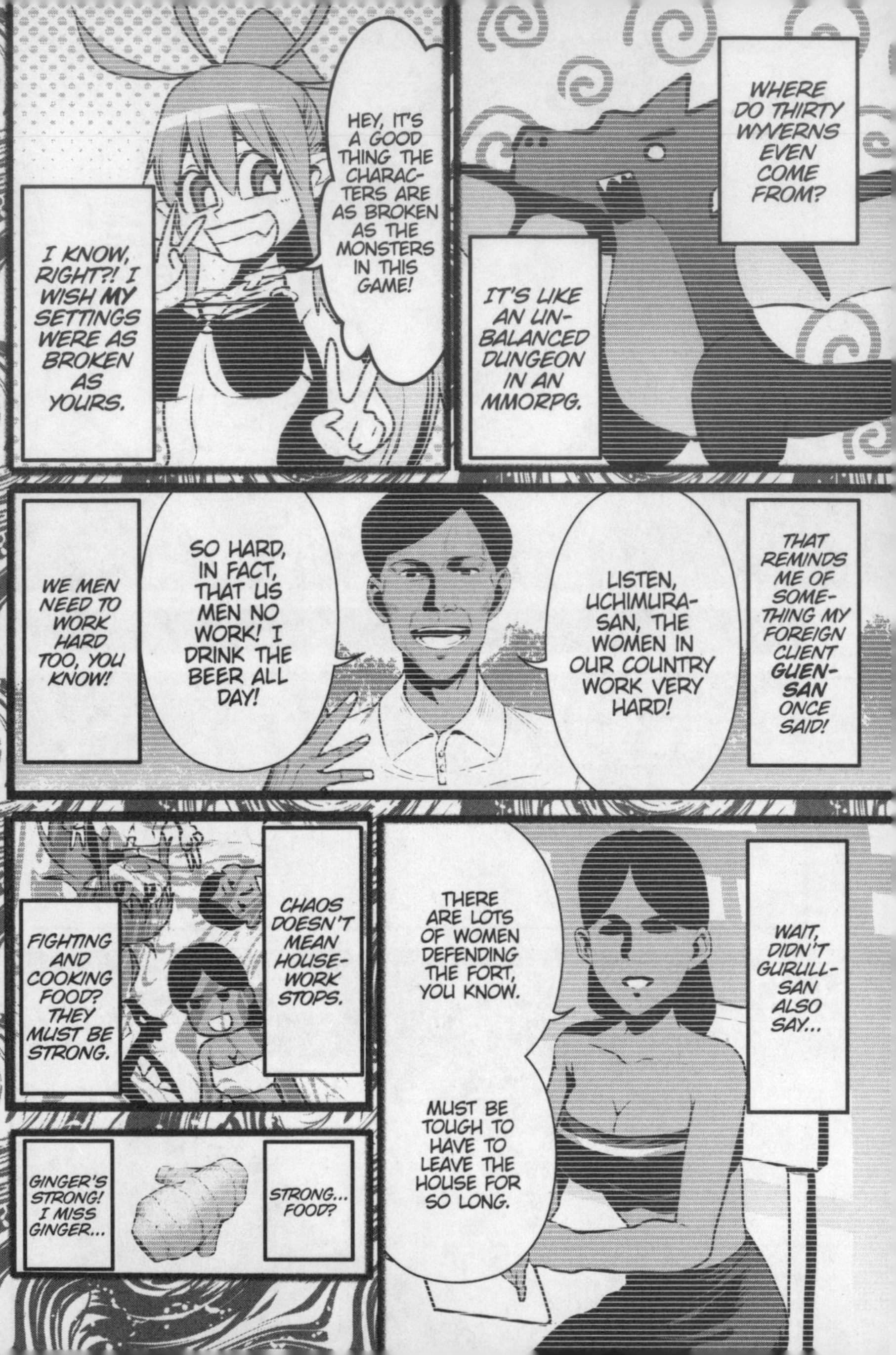
WHERE DO THIRTY WYVERNS EVEN COME FROM?
IT'S LIKE AN UN-BALANCED DUNGEON IN AN MMORPG.
HEY, IT'S A GOOD THING THE CHARAC-TERS ARE AS BROKEN AS THE MONSTERS IN THIS GAME!
I KNOW, RIGHT?! I WISH MY SETTINGS WERE AS BROKEN AS YOURS.
THAT REMINDS ME OF SOME-THING MY FOREIGN CLIENT GUEN-SAN ONCE SAID!
LISTEN, UCHIMURA-SAN, THE WOMEN IN OUR COUNTRY WORK VERY HARD!
SO HARD, IN FACT, THAT US MEN NO WORK! I DRINK THE BEER ALL DAY!
WE MEN NEED TO WORK HARD TOO, YOU KNOW!
WAIT, DIDN'T GURULL-SAN ALSO SAY...
THERE ARE LOTS OF WOMEN DEFENDING THE FORT, YOU KNOW.
MUST BE TOUGH TO HAVE TO LEAVE THE HOUSE FOR SO LONG.
CHAOS DOESN'T MEAN HOUSE-WORK STOPS.
FIGHTING AND COOKING FOOD? THEY MUST BE STRONG.
STRONG... FOOD?
GINGER'S STRONG! I MISS GINGER...

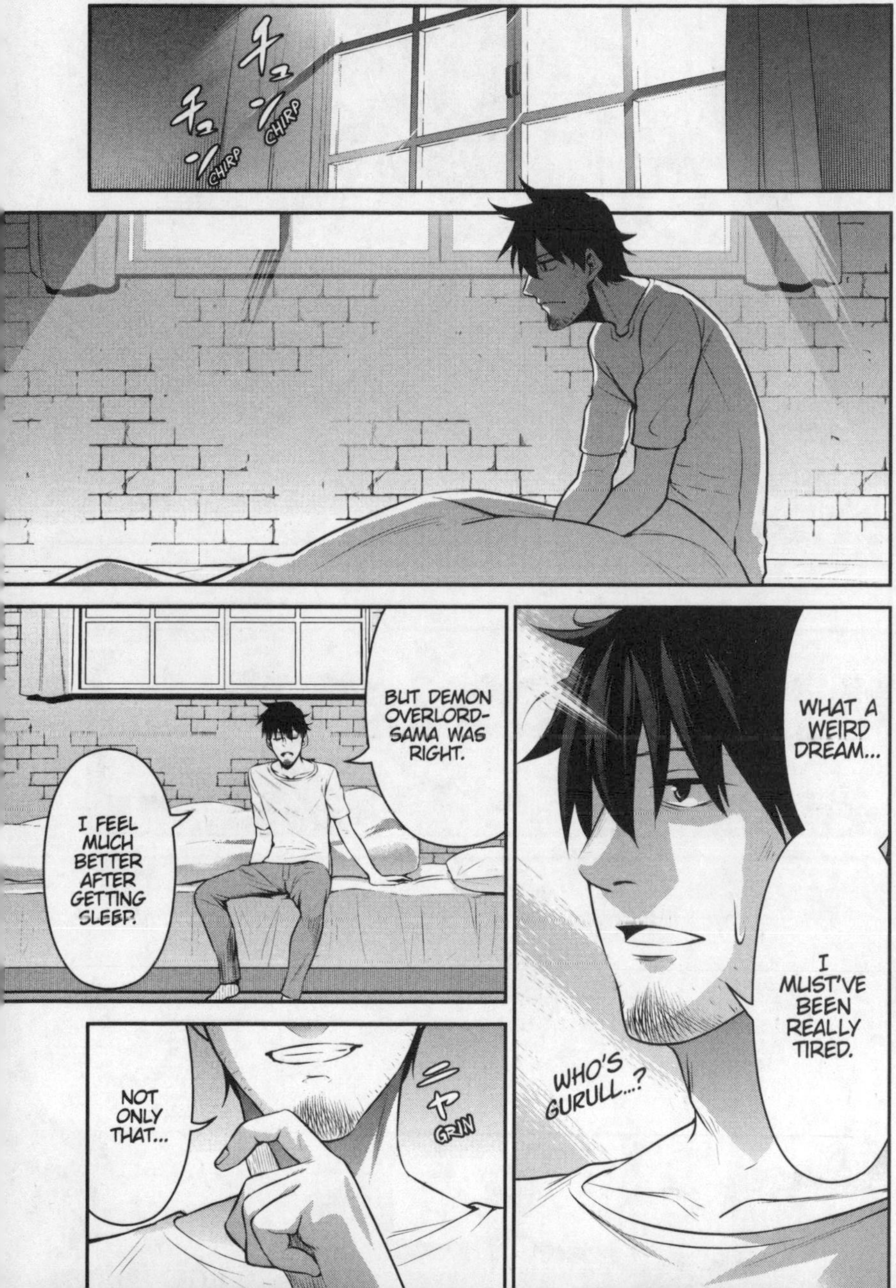
チュン
CHIRP
チュン
CHIRP
WHAT A WEIRD DREAM...
I MUST'VE BEEN REALLY TIRED.
WHO'S GURULL...?
BUT DEMON OVERLORD-SAMA WAS RIGHT.
I FEEL MUCH BETTER AFTER GETTING SLEEP.
ニヤ
GRIN
NOT ONLY THAT...

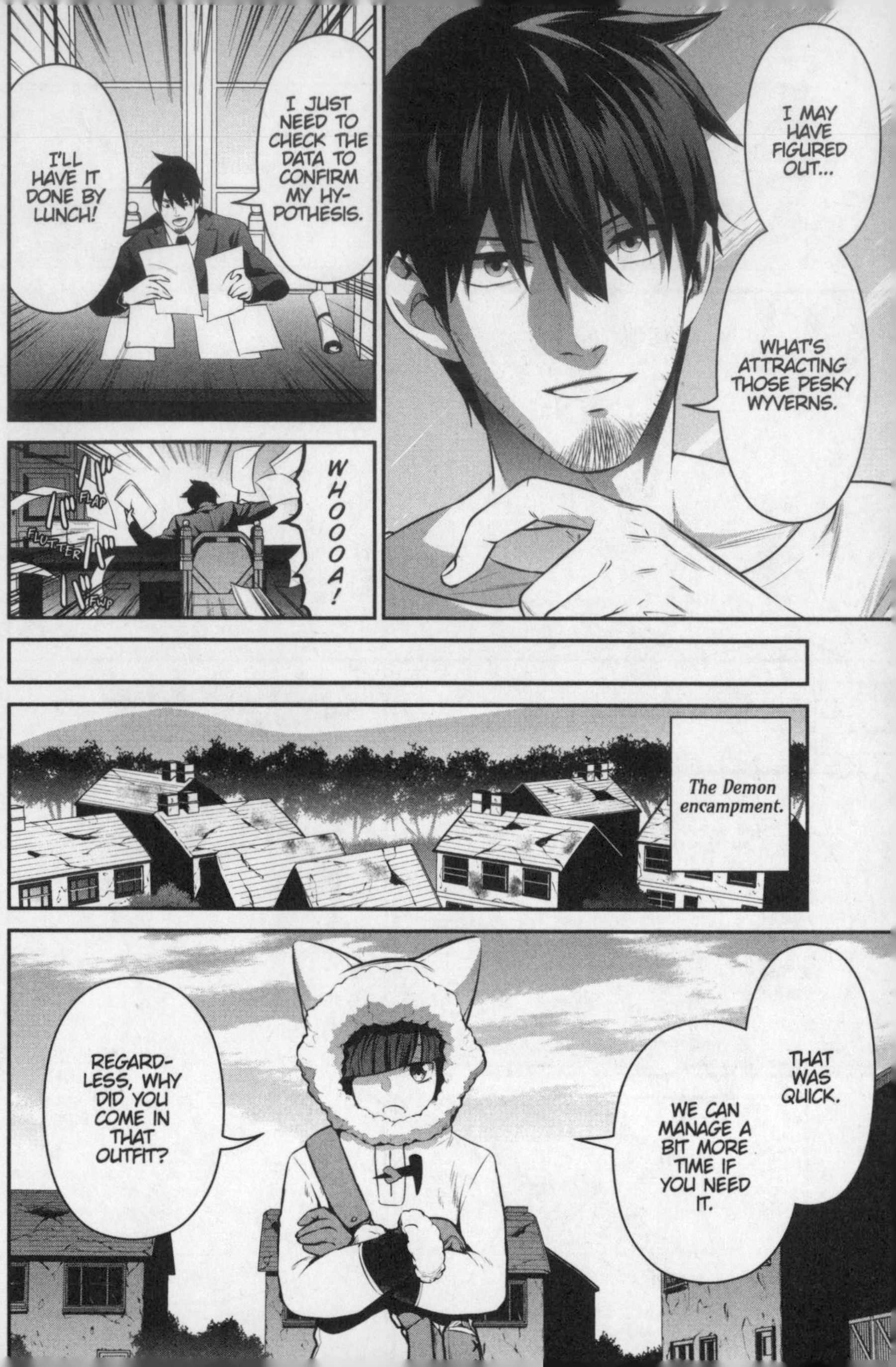
I MAY HAVE FIGURED OUT...
WHAT'S ATTRACTING THOSE PESKY WYVERNS.
I JUST NEED TO CHECK THE DATA TO CONFIRM MY HY-POTHESIS.
I'LL HAVE IT DONE BY LUNCH!
WHOOOOA!
FLAP
FLUTTER
FWP
The Demon encampment.
THAT WAS QUICK.
WE CAN MANAGE A BIT MORE TIME IF YOU NEED IT.
REGARD-LESS, WHY DID YOU COME IN THAT OUTFIT?

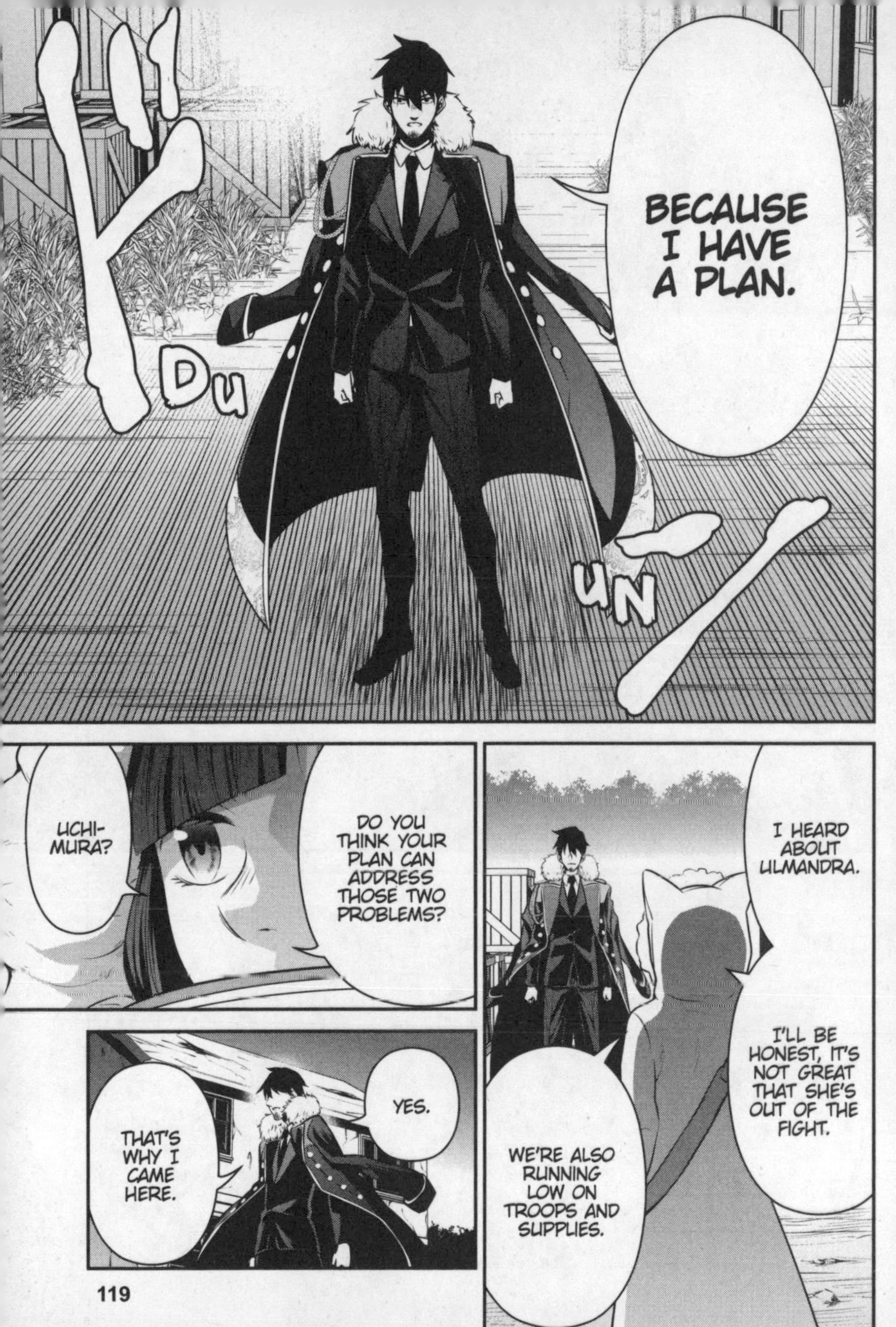
BECAUSE I HAVE A PLAN.
Du
UN
I HEARD ABOUT ULMANDRA.
I'LL BE HONEST, IT'S NOT GREAT THAT SHE'S OUT OF THE FIGHT.
WE'RE ALSO RUNNING LOW ON TROOPS AND SUPPLIES.
DO YOU THINK YOUR PLAN CAN ADDRESS THOSE TWO PROBLEMS?
UCHI-MURA?
YES.
THAT'S WHY I CAME HERE.

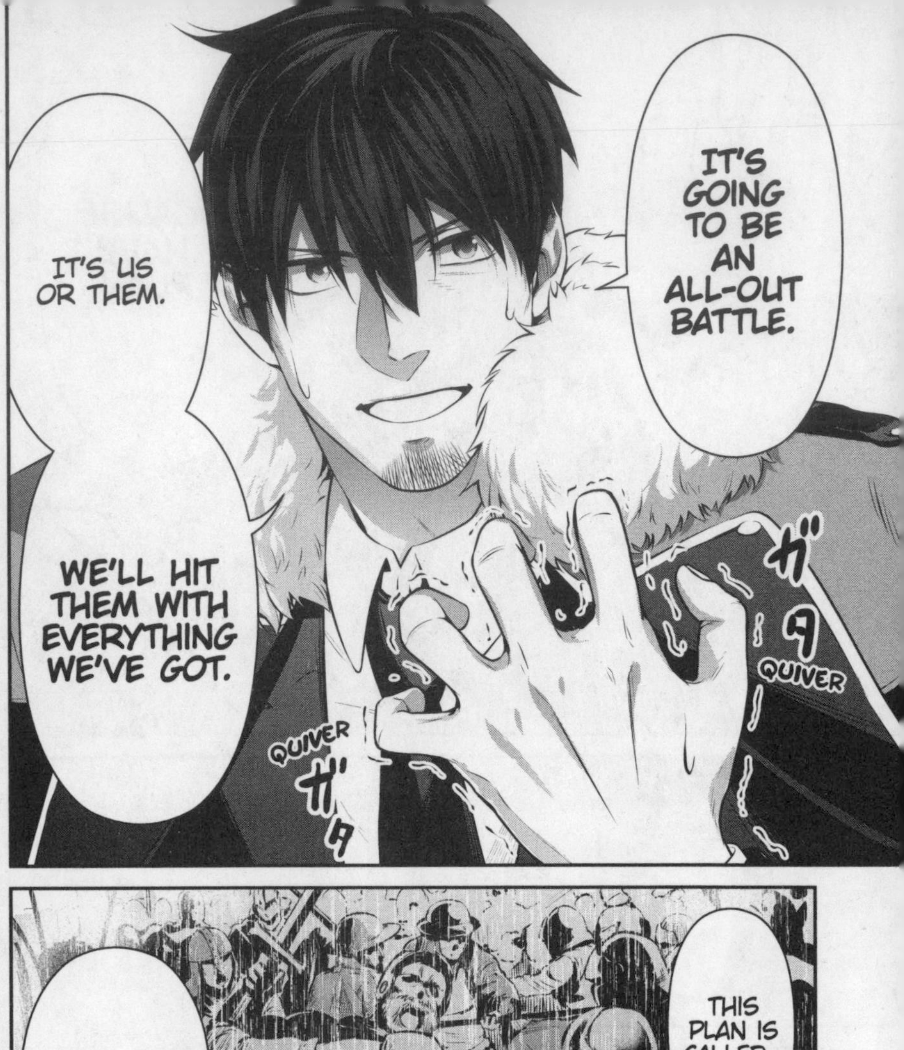
IT'S GOING TO BE AN ALL-OUT BATTLE.
IT'S US OR THEM.
WE'LL HIT THEM WITH EVERYTHING WE'VE GOT.
ガタ
QUIVER
ガタ
QUIVER

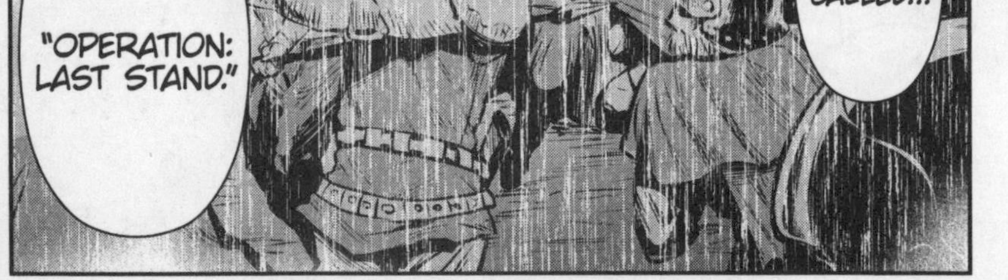
THIS PLAN IS CALLED...
"OPERATION: LAST STAND."

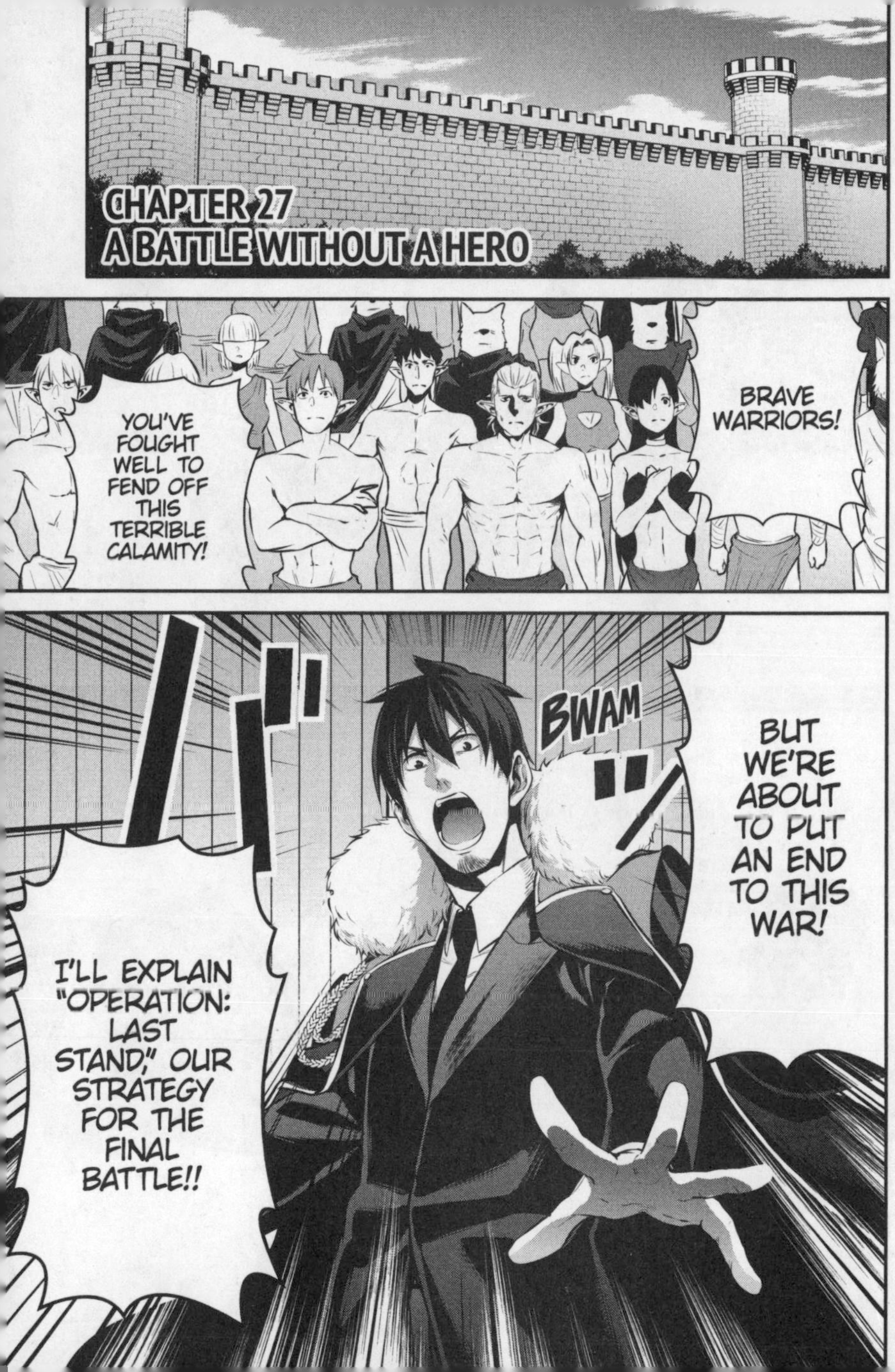
CHAPTER 27
A BATTLE WITHOUT A HERO
BRAVE WARRIORS!
YOU'VE FOUGHT WELL TO FEND OFF THIS TERRIBLE CALAMITY!
BWAM
BUT WE'RE ABOUT TO PUT AN END TO THIS WAR!
I'LL EXPLAIN "OPERATION: LAST STAND," OUR STRATEGY FOR THE FINAL BATTLE!!

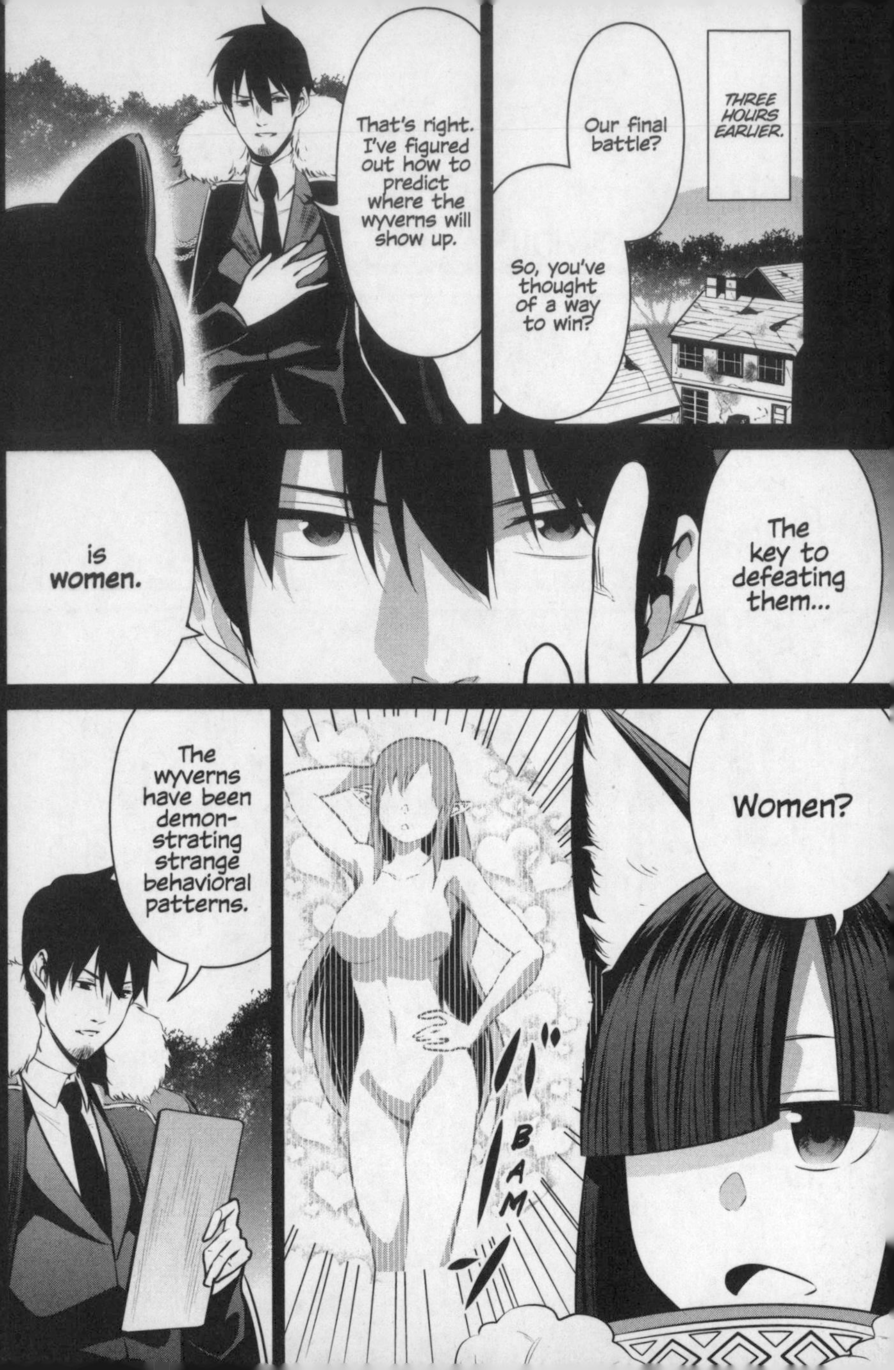
THREE HOURS EARLIER.
Our final battle?
So, you've thought of a way to win?
That's right. I've figured out how to predict where the wyverns will show up.
The key to defeating them...
is women.
Women?
BAM
The wyverns have been demon-strating strange behavioral patterns.

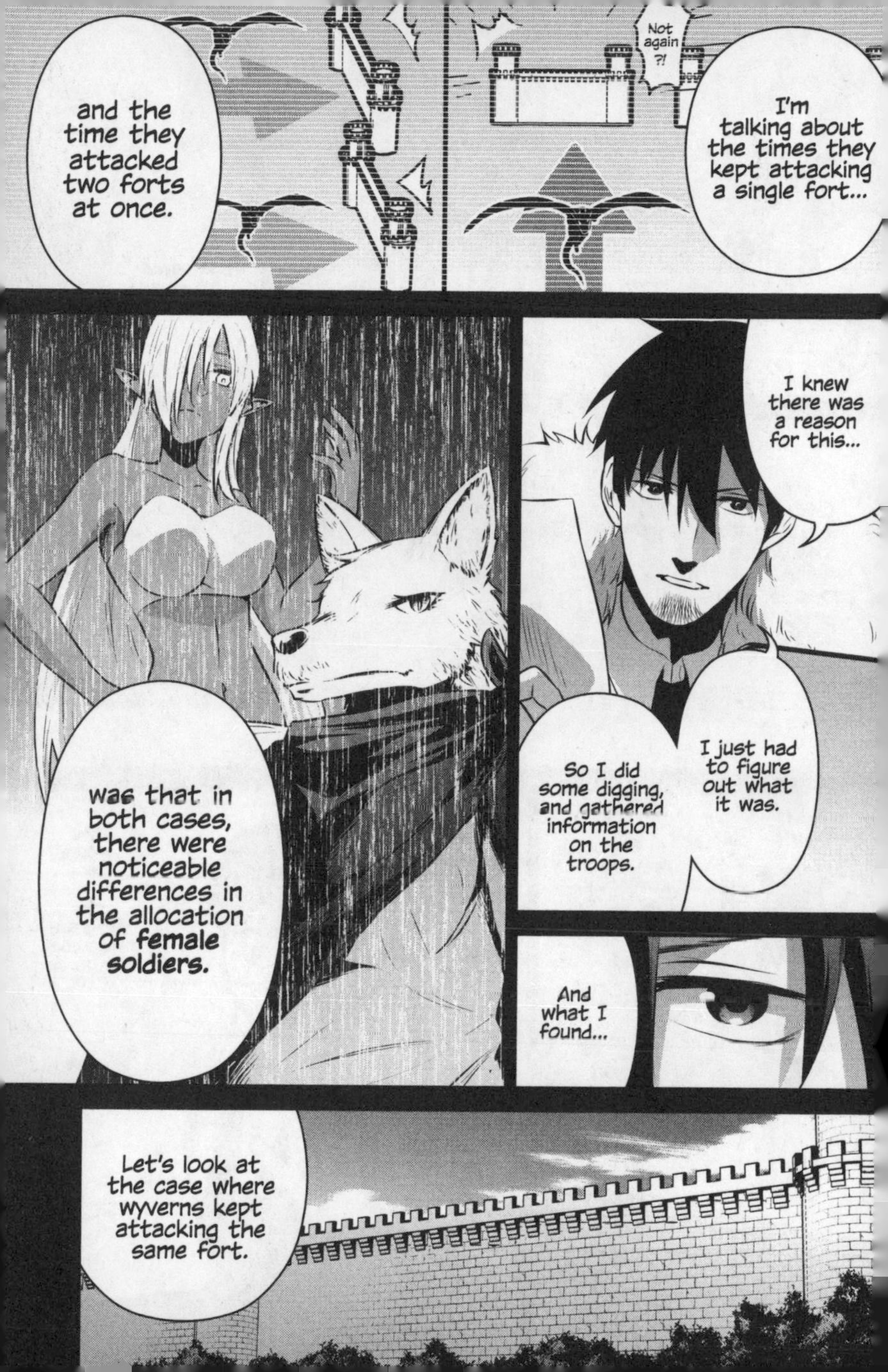
I'm talking about the times they kept attacking a single fort...
Not again ?!
and the time they attacked two forts at once.
I knew there was a reason for this...
I just had to figure out what it was.
So I did some digging, and gathered information on the troops.
And what I found...
was that in both cases, there were noticeable differences in the allocation of **female soldiers.**
Let's look at the case where wyverns kept attacking the same fort.

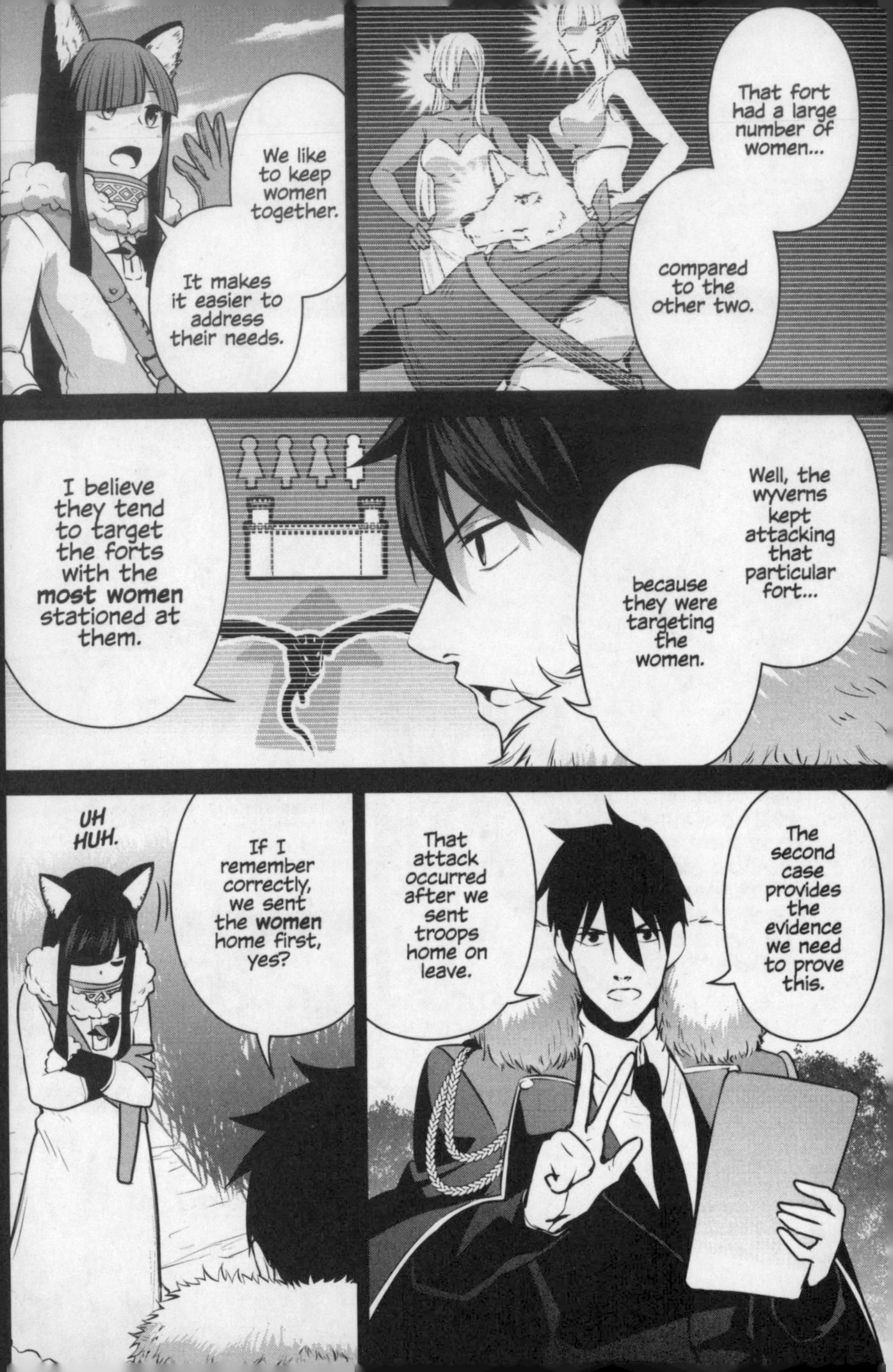

That fort had a large number of women...
compared to the other two.
We like to keep women together.
It makes it easier to address their needs.
Well, the wyverns kept attacking that particular fort...
because they were targeting the women.
I believe they tend to target the forts with the **most women** stationed at them.
The second case provides the evidence we need to prove this.
That attack occurred after we sent troops home on leave.
If I remember correctly, we sent the **women** home first, yes?
UH HUH.

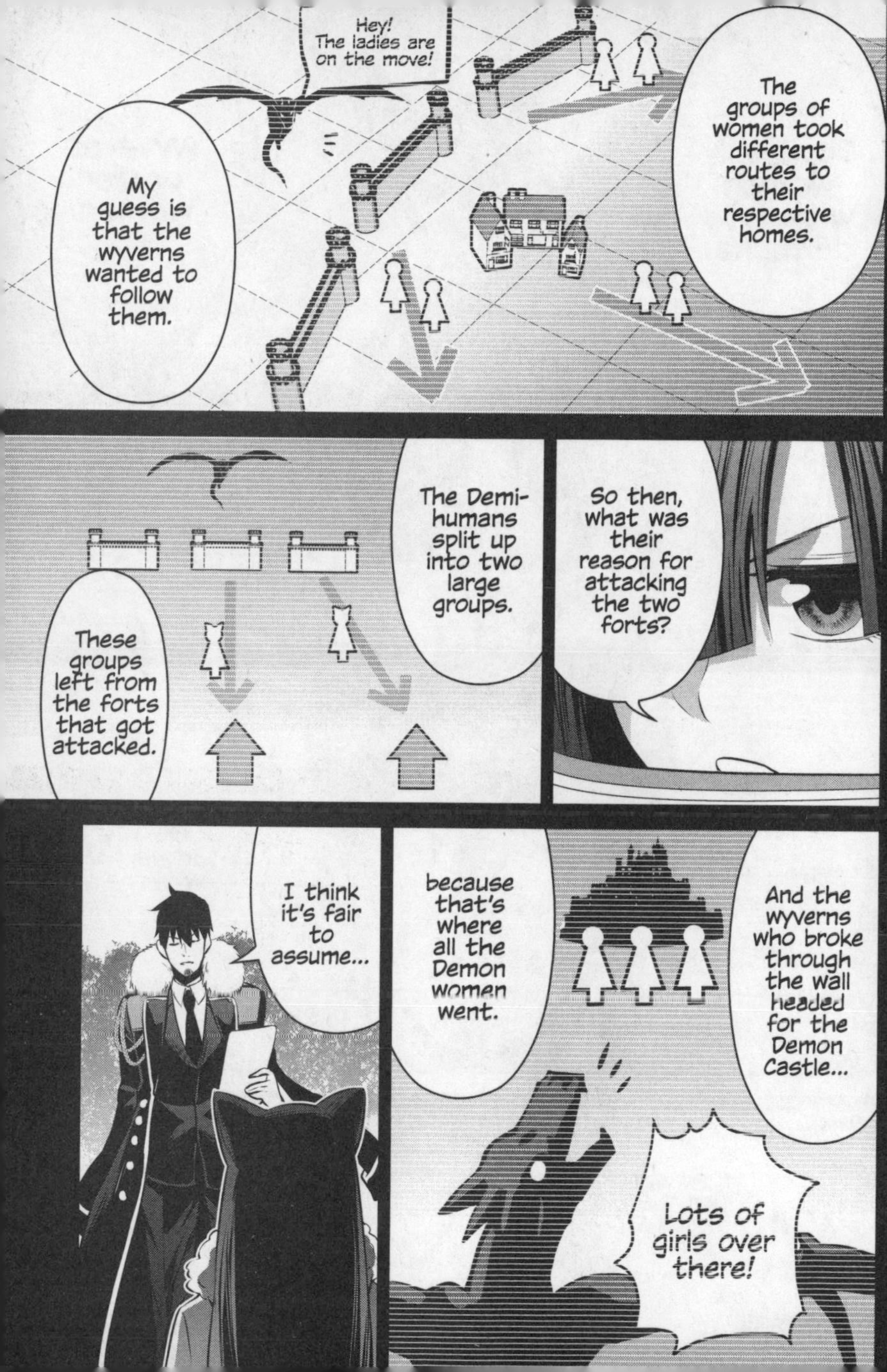
The groups of women took different routes to their respective homes.
Hey! The ladies are on the move!
My guess is that the wyverns wanted to follow them.
So then, what was their reason for attacking the two forts?
The Demi-humans split up into two large groups.
These groups left from the forts that got attacked.
And the wyverns who broke through the wall headed for the Demon Castle...
Lots of girls over there!
I think it's fair to assume...
because that's where all the Demon women went.

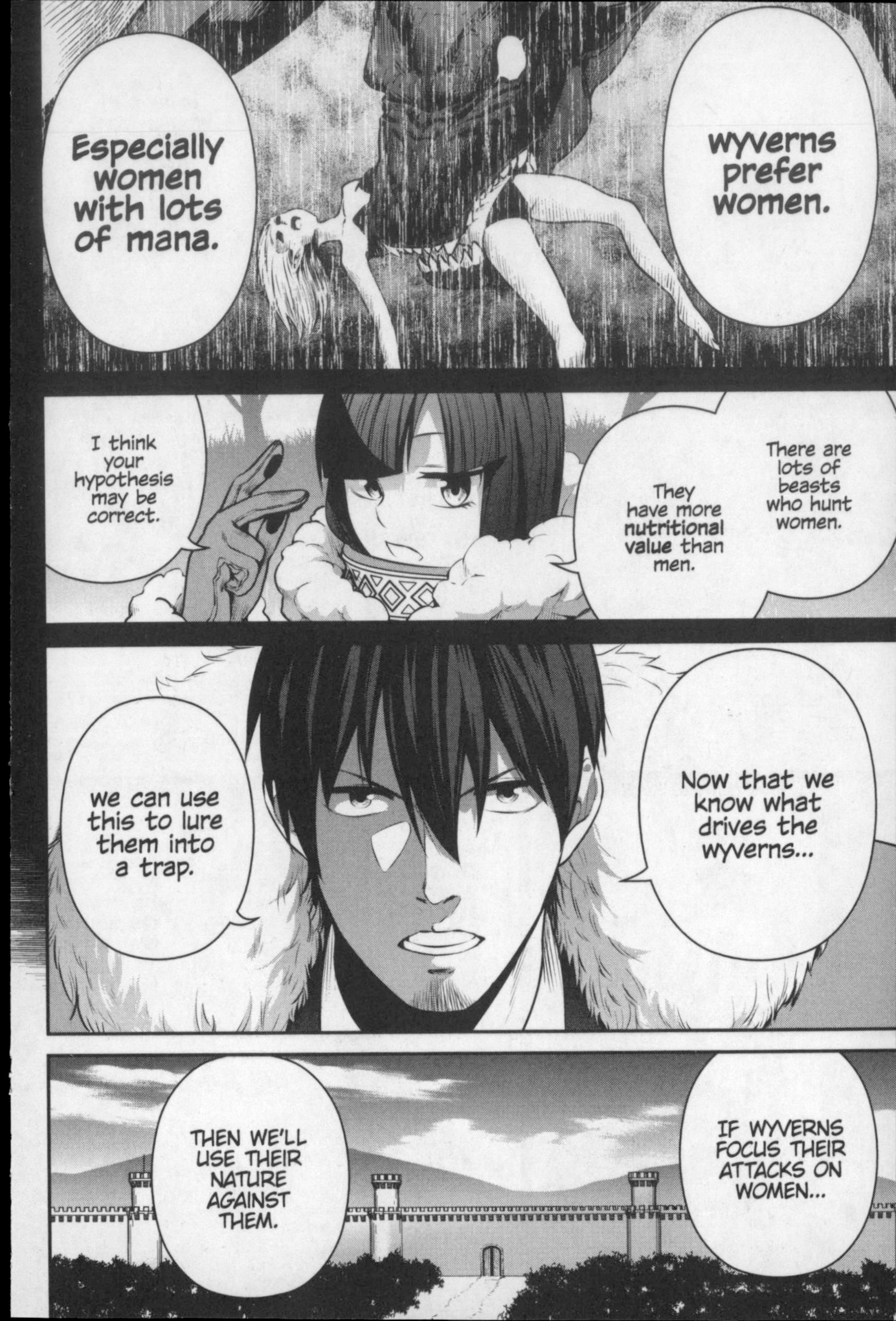
wyverns prefer women.
Especially women with lots of mana.
There are lots of beasts who hunt women.
They have more nutritional value than men.
I think your hypothesis may be correct.
Now that we know what drives the wyverns...
we can use this to lure them into a trap.
IF WYVERNS FOCUS THEIR ATTACKS ON WOMEN...
THEN WE'LL USE THEIR NATURE AGAINST THEM.

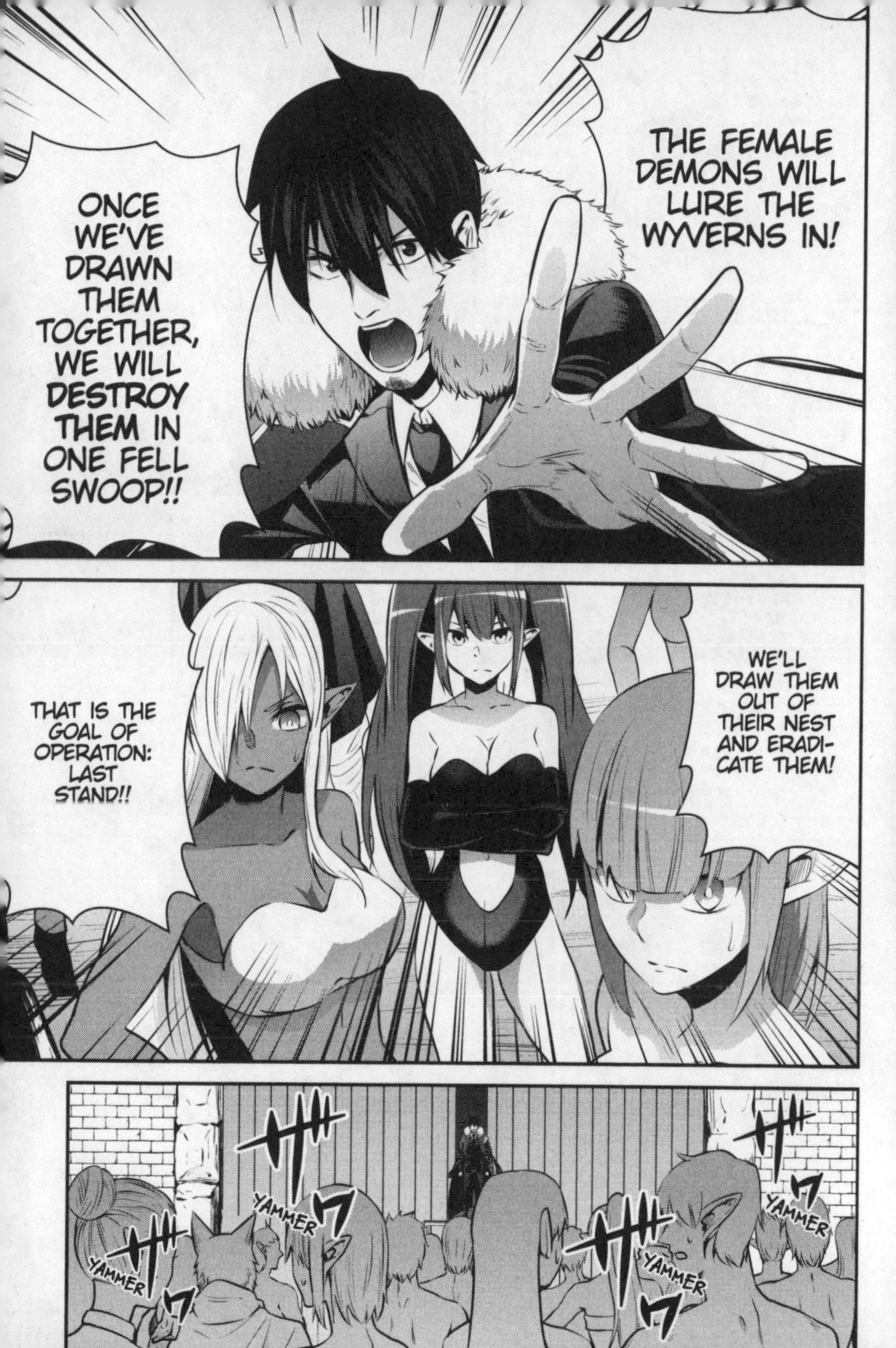
THE FEMALE DEMONS WILL LURE THE WYVERNS IN!
ONCE WE'VE DRAWN THEM TOGETHER, WE WILL DESTROY THEM IN ONE FELL SWOOP!!
WE'LL DRAW THEM OUT OF THEIR NEST AND ERADI-CATE THEM!
THAT IS THE GOAL OF OPERATION: LAST STAND!!
YAMMER
YAMMER
YAMMER
YAMMER

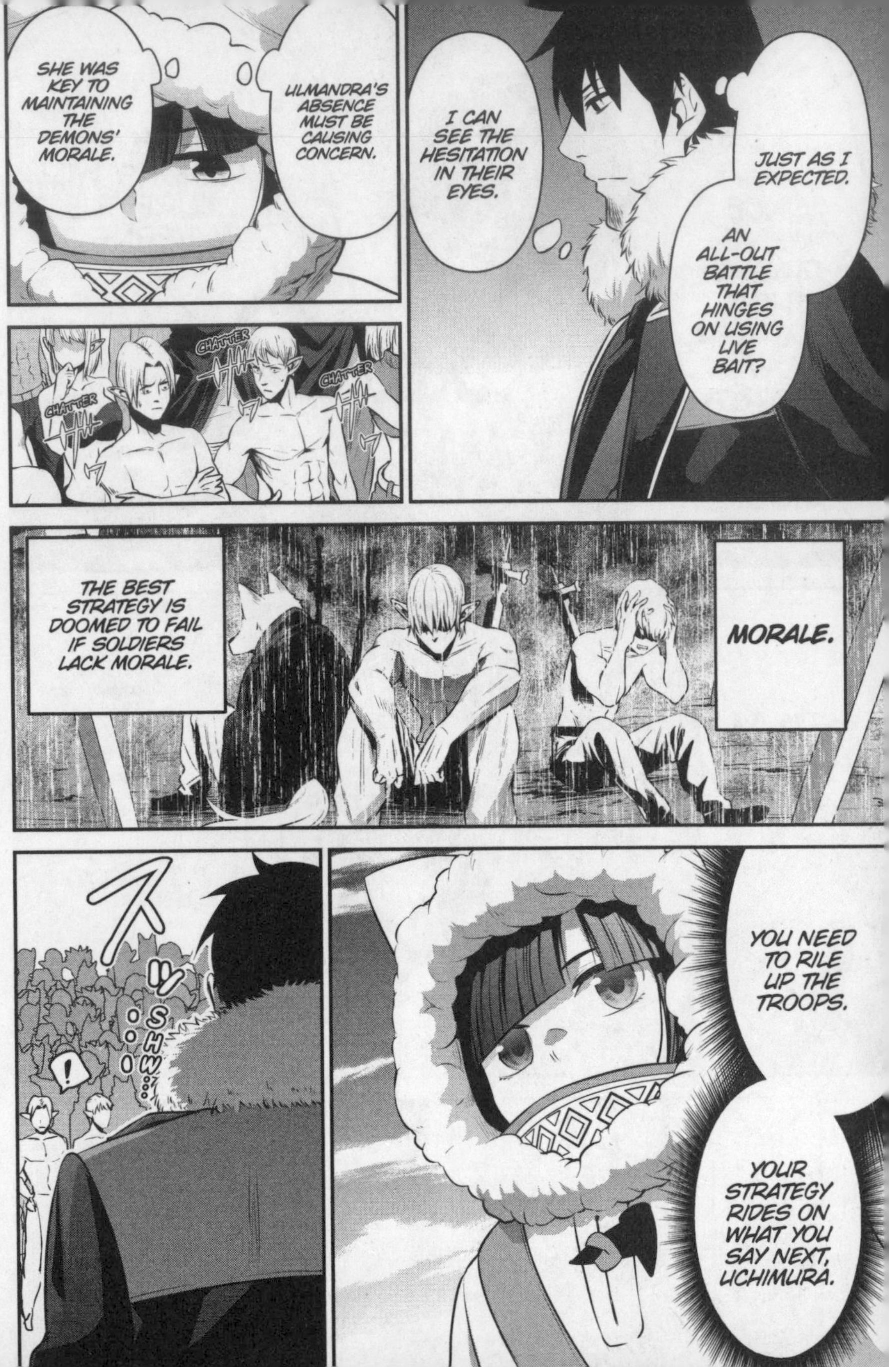

JUST AS I EXPECTED.
AN ALL-OUT BATTLE THAT HINGES ON USING LIVE BAIT?
I CAN SEE THE HESITATION IN THEIR EYES.
ULMANDRA'S ABSENCE MUST BE CAUSING CONCERN.
SHE WAS KEY TO MAINTAINING THE DEMONS' MORALE.
CHATTER
CHATTER
CHATTER
MORALE.
THE BEST STRATEGY IS DOOMED TO FAIL IF SOLDIERS LACK MORALE.
YOU NEED TO RILE UP THE TROOPS.
YOUR STRATEGY RIDES ON WHAT YOU SAY NEXT, UCHIMURA.
SHW...
!

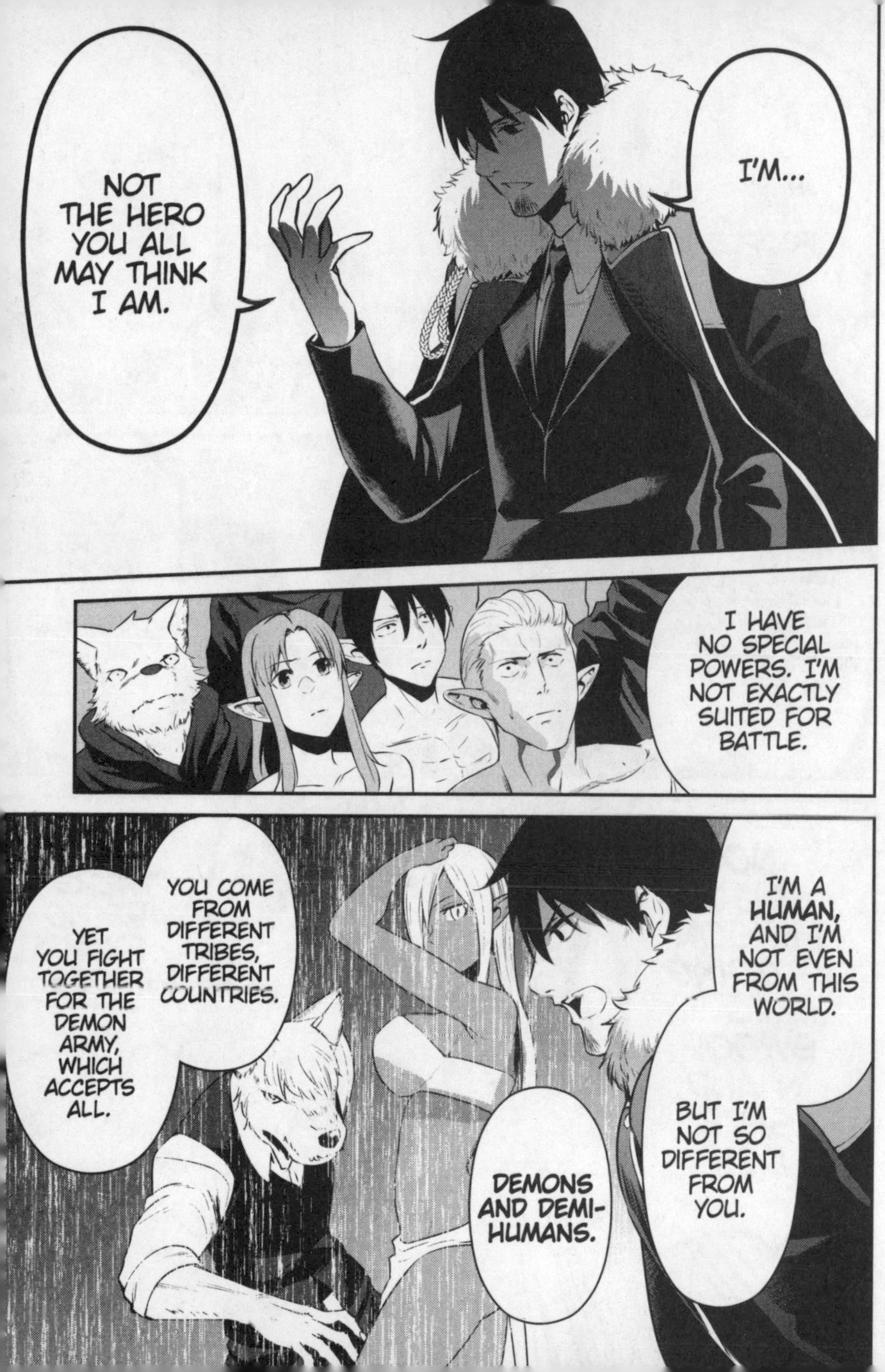
I'M...
NOT THE HERO YOU ALL MAY THINK I AM.
I HAVE NO SPECIAL POWERS. I'M NOT EXACTLY SUITED FOR BATTLE.
I'M A HUMAN, AND I'M NOT EVEN FROM THIS WORLD.
BUT I'M NOT SO DIFFERENT FROM YOU.
DEMONS AND DEMI-HUMANS.
YOU COME FROM DIFFERENT TRIBES, DIFFERENT COUNTRIES.
YET YOU FIGHT TOGETHER FOR THE DEMON ARMY, WHICH ACCEPTS ALL.

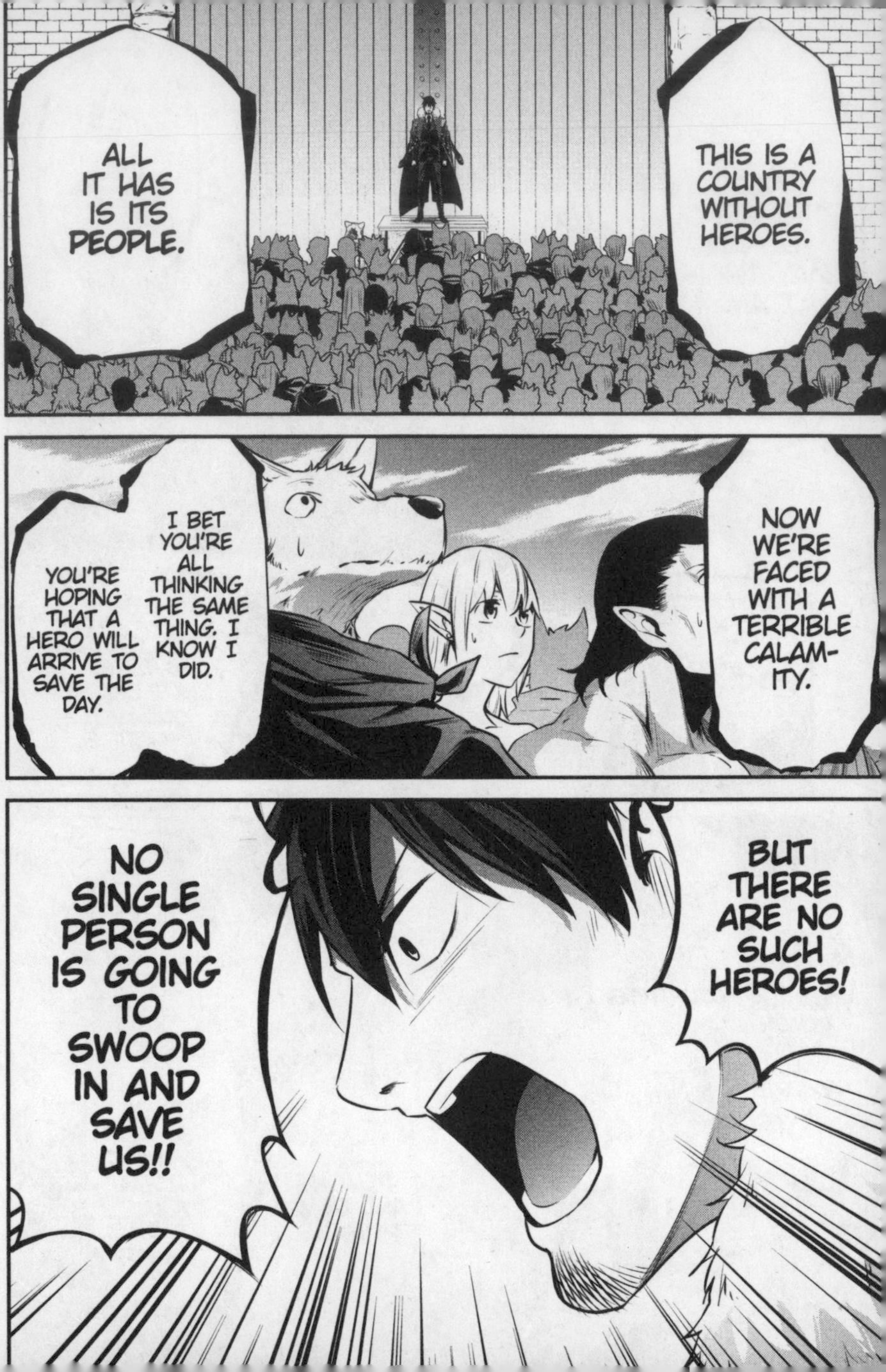
THIS IS A COUNTRY WITHOUT HEROES.
ALL IT HAS IS ITS PEOPLE.
NOW WE'RE FACED WITH A TERRIBLE CALAMITY.
I BET YOU'RE ALL THINKING THE SAME THING. I KNOW I DID.
YOU'RE HOPING THAT A HERO WILL ARRIVE TO SAVE THE DAY.
BUT THERE ARE NO SUCH HEROES!
NO SINGLE PERSON IS GOING TO SWOOP IN AND SAVE US!!

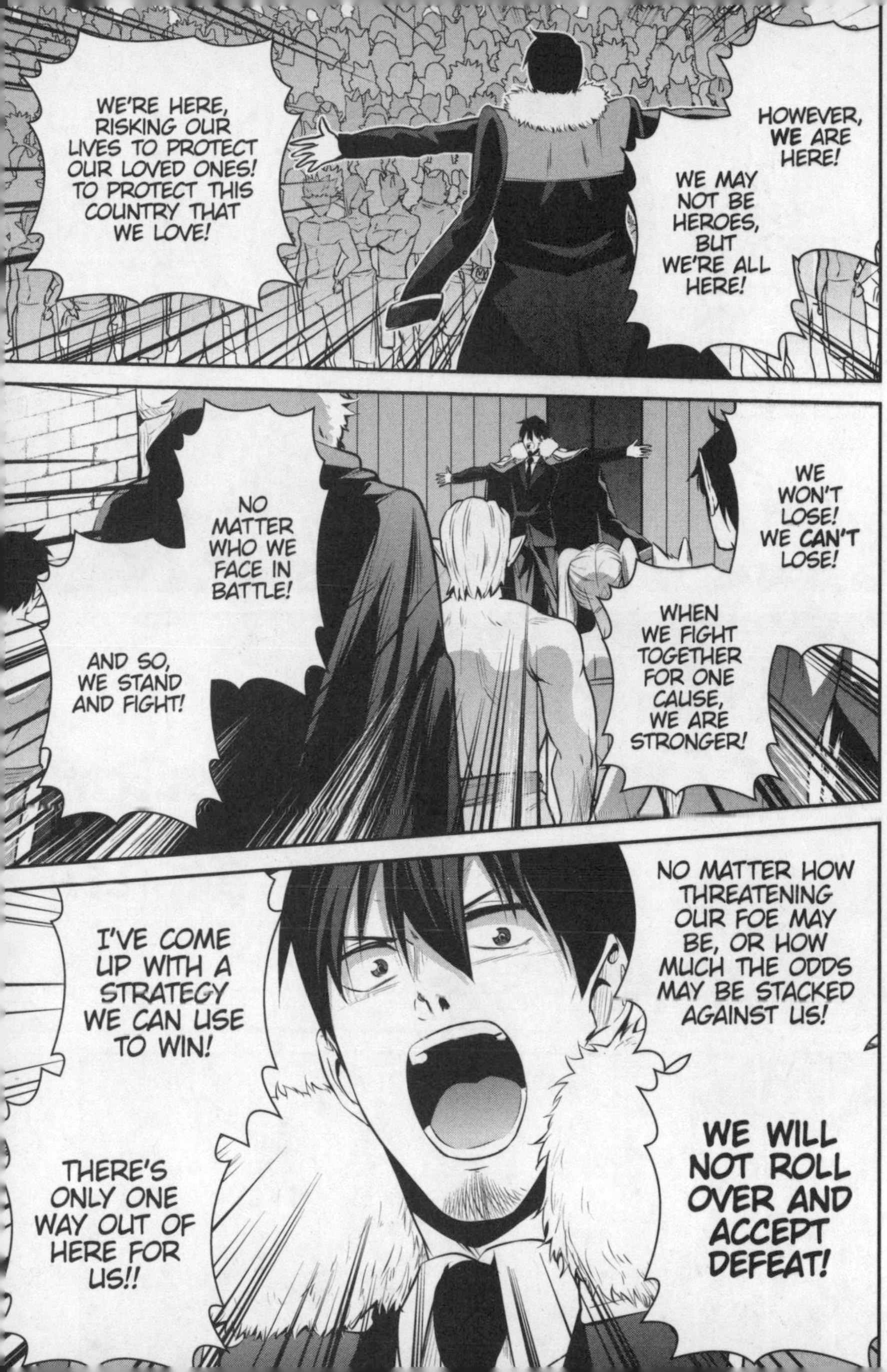
HOWEVER, WE ARE HERE!
WE MAY NOT BE HEROES, BUT WE'RE ALL HERE!
WE'RE HERE, RISKING OUR LIVES TO PROTECT OUR LOVED ONES! TO PROTECT THIS COUNTRY THAT WE LOVE!
WE WON'T LOSE! WE CAN'T LOSE!
NO MATTER WHO WE FACE IN BATTLE!
WHEN WE FIGHT TOGETHER FOR ONE CAUSE, WE ARE STRONGER!
AND SO, WE STAND AND FIGHT!
NO MATTER HOW THREATENING OUR FOE MAY BE, OR HOW MUCH THE ODDS MAY BE STACKED AGAINST US!
I'VE COME UP WITH A STRATEGY WE CAN USE TO WIN!
WE WILL NOT ROLL OVER AND ACCEPT DEFEAT!
THERE'S ONLY ONE WAY OUT OF HERE FOR US!!

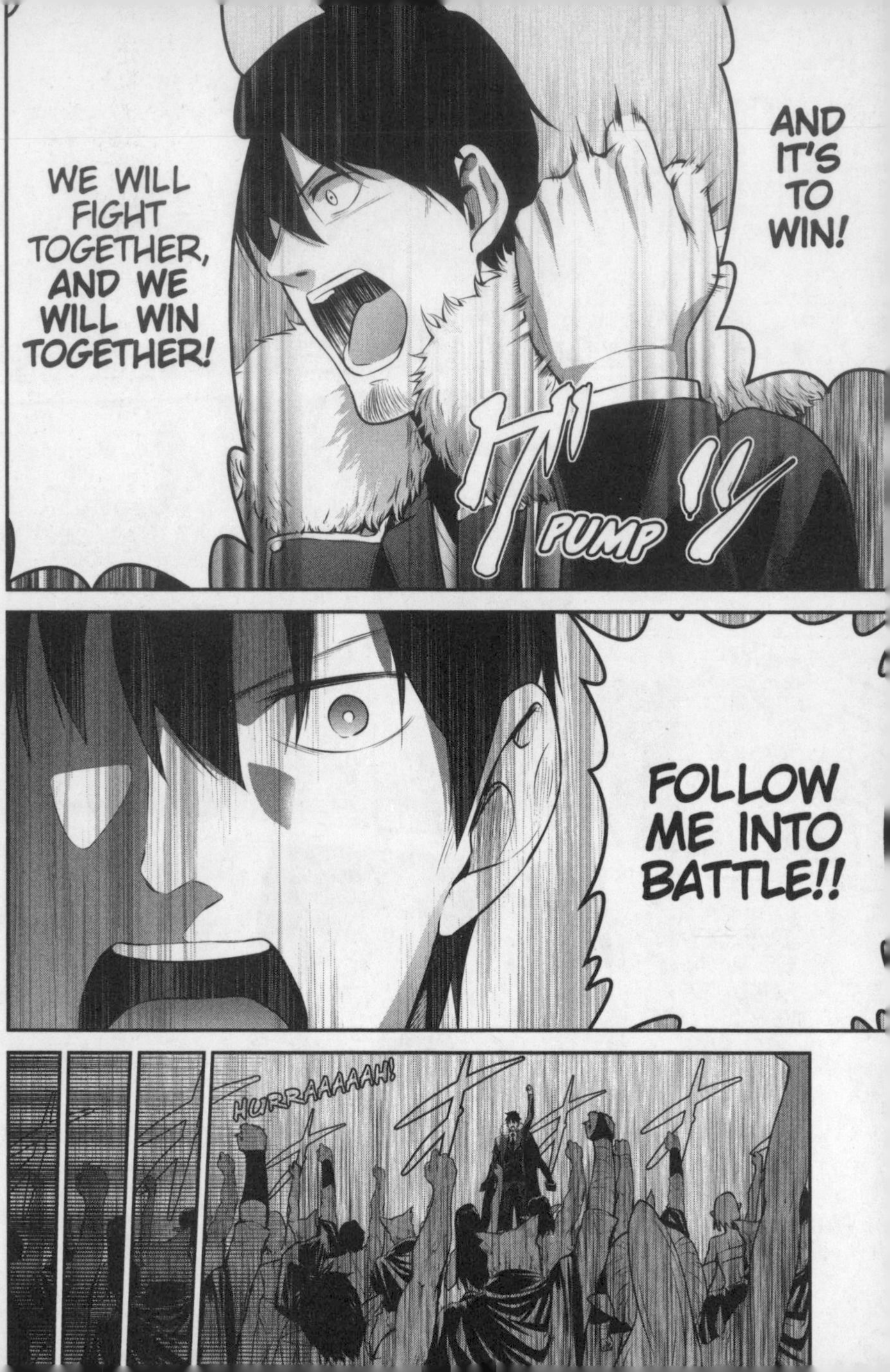
AND IT'S TO WIN!
WE WILL FIGHT TOGETHER, AND WE WILL WIN TOGETHER!
PUMP
FOLLOW ME INTO BATTLE!!
HURRAAAAAH!

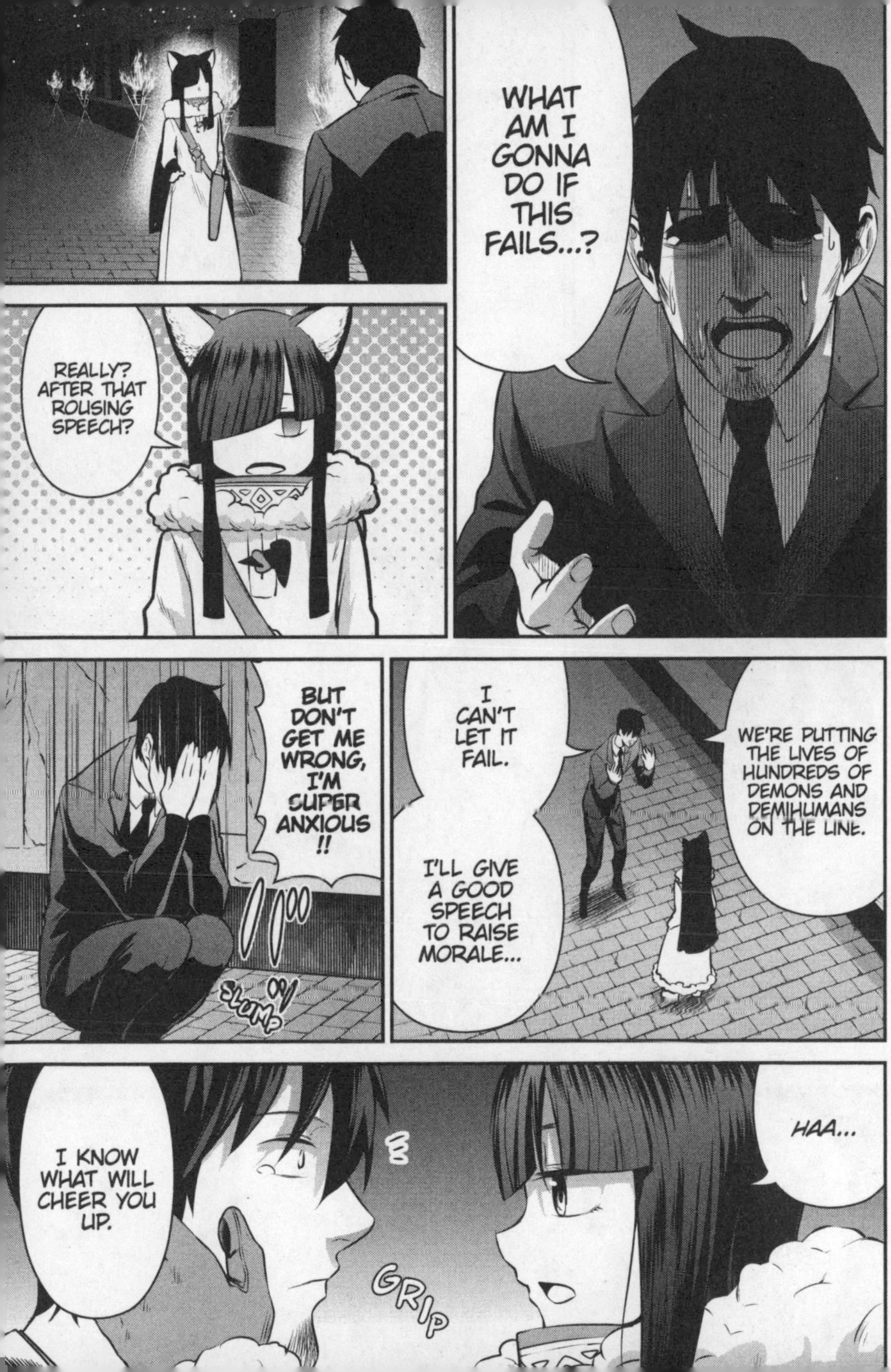
WHAT AM I GONNA DO IF THIS FAILS...?
REALLY? AFTER THAT ROUSING SPEECH?
WE'RE PUTTING THE LIVES OF HUNDREDS OF DEMONS AND DEMIHUMANS ON THE LINE.
I CAN'T LET IT FAIL.
I'LL GIVE A GOOD SPEECH TO RAISE MORALE...
BUT DON'T GET ME WRONG, I'M SUPER ANXIOUS!!
SLUMP
HAA...
GRIP
I KNOW WHAT WILL CHEER YOU UP.

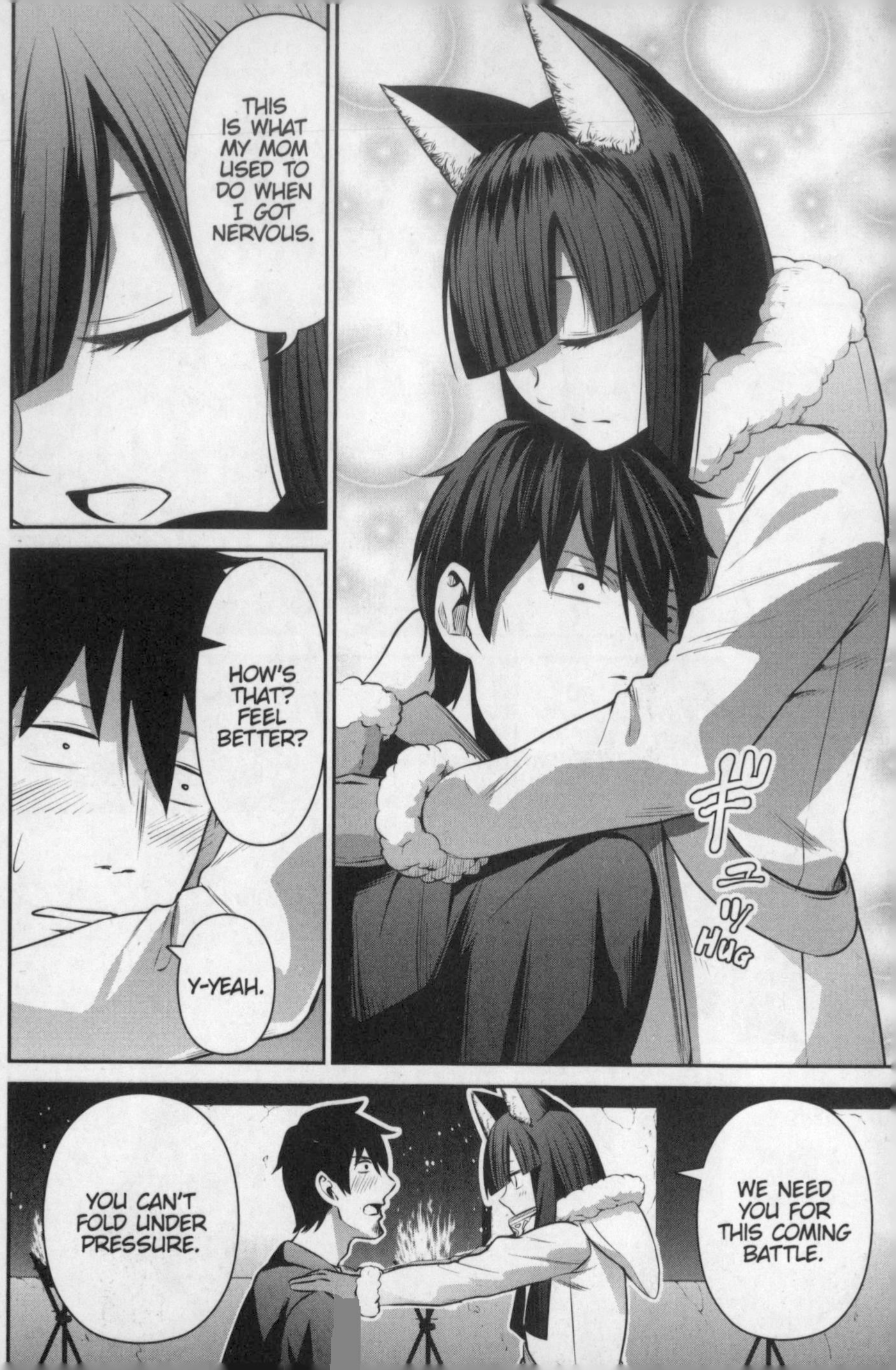

ギュッ
Hug
THIS IS WHAT MY MOM USED TO DO WHEN I GOT NERVOUS.
HOW'S THAT? FEEL BETTER?
Y-YEAH.
WE NEED YOU FOR THIS COMING BATTLE.
YOU CAN'T FOLD UNDER PRESSURE.

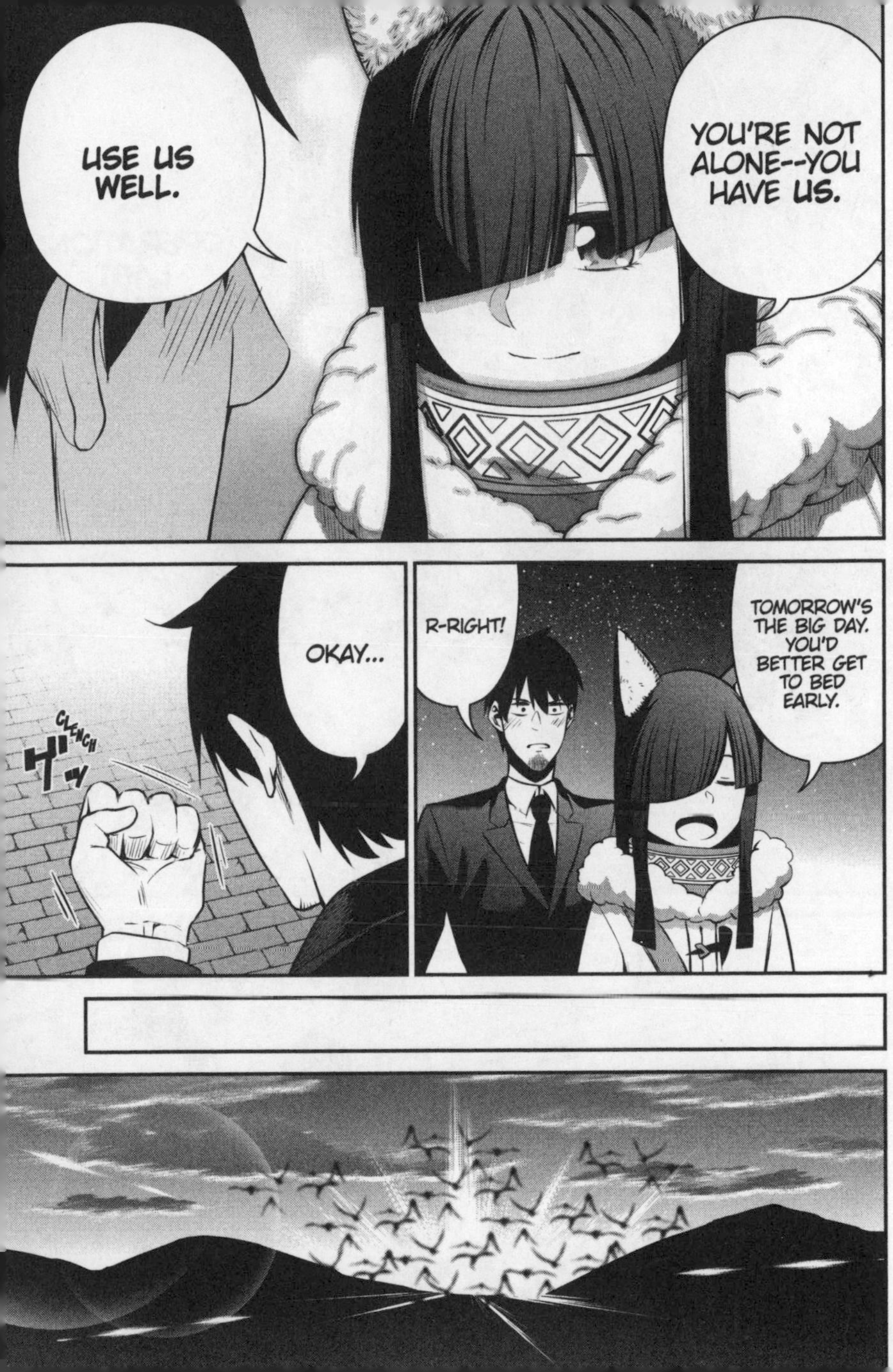
YOU'RE NOT ALONE--YOU HAVE US.
USE US WELL.
TOMORROW'S THE BIG DAY. YOU'D BETTER GET TO BED EARLY.
R-RIGHT!
OKAY...
CLENCH

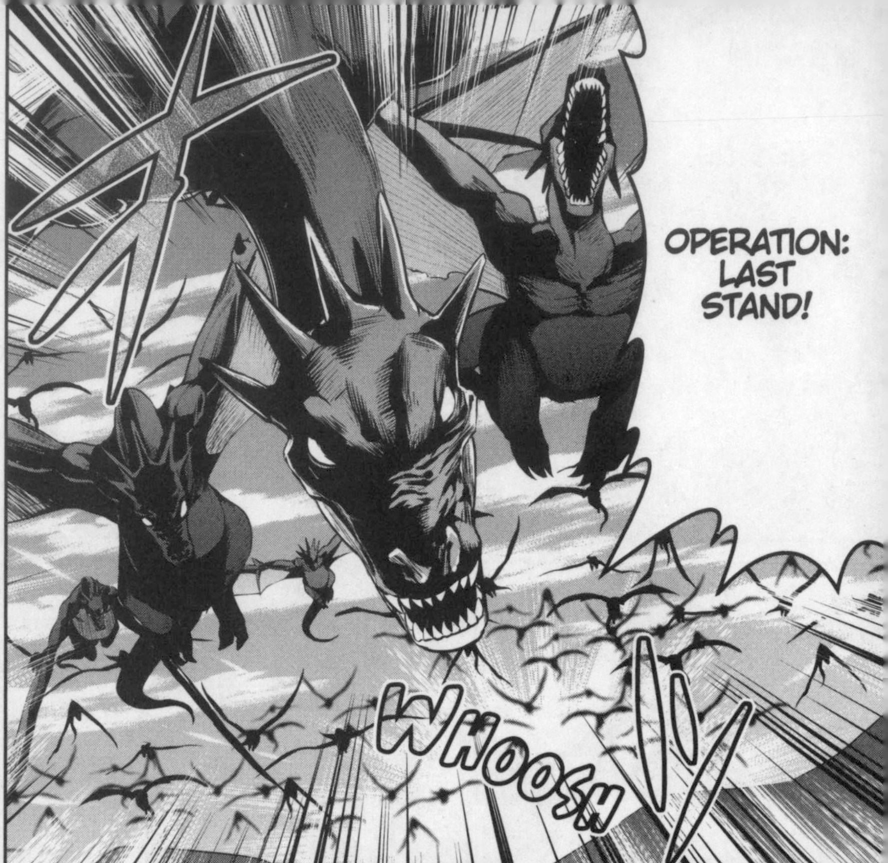
OPERATION: LAST STAND!
WHOOSH
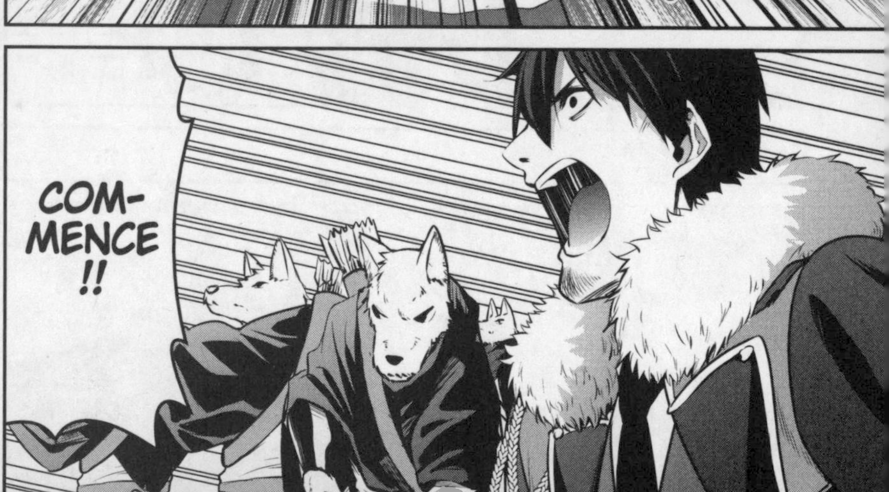
COM-MENCE!!

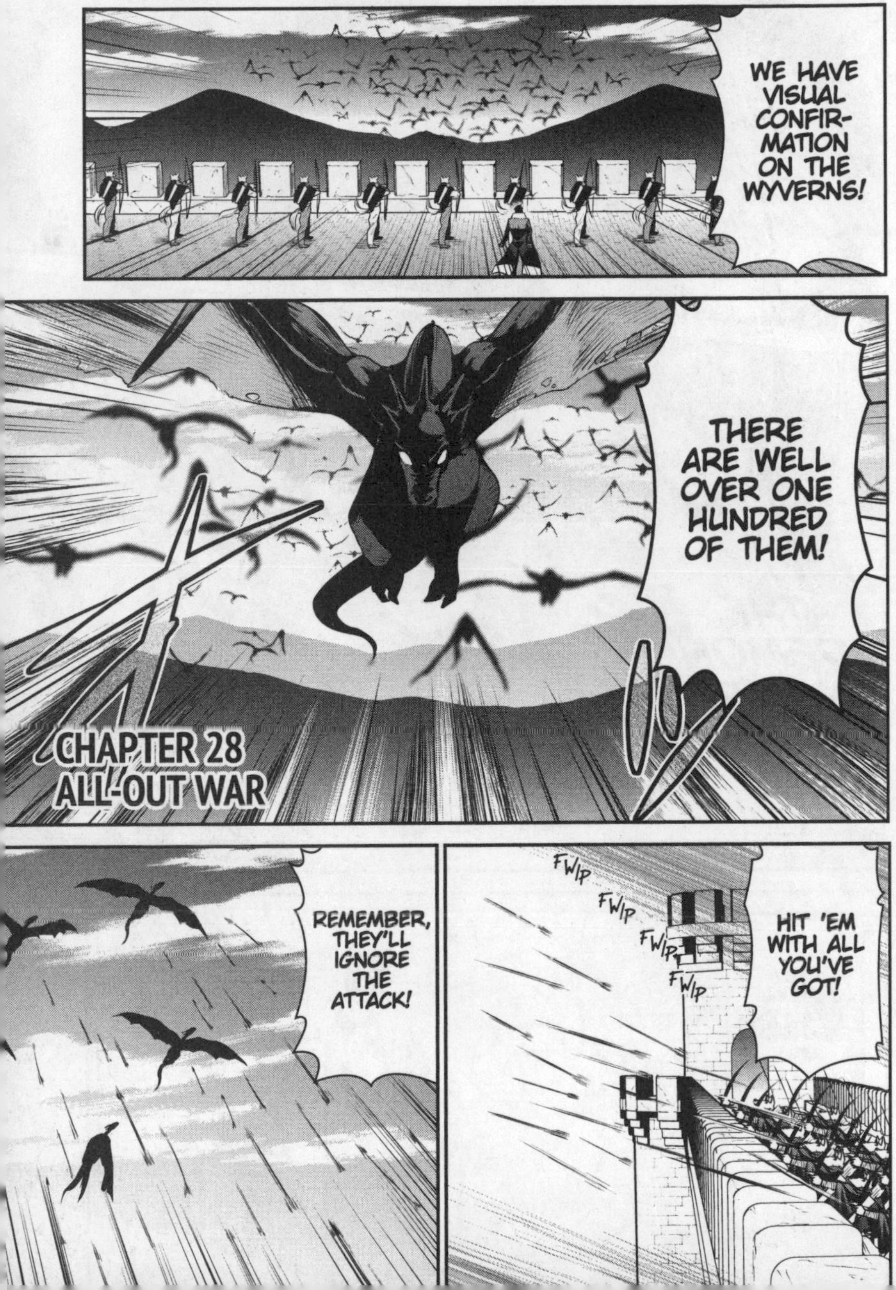
WE HAVE VISUAL CONFIR-MATION ON THE WYVERNS!
THERE ARE WELL OVER ONE HUNDRED OF THEM!
CHAPTER 28 ALL-OUT WAR
HIT 'EM WITH ALL YOU'VE GOT!
FWIP
FWIP
FWIP
FWIP
REMEMBER, THEY'LL IGNORE THE ATTACK!

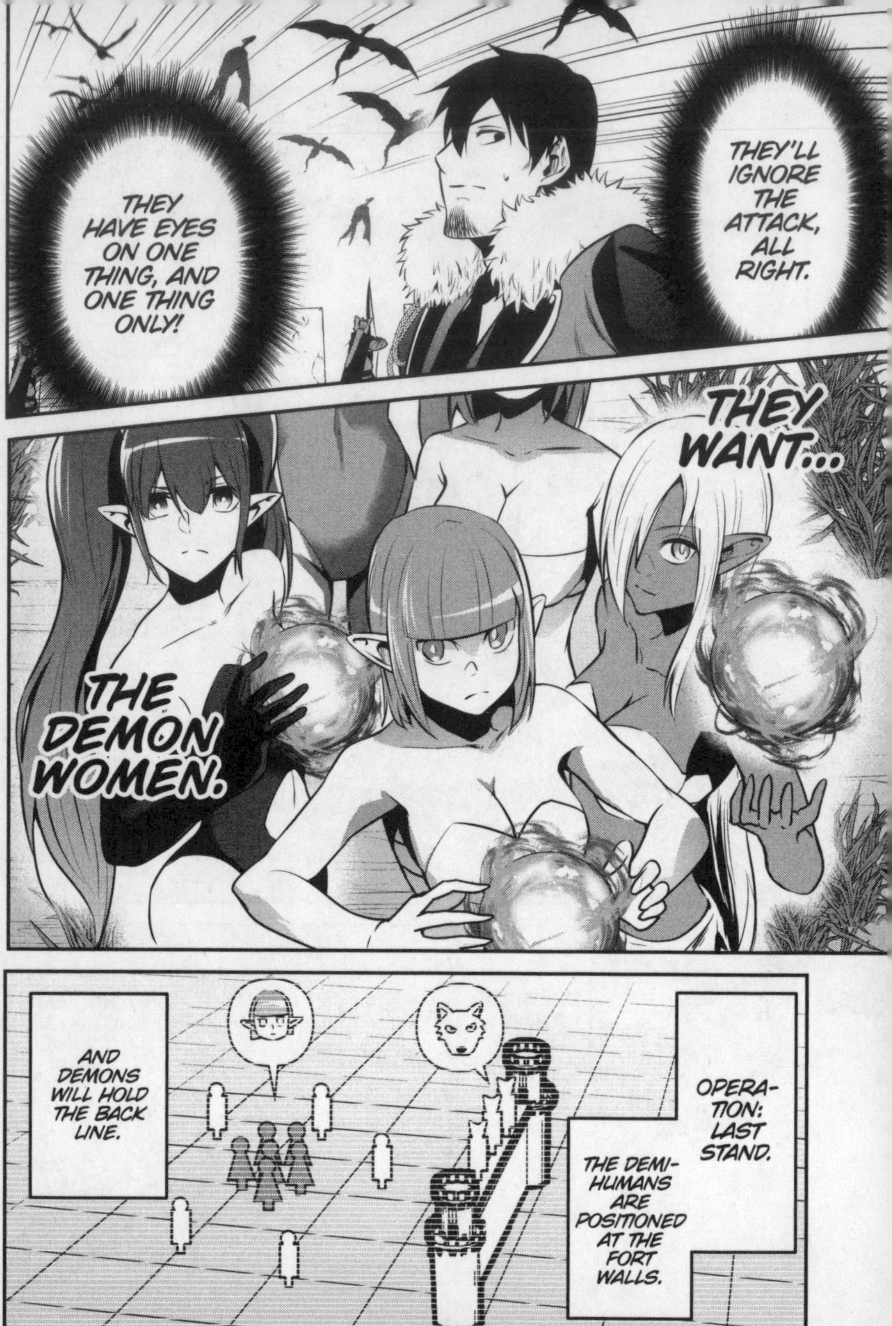
THEY'LL IGNORE THE ATTACK, ALL RIGHT.
THEY HAVE EYES ON ONE THING, AND ONE THING ONLY!
THEY WANT...
THE DEMON WOMEN.
OPERATION: LAST STAND.
THE DEMI-HUMANS ARE POSITIONED AT THE FORT WALLS.
AND DEMONS WILL HOLD THE BACK LINE.

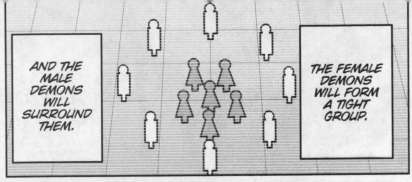

AND THE MALE DEMONS WILL SURROUND THEM.

THE FEMALE DEMONS WILL FORM A TIGHT GROUP.

WHEN THE WYVERNS MAKE THEIR MOVE ON THE FEMALE DEMONS...

WE'LL HIT THEM WITH EVERYTHING WE'VE GOT.

APTER THAT...

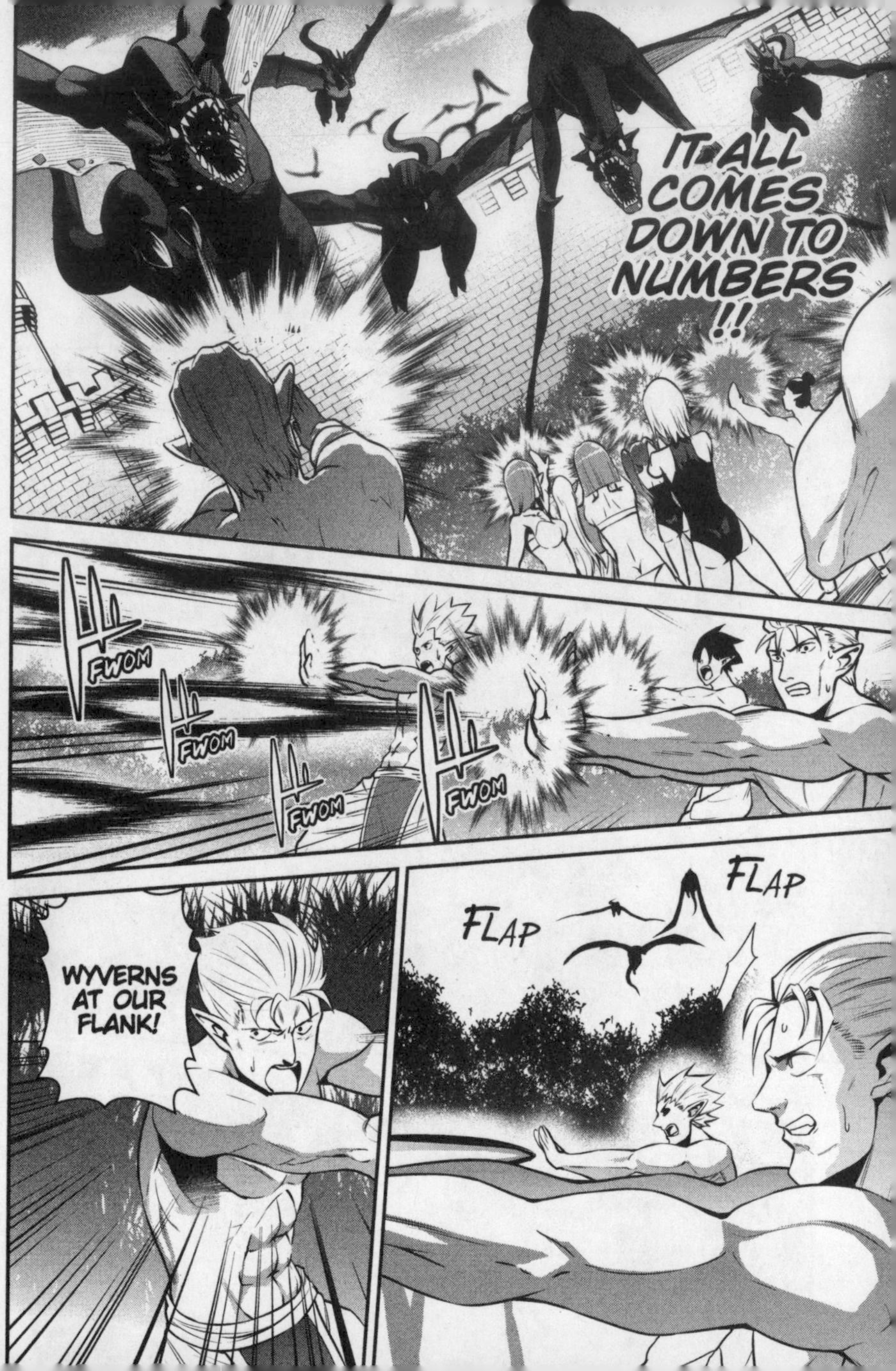
IT ALL COMES DOWN TO NUMBERS!!
FWOM
FWOM
FWOM
FWOM
FLAP
FLAP
WYVERNS AT OUR FLANK!

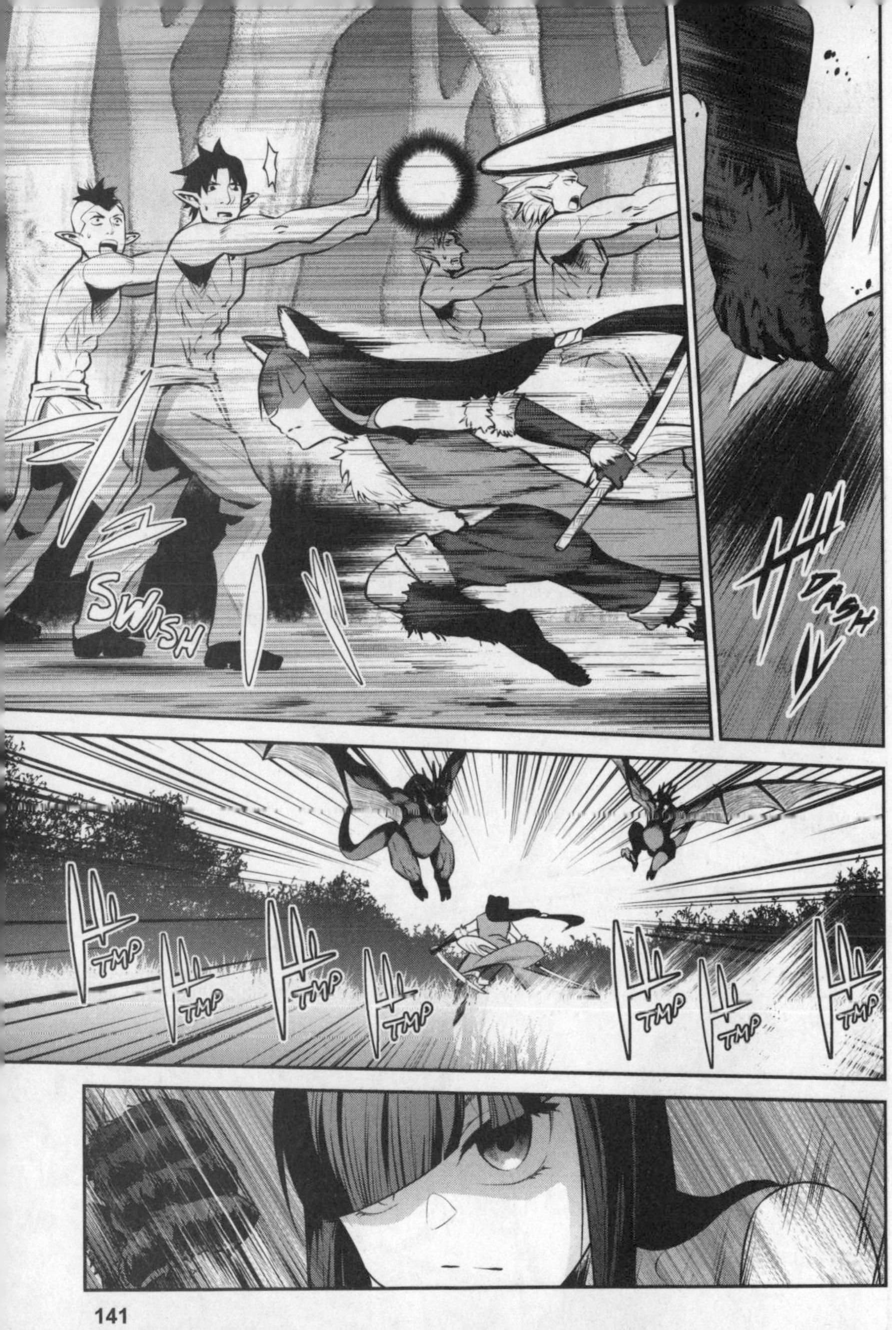
DASH
SWISH
TMP
TMP
TMP
TMP
TMP
TMP
TMP

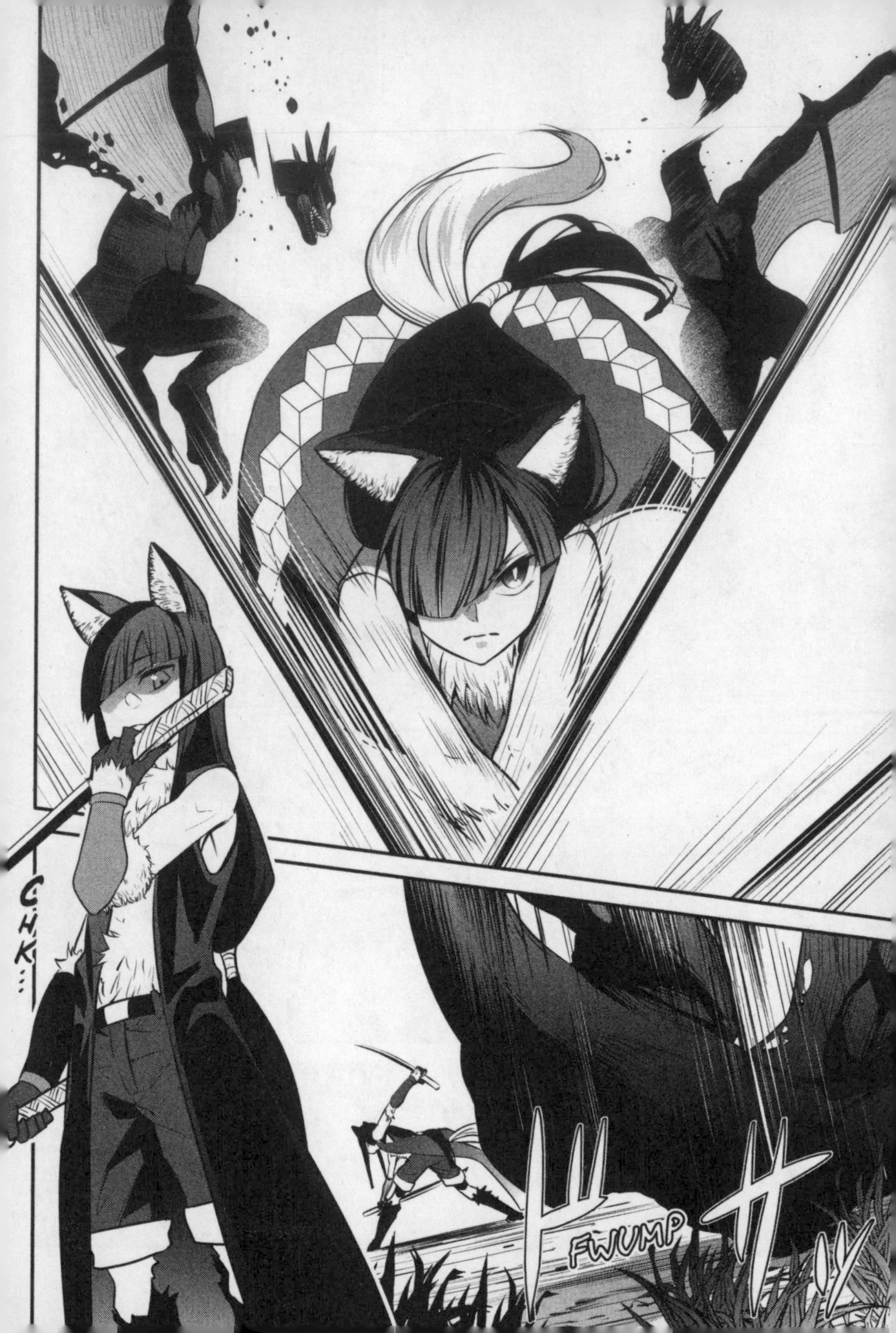
FWUMP
CHK...

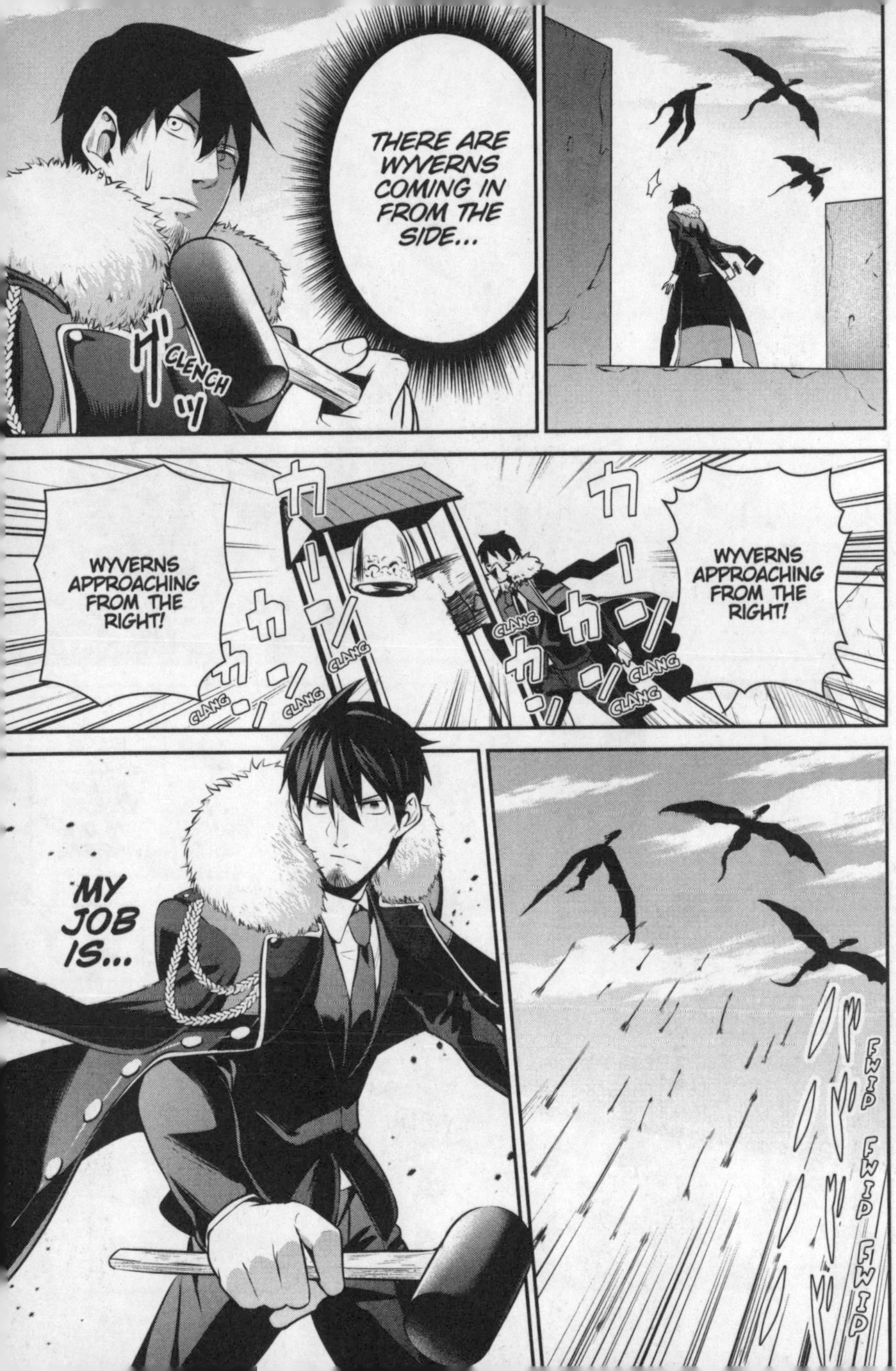
THERE ARE WYVERNS COMING IN FROM THE SIDE...
CLENCH
WYVERNS APPROACHING FROM THE RIGHT!
WYVERNS APPROACHING FROM THE RIGHT!
CLANG
CLANG
CLANG
CLANG
CLANG
CLANG
FWIP FWIP FWIP
MY JOB IS...

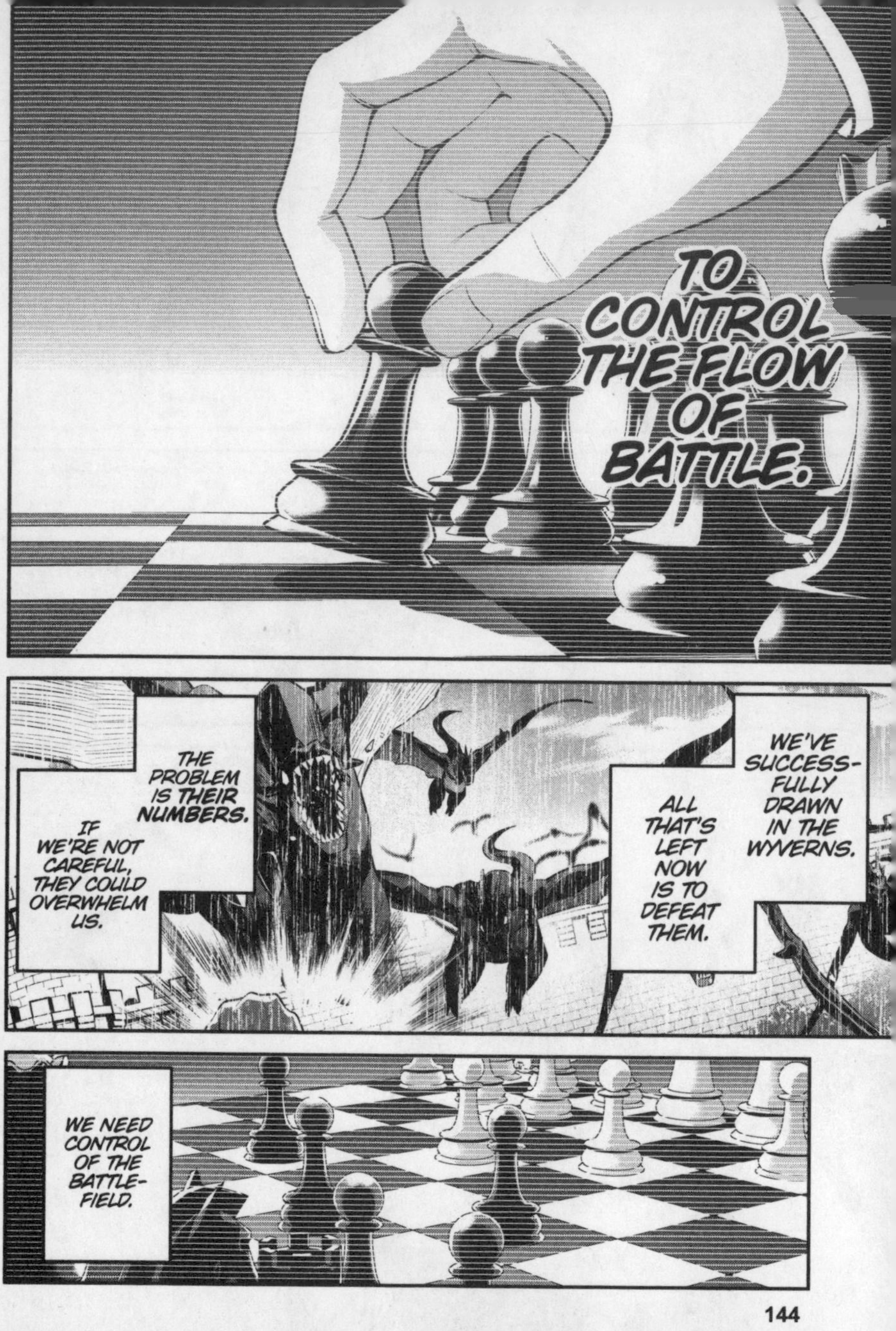
TO CONTROL THE FLOW OF BATTLE.
WE'VE SUCCESSFULLY DRAWN IN THE WYVERNS.
ALL THAT'S LEFT NOW IS TO DEFEAT THEM.
THE PROBLEM IS THEIR NUMBERS.
IF WE'RE NOT CAREFUL, THEY COULD OVERWHELM US.
WE NEED CONTROL OF THE BATTLEFIELD.

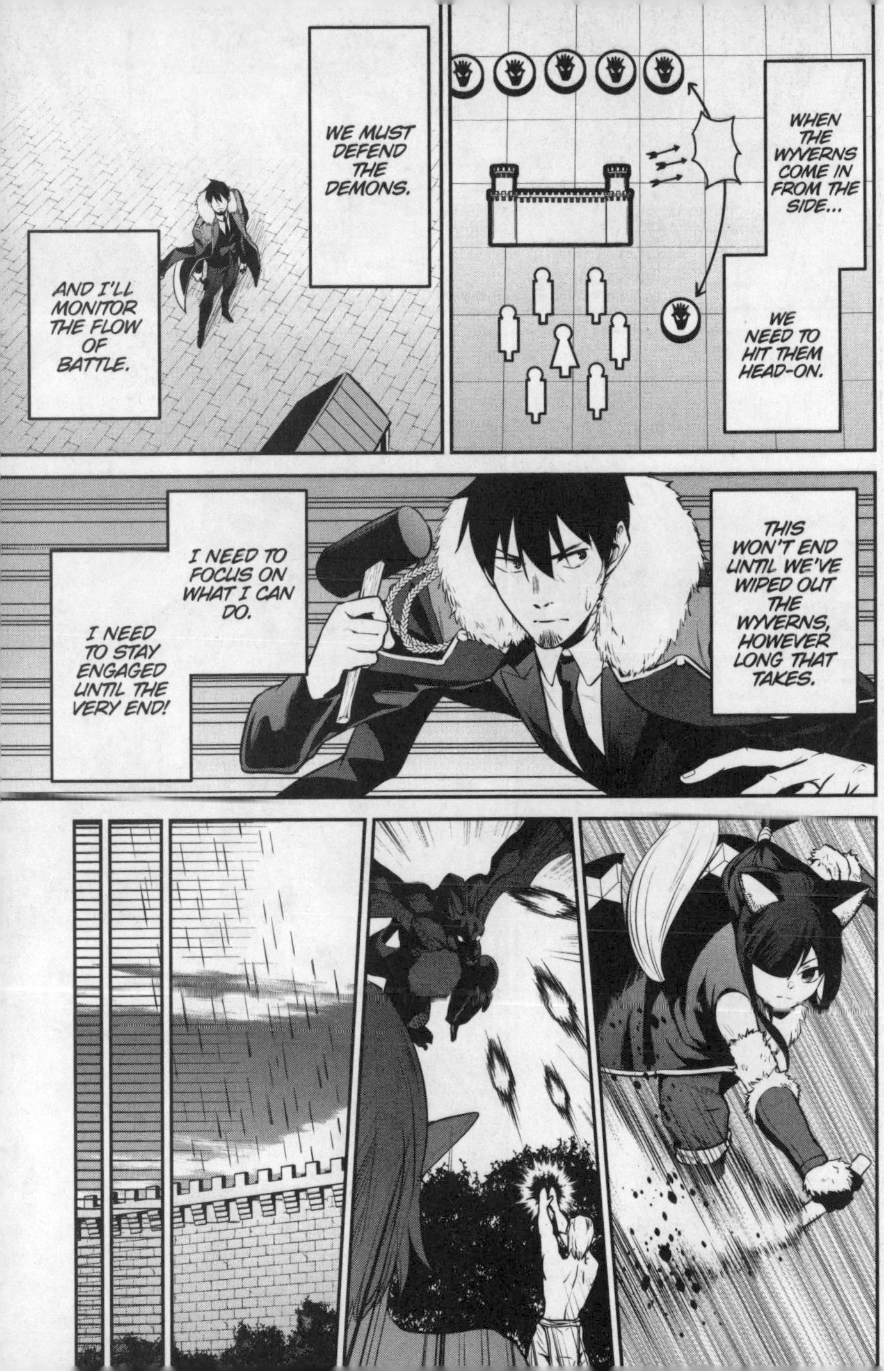
WHEN THE WYVERNS COME IN FROM THE SIDE...
WE NEED TO HIT THEM HEAD-ON.
WE MUST DEFEND THE DEMONS.
AND I'LL MONITOR THE FLOW OF BATTLE.
THIS WON'T END UNTIL WE'VE WIPED OUT THE WYVERNS, HOWEVER LONG THAT TAKES.
I NEED TO FOCUS ON WHAT I CAN DO.
I NEED TO STAY ENGAGED UNTIL THE VERY END!

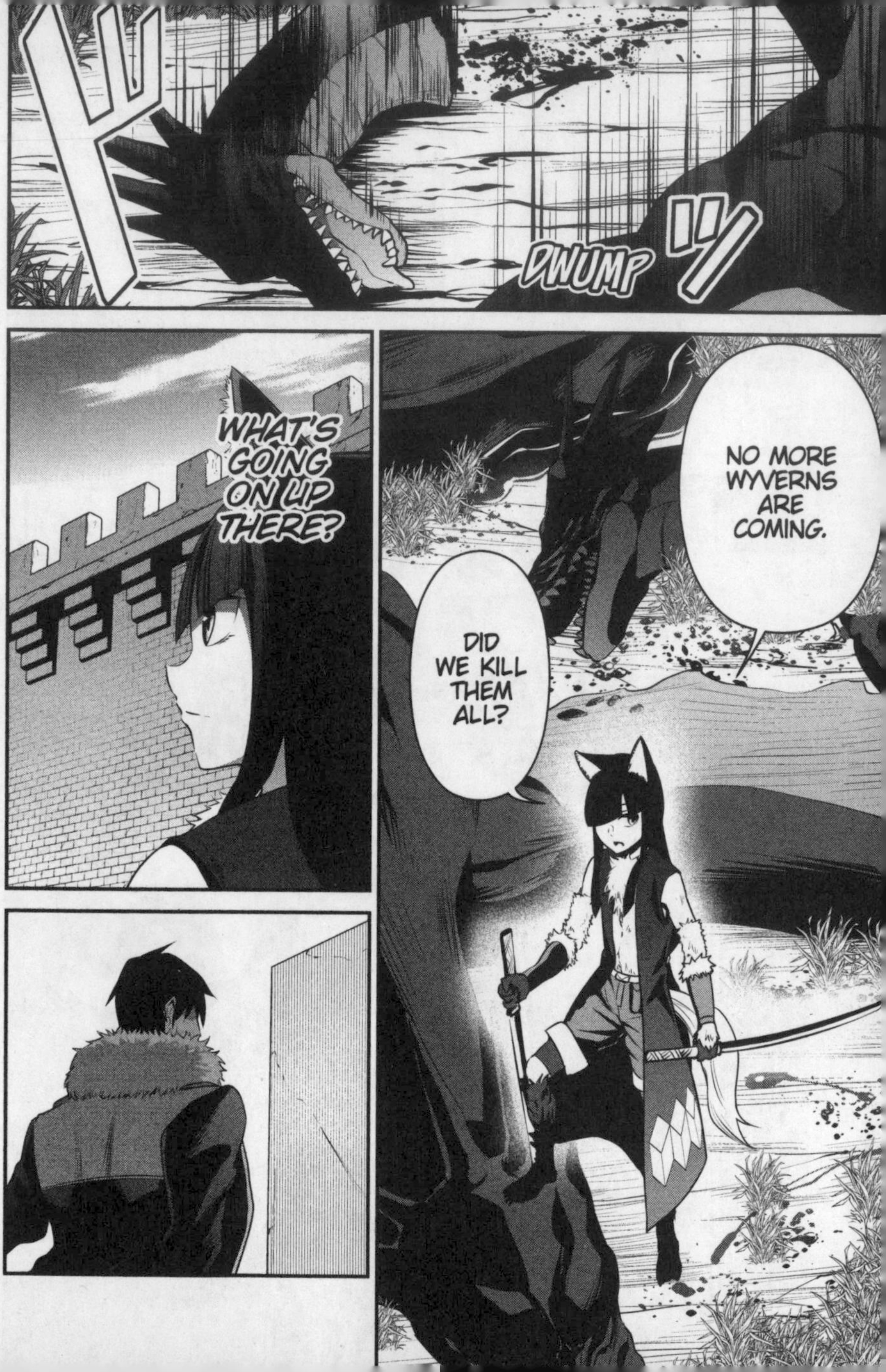
DWUMP
NO MORE WYVERNS ARE COMING.
DID WE KILL THEM ALL?
WHAT'S GOING ON UP THERE?

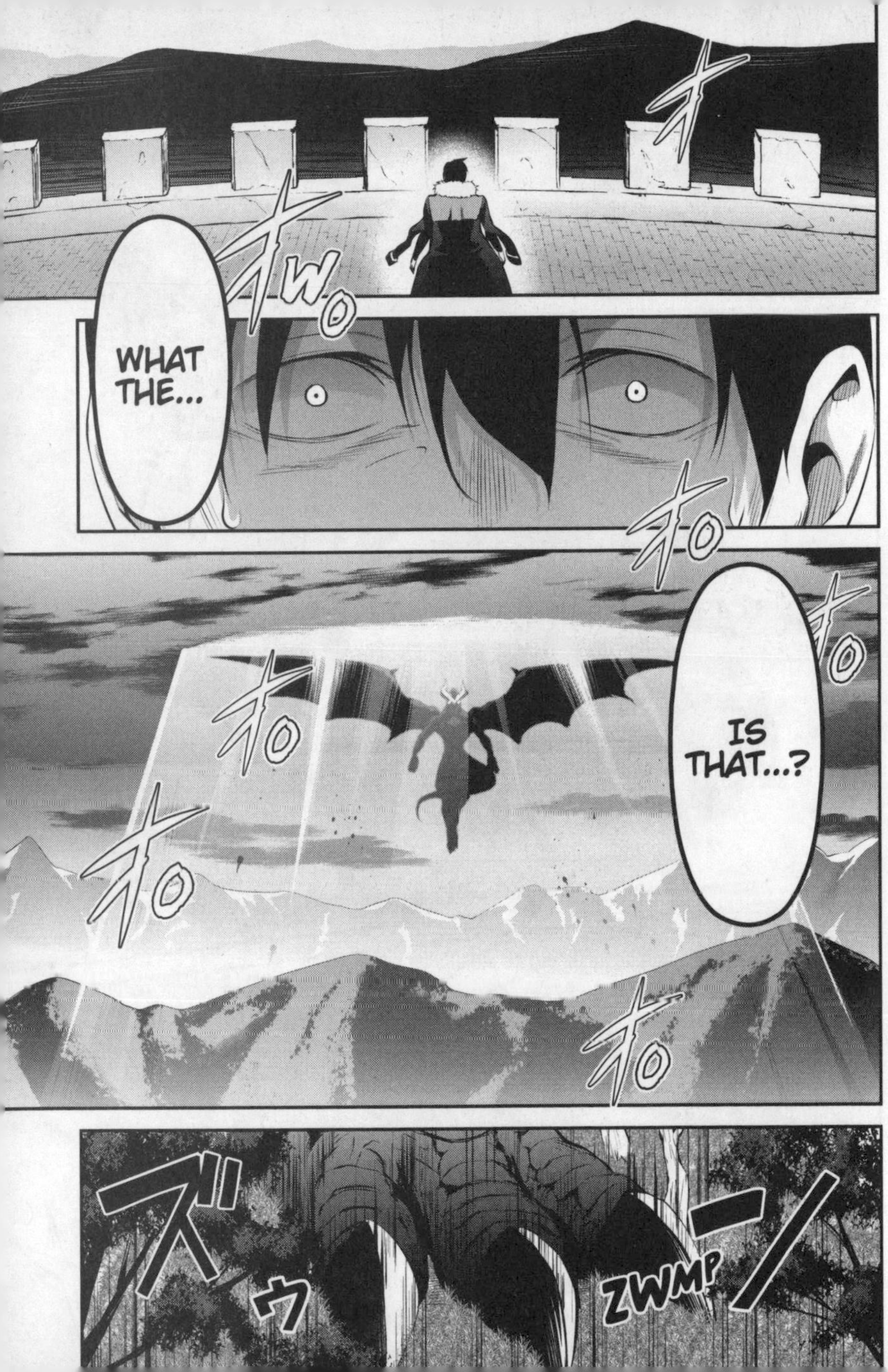
Wo
WHAT THE...
IS THAT...?
ZWMP

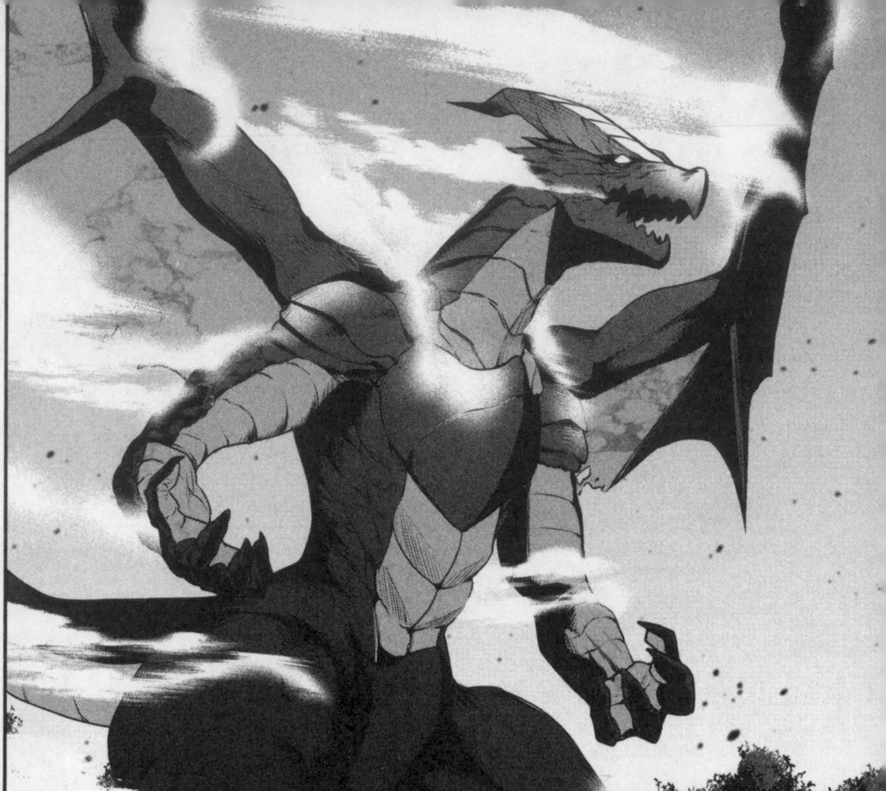

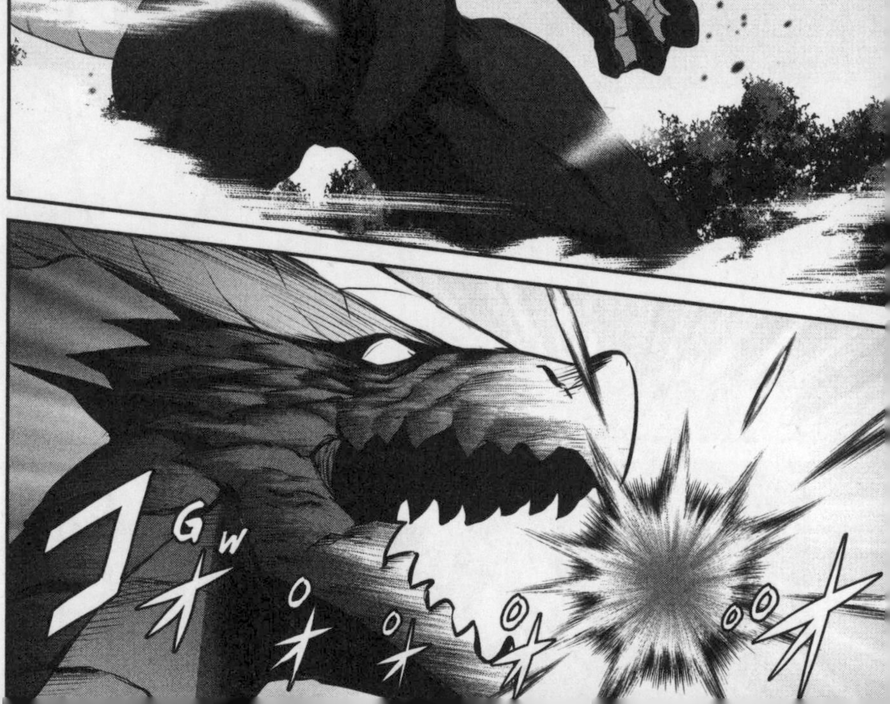
GWOOOOO

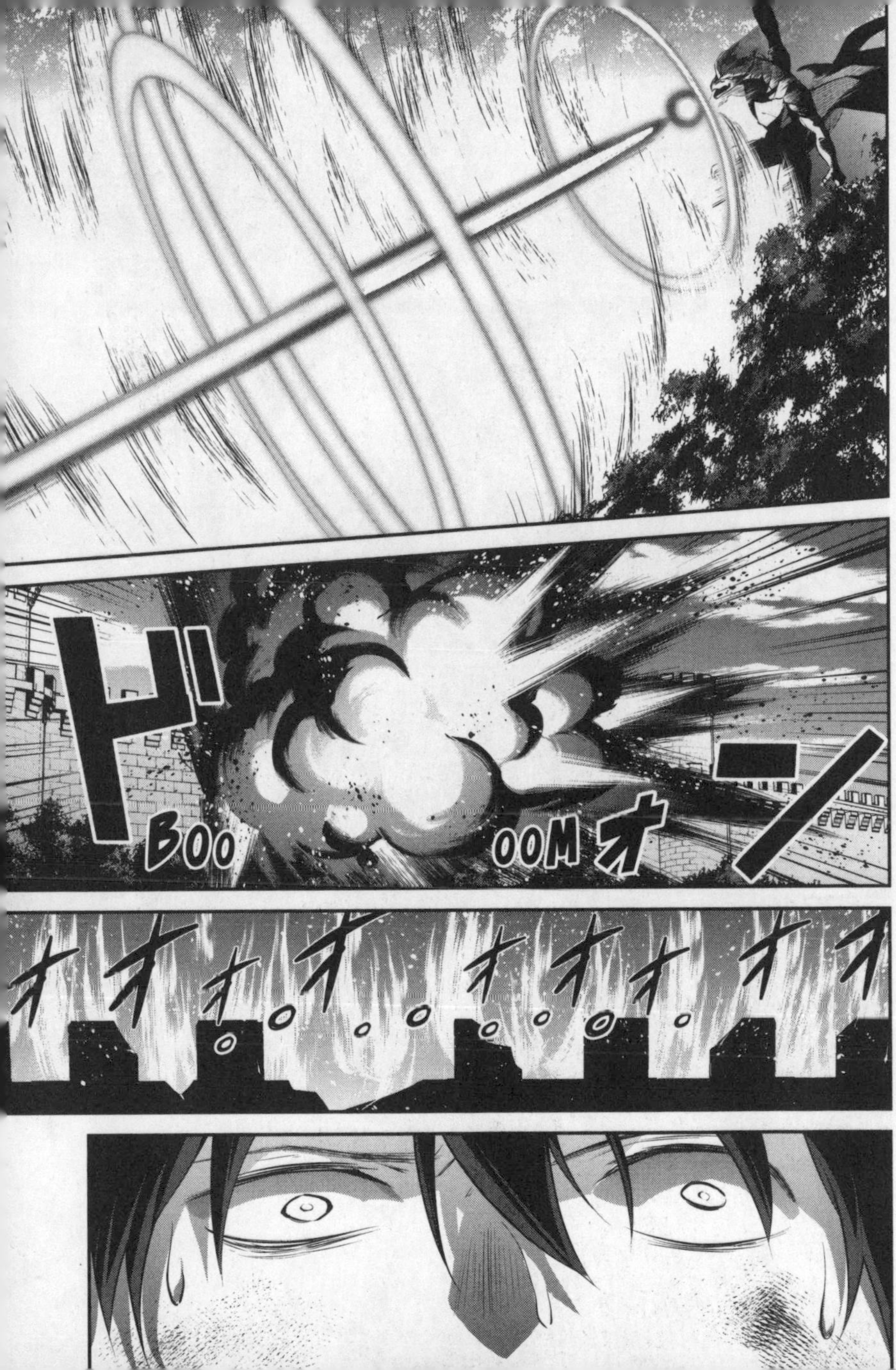
BOO
OOM

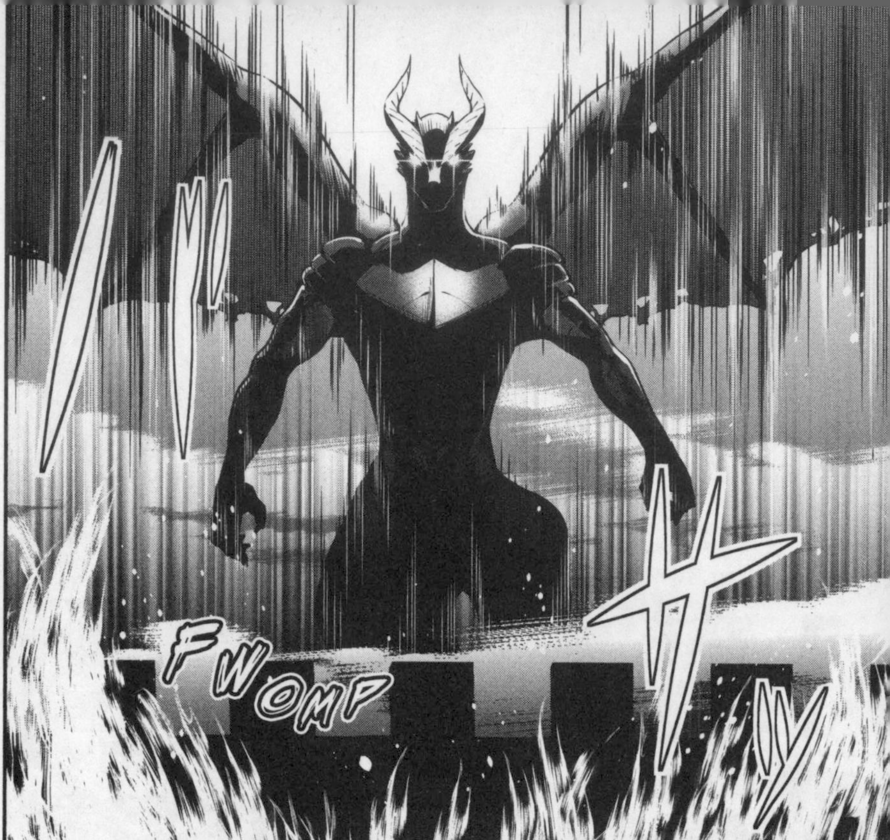
FWOMP

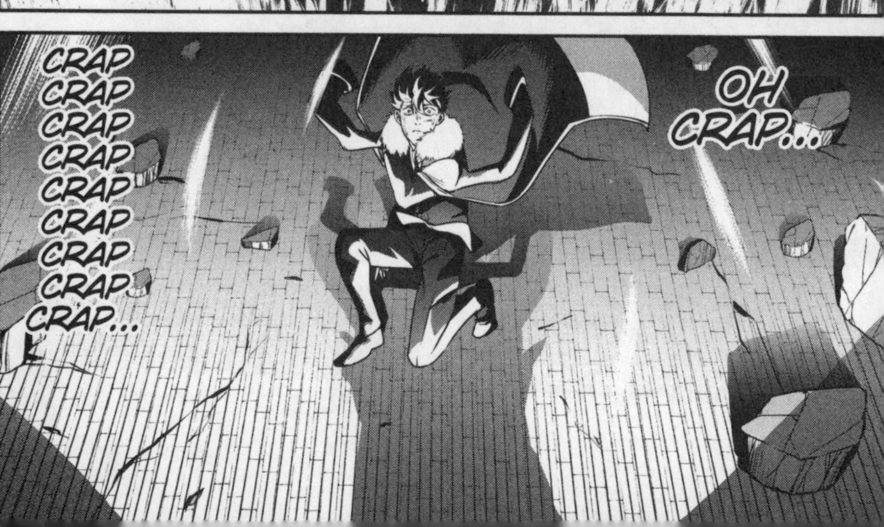
OH CRAP...
CRAP CRAP CRAP CRAP CRAP CRAP CRAP CRAP CRAP...

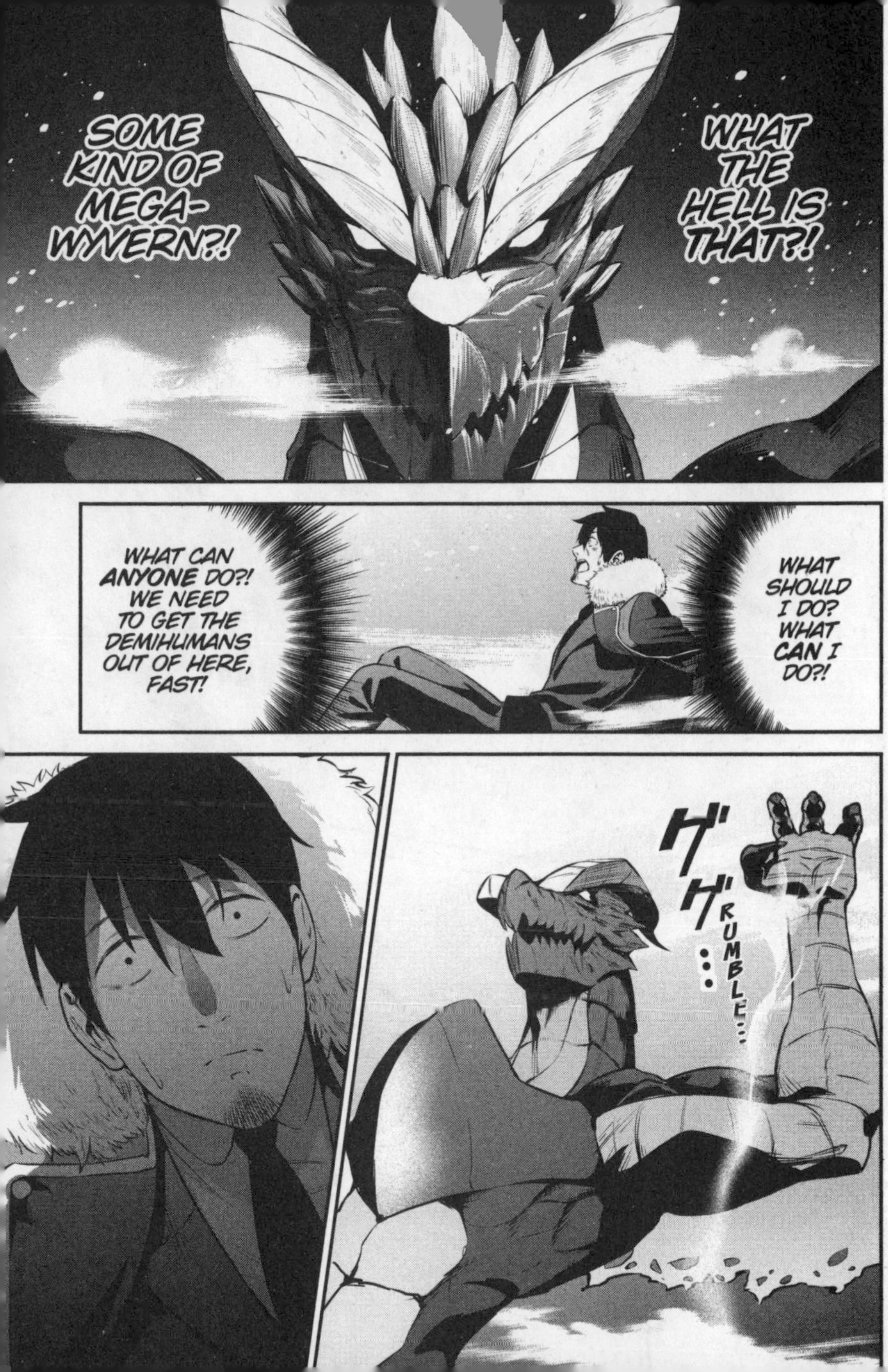
WHAT THE HELL IS THAT?!
SOME KIND OF MEGA-WYVERN?!
WHAT SHOULD I DO? WHAT CAN I DO?!
WHAT CAN ANYONE DO?! WE NEED TO GET THE DEMIHUMANS OUT OF HERE, FAST!
ゴゴ…
RUMBLE...

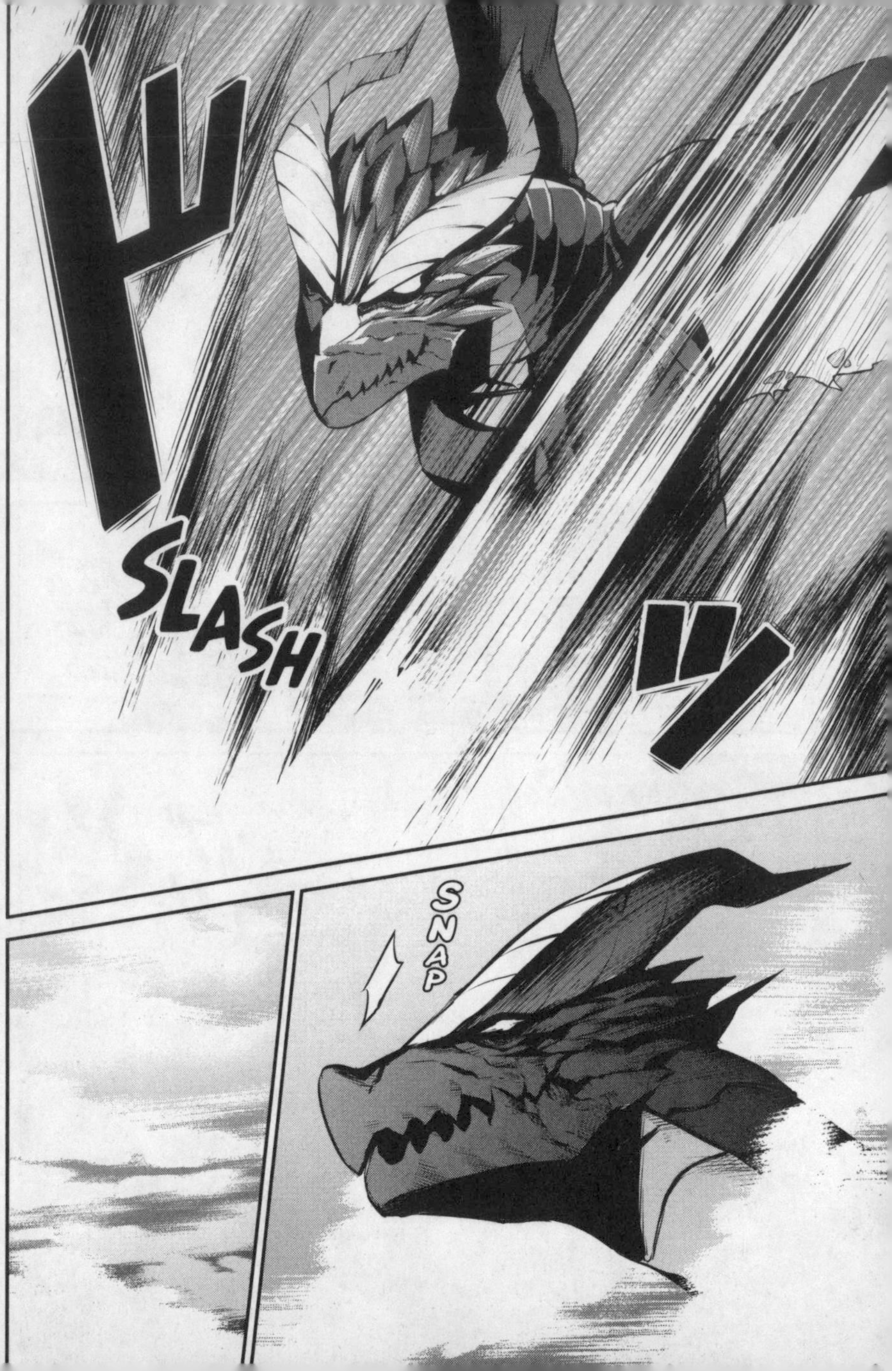
SLASH
SNAP

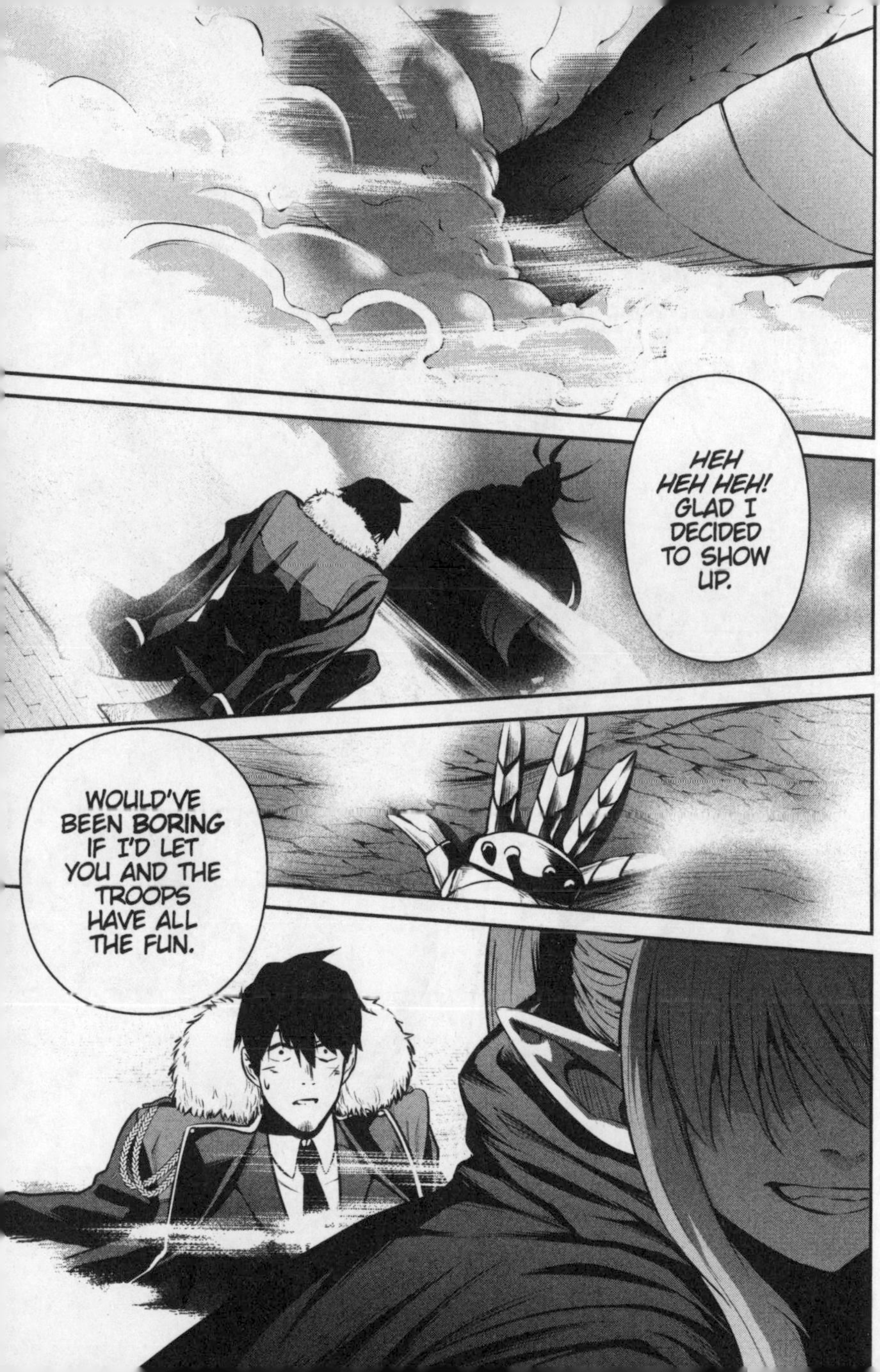
HEH HEH HEH! GLAD I DECIDED TO SHOW UP.
WOULD'VE BEEN BORING IF I'D LET YOU AND THE TROOPS HAVE ALL THE FUN.

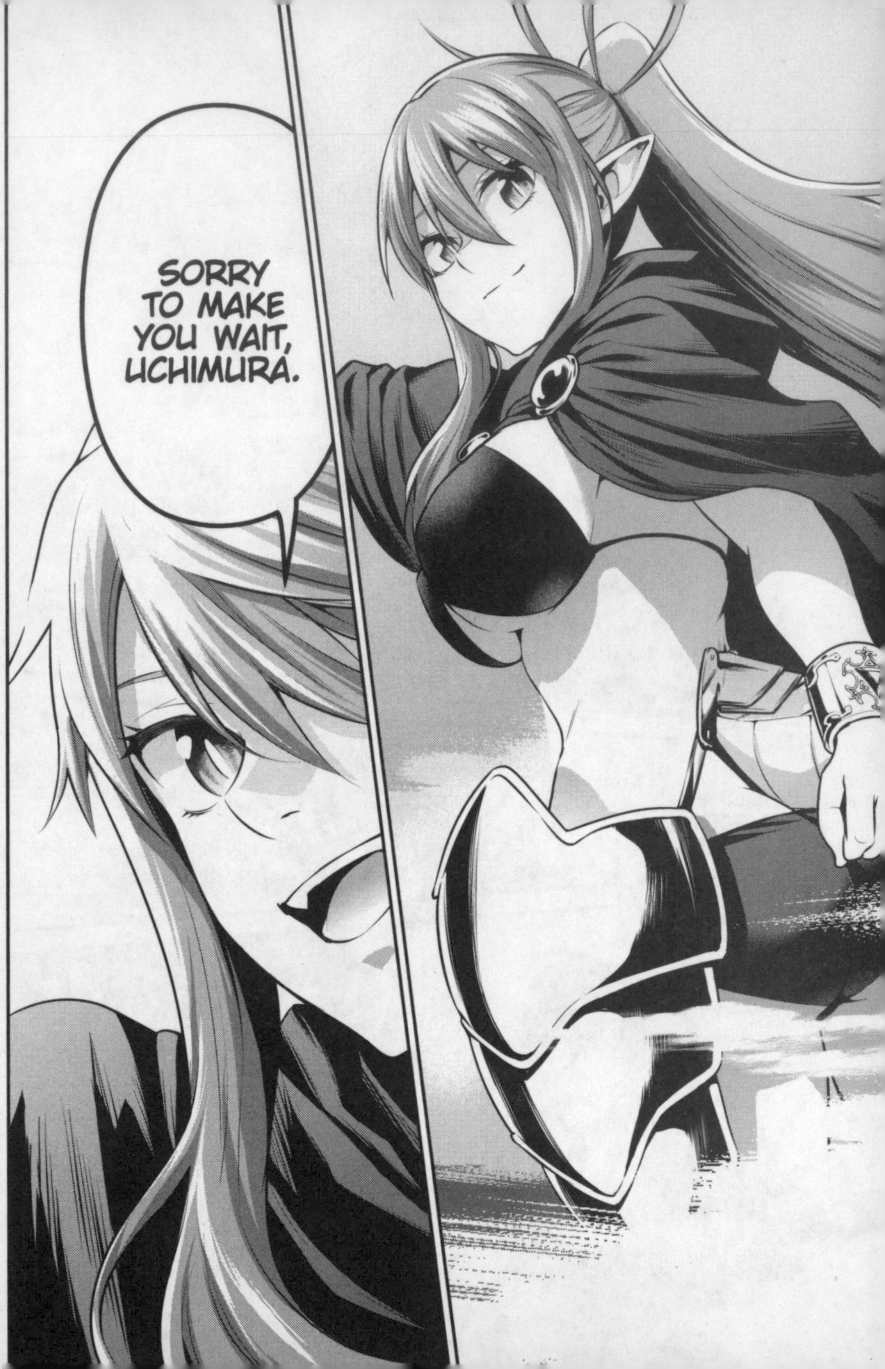
SORRY TO MAKE YOU WAIT, UCHIMURA.

HEAD HUNTED TO ANOTHER WORLD

FROM SALARYMAN TO BIG FOUR!

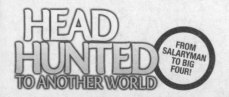

HEAD HUNTED TO ANOTHER WORLD

FROM SALARYMAN TO BIG FOUR!

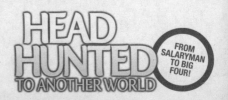

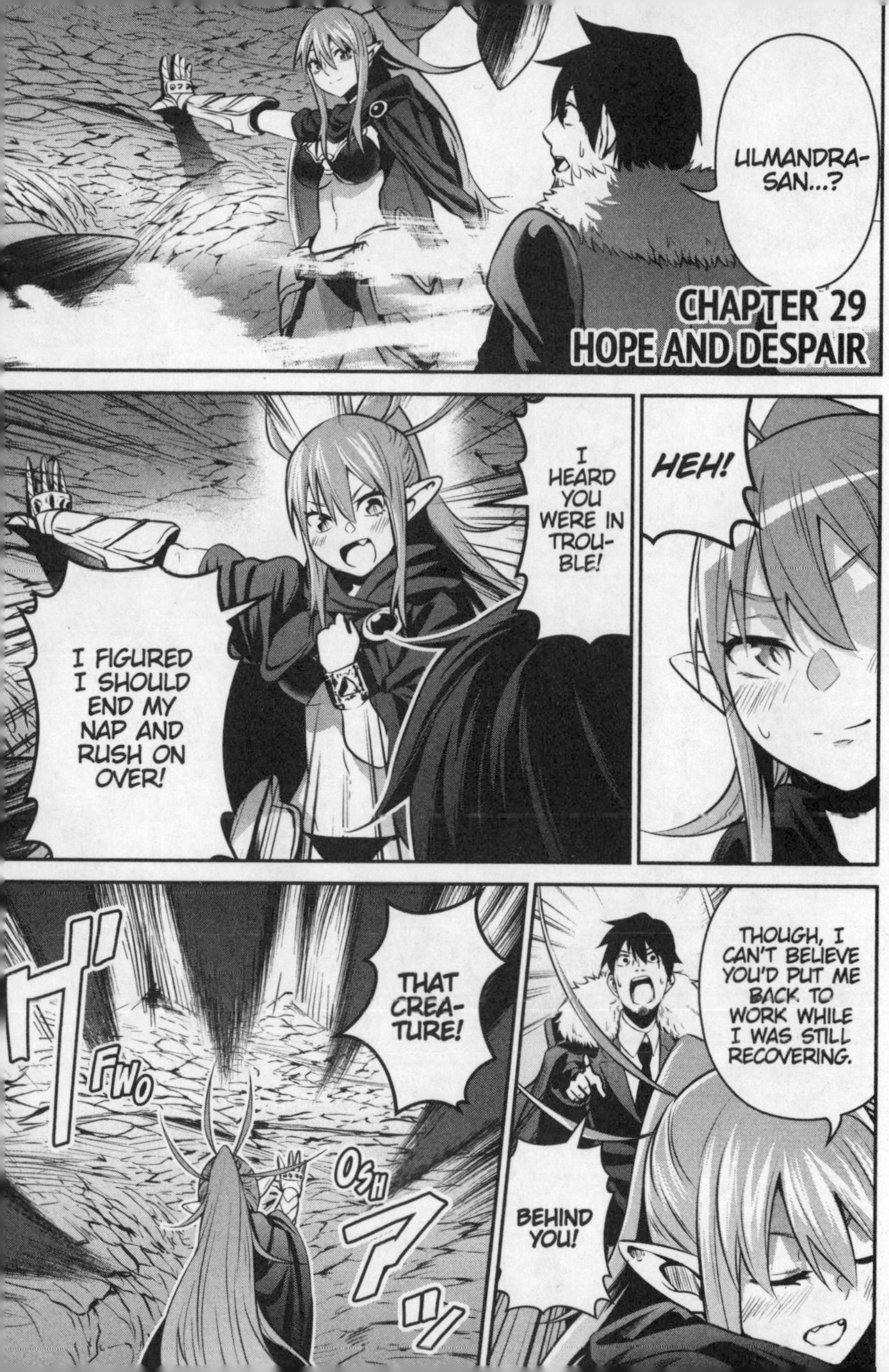
ULMANDRA-SAN...?
CHAPTER 29
HOPE AND DESPAIR
HEH!
I HEARD YOU WERE IN TROUBLE!
I FIGURED I SHOULD END MY NAP AND RUSH ON OVER!
THOUGH, I CAN'T BELIEVE YOU'D PUT ME BACK TO WORK WHILE I WAS STILL RECOVERING.
BEHIND YOU!
THAT CREATURE!
FWO
OSH

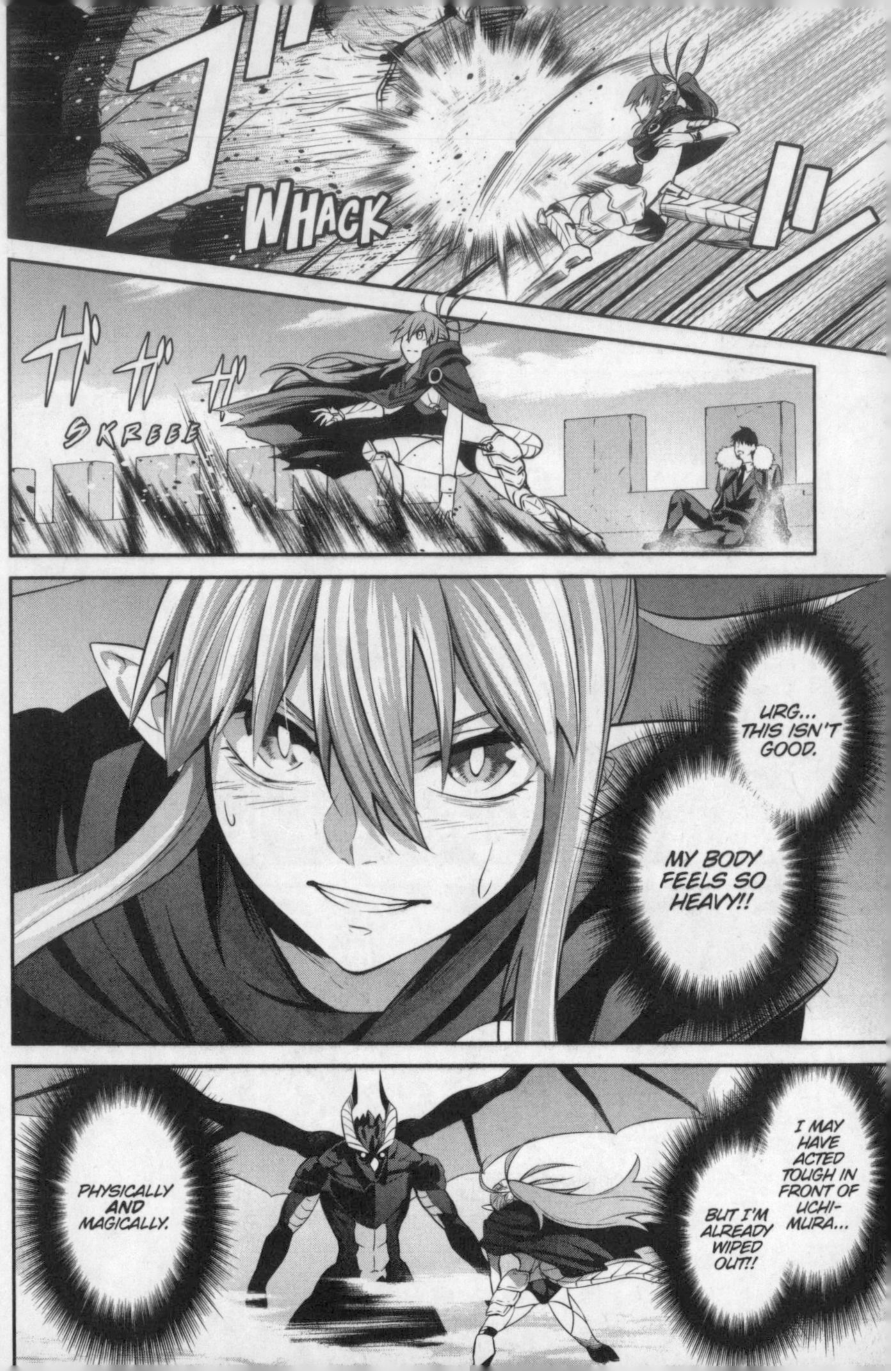
WHACK
SKREEEE
URG... THIS ISN'T GOOD.
MY BODY FEELS SO HEAVY!!
I MAY HAVE ACTED TOUGH IN FRONT OF UCHI-MURA...
BUT I'M ALREADY WIPED OUT!!
PHYSICALLY AND MAGICALLY.

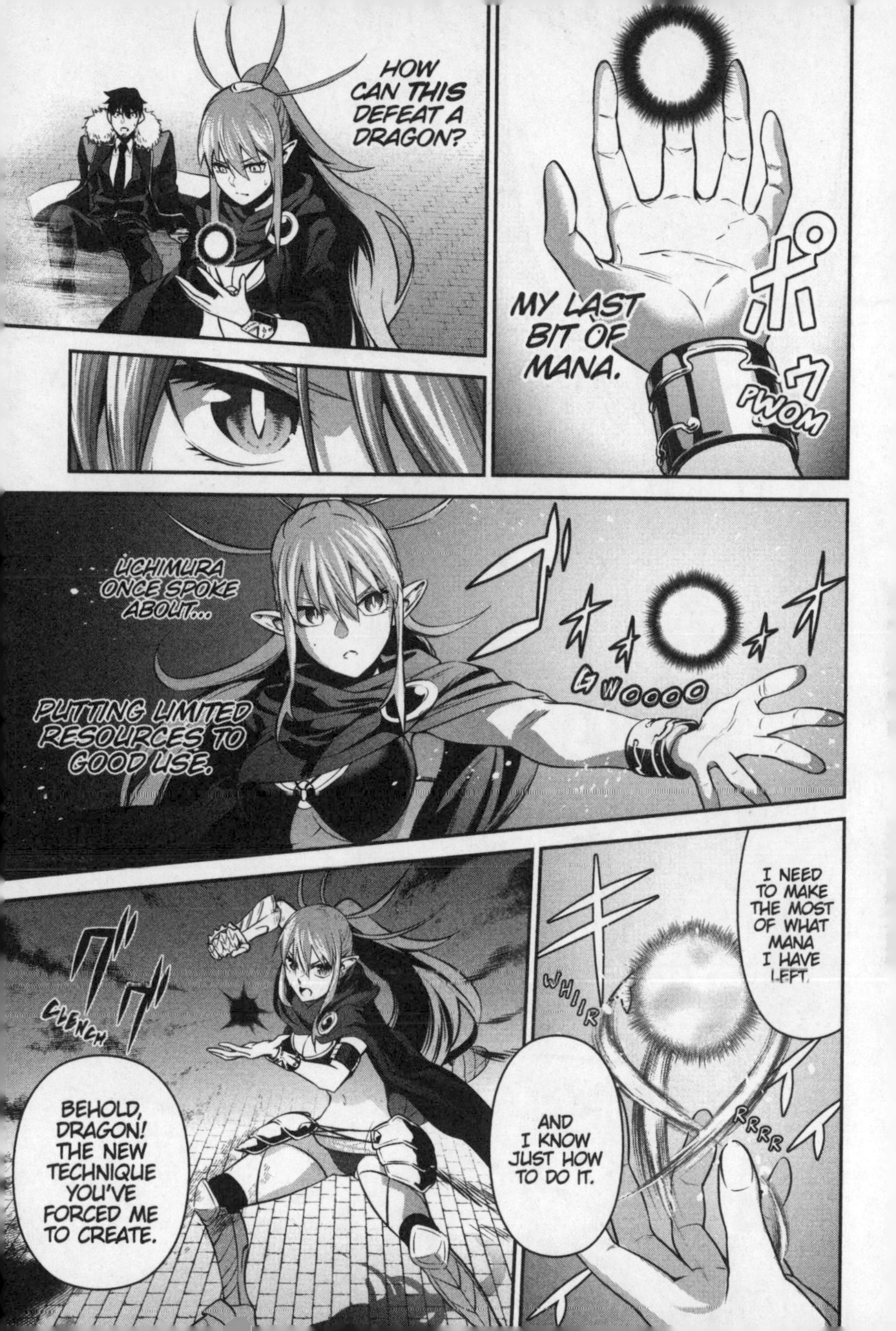
MY LAST BIT OF MANA.
PWOM
HOW CAN THIS DEFEAT A DRAGON?
GWOOOO
UCHIMURA ONCE SPOKE ABOUT...
PUTTING LIMITED RESOURCES TO GOOD USE.
I NEED TO MAKE THE MOST OF WHAT MANA I HAVE LEFT.
WHIRR
RRRR
AND I KNOW JUST HOW TO DO IT.
CLENCH
BEHOLD, DRAGON! THE NEW TECHNIQUE YOU'VE FORCED ME TO CREATE.

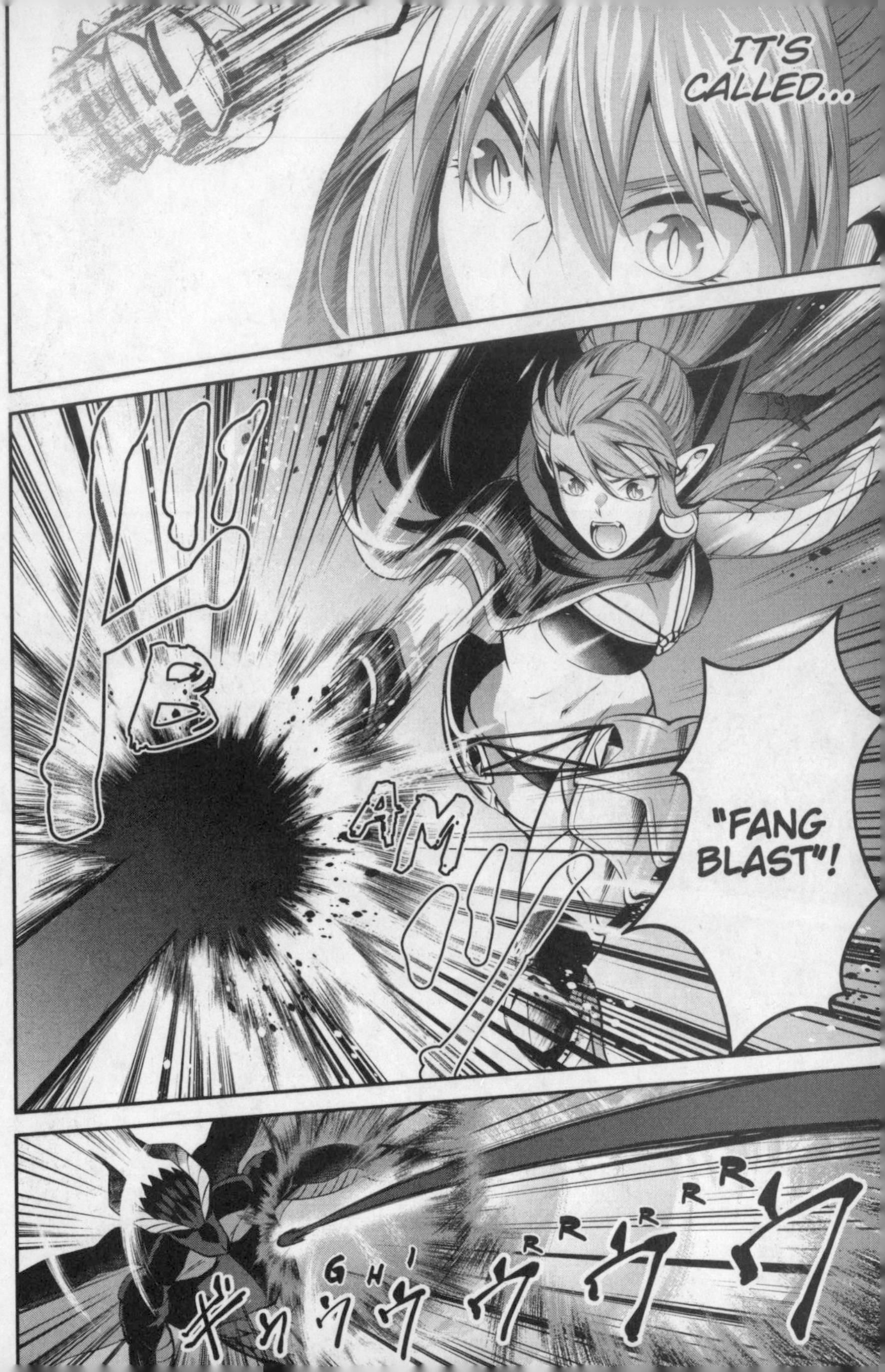
IT'S CALLED...
"FANG BLAST"!
BAM
GHIRRRRR

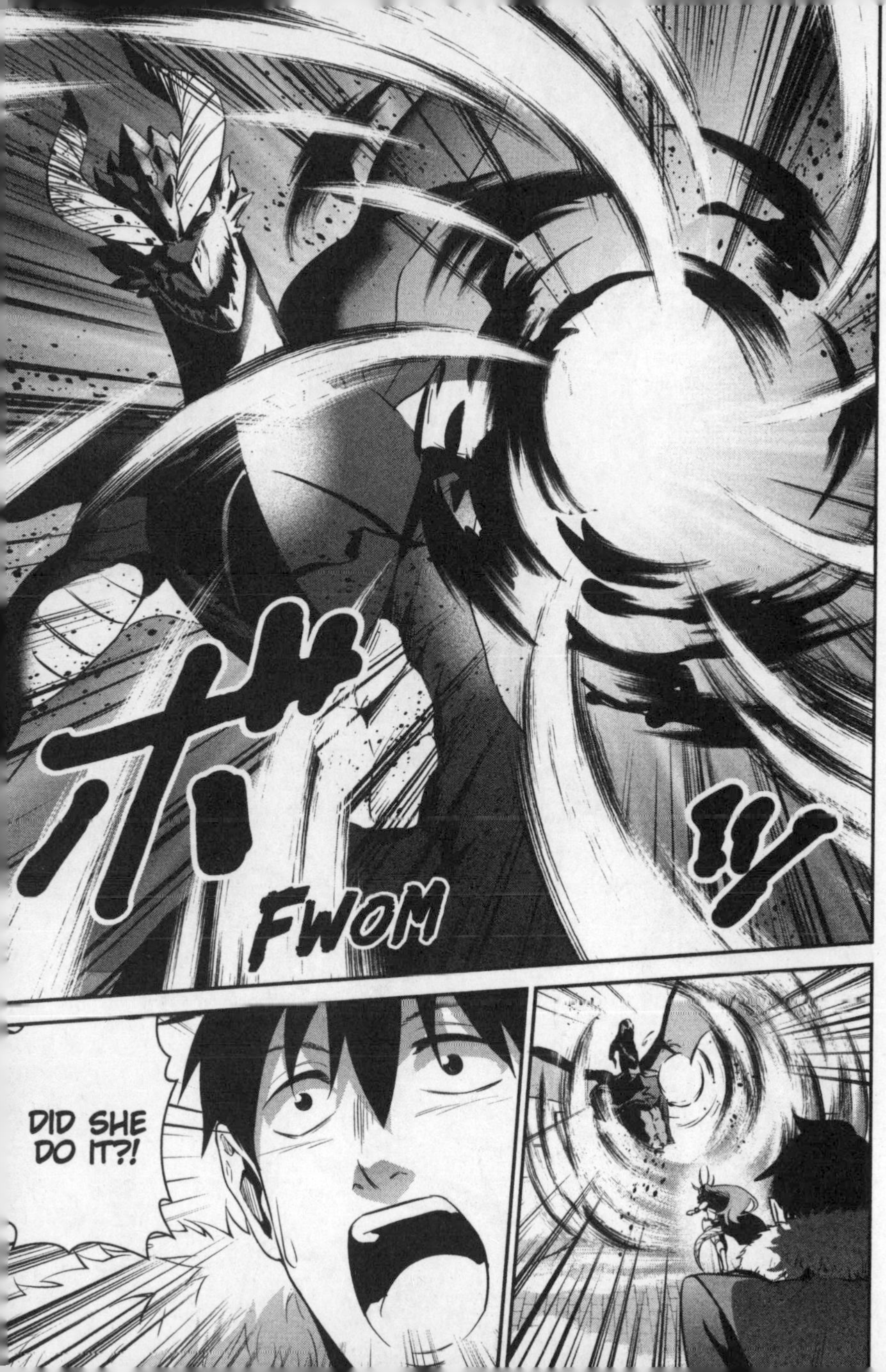
FWOM
DID SHE DO IT?!

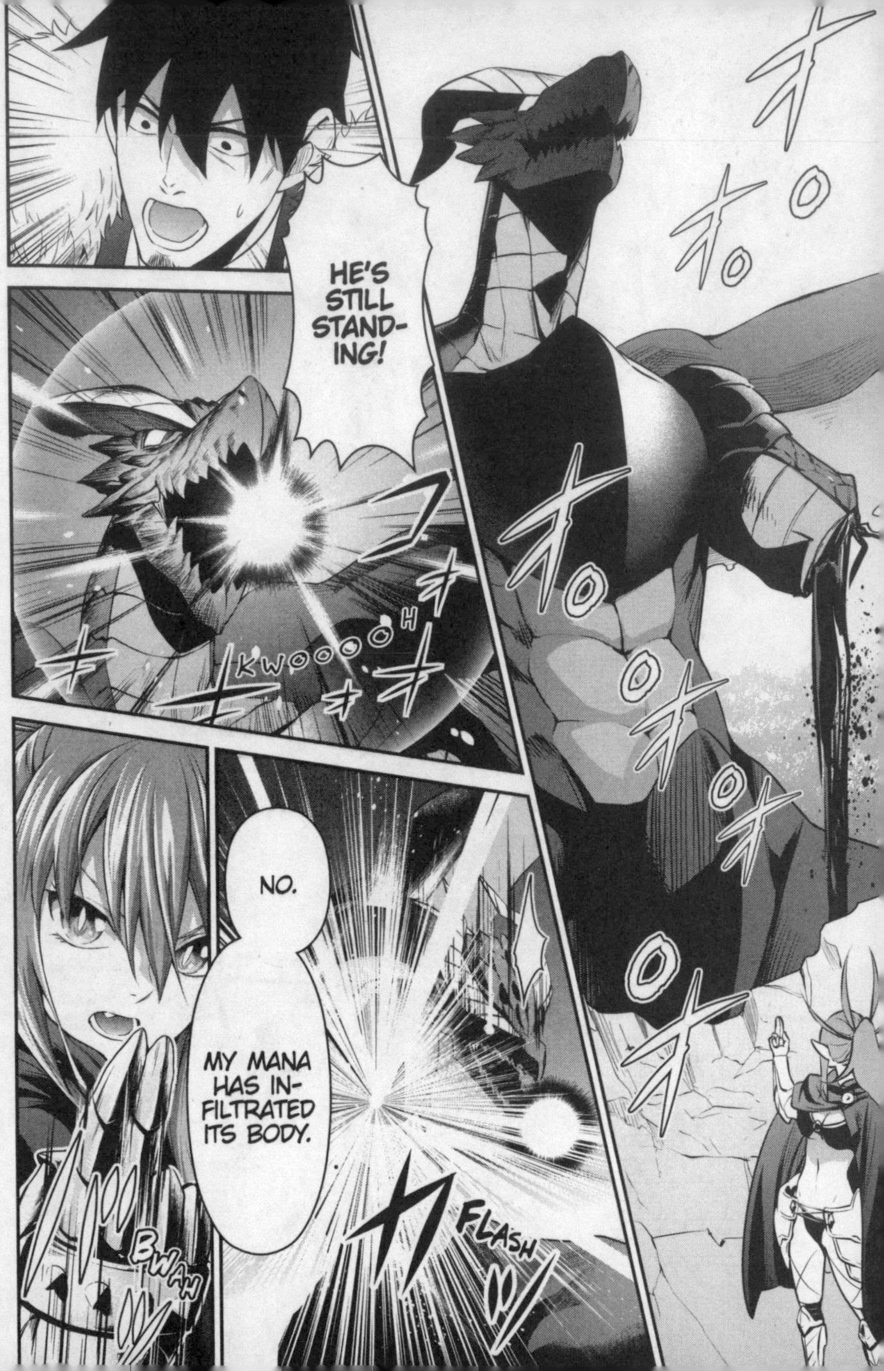
HE'S STILL STAND-ING!
KWOOOOOOH
NO.
MY MANA HAS IN-FILTRATED ITS BODY.
FLASH
BWAH

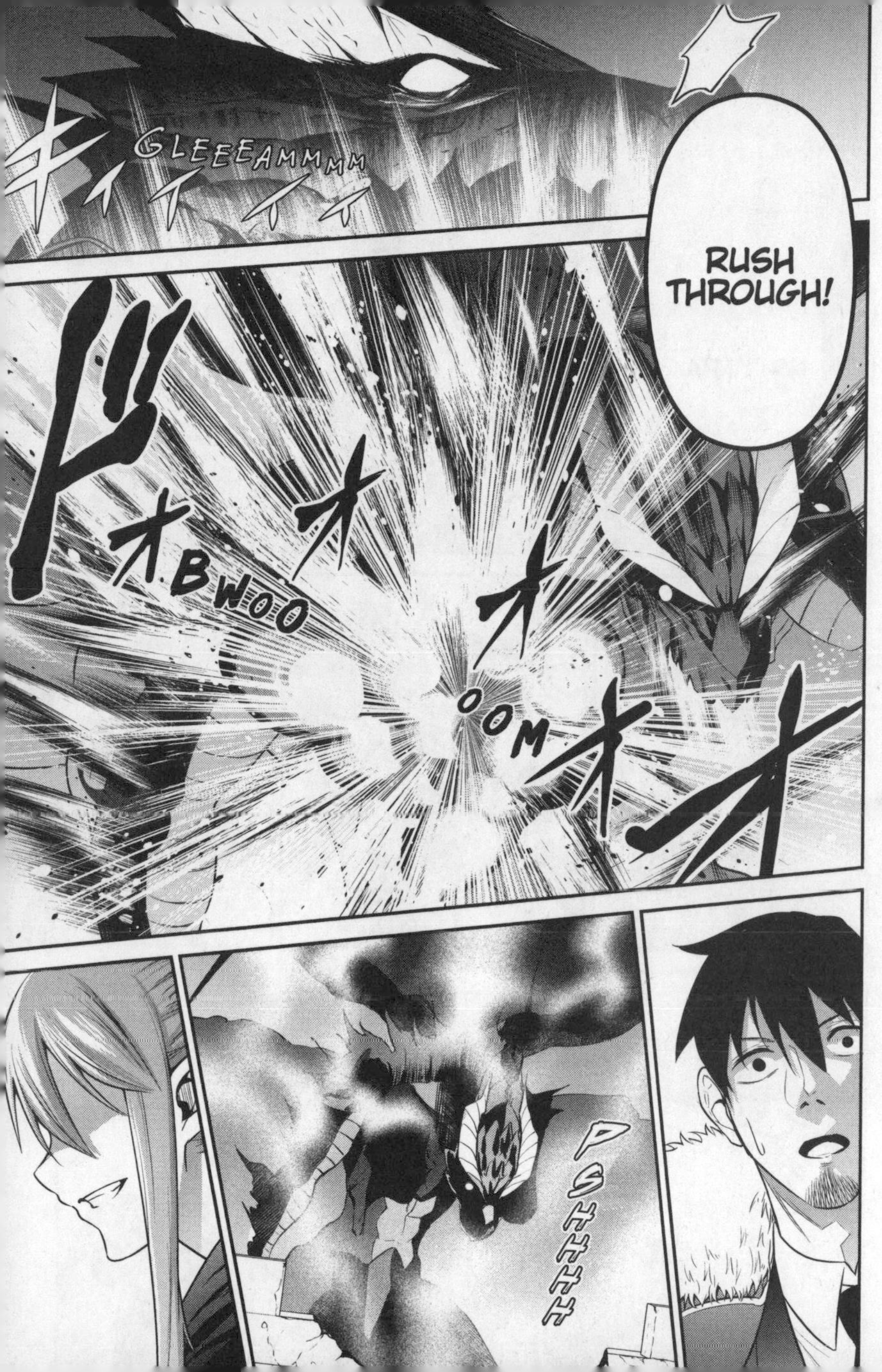
RUSH THROUGH!
GLEEEAMMMM
BWOOOOM
PSHHHH

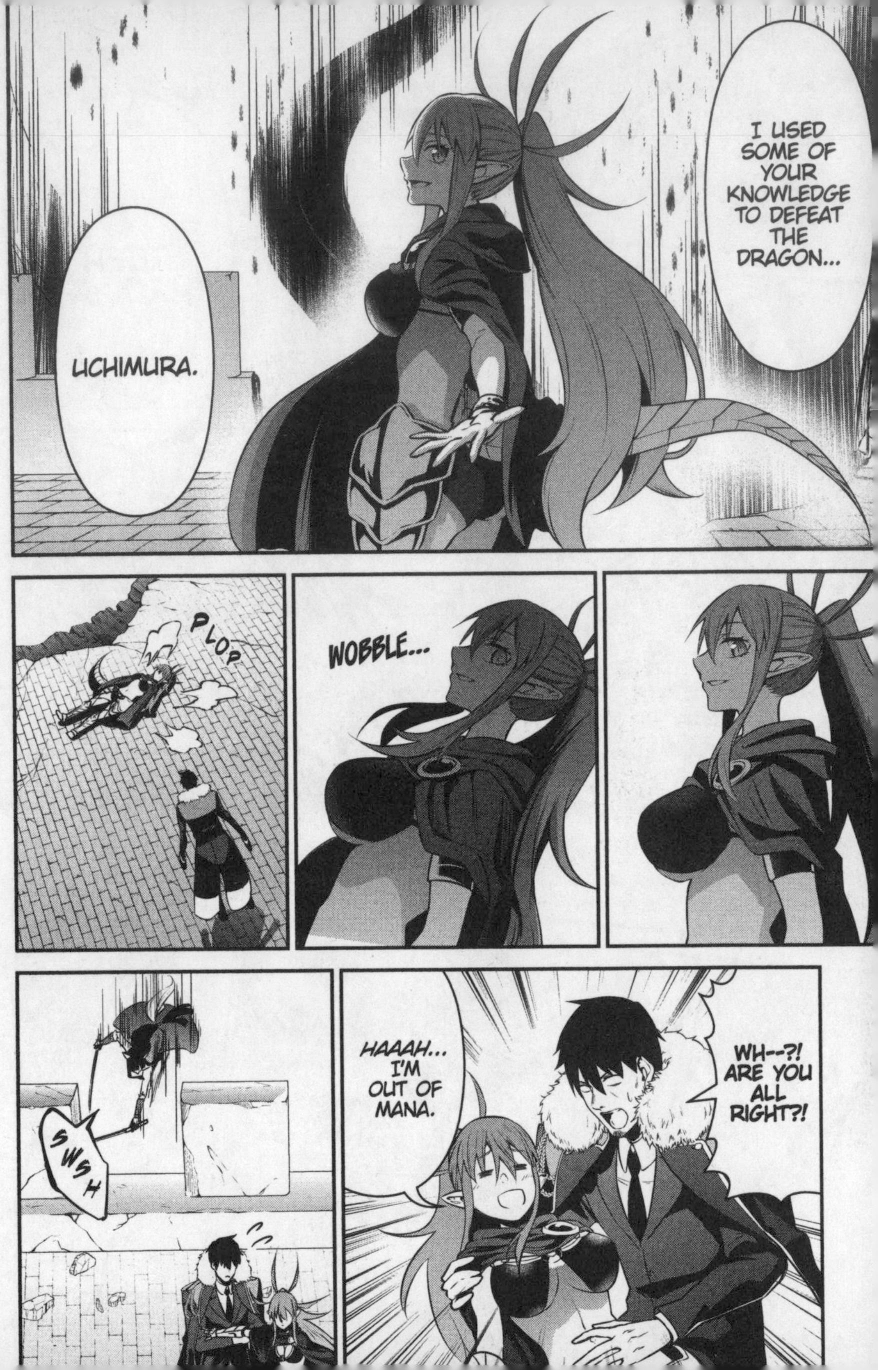
I USED SOME OF YOUR KNOWLEDGE TO DEFEAT THE DRAGON...
UCHIMURA.
WOBBLE...
PLOP
WH--?! ARE YOU ALL RIGHT?!
HAAAH... I'M OUT OF MANA.
SWSH

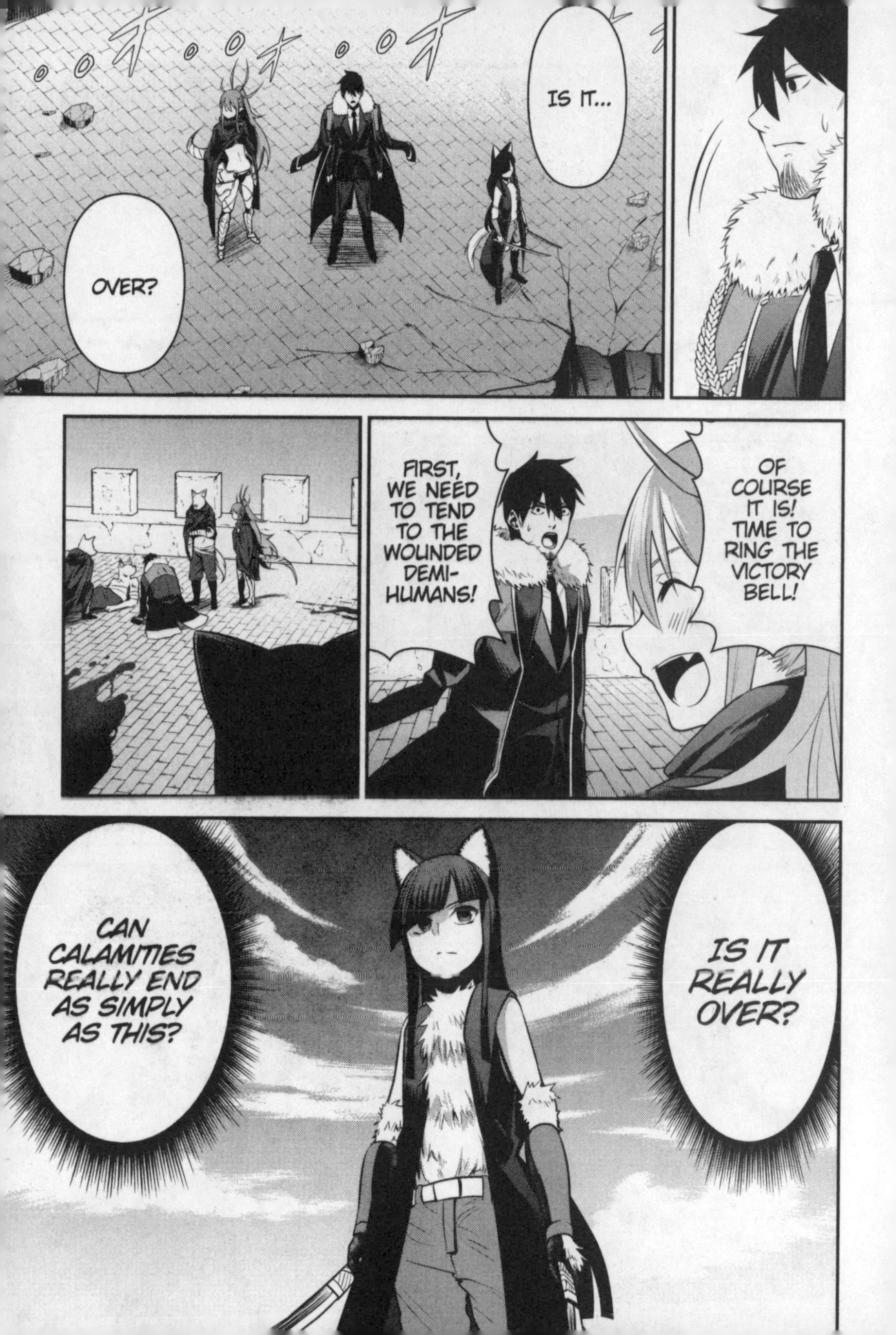
IS IT...
OVER?
OF COURSE IT IS! TIME TO RING THE VICTORY BELL!
FIRST, WE NEED TO TEND TO THE WOUNDED DEMI-HUMANS!
IS IT REALLY OVER?
CAN CALAMITIES REALLY END AS SIMPLY AS THIS?

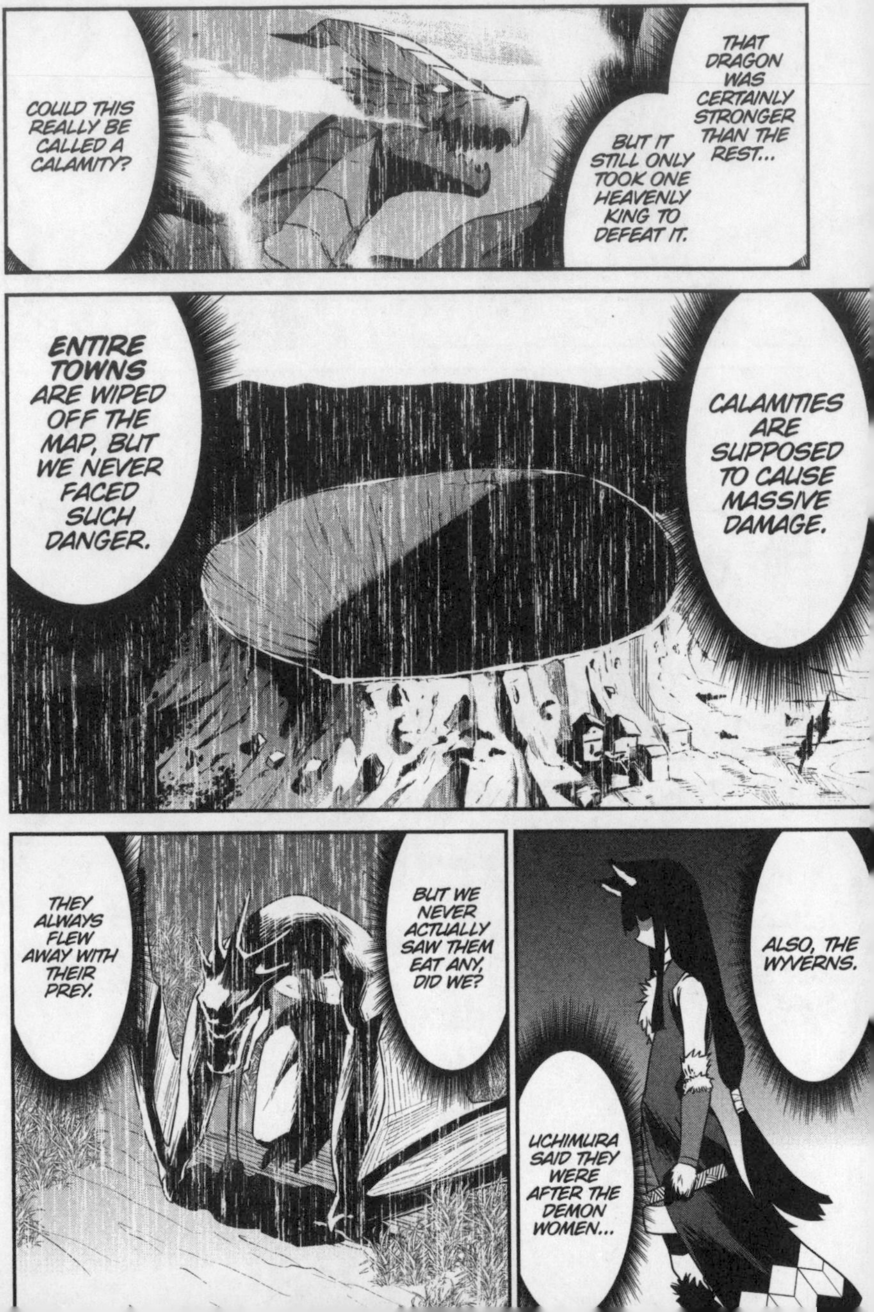
THAT DRAGON WAS CERTAINLY STRONGER THAN THE REST...
BUT IT STILL ONLY TOOK ONE HEAVENLY KING TO DEFEAT IT.
COULD THIS REALLY BE CALLED A CALAMITY?
CALAMITIES ARE SUPPOSED TO CAUSE MASSIVE DAMAGE.
ENTIRE TOWNS ARE WIPED OFF THE MAP, BUT WE NEVER FACED SUCH DANGER.
ALSO, THE WYVERNS.
UCHIMURA SAID THEY WERE AFTER THE DEMON WOMEN...
BUT WE NEVER ACTUALLY SAW THEM EAT ANY, DID WE?
THEY ALWAYS FLEW AWAY WITH THEIR PREY.

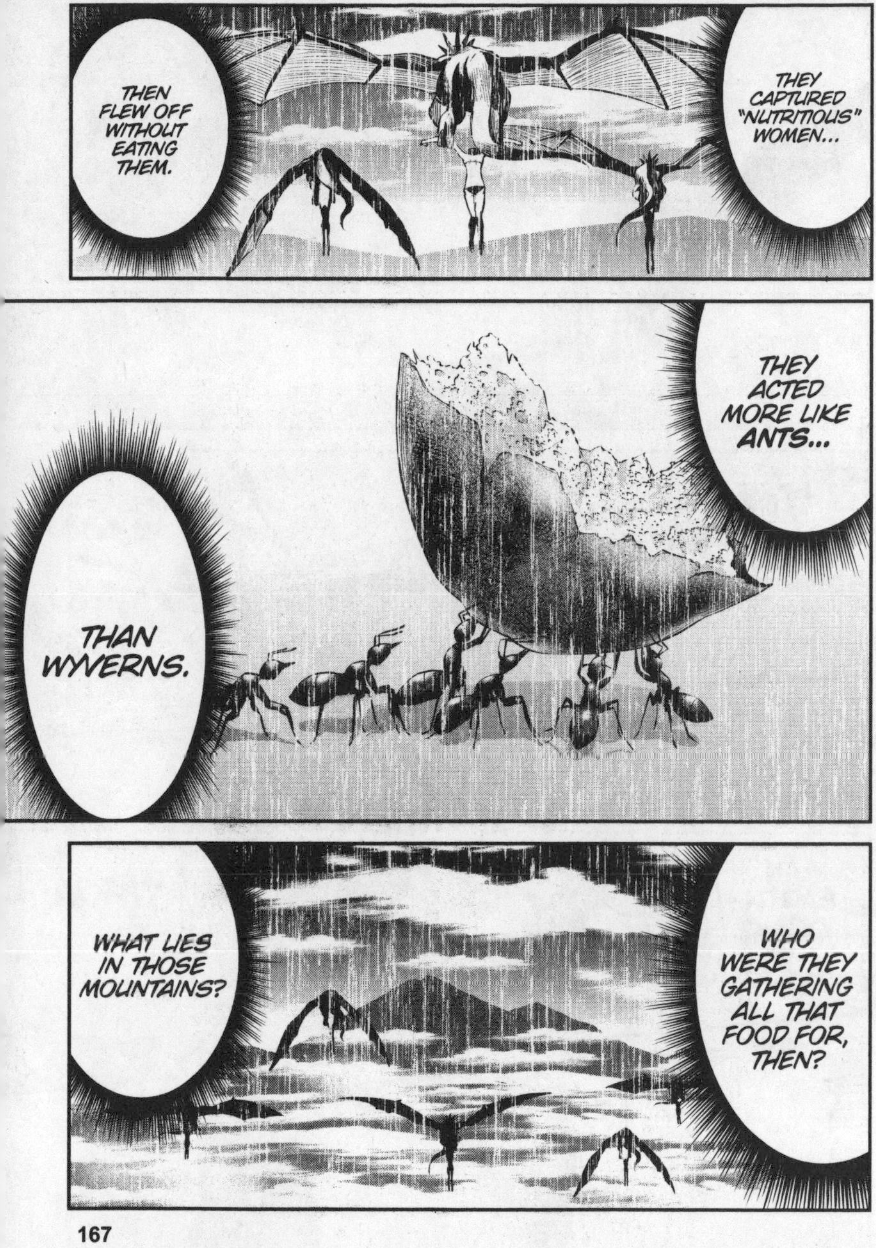
THEY CAPTURED "NUTRITIOUS" WOMEN...
THEN FLEW OFF WITHOUT EATING THEM.
THEY ACTED MORE LIKE ANTS...
THAN WYVERNS.
WHO WERE THEY GATHERING ALL THAT FOOD FOR, THEN?
WHAT LIES IN THOSE MOUNTAINS?

HOW IS THIS A CALAMITY?

CRACK

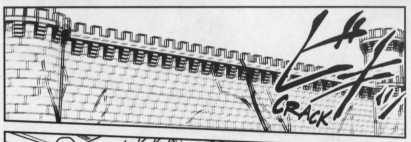

AN EARTH-QUAKE?!

RMB

WHOA!

THE MOUNTAIN!

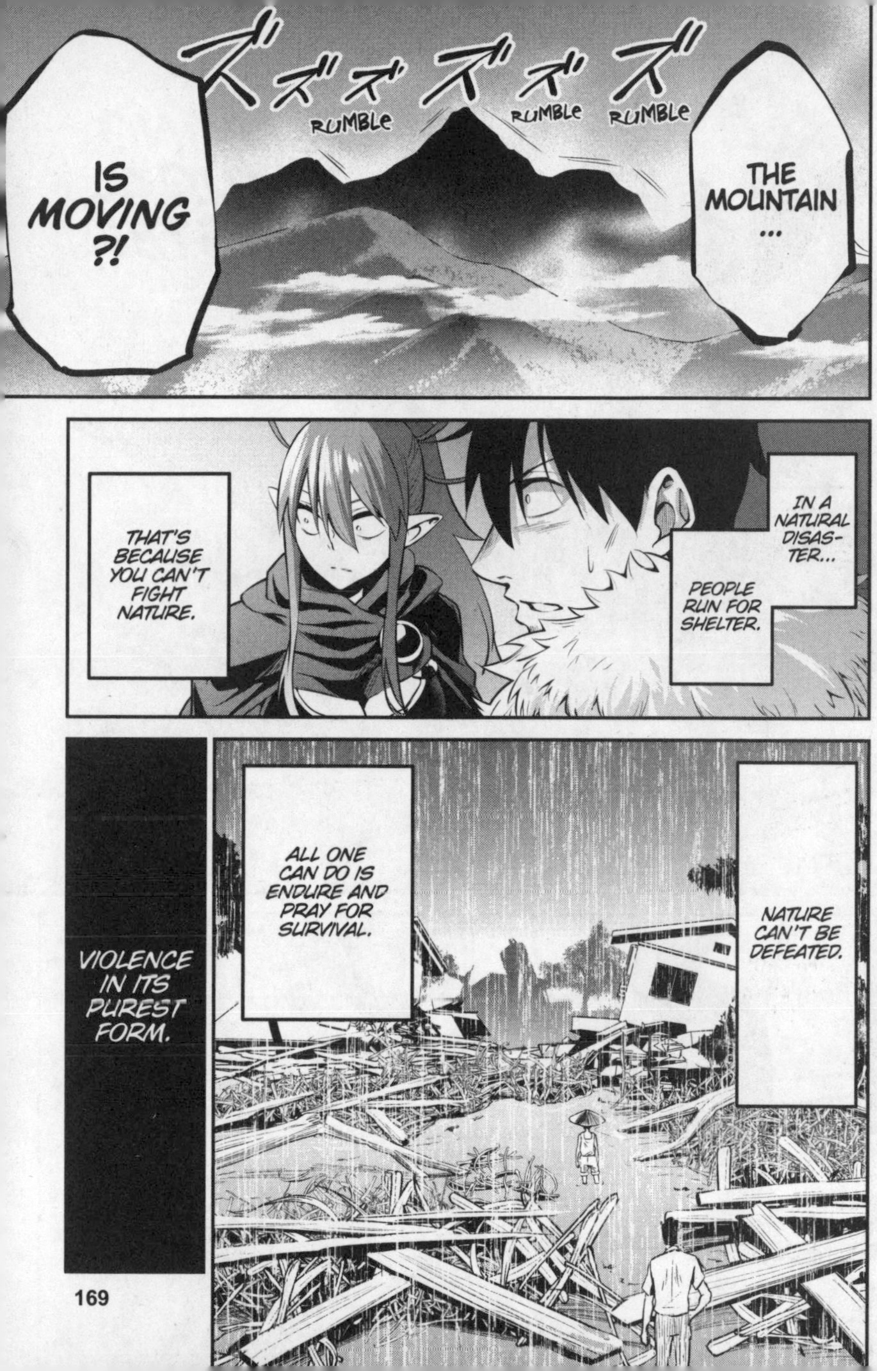
THE MOUNTAIN ...
ズズズズズズ
RUMBLE RUMBLE RUMBLE
IS MOVING ?!
IN A NATURAL DISASTER...
PEOPLE RUN FOR SHELTER.
THAT'S BECAUSE YOU CAN'T FIGHT NATURE.
NATURE CAN'T BE DEFEATED.
ALL ONE CAN DO IS ENDURE AND PRAY FOR SURVIVAL.
VIOLENCE IN ITS PUREST FORM.

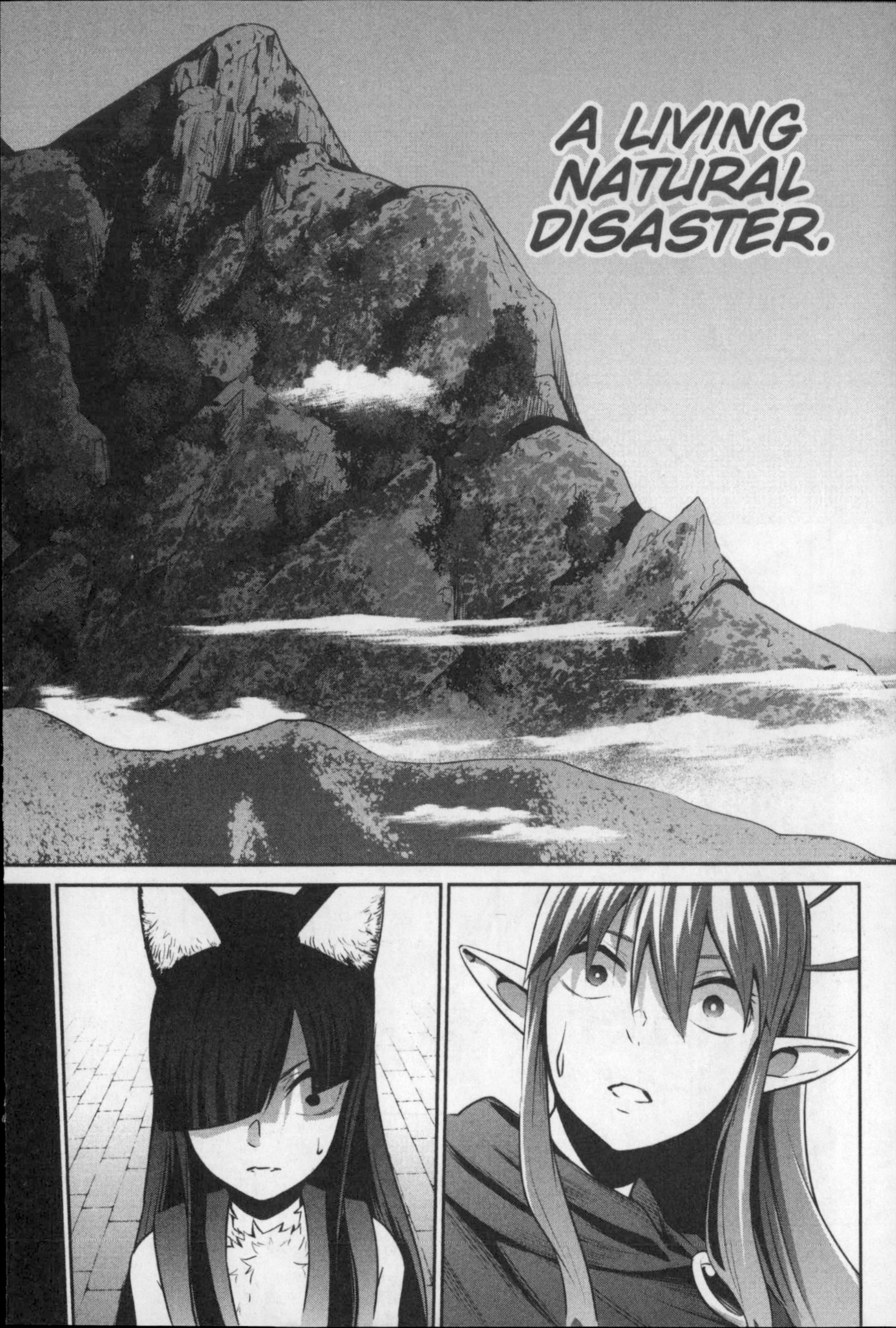
A LIVING NATURAL DISASTER.

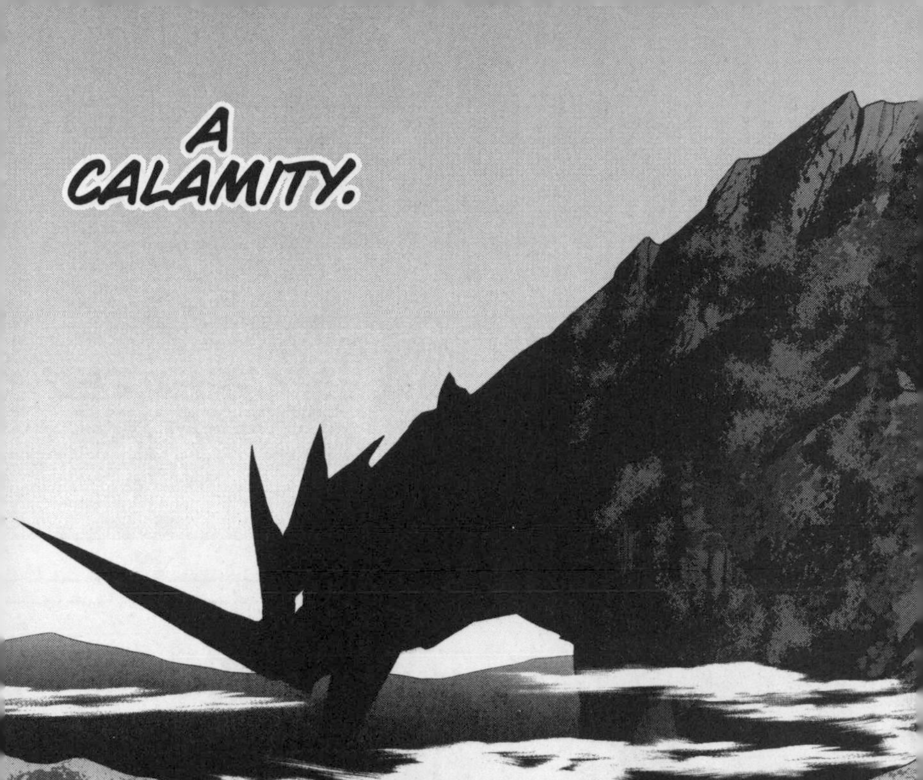
A CALAMITY.

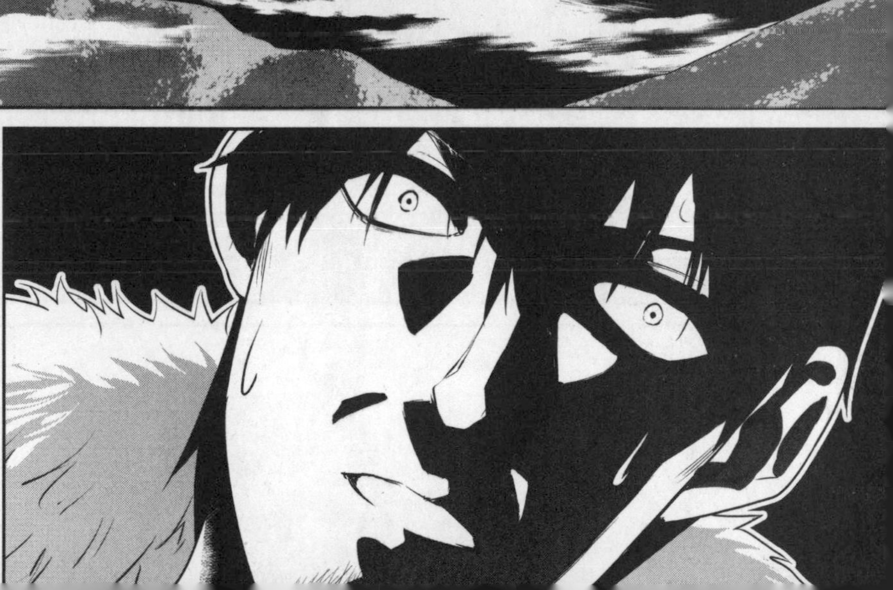

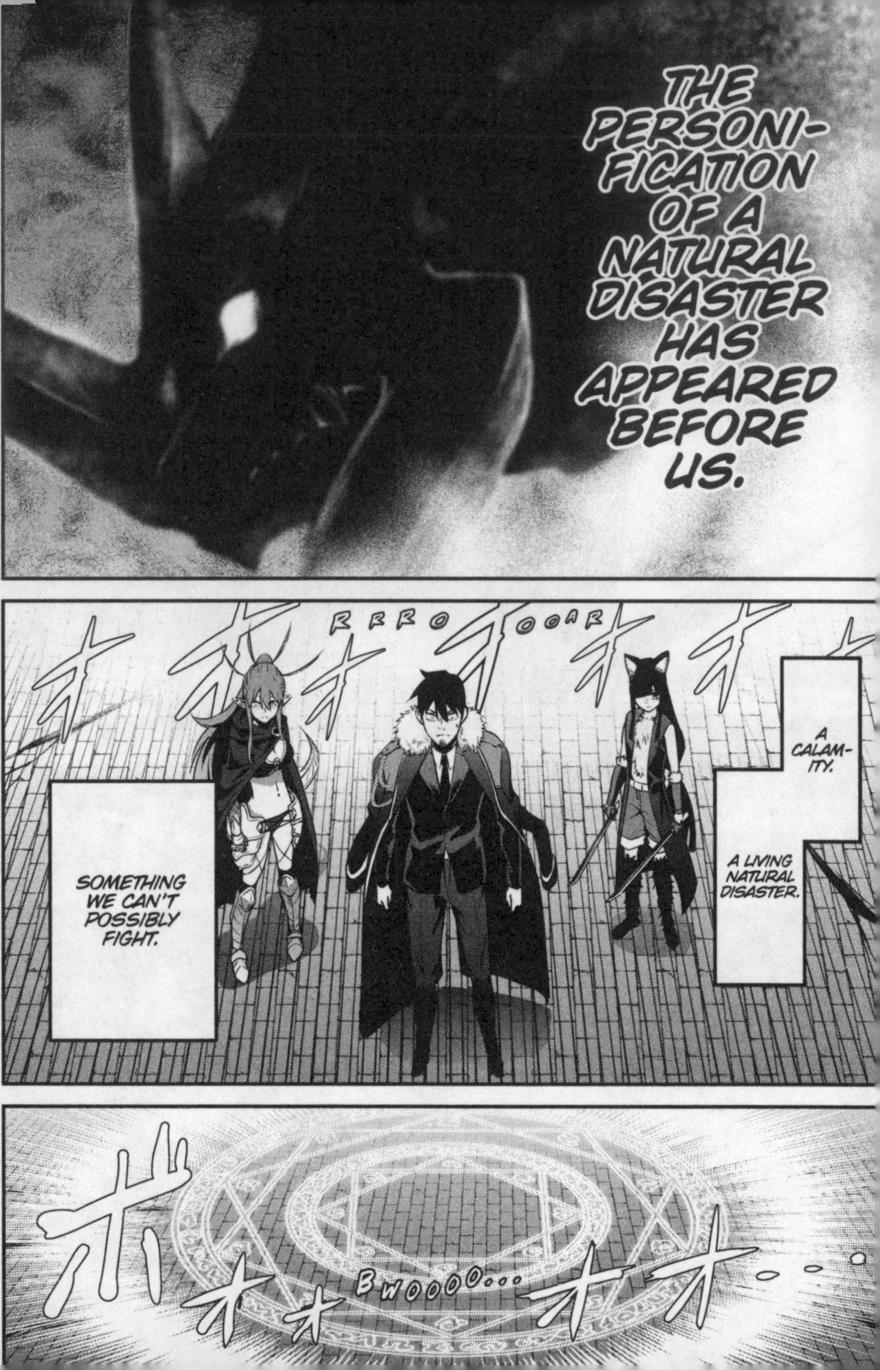
THE PERSONI-FICATION OF A NATURAL DISASTER HAS APPEARED BEFORE US.
RRRO OOAR
A CALAM-ITY.
A LIVING NATURAL DISASTER.
SOMETHING WE CAN'T POSSIBLY FIGHT.
BWOOOO...

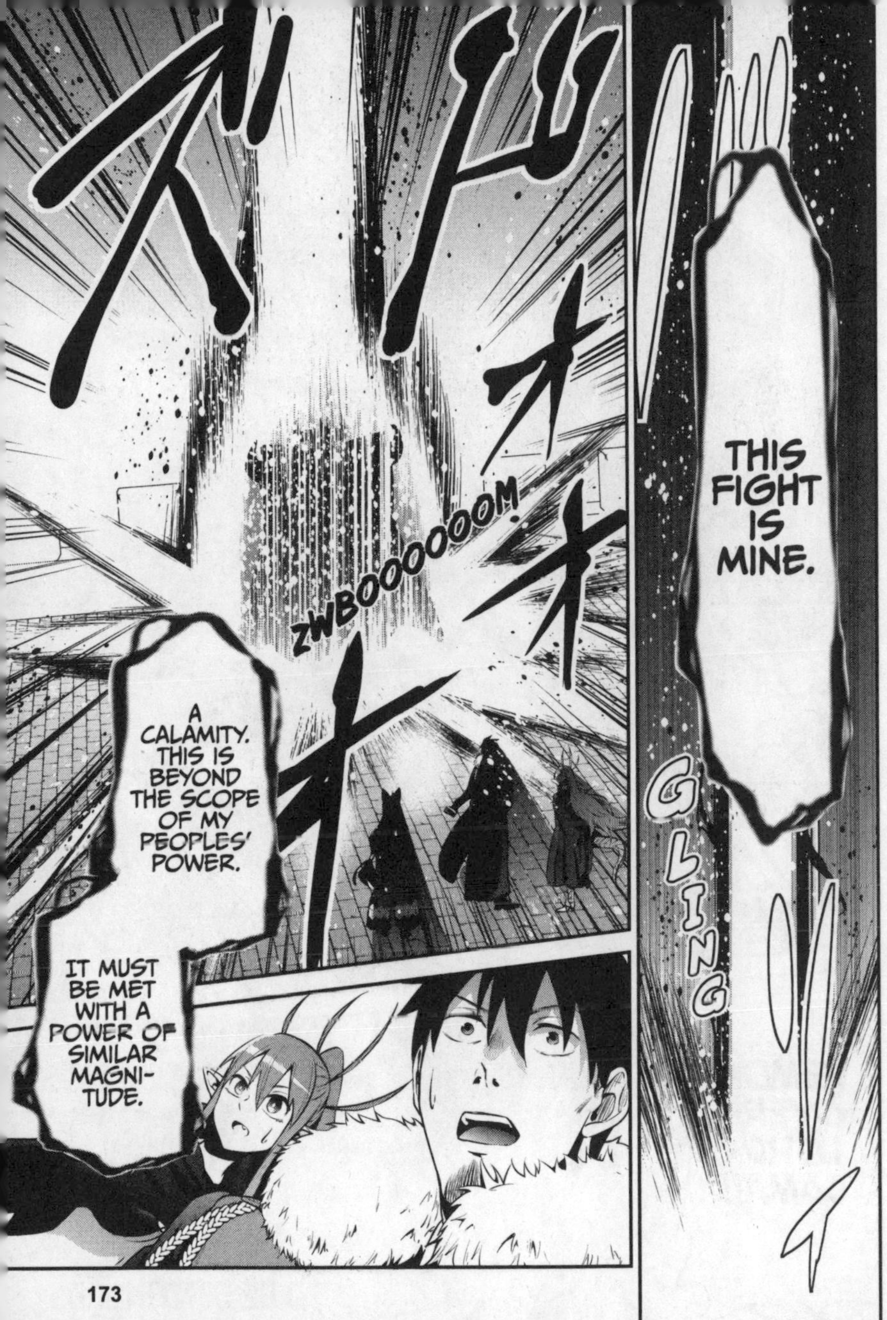
THIS FIGHT IS MINE.
GLING
ZWBOOOOOOOM
A CALAMITY. THIS IS BEYOND THE SCOPE OF MY PEOPLES' POWER.
IT MUST BE MET WITH A POWER OF SIMILAR MAGNITUDE.

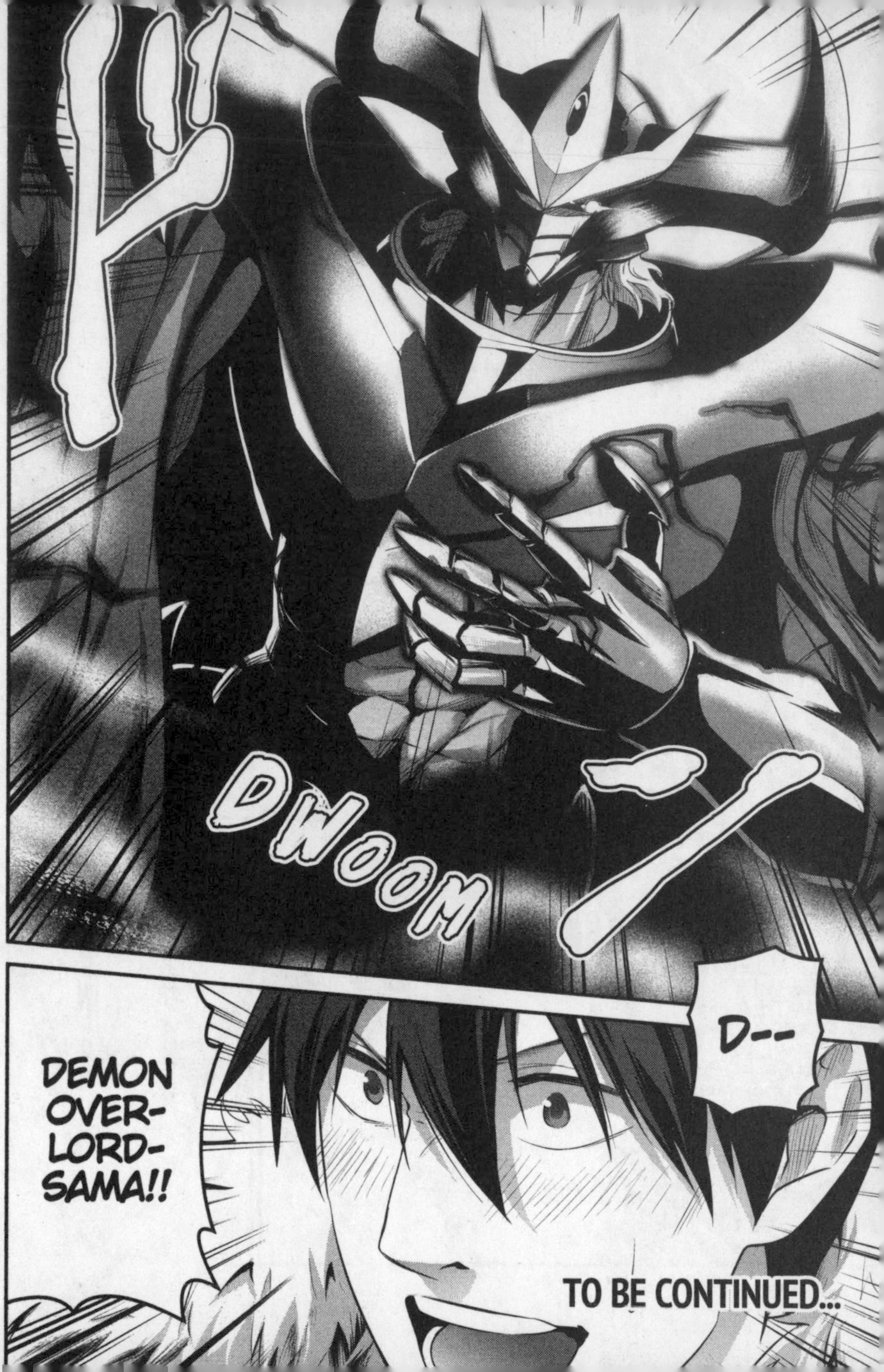
DWOOM
D--
DEMON OVER-LORD-SAMA!!
TO BE CONTINUED...

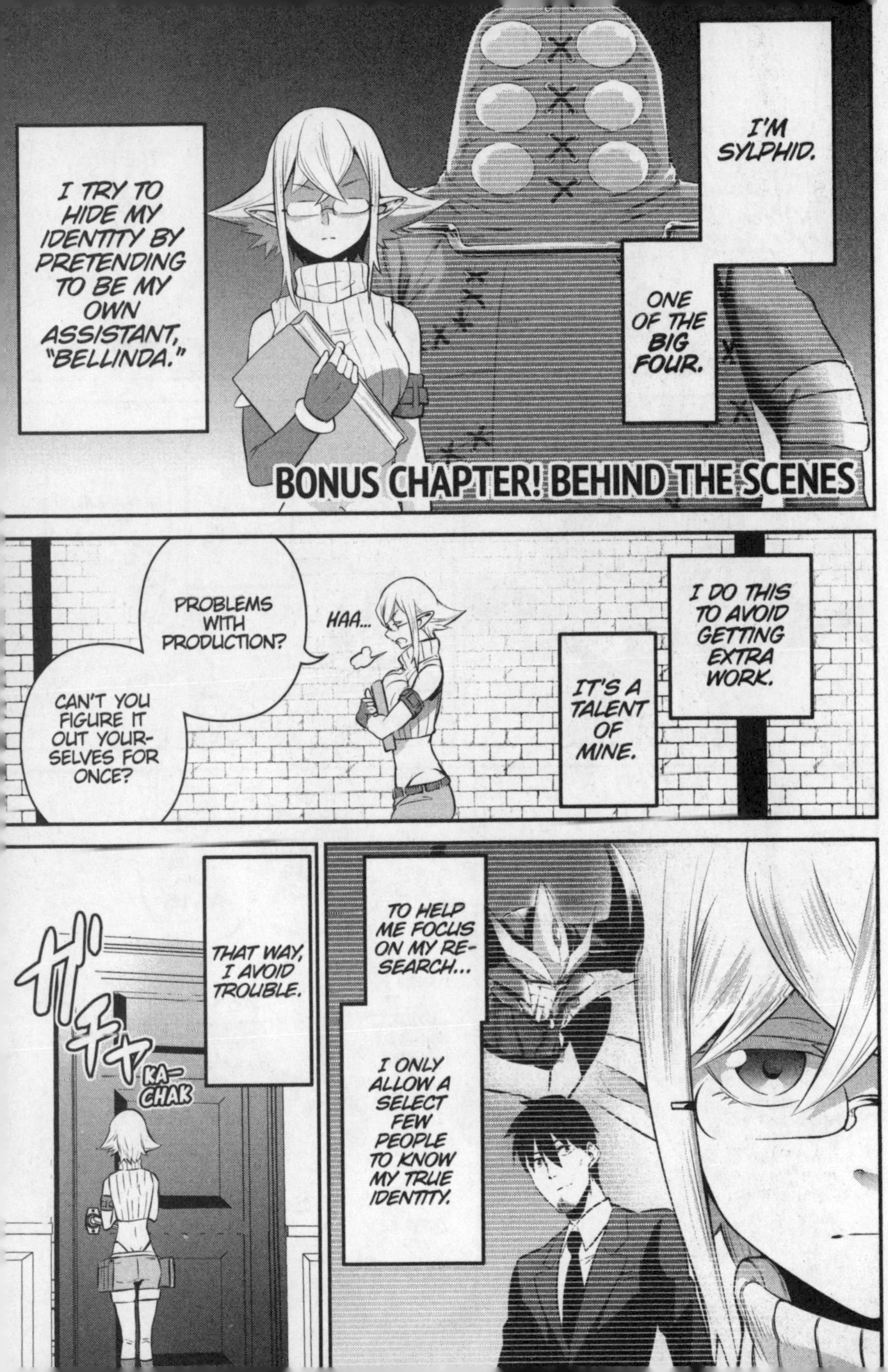
I'M SYLPHID.
ONE OF THE BIG FOUR.
I TRY TO HIDE MY IDENTITY BY PRETENDING TO BE MY OWN ASSISTANT, "BELLINDA."
BONUS CHAPTER! BEHIND THE SCENES
I DO THIS TO AVOID GETTING EXTRA WORK.
IT'S A TALENT OF MINE.
HAA...
PROBLEMS WITH PRODUCTION?
CAN'T YOU FIGURE IT OUT YOURSELVES FOR ONCE?
TO HELP ME FOCUS ON MY RESEARCH...
I ONLY ALLOW A SELECT FEW PEOPLE TO KNOW MY TRUE IDENTITY.
THAT WAY, I AVOID TROUBLE.
KA-CHAK

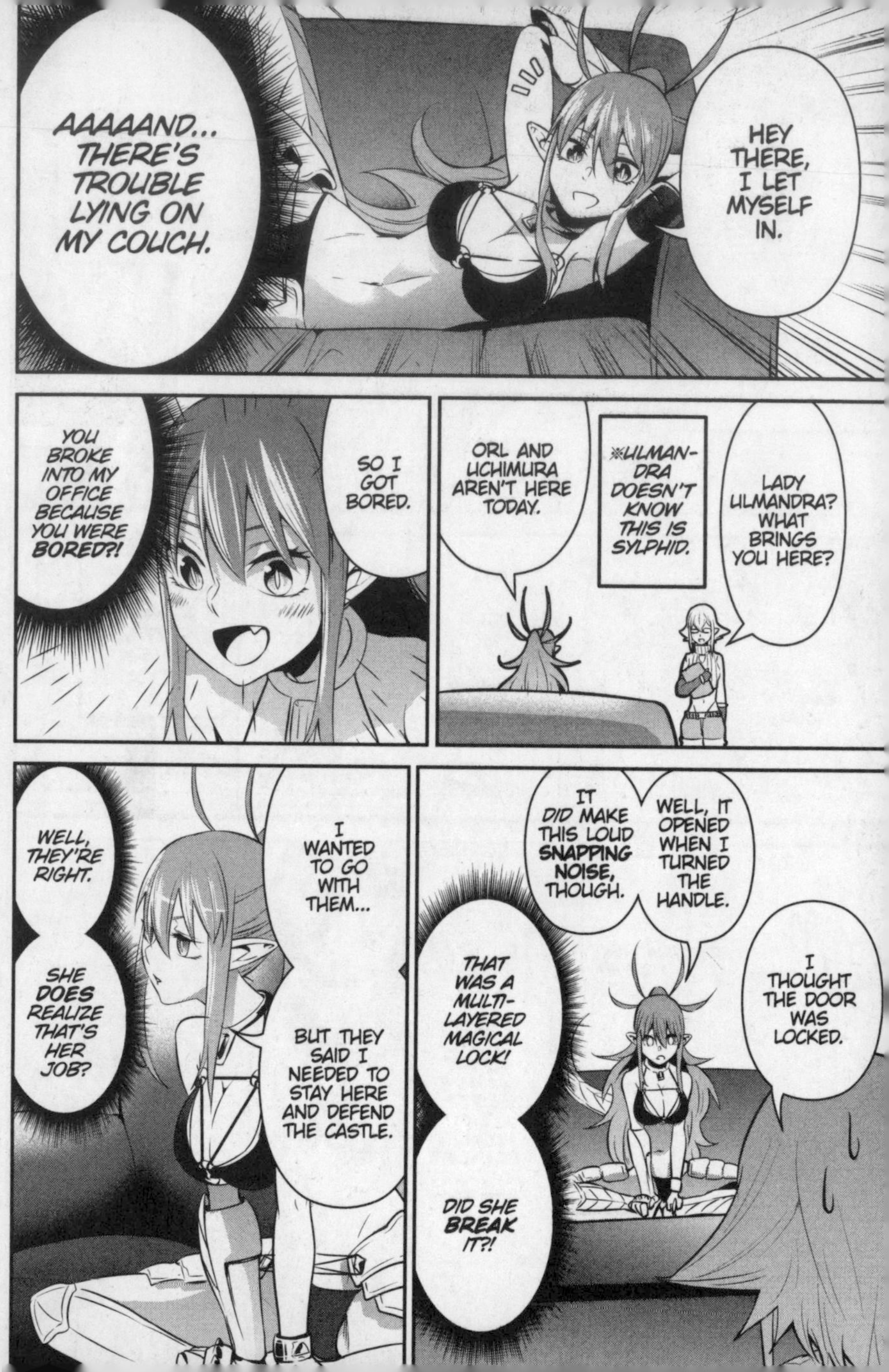
HEY THERE, I LET MYSELF IN.
AAAAAND... THERE'S TROUBLE LYING ON MY COUCH.
LADY ULMANDRA? WHAT BRINGS YOU HERE?
※ULMANDRA DOESN'T KNOW THIS IS SYLPHID.
ORL AND UCHIMURA AREN'T HERE TODAY.
SO I GOT BORED.
YOU BROKE INTO MY OFFICE BECAUSE YOU WERE BORED?!
I THOUGHT THE DOOR WAS LOCKED.
WELL, IT OPENED WHEN I TURNED THE HANDLE.
IT DID MAKE THIS LOUD SNAPPING NOISE, THOUGH.
THAT WAS A MULTI-LAYERED MAGICAL LOCK!
DID SHE BREAK IT?!
I WANTED TO GO WITH THEM...
BUT THEY SAID I NEEDED TO STAY HERE AND DEFEND THE CASTLE.
WELL, THEY'RE RIGHT.
SHE DOES REALIZE THAT'S HER JOB?

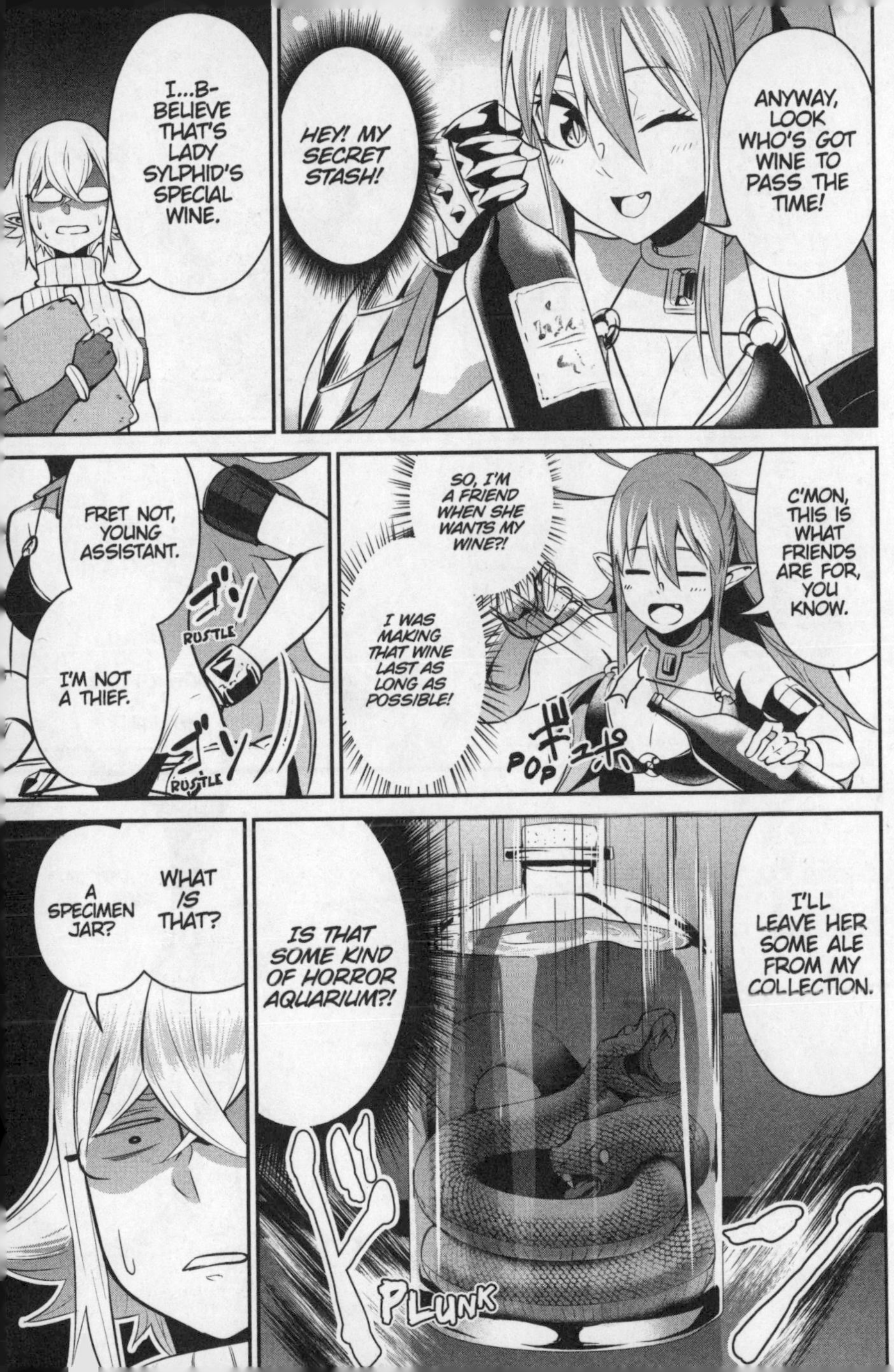
ANYWAY, LOOK WHO'S GOT WINE TO PASS THE TIME!
HEY! MY SECRET STASH!
I...B-BELIEVE THAT'S LADY SYLPHID'S SPECIAL WINE.
C'MON, THIS IS WHAT FRIENDS ARE FOR, YOU KNOW.
SO, I'M A FRIEND WHEN SHE WANTS MY WINE?!
I WAS MAKING THAT WINE LAST AS LONG AS POSSIBLE!
POP
FRET NOT, YOUNG ASSISTANT.
RUSTLE
I'M NOT A THIEF.
RUSTLE
I'LL LEAVE HER SOME ALE FROM MY COLLECTION.
IS THAT SOME KIND OF HORROR AQUARIUM?!
PLUNK
WHAT IS THAT?
A SPECIMEN JAR?

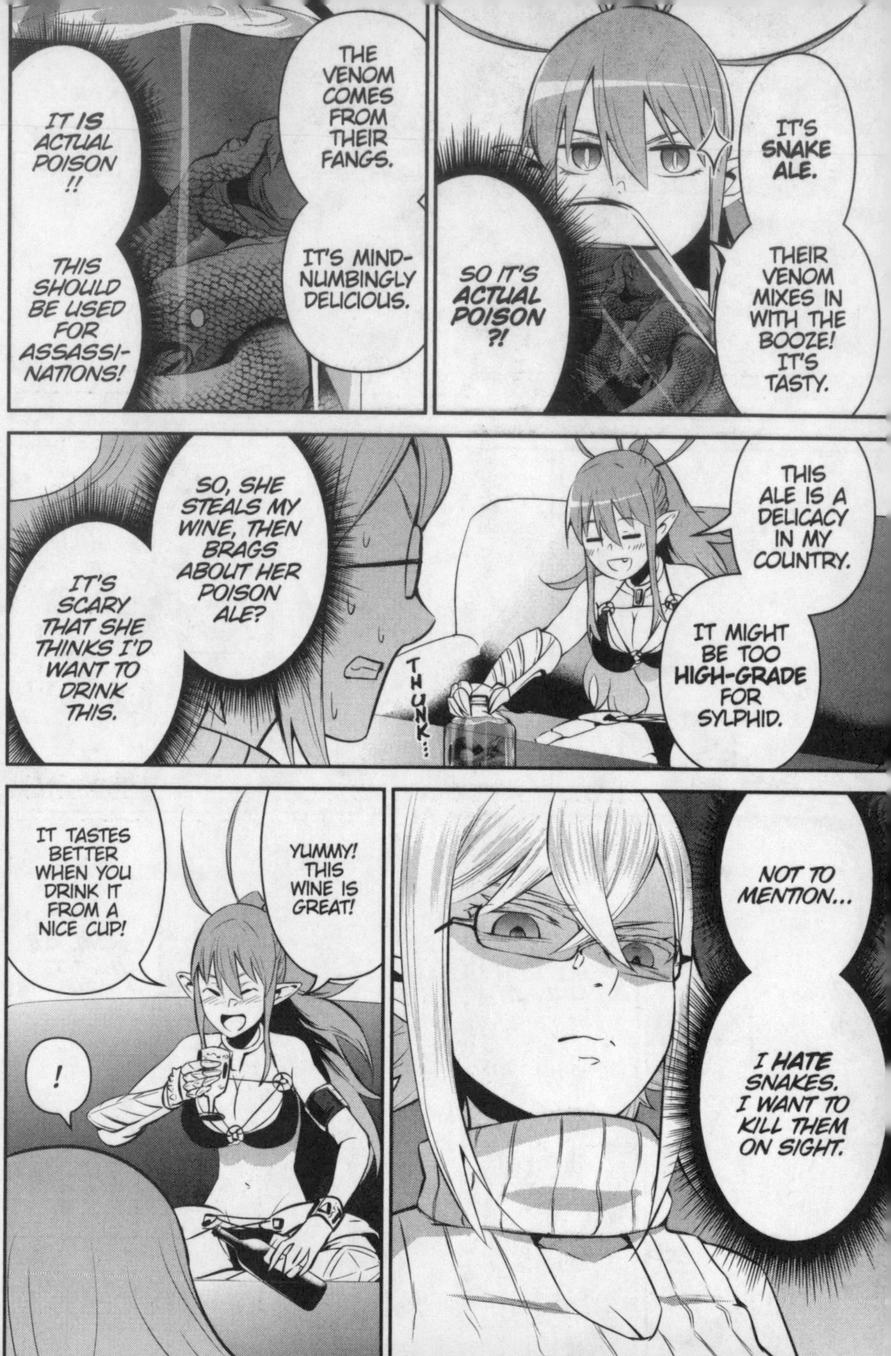
IT'S SNAKE ALE.
THEIR VENOM MIXES IN WITH THE BOOZE! IT'S TASTY.
SO IT'S ACTUAL POISON?!
THE VENOM COMES FROM THEIR FANGS.
IT'S MIND-NUMBINGLY DELICIOUS.
IT IS ACTUAL POISON!!
THIS SHOULD BE USED FOR ASSASSINATIONS!
THIS ALE IS A DELICACY IN MY COUNTRY.
IT MIGHT BE TOO HIGH-GRADE FOR SYLPHID.
THUNK...
SO, SHE STEALS MY WINE, THEN BRAGS ABOUT HER POISON ALE?
IT'S SCARY THAT SHE THINKS I'D WANT TO DRINK THIS.
NOT TO MENTION...
I HATE SNAKES. I WANT TO KILL THEM ON SIGHT.
YUMMY! THIS WINE IS GREAT!
IT TASTES BETTER WHEN YOU DRINK IT FROM A NICE CUP!
!

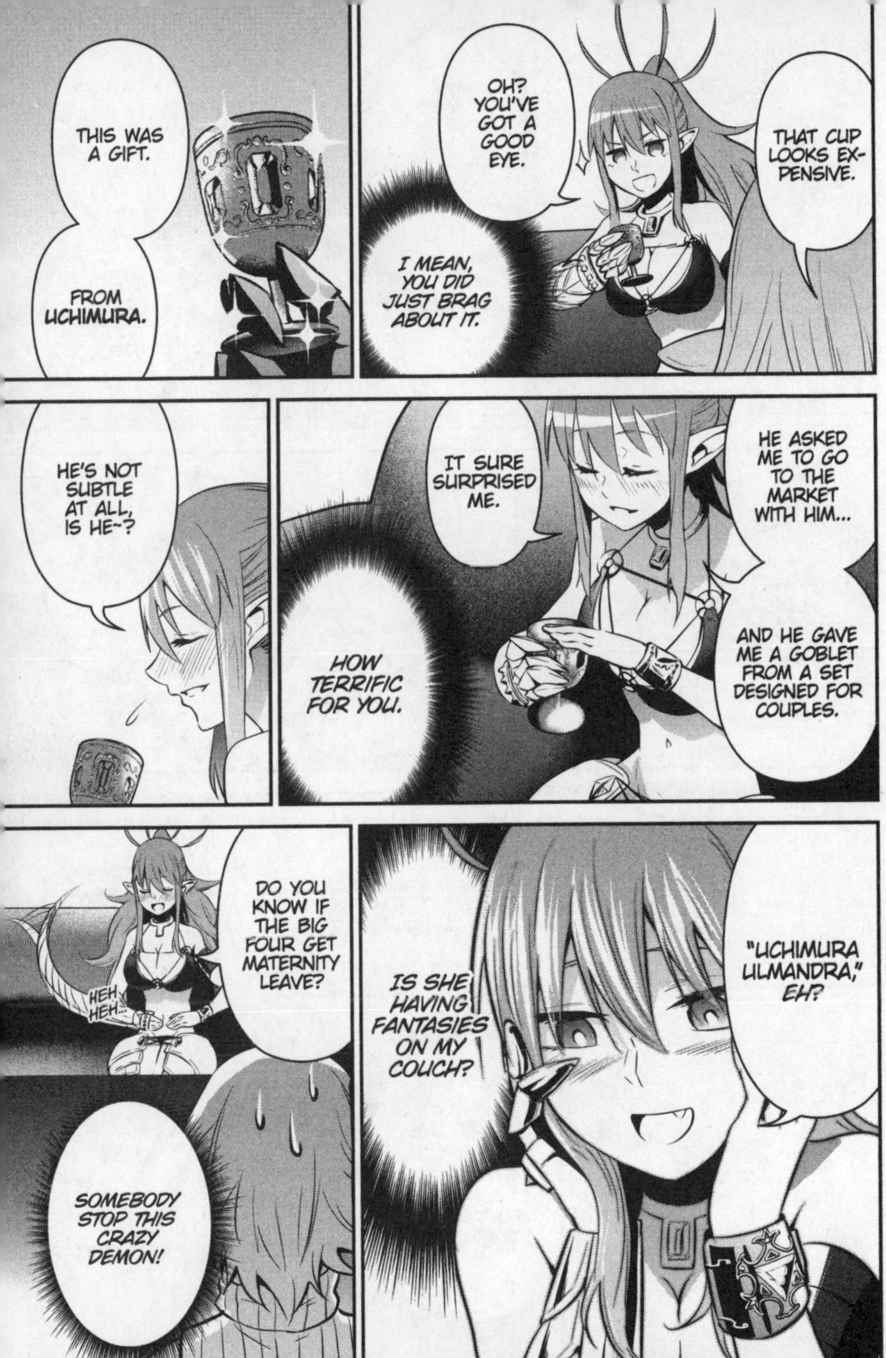
THAT CUP LOOKS EX-PENSIVE.
OH? YOU'VE GOT A GOOD EYE.
I MEAN, YOU DID JUST BRAG ABOUT IT.
THIS WAS A GIFT.
FROM UCHIMURA.
HE ASKED ME TO GO TO THE MARKET WITH HIM...
IT SURE SURPRISED ME.
AND HE GAVE ME A GOBLET FROM A SET DESIGNED FOR COUPLES.
HOW TERRIFIC FOR YOU.
HE'S NOT SUBTLE AT ALL, IS HE~?
"UCHIMURA ULMANDRA," EH?
IS SHE HAVING FANTASIES ON MY COUCH?
DO YOU KNOW IF THE BIG FOUR GET MATERNITY LEAVE?
HEH HEH...
SOMEBODY STOP THIS CRAZY DEMON!

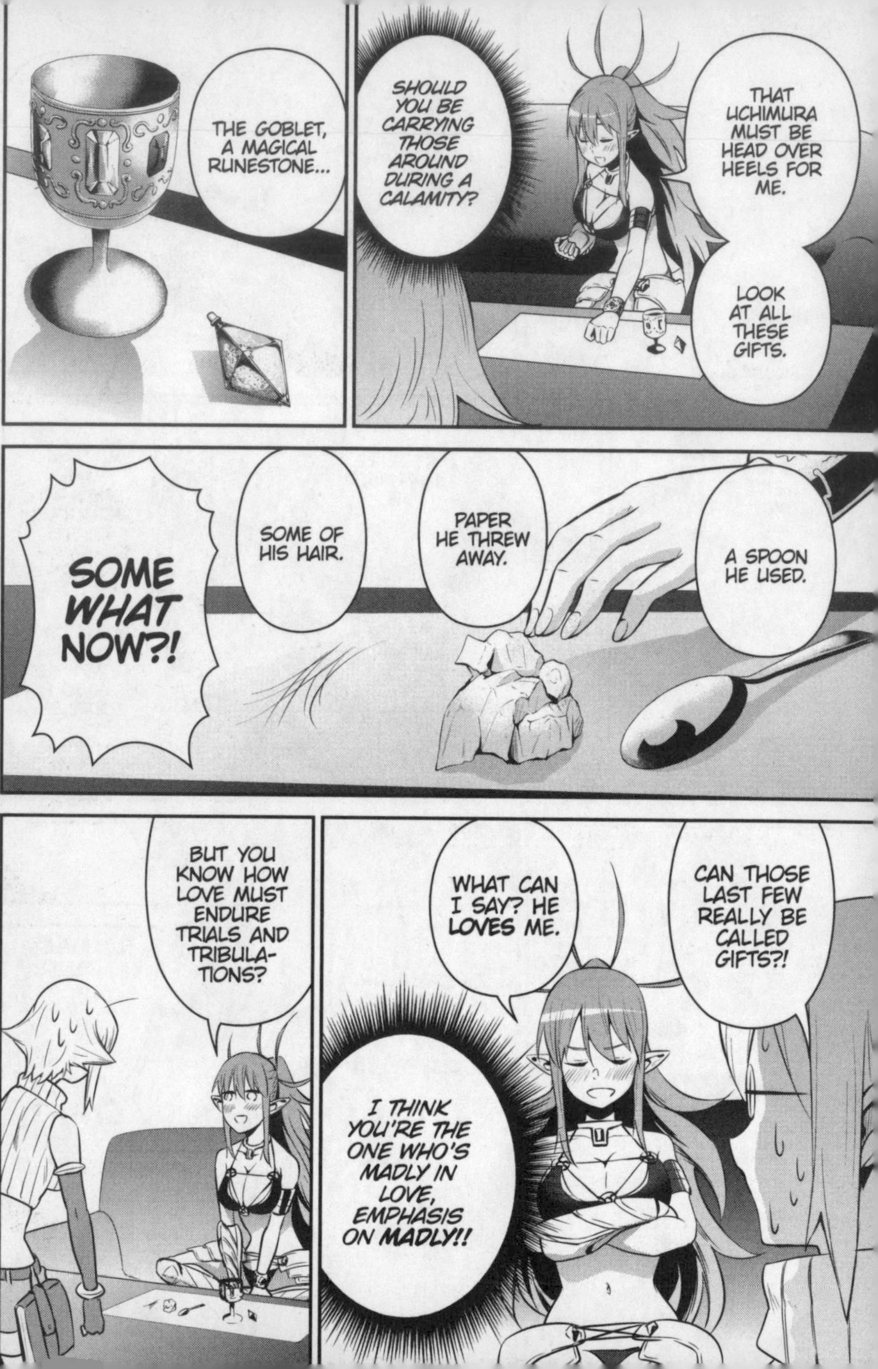
THAT UCHIMURA MUST BE HEAD OVER HEELS FOR ME.
LOOK AT ALL THESE GIFTS.
SHOULD YOU BE CARRYING THOSE AROUND DURING A CALAMITY?
THE GOBLET, A MAGICAL RUNESTONE...
A SPOON HE USED.
PAPER HE THREW AWAY.
SOME OF HIS HAIR.
SOME WHAT NOW?!
CAN THOSE LAST FEW REALLY BE CALLED GIFTS?!
WHAT CAN I SAY? HE LOVES ME.
I THINK YOU'RE THE ONE WHO'S MADLY IN LOVE, EMPHASIS ON MADLY!!
BUT YOU KNOW HOW LOVE MUST ENDURE TRIALS AND TRIBULATIONS?

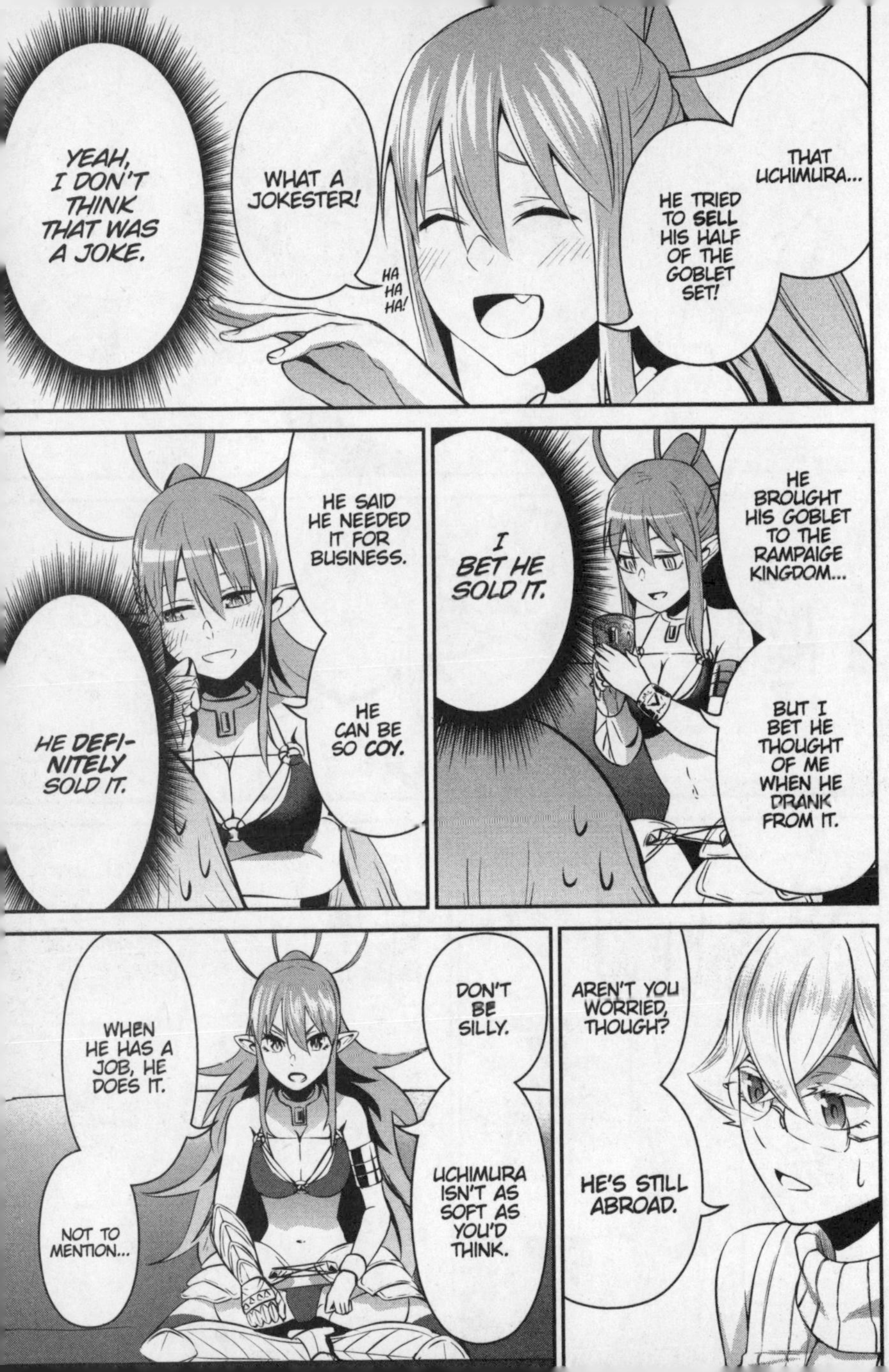
THAT UCHIMURA...
HE TRIED TO SELL HIS HALF OF THE GOBLET SET!
WHAT A JOKESTER!
HA HA HA!
YEAH, I DON'T THINK THAT WAS A JOKE.
HE BROUGHT HIS GOBLET TO THE RAMPAIGE KINGDOM...
BUT I BET HE THOUGHT OF ME WHEN HE DRANK FROM IT.
I BET HE SOLD IT.
HE SAID HE NEEDED IT FOR BUSINESS.
HE CAN BE SO COY.
HE DEFI-NITELY SOLD IT.
AREN'T YOU WORRIED, THOUGH?
HE'S STILL ABROAD.
DON'T BE SILLY.
UCHIMURA ISN'T AS SOFT AS YOU'D THINK.
WHEN HE HAS A JOB, HE DOES IT.
NOT TO MENTION...

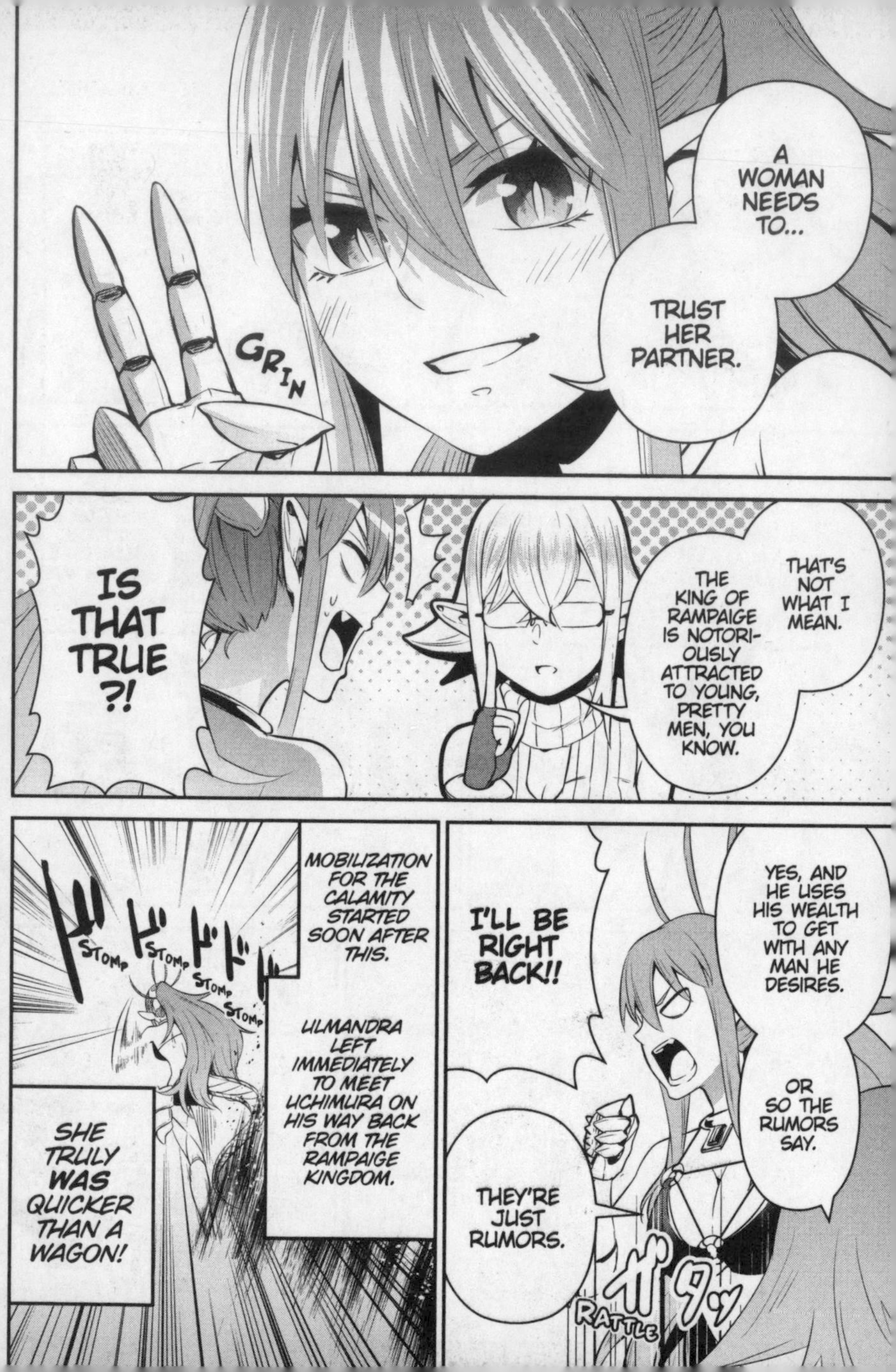
A WOMAN NEEDS TO...
TRUST HER PARTNER.
GRIN
THAT'S NOT WHAT I MEAN.
THE KING OF RAMPAIGE IS NOTORIOUSLY ATTRACTED TO YOUNG, PRETTY MEN, YOU KNOW.
IS THAT TRUE?!
YES, AND HE USES HIS WEALTH TO GET WITH ANY MAN HE DESIRES.
I'LL BE RIGHT BACK!!
OR SO THE RUMORS SAY.
THEY'RE JUST RUMORS.
RATTLE
MOBILIZATION FOR THE CALAMITY STARTED SOON AFTER THIS.
ULMANDRA LEFT IMMEDIATELY TO MEET UCHIMURA ON HIS WAY BACK FROM THE RAMPAIGE KINGDOM.
STOMP STOMP STOMP STOMP
SHE TRULY WAS QUICKER THAN A WAGON!

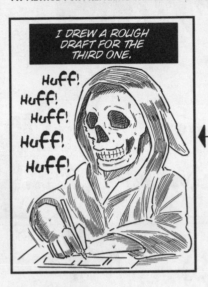

MY METHOD FOR PREPARING THIS SERIES CHANGED WITH THE THIRD VOLUME. --BENIGASHIRA.

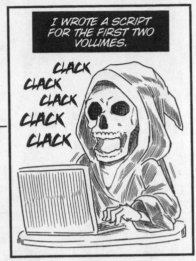

I WROTE A SCRIPT FOR THE FIRST TWO VOLUMES.
CLACK
CLACK
CLACK
CLACK
CLACK
I DREW A ROUGH DRAFT FOR THE THIRD ONE.
Huff!
Huff!
Huff!
Huff!
Huff!

VOLUME THREEEEEEE!!

Volume 3 is here!!
The tumultuous third volume!!!
With its wyverns and dragons. A Calamity? And the Demon Overlord fighting?!

The series is getting so interesting that I can't wait to draw the rest of it!

I feel like my art has gotten better since the first volume, and I intend on working hard to keep getting better as the series continues!
I hope you all continue to enjoy our series from here on out!

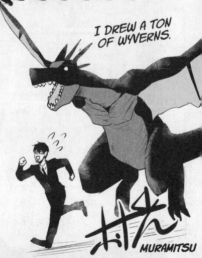

I DREW A TON OF WYVERNS.
MURAMITSU

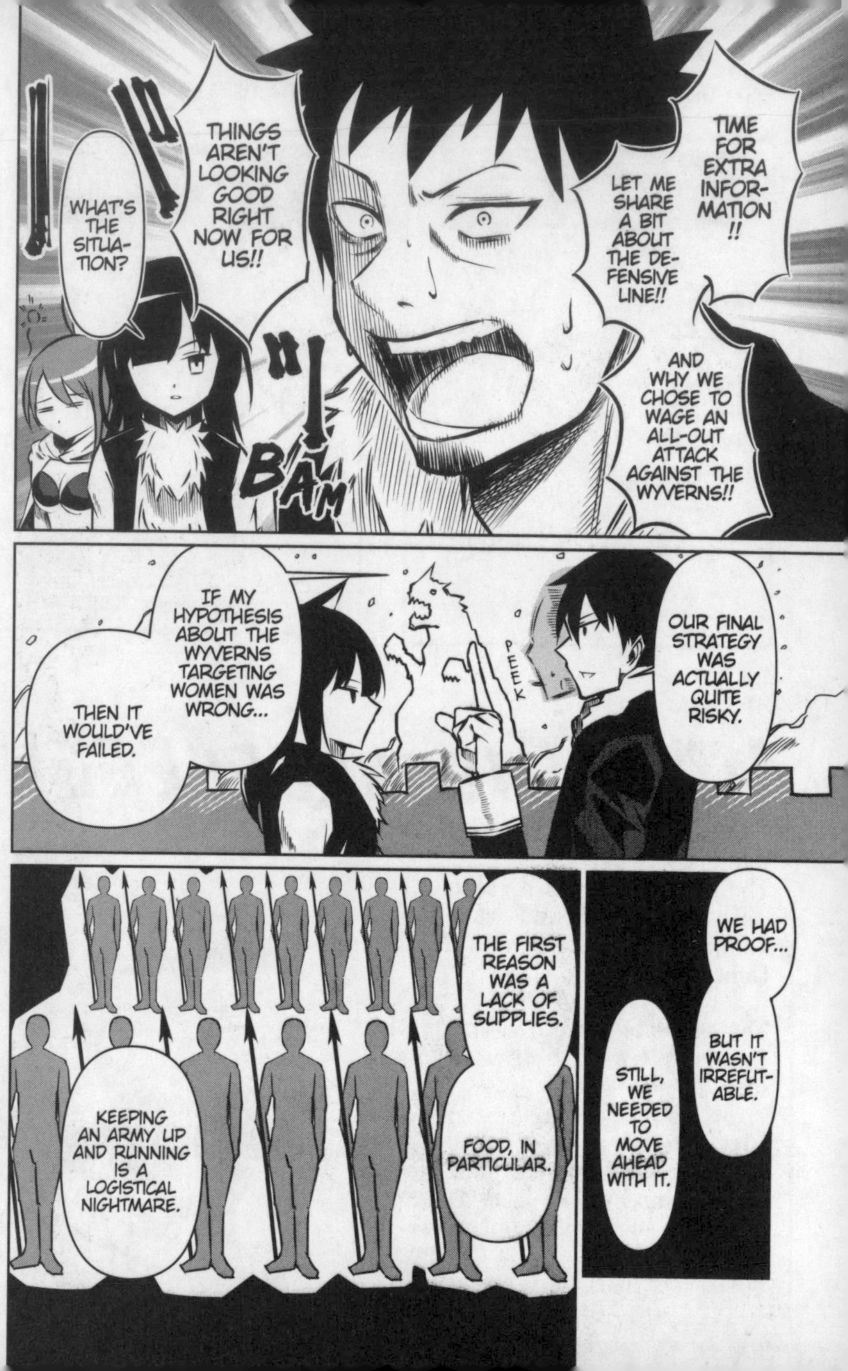
TIME FOR EXTRA INFORMATION!!
LET ME SHARE A BIT ABOUT THE DEFENSIVE LINE!!
AND WHY WE CHOSE TO WAGE AN ALL-OUT ATTACK AGAINST THE WYVERNS!!
THINGS AREN'T LOOKING GOOD RIGHT NOW FOR US!!
WHAT'S THE SITUATION?
BAM
OUR FINAL STRATEGY WAS ACTUALLY QUITE RISKY.
PEEK
IF MY HYPOTHESIS ABOUT THE WYVERNS TARGETING WOMEN WAS WRONG...
THEN IT WOULD'VE FAILED.
WE HAD PROOF...
BUT IT WASN'T IRREFUTABLE.
STILL, WE NEEDED TO MOVE AHEAD WITH IT.
THE FIRST REASON WAS A LACK OF SUPPLIES.
FOOD, IN PARTICULAR.
KEEPING AN ARMY UP AND RUNNING IS A LOGISTICAL NIGHTMARE.

(AUTHOR) BENIGASHIRA

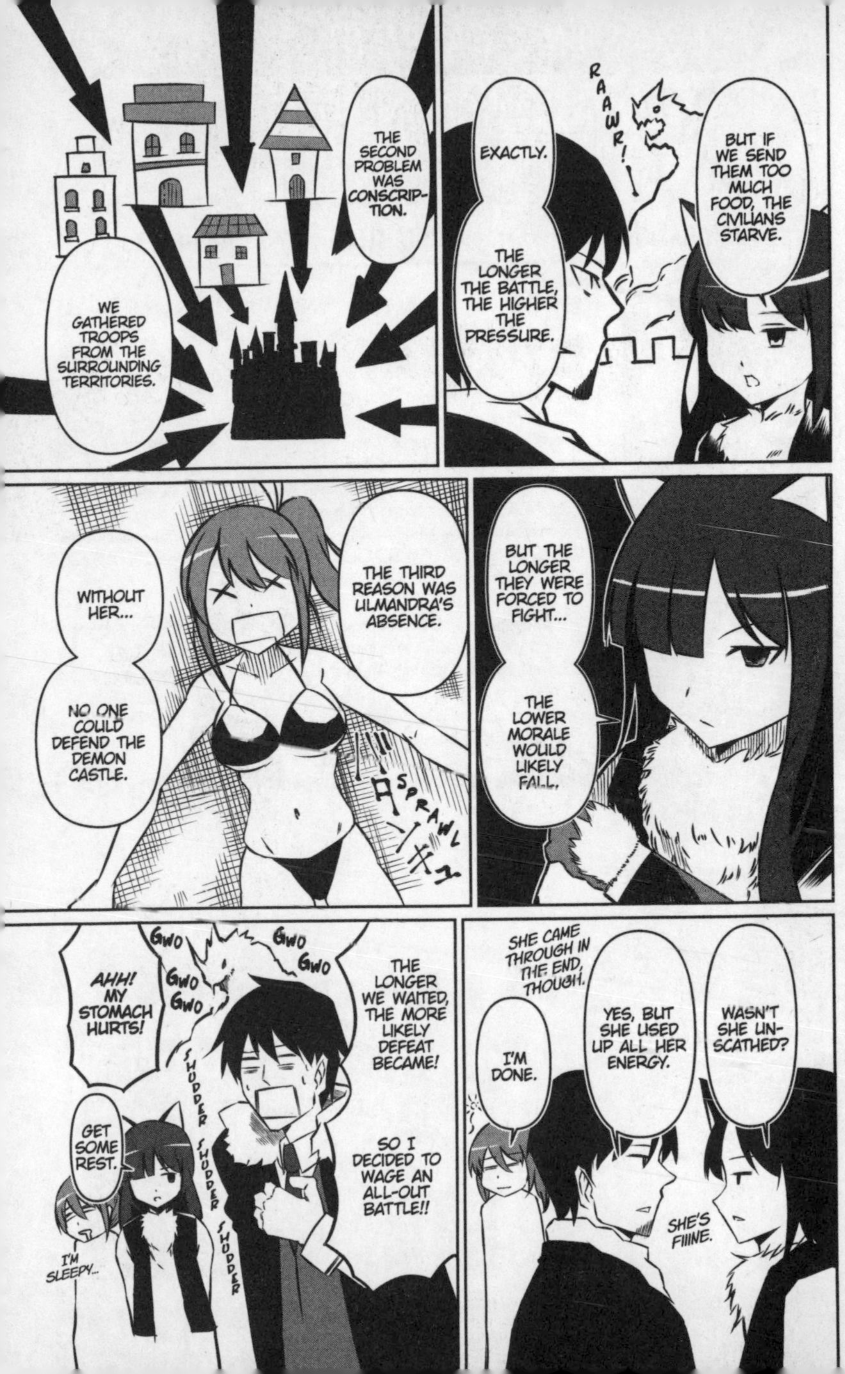
BUT IF WE SEND THEM TOO MUCH FOOD, THE CIVILIANS STARVE.
RAAWR!
EXACTLY.
THE LONGER THE BATTLE, THE HIGHER THE PRESSURE.
THE SECOND PROBLEM WAS CONSCRIPTION.
WE GATHERED TROOPS FROM THE SURROUNDING TERRITORIES.
BUT THE LONGER THEY WERE FORCED TO FIGHT...
THE LOWER MORALE WOULD LIKELY FALL.
THE THIRD REASON WAS ULMANDRA'S ABSENCE.
WITHOUT HER...
NO ONE COULD DEFEND THE DEMON CASTLE.
SPRAWL
WASN'T SHE UNSCATHED?
SHE CAME THROUGH IN THE END, THOUGH.
YES, BUT SHE USED UP ALL HER ENERGY.
I'M DONE.
SHE'S FIIINE.
THE LONGER WE WAITED, THE MORE LIKELY DEFEAT BECAME!
GWO GWO GWO GWO GWO GWO
AHH! MY STOMACH HURTS!
SO I DECIDED TO WAGE AN ALL-OUT BATTLE!!
SHUDDER SHUDDER SHUDDER
GET SOME REST.
I'M SLEEPY...

[AUTHOR] BENIGASHIRA

SEVEN SEAS ENTERTAINMENT PRESENTS

HEADHUNTED TO ANOTHER WORLD

FROM SALARYMAN TO BIG FOUR!

story by **BENIGASHIRA**   art by **MURAMITSU**   **VOLUME 3**

TRANSLATION
Richard Tobin

ADAPTATION
Patrick King

LETTERING
Rai Enril

COVER DESIGN
H. Qi

LOGO DESIGN
George Panella

PROOFREADER
Dayna Abel
B. Lillian Martin

SENIOR EDITOR
Shanti Whitesides

PREPRESS TECHNICIAN
Melanie Ujimori

PRINT MANAGER
Rhiannon Rasmussen-Silverstein

PRODUCTION DESIGNER
Christa Miesner

PRODUCTION MANAGER
Lissa Pattillo

EDITOR-IN-CHIEF
Julie Davis

ASSOCIATE PUBLISHER
Adam Arnold

PUBLISHER
Jason DeAngelis

SARARIIMAN GA ISEKAI NI ITTARA SHITENNOU NI NATTA HANASHI VOL. 3
© 2021 Muramitsu
© Benigashira/OVERLAP
First published in Japan in 2021 by OVERLAP Inc., Ltd., Tokyo.
English translation rights arranged with OVERLAP Inc., Ltd., Tokyo.

Seven Seas press and purchase enquiries can be sent to Marketing Manager Lianne Sentar at press@gomanga.com. Information regarding the distribution and purchase of digital editions is available from Digital Manager CK Russell at digital@gomanga.com.

Seven Seas and the Seven Seas logo are trademarks of Seven Seas Entertainment. All rights reserved.

ISBN: 978-1-63858-187-1
Printed in Canada
First Printing: May 2022
10 9 8 7 6 5 4 3 2 1

READING DIRECTIONS

This book reads from *right to left*, Japanese style. If this is your first time reading manga, you start reading from the top right panel on each page and take it from there. If you get lost, just follow the numbered diagram here. It may seem backwards at first, but you'll get the hang of it! Have fun!!

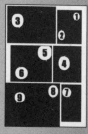

Follow us online: www.SevenSeasEntertainment.com